# Brothers Under the Skin

## REVISED EDITION

## By CAREY McWILLIAMS

The mystic chords of memory, stretching from every
battle-field and patriot grave to every living heart and
hearth-stone all over this broad land, will yet swell to
the chorus of the Union, when again touched, as surely
they will be, by the better angels of our nature.

— LINCOLN

*Boston* · Little, Brown and Company · *Toronto*

*Revised Edition*

A

The author is indebted to The Macmillan Company for permission to
quote from *The Negro in the United States* by Dr. E. Franklin Frazier,
copyright 1949 by The Macmillan Company; to Dodd, Mead & Company
for permission to quote from *Rutherford B. Hayes: Statesman of Reunion*
by H. J. Eckenrode, copyright 1930 by Dodd, Mead & Company; to
Appleton-Century-Crofts, Inc. for permission to quote from *Money Powers
of Europe*, by Paul H. Emden, 1938; to Doubleday & Company, Inc. for
permission to quote from *Caste, Class & Race* by Oliver Cromwell Cox,
copyright 1948 by Oliver Cromwell Cox, reprinted by permission of
Doubleday & Company, Inc.; to The Columbia Studies in History, Economics, and Public Law, and to Dr. Edward N. Saveth, for permission to
quote from *American Historians and European Immigrants* by Edward N.
Saveth, copyright 1948 by Columbia University Press; to Houghton Mifflin
Company for permission to quote from *The Education of Henry Adams*
and from *Letters of Henry Adams*, Worthington Ford, ed., 2 vols. Boston,
1930–38; to Alfred A. Knopf, Incorporated, for permission to quote from
*The Masters and the Slaves* by Gilberto Freyre, 1946; to J. B. Lippincott
Company for permission to quote from *They Came Here First* by D'Arcy
McNickle, 1949; and to the University of Chicago Press for permission to
quote from *French Canada in Transition*, by Everett Cherrington Hughes,
copyright 1943 by the University of Chicago; and *Americans Betrayed* by
Morton Grodzins, copyright 1949 by the University of Chicago.

# Contents

Introduction     3

I   *The Non-Vanishing Indian*     59

II   *The Long-Suffering Chinese*     89

III   *The Forgotten Mexican*     113

IV   *The Hostage Japanese*     140

V   *Hawaii: Island Racial Frontier*     170

VI   *Puerto Ricans and Other Islanders*     195

VII   *The Little Brown Brother*     229

VIII   *"The Negro Problem": A Case History*     250

IX   *The Jewish Minority and Anti-Semitism*     280

X   *Beyond Civil Rights*     312

*Acknowledgments*     347

*Index*     349

# A New Introduction—1964

THE INTRODUCTION to the 1951 edition of *Brothers Under the Skin* was completed shortly before I left California in the spring of that year to join the staff of *The Nation* in New York. Even then I was convinced that today's much-ballyhooed "Negro revolt" was under way. "The year 1950," I wrote, "marks the beginning of the permanent crisis in race relations."

The critical event in this unfolding revolution was the Supreme Court's decision (*Brown* v. *Board of Education*, May 17, 1954), outlawing segregation in the public schools. The case was elaborately argued and reargued; in fact it was not until the court's second decision, a year later, that the manner of implementation was determined. During this period, the Eisenhower Administration did nothing to win public acceptance for the decision, nor did it do anything to facilitate the transition. Even so, the reaction to the decision in the South was more favorable than might have been expected. "All told, the South's reaction has been calm," reported Harry S. Ashmore from Little Rock. In a *Nation* editorial (May 29, 1954), I stressed the fact that the unanimous decision had won an immediate national approval that was "as nearly unanimous as any such verdict is ever likely to be." I noted, too, that the decision was "a fine antidote to the blight of McCarthyism and kindred fevers," as indeed it was.

While this mood prevailed was the time for President Eisenhower to have acted. He could have greeted the decision with enthusiasm. He could have mobilized support for it. He could have urged the Southern governors to plan the transition; he could have offered federal assistance. But he did none of these things. In fact it was not until June 19, 1958, that he had his first face-to-face meeting with a Negro delegation in the White House. Dr. Martin Luther King, Jr., who had been trying for months to see Vice-President Nixon, finally met him when the two men were introduced in Accra at the ceremonies when Ghana became an independent state on March 6, 1957. President Eisenhower did not include any civil rights proposals in his legislative recommendations for 1953, 1954, 1955, and 1956. Belatedly, in 1957, the Administration obtained passage of the first civil rights legislation in nearly a century, but by then it was a question of too little and too late. This incredible record of default in presidential leadership is documented on a day-to-day basis in *Black Man in the White House* (1963), the diary kept by E. Frederic Morrow, Administrative Officer for Special Projects at the White House, the first Negro presidential aide in history. In retrospect it is clear that the lack of strong executive leadership from 1952 to 1960 was a contributing cause of the Negro revolt of 1963.

If I had to select a single event as dating the inception of the revolt, I would fix on the Montgomery bus boycott, which began on December 1, 1955, and continued until November 13, 1956, almost a year later, when the Supreme Court affirmed a lower court decision that segregated buses were unconstitutional. The extraordinary aspect of the boycott was the way Montgomery's 50,000 Negroes responded to it. Few observers thought it could be sustained for any length of time. But by the skillful organization of car pools it was maintained for days, weeks, months. In a *Nation* editorial ("Miracle in Alabama," March 3, 1956), I characterized the boycott as "a major historic development" in American race relations. Overnight, or so it seemed, Southern Negroes had put aside their fears, and the longer they marched the more self-confident they became. For all practical purposes, the boycott was the first mass protest by Southern Negroes against Jim Crow.

Up to this point, desegregation of the schools had been proceeding at a snail's pace. Then, on February 6, 1956, students rioted and national excitement mounted as Miss Autherine Lucy enrolled in the University of Alabama. Caught off balance by the Montgomery bus boycott and Miss Lucy's audacity — and the national reaction to both — the Dixiecrats decided that the time had come to launch a counteroffensive against *Brown* v. *Board of Education*. The Dixiecrat Manifesto, which triggered the counter-revolt, was issued on March 12, 1956, the day Miss Lucy was expelled from the university. Senator Byrd, according to Doris Fleeson, was the "powerhouse" behind the manifesto. The manifesto complained that "amicable relations" (!) between Southern whites and Negroes had been upset by the Supreme Court's decision and urged opposition to the decision by all "lawful means." It was signed by a hundred Southern members of Congress, and all but four were Democrats. Up to this time, Southern opinion had remained relatively calm; there had been no talk of "nullification." "A nod from Byrd," reported Benjamin Muse in the *Washington Post*, would have headed Virginia toward compliance." But after the manifesto, Virginia led the opposition. "Fulminations against the Supreme Court," wrote Muse, "were not emotional indiscretion. Appeals to racial demagoguery were not irresponsible demagoguery. They were part of the established policy of the Commonwealth." These fulminations were not voiced by "red-necks," by ignorant and impoverished "poor whites"; they were voiced by the patricians, by the tidewater aristocrats. An open incitation to nullification, the manifesto silenced the Southern moderates and gave a green light to every demagogue in the South.

But the manifesto was merely one aspect of the South's counterattack. In the period from January 1955 to January 1959 the Southern Regional Council listed 530 specific acts of violence, reprisal, and intimidation in eleven Southern states. Still another phase of the counterattack was the campaign launched in 1956 to cripple the NAACP. Largely because of the disfranchisement of the Southern Negro, the Negro minority has never been able to exert its full political power. Of necessity, therefore, great reliance has been placed on court action, particularly in the federal courts, with the NAACP as the principal vehicle. With a fine record in individual cases, the NAACP had begun to win a series of important court victories against the principle of racial discrimination: legally sanctioned segregation fell first in education (1954), then in public recreational facilities (1955), then in public transportation (1956). But the Southern segregationists, with easy access to state courts, state legislatures, and the power in Southern state capitols, exploited this advantage in a series of harassing actions and enactments aimed at crippling the NAACP. Placed on the defensive, the NAACP had to divert limited funds, energies and personnel from civil rights litigation to self-protective measures. Fortunately it still had access to the federal courts, where, usually on appeal, it managed to ward off some of the attacks. All the same, the attacks hurt: membership fell almost 38,000 in 1957.

But the overall effect of the Southern counteroffensive was to stiffen Negro morale. The attacks against the NAACP merely shifted the fight from the courts to the streets — with disastrous consequences for the Bourbon South. Television cameras are not permitted in most courtrooms. But a television camera trained on a street demonstration is a powerful instrument of national public enlightenment. Also, tactics seen in one place can be immediately applied somewhere else. Prior to 1956, Southern Negroes complained that they had great difficulty in breaking through the communications barrier, but the complaints have abated since then. In fact, Governor Ross Barnett of Mississippi is close to the truth in calling the Negro revolt of 1963 "the television revolution."

In retrospect, one aspect of the South's counterattack merits emphasis. The violence of it is the best proof that it constituted a countermovement, not a popularly based reaction. It suggests that the leaders knew, and had good reason to know, that the changing mores of the South do not in fact support segregation. "We may suspect," writes Lewis M. Killian (*Phylon Quarterly*, second quarter, 1957), "that the vigor with which the movement is being prosecuted reflects the suspicion that a significant portion of both the white and Negro population of the South are no longer convinced of the absolute rightness of segregation. It is not just a movement to repel an invasion of new, nontraditional ideas; it is also a movement to restore and secure traditional values that are beginning to lose their hold in the society. . . . The fundamental strategy of this countermovement is to fight a long series of delaying actions . . . designed to exhaust the resources of the integration movement; to weaken its morale by making success seem increasingly remote; and to sustain morale in the segregationist countermovement. The last objective is served by diverting attention from the conflict of values which is the central issue. . . . In fact, the countermovement seems to have no long-range program but to depend upon one expedient after another."

In a way the stage had been set for the 1956 counteroffensive by the illness of President Eisenhower in October 1955, which had in effect advanced the presidential election by almost a year. "Relieved of the necessity of dealing with the magic of Ike's name," wrote Oscar Handlin (*Commentary*, November 1957), "and cheered on by discontent in the farm belt, the Democrats imagined they could readily regain their primacy of the 1930s and 1940s. The congressional elections of 1954 seemed to confirm that estimate. . . . It therefore seemed more important to concentrate on the nomination than on the election. Stevenson had few doubts that he could be nominated, but he wished to lead a united party that would be certain to win in November. And to keep the party united meant to appease the Southerners who had bolted openly in 1948 and defected surreptitiously to the GOP in 1952." By the time it became apparent that President Eisenhower would run again, it was too late for the Democrats to shift the grounds of the campaign.

The 1956 campaign offered the first chance for both parties to take a stand on the issues raised by the Supreme Court's decision in *Brown* v. *Board of Education*. A strong stand by either party in support of the decision would have encouraged a strong stand by the other. The Democratic platform rejected "all proposals for the use of force to interfere with the orderly determination of these matters by the courts." The Republicans were even more solicitous of Southern feelings and equated force by an official agency with mob violence. The Democrats left enforcement to the courts alone; the Republicans advocated nothing more than "intelligent study, understanding, education and good will." Thus the stage was set for Governor Orval Faubus's mock-heroics at Little Rock in the fall of 1957. As a postscript, the appeasement of the Dixiecrats — against which we had warned in a special issue of *The Nation* ("Time to Kill Jim Crow," July 7, 1956) — did not help the Democrats; party unity was maintained, but Eisen-

hower coasted to victory in November and captured several
Southern states in the process. However, the 1956 election did
mark the beginning of the end of the bipartisan moratorium on
civil rights which had been maintained since 1948. In response
to mounting national concern and a groundswell of Negro protest, a civil rights act was adopted in 1957.

As part of the South's counteroffensive, the Dixiecrats needed
to stage a dramatic holding operation against the Supreme Court's
decision, first, to keep the border states from slipping into the
enemy's camp (standing alone, the Deep South states are relatively insignificant, as the 1948 election demonstrated); and, second, to force the Administration to use federal troops in the hope
that their use would release a wave of popular resentment of
such volume as to discourage further efforts to enforce the decision. Little Rock provided ideal political terrain for such an
operation. Arkansas is neither a border nor a Deep South state
but a link between the two. Only about 23 per cent of the state's
population is Negro. Little Rock itself was one of the least likely
places for open defiance to take place. Three days after the
Supreme Court's decision, the Little Rock Board of Education
had announced that it would comply. A plan of integration,
which seemed to have general community acceptance, was
scheduled to go into effect in the fall of 1957. A big razzle-dazzle
show of resistance in such a relatively enlightened community
was certain to make big news, and it did. By universal judgment
it was the second biggest news story of 1957, topped only by
Sputnik.

The stage had been carefully set. In November 1956 the voters
approved two measures: a resolution calling for an amendment
to the United States Constitution which would prohibit the
federal government from exercising any control over operation
of the public schools; and an amendment to the Arkansas constitution which would require the state legislature to oppose the
Supreme Court's decision in every constitutional manner. The
package was approved by 55 per cent of the electorate; in Little
Rock the division was almost exactly 50–50. The legislature then
passed an act which would make it illegal to require any child to

attend a school in which both white and Negro children were enrolled. A month before the Little Rock schools were to open, a group calling itself the Mothers League of Central High was formed to resist desegregation, and two days later Governor Marvin Griffin and Roy Harris, both prominent and influential Georgia Dixiecrats, arrived to organize a broader opposition and to convince Governor Faubus that he might become a national figure if he would lead it. On "Black Monday," September 23, 1957, nine Negro students succeeded in entering Central High but were soon forced to leave. Until Faubus began to make televised speeches, there had been no trouble. He had not been asked by the mayor or the chief of police to call out the National Guard. But once the opposition had formed, in response to his constant agitation of the issue, he cited it to justify his action in mobilizing the Guard. The President then had no alternative but to federalize the Guard and send in federal troops, which were under the command of Major General Edwin Walker. The flash of sunlight on their bayonets was enough to restore order. Central High remained open that year, under guard; but Faubus closed the high schools in the fall of 1958, and it was not until 1959 that they reopened, on a placement, or "token," integration basis. This time the police handled the situation without much trouble. They arrested twenty-one troublemakers, mostly teenagers, and that, as one reporter said, "was the end of it."

The melodrama of Little Rock tended to obscure an important aspect, noted by Harry S. Ashmore (*Look*, July 16, 1963); namely, that even with the governor's strongly implied blessing in 1957, "considerable effort was required to assemble a mob sufficient to overwhelm a small force of dispirited policemen. . . . The Arkansas mob had about as much spontaneity as the regiment of U.S. airborne infantry that arrived to clear the streets in a brisk action of fifteen minutes' duration. . . . Superior federal force and a demonstrated willingness to employ it obviously are controlling factors. But perhaps more significant is the absence of adverse mass reaction to such intervention. The psychological warfare experts among the architects of massive resistance calculated that occupying federal troops would solidify their support by stirring atavistic memories among the sons and daughters of the Lost Cause. Orators still cry out in the tone of Confederate bugles, but in fact the arrival of the Army has been greeted everywhere with a general feeling of relief that the situation is once again in hand." Neither side won a clear-cut victory in Little Rock, but it was the segregationists who withdrew.

On February 1, 1960, the Southern Negro's revolt was advanced another step with the sit-ins in Greensboro, North Carolina, staged by Negro students of the all-Negro Agricultural and Technical College. From Greensboro, the sit-ins spread rapidly across the entire South. Thousands of Negroes, students and adults, took part in these demonstrations; scarcely a major area in the South was unaffected and the arrests ran into the thousands. Out of the initial sit-ins came the Raleigh Conference in April 1960, at which SNCC was born — the Student Nonviolent Coordinating Committee — a dynamic new force in the civil rights movement.

In essence the sit-ins were a revolt against tokenism (see the article by James McBride Dabbs, *Nation*, April 2, 1960). Massive resistance to desegregation had finally bred massive determination. At a deeper level, the sit-ins were an eloquent statement of the demand of young Southern Negroes for recognition of their dignity as human beings. "The lunch-counter demonstrations," I wrote in *The Nation* (March 12, 1960), "are not 'student strikes' for this or that concession; they are eloquent assertions of the New Negro's sense of his own dignity as a human being. He is demanding more than 'service'; he demands respect." In part, too, the sit-ins were a protest against an older, more cautious Negro leadership. And the next year came the Freedom Rides, organized by CORE (Congress of Racial Equality) as a protest against segregation in interstate transportation. Both the sit-ins and the Freedom Rides stemmed, of course, from experiments in the use of nonviolent demonstrations against racial discrimination dating back to the early period of World War II (see article by Carleton Mabee, *Nation*, August 12, 1961).

The sit-ins and the Freedom Rides helped to clear the air in the South. They dramatized discrimination and brought it directly to the attention of a national audience; by forcing hostility to the surface, they revealed some of the uglier aspects of the Southern scene and character. They also sustained the tempo of the civil rights movement when it had begun to lag. Both types of protest succeeded, as probably nothing else has, in causing white Southerners to see Negro Southerners as individuals; in some instances even the jailers have been impressed. The protests relieved frustration by suggesting that there were things an individual could do to communicate his sense of the right and wrong of social issues. Students, in particular, were drawn to these protests, which gave them something to do. The sit-ins also provided a bridge to the older Negro generation; as the idea caught on, initial adult disapproval in many instances turned into pride and personal participation. The sit-ins also made it possible for the uneducated, lower-class Negroes to participate. Even women and children could participate without much risk of serious bodily injury. Nonviolent direct action is an excellent technique, also, to make the wrongdoer and passive observer conscious of a wrong. The commitment to nonviolence is of critical importance in rural areas of the Deep South, where Negroes have been terrorized for years and live in constant fear of violence. Nonviolence also provides a bridge to the Negro church, a key institution.

In a sense the Black Muslim movement in the North, like the sit-ins in the South, represents a protest against the slow pace of gradualism. Like the Garvey movement of the 1920s, its main appeal is to lower-class urban Negroes. Its leaders scorn nonviolence and reject the concept of integration. Melodramatic, nationalistic, urging a separate Negro state, the Black Muslims are working against the grain of Negro aspiration, which is overwhelmingly for full participation and against separatism. In a sense the Black Muslims are a reflection of the swift emergence of a new black state in Africa. Ten years ago there were only four sovereign states in Africa; four more were added by 1958; and then, within a two-year period, an additional twenty emerged, each of which took its place in the United Nations. A side effect, of course, was the encouragement of "black nationalism" here. The Black Muslims represent a significant protest just as the Garvey movement did, but unless they change their tactics and their strategy, they are not likely to become a major influence. The more they succeed in frightening whites with their bitter denunciations of the white world, the more willing whites become to support·the civil rights movements which the Muslims despise.

President Kennedy, who probably owed his election to his skill in holding the Negro vote, had promised that Negroes would be given their full civil rights as citizens. But according to Dr. James T. Crown (*Kennedy in Power*, 1962), an agreement had been made, in order to keep the South in line, that civil rights legislation would not be requested in the first session of Congress. But the President felt compelled to use the executive power to give support to the civil rights movement, and by and large his record on this score was impressive. He used executive power to enroll James H. Meredith in the University of Mississippi and kept him there, at the cost of two lives, with the use of a total of 25,700 federal troops and U.S. marshals. But the better the Administration performed — the more executive power and support it placed behind the civil rights movement — the more militant the movement became. The initiative no longer rested with the President or the Congress or with the leadership of either party; it rested with the leadership of the civil rights movement, which began to produce crises each of which required the Administration to act and thereby placed it increasingly in opposition to the Dixiecrats.

Throughout the spring and summer of 1963 tension rapidly mounted. Governor George Wallace staged his token show of opposition at the University of Alabama; William L. Moore, a white Baltimore postman, was assassinated at Keener, Alabama; Medgar W. Evers was murdered by a sniper's bullet on June 12; a savage protest movement flared up in Cambridge, Maryland. In May, June and July, 1963, an estimated 12,500 civil rights demonstrators were arrested. (Incidentally, the Department of Justice estimated that in a three-month period 275 of 574 communities of 10,000 or more population in the South desegregated one or more facilities.) But it was the protest in Birmingham, which Martin Luther King, Jr., launched on April 12, that dominated the headlines. Huge rallies and marches were staged in other cities in support of Southern Negroes: 16,000 marched in Cincinnati, 100,000 in San Francisco, 125,000 in Detroit. A settlement of a sort had been reached in Birmingham on May 10, but a series of bombings, in one of which four Negro girls were killed while attending Sunday school, put Birmingham back in the headlines in September.

Television crews were kept busy in the spring and summer and fall, but principally people remembered Birmingham: the police dogs, the fierce water hoses, the electric prod poles, "Bull" Connor, the Negro children in best bib and tucker marching sweetly off to jail. Birmingham, said Ralph McGill, editor of the *Atlanta Constitution*, "enabled people all over this country to see what was going on"; it changed "the pattern almost overnight." In an NBC program, Frank McGee summed up its importance: "For nearly a decade after the Supreme Court ordered school desegregation ended 'with all deliberate speed,' the United States witnessed and even became accustomed to an annual autumnal rite — the enrollment of a few Negro students in previously all-white schools. Sometimes it was enacted against a background of howling mobs and bayonets; sometimes it occurred peacefully. But either way, most white Americans felt the Negro was making progress. It was not until the spring of 1963 that this illusion was shattered. Suddenly aroused, but not fully awakened, most of us were baffled by the new character of the 'struggle.' Schools were no longer the prime target. . . . Federal court orders were no longer the prime weapons. The movement had vaulted over these and Negroes were invoking the Constitution itself. Negotiations no longer prevented or halted demonstrations. Noticed but fitfully by the country as a whole, the Negro had spilled his cause out of conference rooms and court into the streets; and a movement burst its seams and became a revolution."

The President read the meaning of Birmingham correctly; on July 19, 1963, he sent his Civil Rights Message to Congress. It had been clear, as the centennial of the Emancipation Proclamation year approached, that he was anxious to avoid a clash with Congress over civil rights until after the 1964 election. But after Birmingham, he knew that a "crash" legislative program was needed.

In the wake of Birmingham, at the end of the long hot summer of our discontent, 250,000 marchers assembled in Washington. Not only was it unplanned; it was definitely not wanted. On August 26, the Gallup Poll indicated that only 22 per cent approved the idea of the March, 63 per cent were unfavorable and 15 per cent undecided. But the March came off without a hitch and the centennial was finally given appropriate observance. Of 250,000 marchers, 200,000 were Negroes. The proceedings were orderly and dignified, the spirit admirable. "A profoundly moving demonstration," reported Robert S. Bird in the *New York Herald Tribune*, "so big, so orderly, so sweet-singing and good-natured, so boldly confident and at the same time so relaxed, so completely right from start to finish that America was done proud beyond measure." "No one," reported Russell Baker in the *New York Times*, "could remember an invading army quite as gentle as the 200,000 civil rights marchers who occupied Washington today. For the most part, they came silently during the night and early morning, occupied the great shaded boulevards along the Mall, and spread through the parklands between the Washington Monument and the Potomac. . . . But instead of the emotional horde of angry militants that many had feared, what Washington saw was a vast army of quiet, middle-class Americans who had come in the spirit of a church outing. And instead of the tension that had been expected, they gave the city a day of sad music, strange silences and good feeling in the streets."

The day before the March, Dr. W. E. B. Du Bois, ninety-five years of age, died in Ghana, "a lonely casualty," as Roy Wilkins said, "in a cause he did so much to promote."

And then, of course, came the rifle shots in Dallas on November 22, and the President was dead. In an odd way, his death seemed to place the ugliness, the brutality, and the sound and fury in proper perspective. The petty demagogues — Faubus, Wallace, Barnett — seemed very petty indeed. Just as the President had been forced, rather against his customary caution, to acknowledge the unavoidable implications of the civil rights issue, so the nation, through him and through his death, finally was forced to face the issue it had successfully been avoiding since the founding of the Republic. The implications are numerous, but essentially the issue is quite simple: Is the Negro a member of the human race? *The Nation* stated this issue, as clearly as it has ever been stated, in an editorial of October 26, 1867: "We boast of having gone beyond others in social and political science, but we have at last come to a place where the claim is to be more solemnly tested. The question of race is put before us as a stone of stumbling, or a rock of exaltation. . . . We have boasted of our land as the free home of all races. We have insulted other nations with the vehemence of our declamation. And now we are brought face to face with a question that will test it all. . . . Is the Negro a man? Say what you will, this is the real issue of the controversy respecting him."

But there is another dimension to the problem — a specific constitutional issue. The failure to eliminate all vestiges of chattel slavery left us with a situation in which the guarantees of the Constitution, by tacit bipartisan accord, were permitted to lapse so far as most Negroes were concerned. Today we find it difficult to believe, but it is a fact, that Jim Crow discriminations represent vestiges of the system of chattel slavery. Similarly we find it hard to believe that certain traits observed in some Negroes, such as a tendency to infantile behavior, to overdependency, etc — none of which has anything to do with biological inheritance — could be, as they are, carryover aspects of the culture of chattel slavery. Granted that law cannot force one person to acknowledge the humanity of another, still the law can compel townships, cities, counties and states to respect rights secured by the Constitution. A government that cannot compel respect for its writ, a government that permits and even connives at flagrant, massive denials of basic civil rights under color of state action, scarcely deserves to be called a government.

Now, of course, another dimension has been added to the problem. While there is a sizable Negro elite and a large and growing Negro middle class, the fact is that Negroes have become a kind of lower class making up about 20 per cent of the population. Economic improvement has occurred, but not fast enough to enable Negroes to adjust to an economy whose rate of change is cumulative and intense. In the twenty years since *Brothers*

*Under the Skin* was first published, the economic position of the Negro relative to whites has not improved and may actually have deteriorated. The Negro movement out of the South, which will accelerate, has concentrated Negroes in the core areas of the cities in which they have settled. The effect is to convert these areas into enlarged ghettoes. Adoption of a civil rights program will not, of itself, offset the disadvantages under which Negroes live today. "If all the discriminatory laws in the United States were immediately repealed," writes Michael Harrington (*Commonweal*, June 7, 1961), "race would still remain one of the most pressing moral and political programs in the nation." (See also "Freedom Now — but What Then?" by Loren Miller, *Nation*, June 29, 1963, and the article by Charles Silberman in *Fortune*, September 1963.)

In this perspective it is clear that Negroes must more and more turn to political action. Despite their strategic distribution, which enables Negroes to be the balance of power in national elections, they still lack the political power to achieve their long-term objectives — alone. They have not, despite their growing political power North and South, been able to significantly affect the character of Congress. But if Negroes seek their natural allies, if they develop a political leadership as skillful as the leadership of the civil rights movement, if they can succeed in bringing out the untapped Negro vote potential, they will be able to mobilize the power needed to have their major demands met (see *The Era of Politics* by Herman H. Long, 1958, p. 45).

To date, the Negro revolution is aimed at the achievement of middle-class status; continued opposition could divert it into other channels, but this is not likely to happen. "Revolutionary radicalism, whether of the nationalist or the Marxist variety," writes August Meier (*New Politics*, Vol. II, No. 3), "seems to be an unlikely haven for the majority of Negroes, simply because, in contrast to Africans, they are a minority too small and too dispossessed to obtain freedom and dignity by either of these methods. But they are numerous enough to be a crucial factor in national and in many state and local elections; they are numerous enough to disrupt the normal operations of city life by demonstrations; and they are numerous enough and prosperous enough to wield a mighty economic threat through the power of selective patronage. The future success of the Negro protest movement therefore lies in the use of economic and political pressures, dramatized by nonviolent demonstrations, that will compel the politicans and the businesss community . . . to accord equal treatment to Negroes in American society."

CAREY McWILLIAMS

*New York, January 1964*

*Brothers Under the Skin*

*To Angus Cameron,*
*in appreciation*

# Introduction

*Brothers Under the Skin* was released on April 23, 1943 — roughly the mid-point of World War II. Almost before the first reviews had begun to arrive, the racial tensions which had been steadily mounting since 1940, tensions given detailed description in the introduction to that first edition, suddenly exploded right under my nose — in Los Angeles. The week-long "zoot-suit" race riots which began in Los Angeles on June 3, 1943, touched off a chain reaction of riots across the country. Similar disturbances were reported in San Diego on June 9; in Philadelphia on June 10; in Chicago on June 15; and in Evansville on June 27. Between June 16 and August 1, large-scale race riots occurred in Beaumont, Texas, in Detroit, and in Harlem. The Detroit riot of June 20–21 was one of the most costly and bitter of the century: 25 Negroes and 9 white persons were killed and property worth hundreds of thousands of dollars was destroyed.[1] The Harlem riot of August 1–2, 1943, was the most severe in the history of New York's Negro community: 5 Negroes were killed, approximately 565 persons received hospital treatment, over 500 arrests were made, and property damage was estimated at $5,000,000.[2] Nor were these the only disturbances of those tense weeks in midsummer 1943.[3]

Before the zoot-suit riots in Los Angeles were over, I found

[1] *Race Riot*, by Alfred McClung Lee and Norman Wayne Humphrey, 1943.

[2] *The Harlem Riot: A Study in Mass Frustration*, by Harold Orlansky, Social Analysis, 1943, Report No. 1.

[3] "The Race Riots," by Thomas Sanctum, *New Republic*, July 5, 1943.

myself in the position of writing a report on the disturbances
for a committee appointed by Governor Earl Warren and,
some weeks later, of preparing a report for the Attorney
General of California on race riots and the role of the police.[4]
If I had not realized its meaning before, I now knew the
fateful import of the phrase: "He wrote a book"! Before the
war was over, I had been catapulted out of the profession
in which I had been trained, and which I had practiced for
twelve years, and found myself embroiled — how I scarcely
knew — in what can only be described, in retrospect, as a
rapidly emerging revolution in group relations in the United
States.

For a revolution of a sort has occurred in the last decade
in the field of what we still call "race relations" in the
United States. Not until I sat down to write this new introduction had I fully realized the enormous impact of the war
on America's "racial problem." Not in this introduction,
surely, and not for many years to come, will it be possible
to tell the amazing story of the developing protest against
racial discrimination in the United States of the last seven
or eight years. The facts are not yet fully known; the materials are of enormous extent; and the implications are far-
reaching. In the period from 1943 to 1950 more has happened
in the field of race relations in this country — more interest
has been aroused; more has been said and written; more proposed and accomplished — than in the entire span of years
from the end of the Civil War to 1940. Of this there can be
no doubt.

In writing the introduction to the first edition I was almost
entirely concerned with the gathering tensions, the ever-
widening perspective, and the radically different dimensions
which the racial problem had suddenly assumed in American
life with the onset of World War II. There is no need to

[4] Interim Report of Peace Officers Committee on Civil Disturbances, State
Printing Office, Sacramento, December 15, 1943.

repeat this material now; it belongs to the period of the war and has long since become part of everyone's thinking, more or less, on racial issues. What I have sought to do, therefore, in this new introduction is to place the events of the period from 1943 to 1950 in a perspective which will doubtless have to be adjusted, here and there, at a later date, but which should serve to indicate how far we have gone, and in what directions, and with what prospects for the future in the solution of America's most persistent and pernicious domestic social problem.

## 1. Storm Signals

The search for a new perspective on America's racial problem might well begin by a comparison of the race riots of World War I with those of World War II. Both wars had a revolutionary impact on the scheme of race relations and the riots which occurred were the signal fires of social change. For, as Dr. Robert C. Weaver has pointed out, "A war is a social revolution. . . . For society it means dislocation of temporary equilibriums incident to fundamental problems. In such a period, the basic, unsolved problems come to the fore and force our attention to them. We discover that many of the issues we had kept under cover can no longer be ignored." [5] We have somehow forgotten, in the shock and excitement of the race riots which came midway of the last war, that the riots of World War I were of much greater violence and destructiveness.

The first major riots of World War I occurred in East St. Louis, Illinois. The first of these riots, which started on May 28, 1917, lasted for two days and two nights, without an hour's cessation, and did not end until martial law was finally declared. The second riot, which began on July 1, was infinitely more violent. Witnesses, including a congressman and

[5] *Racial Tensions in Chicago*, by Robert C. Weaver, reprinted from *Social Service Year Book*, Chicago, 1943.

an army officer, told a congressional committee of inquiry that over 500 Negroes were killed in this, the most savage of all American race riots. "Negroes were hunted through the streets like wild animals. A black skin became a death warrant." [6] The next major riot of World War I took place in Houston on August 16, 1917, when Negro troops at Camp Logan, enraged by reports of the mistreatment of Negro civilians, armed themselves and marched into the city. Thirteen people were killed but, for a change, all but one were whites. In the savage reprisals which followed, 13 Negro soldiers were executed — presumably a life for a life — and 41 were given life imprisonment. Later in 1917, riots were reported at Chester, Pennsylvania, at Lexington, Kentucky, and at Waco, Texas.

In the year 1919, twenty-six race riots were reported in American communities, the first major riot occurring at Longview, Texas, on July 10, 1919, with 11 deaths being reported. Then, in rapid succession, came the race riot in Washington, D. C., of July 18 in which 7 persons were killed; the disastrous Chicago riot of July 27–August 2 in which 38 persons were killed; the "sharecroppers' riot" which took place in Phillips County, Arkansas, on October 1, with 30 deaths (12 Negroes were later sentenced to death and 80 to long prison terms as punishment for the Negro participation in a riot in which no whites were arrested); and a final riot in Omaha in which federal troops were used to restore order. [7] Although the statistics are incomplete, it is quite clear that the riots which occurred during and after World War I, and the great postwar upsurge of the Ku Klux Klan, were far more serious than the comparable disturbances which occurred during and after World War II.

[6] *Current Opinion*, vol. 63, pp. 75–77.

[7] "Race Riots During and After the First World War," by Edgar A. Schuler, *The Negro History Bulletin*, April 1944; *The Negro in Chicago*, 1922; and "The Houston Race Riot, 1917," by Edgar A. Schuler, *Journal of Negro History*, July 1944.

World War II, however, had a much greater social, economic, and political impact on race relations than World War I. The Second World War, for example, completely upset the regional "balance" of the racial problem. Right off, approximately 110,000 Japanese-Americans were evacuated from the three West Coast states, creating a special shortage in an already tight wartime labor market and thereby stimulating a Negro migration from the states of Texas, Louisiana, and Oklahoma to the Pacific Coast. During the war it is estimated that 600,000 Negroes moved from rural to urban areas in the South, 300,000 Southern Negroes moved into the border and Northern states, 100,000 Negroes moved from the border states into other areas further north or west, and 250,000 Negroes moved to the West Coast. A large number of the Japanese-Americans have returned to the West Coast states but few Negroes have returned to the South. In general this shifting of residence on the part of approximately 1,250,000 Negroes, like the similar migration of nearly 1,000,000 Negroes in the period from 1916 to 1929, has been a one-way movement with multiple consequences and interrelated effects.

During World War II, the West Coast suddenly became the nation's new racial frontier. As late as 1940, there was only one important Negro community in the eleven Western states — in Los Angeles. The other Negro communities were primarily small, isolated "Pullman car" colonies at the terminal points of the various transcontinental rail lines. Negroes constituted only 1½ per cent of the total population of the three West Coast states in the prewar period; but they made up 10 per cent, or more, of the 2,000,000 migrants who entered the region after 1940. Of ten major wartime production areas showing a 49 per cent increase in the number of Negroes, five were located on the West Coast. Between 1940 and 1945, the Negro population in Los Angeles increased from 75,000 to 135,000 (it is much larger today); in San Francisco from 4800 to 20,000; in Portland from 1931 to 22,000;

in Seattle from 3789 to 16,000; in Vancouver (Washington) from 4 to 4000; in Bremerton from 17 to 3000. It should be noted, also, that Negroes have made a quicker and on the whole a far more satisfactory adjustment in the rapidly growing cities of the West Coast than in any area to which they have migrated. The West Coast migration has major historical significance for it means that nowadays every major region of the nation for the first time has a significant Negro population; "the problem," in short, is now clearly nation-wide. Today Negroes outnumber all other racial minorities in the three West Coast states.[8]

It would take a volume to spell out the various social, economic, and political implications of these interregional shifts in the Negro population. Here I would merely point out, in passing, that the migration of Negroes to the West Coast has *reduced* the population of certain Southern states while, at the same time, it has *increased* the population of the three West Coast states. Not only does this mean more Negro voting strength in an area where Negroes can freely vote, but it also means greater representation in Congress, in the Electoral College, and in party conventions for areas outside the Deep South, and by the same token and to the same extent, a cut in the representation of the Bourbon Democrats.

The economic and industrial gains scored by Negroes in World War II completely dwarfed the comparable gains of World War I. The economic and industrial gains of World War II, moreover, were buttressed by important developments which had taken place during the period between the two wars, such as the birth of the CIO, the various New Deal health, housing, and education programs, including the effect of unionization and wage-and-hour legislation on wage rate differentials. These supporting factors gave great meaning to

[8] *Common Ground*, Spring 1949; *Journal of Educational Sociology*, November 1945; series of articles by Horace R. Cayton, *Chicago Sun*, October 14, 15, 16, 1943; "The Negro in Portland," report of Portland City Club, July 20, 1945; "The Negro War Worker in San Francisco," May 1944.

the sudden and spectacular economic advances which racial minorities, and Negroes in particular, made in the period from 1940 to 1944. Over 1,000,000 Negroes entered civilian employment during this period; the number of Negroes employed at skilled jobs doubled as did the number of single-skilled and semiskilled colored workers; the number of Negro women employed as domestics was sharply curtailed; and, most important of all, thousands of Negroes began to enter industries and plants and occupations in which few Negroes had been previously employed. The number of Negro trade-union members was probably in excess of 1,000,000 by the end of the war. "These changes in a period of four years," reports Dr. Robert C. Weaver, "represented more industrial and occupational diversification for Negroes than had occurred in the seventy-five preceding years." [9]

Although the employment and upgrading of Negro labor was impeded at first, it began to reach significant proportions by 1943 as witness the "hate strikes" in many industries in the spring of that year. As a matter of fact the race riots of midsummer 1943 are in part to be explained by the exceptionally rapid, and large-scale, industrial gains which Negroes were making. Every economic gain which Negroes scored during this period — every recognition which they achieved in the trade-union movement — automatically tended to augment their political power. The more political power Negroes acquired, the more jobs were opened to them, and as more and more Negroes moved into metropolitan industrial centers, in which industrial trade-unionism was a major social force, community attitudes toward the Negro began to change.

In World War I approximately 371,710 Negroes served in the armed forces (200,000 serving overseas); but in World War II, approximately 750,000 served in the Army (411,368 overseas), 100,000 in the Navy, 16,000 in the Marine Corps,

[9] *Negro Labor: A National Problem*, by Robert C. Weaver, 1946, p. 78.

and about 3600 in the Coast Guard.[10] With the accompanying enhancement of political bargaining power and improvement in the quality of Negro leadership, it is not surprising that the fight for integration at all levels, in all branches of the services, including the auxiliary services, should have completely dwarfed the similar agitation of World War I in both volume and effectiveness.

On the eve of the Houston race riot of 1917, Senator James K. Vardaman of Mississippi had told his colleagues that ". . . one of the horrible problems which will grow out of this unfortunate war . . . is the training as a soldier which the Negro receives. Impress the Negro with the fact that he is defending the flag, inflate his untutored soul with military airs, teach him it is his duty to keep the emblem of the Nation flying triumphantly in the air — it is but a short step to the conclusion that his political rights must be respected. . . . It was a mistake, against which I warned the administration when the President of the United States and the Congress called the Negroes of this country to arms." [11] The fears that Vardaman voiced in 1917 were echoed, of course, by Bilbo and Rankin in 1943. At the same time, the logic of the situation, which had compelled the *New York World* to observe in the wake of the Washington riot of 1919 that "the Negro citizen is going to have his day in court; it ought not to be necessary for him to fight for it," compelled a similar admission, and from the same general sources, immediately following the race riots of midsummer 1943.

In World War II the general ideological ferment began to create a triple reaction: a great surge of hope and new aspiration among the racial minority groups; a somewhat similar reaching out for understanding and integration on the part of elements of the white majority; and a reflexive stiffen-

[10] *Leadership and the Negro Soldier*, Washington, D. C., 1944, p. 9.
[11] *Congressional Record*, 55:6063.

ing of resistance to change on the part of the traditionally most biased sections of the population. Each phase of this triple reaction affected every other: the more militantly Negroes pressed for their rights, the more active their white allies became and the more defensive and "touchy" the Deep South became in its attitude. Conversely each new affront to Negroes by the Bilbos and Rankins only spurred Negroes, and their allies, to greater efforts to win complete equality, not at some remote period, but here and now. American Negroes owe a great and most ironic debt to Bilbo and Rankin — gargoyles of Southern reaction inviting nationwide ridicule and scorn. At the same time, American Negroes began to find a new kind of ally quite unlike the philanthropists, the "gradualists," and the pussyfooting mediationists of the pre-war period. For example, it would be impossible to exaggerate the importance of the role which Wendell Willkie played during the war years in forcing an honest approach to the problem of discrimination in American life. The series of syndicated articles that he wrote in 1944, on the eve of the party conventions, not only had great influence but represented the most statesmanlike approach to the problem of discrimination to be voiced by an American politician in our time. In large part, moreover, Willkie was a symbol of the way in which a large element of the white majority was responding to the challenge of the times; he was driven to his conclusions by the pressure of events. "When we talk of freedom of opportunity for all nations," he said, "the mocking paradoxes in our own society become so clear that they can no longer be ignored. . . . Our world is breaking to pieces. And with the break-up arises the opportunity to fashion a newer and a better life." [12]

[12] *PM*, July 21, 1942.

## 2. *The Science of Equality*

With the structure of race relations being undermined by such processes as migration, urbanization, and industrialization, it is not surprising that the ideology of race relations should also have begun to change during the war. As late as 1940, the state of American social theory on race relations was more than unsatisfactory: it was scandalous. Although the first sociological treatises published in the United States were concerned with race relations, social theory had pretty consistently tended to rationalize the racial *status quo* prior to World War II. For example, William Graham Sumner's theory of the mores could hardly have been more effective in inhibiting social action in the improvement of race relations if this had been its author's conscious intention. By and large, the social thinking of the period from 1900 to 1940 was based on the assumption that *the Negro* was the problem in race relations — not the relationships between Negroes and whites; not the techniques by which white supremacy was maintained to the clear advantage of the white majority; not the myth of racial purity. As long as the Negro — and Mexican, Japanese, or Indian could be substituted — was regarded as the source of the trouble, social illusions were certain to flourish since the observers could always find what they were looking for, namely, evidences that the racial minority groups were inferior. During this forty-year period, a majority of the American people believed that the attempt to make the Negro a citizen had been a mistake and, for the most part, the social scientists agreed.[13]

But once Negroes began to break through the intellectual isolation which was the counterpart of segregation they began to ask the social theorists some embarrassing questions and

[13] *American Journal of Sociology*, June 1947, pp. 265–271.

to challenge the glib assumptions on which so much of the social theory of the period from 1900 to 1940 had rested. Caught up in the ferment for equality, social scientists began to take a second look at the prevailing theories of racial prejudice and discovered, of course, that these theories tended to rationalize prejudicial attitudes. The pressure of events — not scientific curiosity per se — forced this reconsideration of the facts. The results have been amazing for, within the last decade, the whole mythology of race as a determinant of culture has been demolished with interacting and far-reaching consequences. Encouraged by new scientific findings, the spokesmen for equality became increasingly insistent that the old barriers should be removed, and at the same time the defense of these barriers began to assume a ludicrous quality, shrill, falsetto, croaking. The more support these new scientific findings provided for the American creed of equality, the more interest they aroused — with the result that the myths formerly used to rationalize prejudiced attitudes have lost their power to coerce people's thinking about race relations. Even those who advocate white supremacy are today aware of the fact that they speak as poets of hatred and not as scientists. The effect has been to make them look ridiculous and, at the same time, to strengthen the appeal which the creed of equality has always had in this country.

In the last eight years, the race question has been given its first real public airing in the United States — in the newspapers, over the radio networks, in motion pictures, books, pamphlets, magazines; in legislative halls, political conventions, and in public forums of all kinds. By and large, this outpouring of information and factual material has been dictated by the new public interest in the problem rather than the other way round. Indeed the manner in which the racial question has moved from a marginal interest to a major national concern is one of the striking intellectual "facts" of the last decade. A listing of the books published in the last decade, dealing with one or another aspect of the minority question, with a tabulation of their sales, would provide a fairly accurate measure of this new interest. Even the large circulation weeklies and the women's magazines have finally yielded to the new interest in the racial question and have begun to run articles dealing with phases of the problem of discrimination. The concrete social advances for the period do not, of course, measure the extent of this interest (public interest must always precede social reform); but the existence of the interest, and its scope and volume, are realities which can be measured.

The fact that this new interest exists is, indeed, one of the major advances which have been made in the field of race relations. In the past, the public's acceptance of the folklore about race, which, by its nature, has ruled out the possibility of effective social action, has been one of the most serious barriers to be overcome. As recently as 1944, one finds the distinguished social scientist, Dr. James G. Leyburn, writing that there can be no solution to the racial problem "until intermarriage has wiped out all distinguishing marks of race in this country," and then adding, with dark pessimism, that "this will hardly occur for centuries"! [14] Before any significant improvement in race relations could occur, it was essential that people's thinking about the nature of the problem should be transformed. As long as *race* per se was regarded as the essence of the problem, there could be little improvement for there is not much anyone can do about race. But in all political and social questions, as Dr. Robert Redfield has pointed out, race enters as a social rather than a biological phenomenon. "It is," he writes, "what men think and feel about racial differences that matters. . . . We might regard racial antipathies as biologically rooted obstacles to peace except for the serious doubt that such antipathies are bio-

[14] *Foreign Influences in American Life*, 1944, p. 66.

logically rooted." [15] In the last decade, science has forced a substitution of the social for the biological view of the racial question and this substitution has opened the way for social action. "If men define situations as real," wrote W. I. Thomas, "they are real in their consequences." A change in the public's definition of the nature of the problem, therefore, has always been the first condition to any improvement in race relations in the United States. That change has now taken place and it is, beyond any doubt, the most significant development in race relations since the Civil War.

The significance of this change is strikingly apparent in the impact of social theory on judicial thinking. Court decisions on racial questions have always reflected the prevailing ideology — that is, the dominant opinions, attitudes, and values. For example, the decision on which the whole structure of segregation has long rested, *Plessy* v. *Ferguson* (163 U. S. 537), is based upon the clearly stated assumption: "If one race is inferior to the other socially, the Constitution of the United States cannot put them upon the same plane." Indeed the correlation between social theory and judicial assumption has been consistently close. Racial prejudice, writes Dr. Ellsworth Faris, the sociologist, is relatively independent of formal legal sanction: "It is a matter of the *mores* and not of the law." [16] This, of course, has long been the legal theory. "This prejudice," the California Supreme Court once stated, "if it exists, is not created by law and probably cannot be changed by law." [17] In point of fact, however, the laws and the mores have never been more weirdly out of relation than on racial issues; it is this discrepancy which has created the "American dilemma."

In the period from 1868 to 1936, as Morroe Berger has pointed out, the law was used to buttress the caste order in

[15] "Peace as a Problem of Ethnology," by Robert S. Redfield, Walgren Foundation Lecture, February 2, 1944.
[16] *American Journal of Sociology*, March 1944, p. 461.
[17] 48 Calif. 36.

those respects in which custom no longer sufficed to maintain traditional patterns of race relations.[18] In this period,
Negroes won only two of fourteen cases before the Supreme
Court in which they sought to use the same public facilities
as whites, and only six of sixteen cases in which they sought
to obtain federal protection of their right to vote. In retrospect it can hardly be denied that the Supreme Court played
an enormously important role, in this period, in keeping
Negroes in their place. On this point, Mr. Berger's conclusion
is unassailable: ". . . from 1868 to about a decade ago the
Supreme Court supported those laws tending to enforce the
separation of Negroes and whites and weakened the operation
of those tending to facilitate the meeting of the two groups
except in situations clearly maintaining the superiority of the
whites." [19] The new trend in the Supreme Court's decisions
on racial issues dates from about 1937 and reflects, in large
part, the change in social theory. In other words, the legal
"definition of the situation" has been consistently influenced
by the scientific definition and has changed as that definition
has changed. Few developments of the last eight years, therefore, have been more significant than the series of victories
which racial minorities have won in the Supreme Court. By
and large it can be said that racial minorities have won every
important issue before the court in this period. The court
decisions, of course, have profoundly influenced public
opinion and have set the stage, so to speak, for legislative
action. The trend of decision in the United States Supreme
Court since 1937 is of exceptional historical importance since
it implies a reversal of the series of decisions by which, in the
post-Civil War period, the court sanctioned the segregation
and, later, the disfranchisement of Negroes.[20]

[18] "The Supreme Court and Group Discrimination Since 1937," by Morroe
Berger, *Columbia Law Review*, February 1949.
[19] Berger, *Ibid.*
[20] "The Upgrading of the Negro's Status by Supreme Court Decisions,"
by Raymond Pace Alexander, *Journal of Negro History*, April 1945; "The

## 3. The Civic Unity Movement

With changes in the underlying social factors and the ideology of race relations being accelerated by the war, it took only the shock of the race riots of 1943 to set in motion, on a scale and with an enthusiasm previously unmatched, the first seriously undertaken attempt "to do something about" the racial problem. From the restoration of Bourbon supremacy until about 1940, there had been little effective social action in the field of race relations anywhere in the United States, North or South. True, there had been certain philanthropical endeavors and attempts had been made, here and there, to deal with the consequences of discrimination, but nothing in the way of a frontal attack on the problem itself had been undertaken.

Race riots had been anticipated at the end of World War II: not at the end of the North African campaign. This sudden "premature" epidemic of open racial violence shocked America into action. Most of the action taken was improvised, unco-ordinated, and not too effective, but important gains were made in organizing, for the first time, a public opinion on the subject. Today there are over 500 local, state, and national organizations working in the field of group relations, of which half or more have been established since June 1943.[21] Organized activity has been reported in 33 states and the District of Columbia. By January 1, 1948, there were approxi-

Negro in the Supreme Court," by Edward V. Waite, *Minnesota Law Review*, March 1946. On the subject of the mores and the law see my article "Race Discrimination and the Law," *Science and Society*, Vol. IX (Winter 1945). The interest that this article aroused — it was reprinted as a pamphlet and appears in many source books — is an indication of the fact that it had never occurred to many people that the law had been used to influence the mores. See *When Peoples Meet*, edited by Alain Locke and Bernhard J. Stern, Revised Edition, 1946, pp. 768–777.

[21] *Directory of Agencies in Race Relations*, 1945, issued by Julius Rosenwald Fund, Chicago.

mately 48 officially constituted local agencies, not to mention any number of official state commissions. A measure of effective co-ordination has been achieved, also, through such organizations as the California Federation for Civic Unity; the Southern Regional Council (formed in 1944); and the American Council on Race Relations, formed in the summer of 1944.

The mushrooming of these agencies is one of the most remarkable developments in the field of community social action of the last quarter century. Today a large number of these local councils have full-time paid secretaries and the personnel combined, some time ago, to form the National Association of Intergroup Relations Officials. In a sense, the way was paved for the "civic unity" movement by the practice of certain New Deal agencies, dating from the middle 1930's, of appointing Negro "race relations advisors." At one time or another, Dr. Robert C. Weaver, William Trent, Mary McLeod Bethune, Alfred Edgar Smith, E. M. Lancaster, William Hastie, Theodore Poston, Henry Lee Moon, T. Arnold Hill, Frank Horne, Thomas Roberts, and Theodore Berry served in this capacity for various federal agencies and exerted a very real influence on federal policy. It was this group which formed the much-discussed "Black Cabinet" of the late thirties. In a number of instances, former federal race relations advisors became executive directors of civic unity councils.[22]

The chief historical importance of the civic unity movement, as Dr. Robert C. Weaver has pointed out, is that it represents, for the first time, an official recognition of the race problem in areas outside the Deep South.[23] A generation ago Northerners discussed "the racial problem" with detachment; after 1943 it became an urgent concern. While it is true that

[22] *In a Minor Key*, by Ira de A. Reid, 1940, p. 110.
[23] "Whither Northern Race Relations Committees?" by Robert C. Weaver, *Phylon*, vol. V, no. 3, p. 205.

many of the civic unity councils were inspired by fear and were products of "crisis patriotism," it is also true that they have come to represent something new in group social action. Scores of communities, from coast to coast, have undertaken self-surveys, "social audits," and investigations since 1943 which have added not only to the available information on race relations but to our knowledge of community organization in general. Not only have thousands of individuals received an intensive social education from the findings of these surveys, and from participation in them, but entire communities have been made aware of factors in their growth and organization of which little had been previously known. To assess the importance of the civic unity movement, therefore, it is important to realize that a community's pattern of race relations illuminates nearly every phase of its civic life. Thus a "social audit" on race relations, if properly conducted, cannot fail to point up general problems of housing, health, education, employment, and similar issues. In many cities, audits and surveys of this character have suddenly taken on an extraordinary social and political importance. More than one conniving mayor has appointed a "civic unity council" as a means of appeasing organized racial minorities, only to discover that he has given the community a most effective means of pressuring him not on one but on a dozen different issues.

The formation of civic unity councils, also, has had an important influence on community organization generally. The simplest kind of organized activity in the field of race relations immediately raises basic problems of community organization. To do anything about race relations in a community, you must know something about the community and also something about community organization, a field in which our knowledge is still largely on an intuitive and rough empirical level. The civic unity movement has provided an all-important field for experimentation in community organization and in the training of community leaders. The experience that has already been accumulated is of immense value. For example, in such publications as *To Secure These Rights in Your Community* (American Council on Race Relations, June 1948) and *Towards Better Race Relations* (Michigan Council of Churches, September 1945), communities have been provided with excellent practical manuals and guidebooks in community organization and social action. In many conferences held since 1943, such as the Institute on Race Relations and Community Organization held at the University of Chicago June 18–29, 1945, hundreds of civic leaders have been given excellent training in community organization. More than one civic unity council, formed to cope with the disturbing events of 1943, has already begun to define its functions, in terms not of race relations, but of "group relations" generally or "human relations." Indeed what people who have participated in the civic unity movement have learned about race relations and racial conflicts has thrown a great deal of light on other conflicts and relationships and, above all, it has been a great aid to self-knowledge on the part of groups and communities as well as individuals. In more than one case, communities have been able to achieve general over-all civic organization, for the first time, around the issue of civic unity.

It is also true, however, that many local civic unity councils have been wholly ineffective; that others have been used by politicians to manipulate racial minorities; and that still others have become "centers of organized local futility." Discount the achievements as one will, however, the record of the civic unity movement is truly impressive and it shows what can happen, and with what swiftness, once people acquire a feeling that "the racial problem" is not an insoluble biological dilemma. As fairly typical of the concrete achievements of civic unity councils of the more active variety, consider the report of the Toledo Board of Community Relations for an eighteen-month period. Listed among the accomplishments for the period are the following:

1. Five nurse training schools now accept Negro trainees.
2. Practical-nurse training programs are now open to all applicants.
3. Toledo Ohio Bell Telephone Company now employs Negro operators.
4. Red Cab Company now hires Negro drivers.
5. Toledo hotels will make accommodations available to all persons.
6. Segregated dressmaking classes eliminated in the commercial school program.
7. The University of Toledo declined to recognize a social-professional fraternity that excluded certain groups from membership.
8. The National Association for the Advancement of Colored People participated fully in the Lucas County March of Dimes campaign.
9. The City Civil Service Commission modified application forms to eliminate questions of race and creed.
10. Negro veterans were accepted in the federal housing project without incident.
11. City ordinances were passed prohibiting discrimination by operators of any municipal franchise.
12. Split bus service involving segregation of Negroes was eliminated.
13. The Board of Education began to eliminate discrimination from school programs.
14. An interracial program was initiated at East Toledo Neighborhood House.[24]

It will be noted that there is nothing very spectacular about any of these achievements and that most of them can best be appraised as "token" or "symbolic." Achievements of this sort are not too important in themselves but the cumulative

[24] *New York Times*, November 6, 1949.

effect on public opinion, and on attitudes, is probably quite influential.

## 4. *From Civic Unity to Fair Practices*

Once people, including the racial minorities themselves, were convinced that the race problem was not an insoluble riddle, the question immediately arose: What form should action take? Of the various answers given to this question none has been more far-reaching in importance than the notion of "fair practices." Today the conception of fair, that is, nondiscriminatory, practices has been extended to many fields other than employment. One hears, for example, of fair housing practices, fair public health practices, fair educational practices, and, currently, the NAACP has proposed a federal "fair elections" act.[25] Certainly the idea that constitutional guarantees of equal treatment can be implemented by action aimed at preventing discrimination is the most fruitful suggestion for social action that has emerged from the debate and discussion of the racial question since 1940.

The idea of fair practices derives, of course, from the civil rights legislation which Congress adopted in the period from 1866 to 1875, most of which was held unconstitutional in 1883. This legislation was aimed at safeguarding constitutionally sanctioned rights by affirmative legislation. In essence, "fair employment practices," and similar measures, represent merely an extension of the policy of insuring equal treatment to all citizens in the domain of public life. World War II created both the necessity and the opportunity for carrying this idea into effect. The responsibility of the federal government was clearly defined. Most of the friction incidents stemmed directly from the mistreatment of Negro soldiers by civilians or from discrimination in the armed services. The government, moreover, was not only the chief employer

[25] *Ibid.*, October 6, 1947.

of labor but it was in a position to influence general employment policies and it had the most compelling reasons for insisting upon the fullest and most efficient utilization of all manpower resources. Aside from one or two perfunctory gestures, however, the government failed to act.

Then, early in June 1941, it was announced that the March-on-Washington Movement, led by A. Philip Randolph, Walter White, A. Clayton Powell, Jr., and Frank Crosswaith, intended to rally at least 50,000 Negroes in Washington on July 1 to demand federal action aimed at minimizing discrimination in the defense industries and in the armed services. Nearly everyone was "alarmed"; even Mrs. Roosevelt stated that "the March will be a very grave mistake." But the March got action which two years of polite exhortation had failed to produce. On June 25, 1941, President Roosevelt signed Executive Order No. 8802, creating the Fair Employment Practices Commission — the most significant executive action in the field of race relations since President Lincoln issued the Emancipation Proclamation.

Indeed the importance of this action can hardly be exaggerated for it marked a reversal of the policy which the federal government had followed since the original civil rights legislation had been invalidated in 1883, namely, a laissez-faire policy based on the assumption that there was nothing the federal government could do to protect the civil rights of citizens of the United States. Even the fairly obvious notion that the federal government might itself refrain from discrimination failed to muster much support. Once the FEPC order was issued, however, the disastrous hypnotic illusion that government was powerless to prevent discrimination was destroyed and proposals for similar action by cities and states, and in other fields too, came thick and fast. On March 5, 1945, New York adopted the Ives-Quinn antidiscrimination measure and other states and a number of municipalities have since taken similar action. Nor was it long before the idea of fair practices began to find reflection in such statutes as the Fair Educational Practices Act which was adopted in New York on September 15, 1948.

The fight for a permanent FEPC marks the fullest expression of the wartime "crisis patriotism" and the abolition of the commission is the division point between the ferment of the war years and the backwash of "peace." The battle for the FEPC, now in its tenth year, throws into bold relief the strength and weakness of the conflicting social forces which have joined issue on the race question in the United States. In some respects, the dynamics of the struggle follow the general outline of the battle over Reconstruction.[26]

President Roosevelt's executive order creating the FEPC was issued during the period of national emergency proclaimed after the fall of France. Although we were not then at war, the order was issued pursuant to the emergency powers which had been conferred on the President, and, in this respect, the order was issued under circumstances analogous to those under which President Lincoln had issued another famous executive order, namely, the Emancipation Proclamation. One year later, however, Vito Marcantonio introduced a bill to create a permanent FEPC with statutory powers, but the bill died in committee. Although it lacked clearly defined powers, the President's committee held a series of successful hearings and had scheduled a crucial hearing on the discrimination practiced by the railroad brotherhoods for January 1943. This hearing had hardly been announced before the chairman was forced to cancel it and the FEPC began to disintegrate rapidly. It was this new crisis which compelled President Roosevelt to issue Executive Order No. 9346 on May 27, 1943, giving a broader definition of the committee's powers and appointing Bishop Francis J. Haas as the new chairman. The railroad hearings were then rescheduled and

[26] "FEPC – A Case History in Parliamentary Maneuver," by Will Maslow, *University of Chicago Law Review*, June 1946.

held but the fight to abolish the FEPC really dates from this period.

Up to this time, the FEPC had been financed by extremely modest appropriations from the President's emergency war funds, but in March 1944 Senator Richard B. Russell of Georgia succeeded in forcing the adoption of an amendment to an appropriations bill the effect of which was to make the FEPC look exclusively to Congress for future appropriations. A bitter battle then ensued over an appropriation for the committee, culminating in an interim appropriation for one year. In the meantime, bills introduced in both the House and the Senate to create a permanent FEPC had died in committee.

The next year the matter of an appropriation was again before Congress. For six weeks or more, the House and Senate wrangled over the question of an appropriation, with the Southern contingent indulging in every parliamentary trick and maneuver, including an abortive filibuster, to prevent a clear-cut vote. On July 15, 1945, both houses finally agreed on a measure which gave the FEPC an appropriation for the purpose of winding up its affairs. The friends of the FEPC still hoped that the agency might be given permanent statutory status before the appropriation expired, but on January 17, 1946, the Southerners launched a filibuster which lasted through February 9, when a resolution to invoke cloture was defeated by a vote of 48 to 36, 24 votes less than the requisite two thirds. There was then nothing for Malcolm Ross, executive director of the FEPC, to do but to call Archives "to come cart away the nonhuman remnants" and thus the FEPC died, not with a bang but a whimper.

Future historians, surveying the record up to this point, are almost certain to agree with the conclusion of Senator Wayne Morse, namely, that Congress had played ". . . a very interesting game of ducks and drakes . . . on a matter of vital importance to our country politically — whether or not we are going to demonstrate that under a democracy minority rights can be protected." In those great months in the spring of 1945 — with V-E Day in sight — here was the American Congress wrangling for weeks on end over a matter of basic, simple, democratic morality. At one point, the Senate took time out to wish Senators Vandenberg and Connally godspeed on their way to San Francisco to help draft a new charter of human freedom — and then promptly resumed the dirty business of killing the FEPC, not openly, not directly, but by parliamentary trickery. The worst of the maneuvering took place at a time, as Malcolm Ross has pointed out, when the fleets were moving in on Japan and Hiroshima was but a few weeks away.[27] Almost at the very moment when the delegates in San Francisco were announcing the adoption of the charter of the United Nations — with Article I, Paragraph 3, clearly enunciating a policy of freedom "without distinction as to race, sex, language or religion" — the Southern contingent in Congress, in unholy alliance with members of the Republican Party, was strangling the FEPC. There was more than irony in this spectacle: it held the shape of things to come; it pointed up, as nothing else could, the fact that the American people were not yet prepared to honor their commitment to human freedom; it was a signal for the resumption of prejudice-as-usual.

But there was something else that was significant about this sad spectacle. Up to this time, there had never really been *a vote* on the FEPC: the measure was killed by maneuver; by trickery; by a perversion of democratic processes. In 1944 both Roosevelt and Dewey had in effect endorsed the FEPC, yet neither party stood by its implied commitments. Malcolm Ross is authority for the statement that there was at all times "a technical majority in both the Senate and the House" in favor of the FEPC.[28] The humiliating fact is that the FEPC

[27] *All Manner of Men*, by Malcolm Ross, 1948.
[28] *Ibid.*, p. 305.

was killed, not by its enemies, but by the lack of conviction of its sponsors. "The FEPC filibuster," writes Malcolm Ross, "was never really fought, except with light blows which fooled no one." Denouncing the "Chesterfieldian attitudes" of the sponsors of FEPC, Will Maslow has this to say of their attempt to break the 1946 filibuster: ". . . the friends of FEPC, with only a few exceptions, showed no capacity for fighting back at the Southern bloc. . . . The friends of FEPC made only half-hearted attempts to break this one [the filibuster]. The struggle against the filibuster seemed to many political observers a sham, if not a fraud. The supporters of the FEPC on both sides of the aisle conducted the fight in a Marquis of Queensberry atmosphere. Every courtesy was extended to the opposition and no effort put forth to make their task more difficult. To many, the struggle of the FEPC bloc seemed almost like a political chore, a disagreeable duty to be got over with as soon as possible." [29]

Nor has the situation changed. Four days after President Truman, speaking in the Chicago Stadium on May 15, 1950, reaffirmed his pledge, and the pledge set forth in the 1948 platform of the Democratic Party, to make an all-out fight for "laws that will guarantee all our citizens equal rights," the Democrats managed to produce *exactly 19 votes* for cloture on the FEPC in the Senate. On July 12, with the headlines reading "Battered U. S. Line Holds in Korea," and "Draftees Slated to Be Called," the Senate by a vote of 33 to 55 refused to limit debate on the measure. The fact that it took *eight years* to get even a roll-call vote on the FEPC, not to mention the subsequent defeats, is some measure of the strength of the hidden social forces which support discrimination.

The truth which the ten-year struggle for the FEPC so clearly reveals is that a majority of the American people are for racial equality "in principle" but are not prepared to fight

[29] Maslow, *op. cit.*, p. 440.

for this principle in action. This inconsistency is glaringly evident in the schizophrenia of the Democratic Party on the question of civil rights legislation. Senator Lister Hill of Alabama is a leading spokesman for the Democratic Party and a loyal supporter of President Truman. Yet here are some excerpts from a re-election campaign speech which Hill made in Alabama in April 1950: "I tell you it is the power and influence of your [the South's] Senators and Congressmen that has made possible the defeat of the FEPC and other so-called civil rights bills. The anti-poll-tax bill is bottled up today in a subcommittee of the Senate Rules Committee of which Senator John C. Stennis [Democrat, Mississippi] is chairman. . . . The general civil rights bill is bottled up today in a subcommittee of the Senate Judiciary Committee of which Senator Jim [James O.] Eastland [Democrat, Mississippi] is chairman. . . . I led the fight in committee against the FEPC bill, and the committee dropped it like a foundling on the Senate's doorstep — without a word in its favor." Charged with rank hypocrisy by Senator Robert C. Hendrickson of New Jersey, Hill's only comment was: "I was speaking to the people of Alabama." [30]

The defeat of the FEPC symbolized more than the fact that by the spring of 1945 the wartime wave of crisis patriotism had begun to subside; it also implied that an effort would be made to wipe out the gains of the war years. By failing to insist on the passage of the FEPC, a majority of the American people made it possible for reaction to use the racial issue to strike down advocates of fair treatment and equality. For example, in the first North Carolina primary in 1950 Senator Frank P. Graham led in 63 of 100 counties, acquiring a lead of 53,000 votes; but in the run-off his opponent reversed the tables, captured 61 counties, and won the nomination by 20,000 votes. In the first campaign, the race-baiting was mild but in the second all the stops were pulled. The racial issue

[30] *New York Times*, April 15, 1950.

"spread like wildfire" and Senator Graham was defeated.[31]

As a premonition of troubles ahead, a wave of "hate strikes" broke out in the schools which coincided almost to the day and hour with the achievement of victory. On September 15, 1945, a strike at the Froebel School in Gary, Indiana, touched off a nation-wide series of disturbances. Similar "hate strikes" were reported in Chicago on September 26, in New York on September 27, in Los Angeles on October 11 and in a number of other communities. It was as though the accumulated tensions of the war years were finding initial expression in the area where, perhaps, the repressions had been most keenly felt, namely, among teen-age youngsters, too young to have worked in war plants or to have served with the armed forces but old enough to have experienced all the strains and tensions of the war. Here, as an editorial in the *Michigan Chronicle* pointed out, was "young America going crazy on the race issue at the very moment in our national history when we were celebrating a great victory over the enemies of democracy."

## 5. The Crisis of 1946

The effort to invoke cloture on the FEPC was defeated, it will be recalled, on February 9, 1946. Almost as if in response to this fact — as though the traditionally biased elements somehow sensed that the wartime ferment had spent its force — the first major postwar race riot occurred on February 25, 1946, at Columbia, Tennessee. On the morning of that day, Mrs. Gladys Stephenson, a Negro, and her son James, a nineteen-year-old veteran, entered a radio repair shop. In the argument which ensued, the white proprietor struck and kicked Mrs. Stephenson and her son promptly intervened. The police, however, arrested only the Stephensons. When a white mob sought to invade the Negro section that night, it

[31] *Ibid.,* June 26, 1950.

was driven back by gunfire. Troops were then sent in "to restore order" but stayed to riot. They broke the windows of buildings in the Negro section and sprayed the interiors with machine gun fire. Not a business establishment in the area escaped damage. In the aftermath, about a hundred Negroes were arrested, held incommunicado for periods ranging from three to eight days, and were denied the right of counsel at their preliminary hearing. Any number were beaten in jail and two were shot and killed inside the jail. Although the Negroes indicted were finally acquitted, the riot was an omen that now that the war abroad was over, the war at home might be resumed. Even before the Columbia riot, Isaac Woodard, Jr., a Negro veteran, was removed from a bus in South Carolina and, in the course of a merciless beating, permanently blinded. Congressional debate on the FEPC was responsible it was said for the first postwar emergence of the Ku Klux Klan on October 10, 1945, with the burning of a fiery cross on Stone Mountain near Atlanta. Following the defeat of cloture, officials of the Klan paid corporate registration fees in Atlanta on March 21, 1946, and announced that the KKK was being revived.

In large part, however, the crisis of 1946 was precipitated by an 8 to 1 decision which the Supreme Court had handed down on April 4, 1944, at a time when the nation awaited word of the impending invasion of Europe. The decision in this case — *Smith* v. *Allwright* — struck down, once and for all time, the "white primary" of the Southern states. Almost immediately, the Solid South was faced with an internal split for the first time since the Civil War. The impact of the decision, however, was not felt until 1946 when Negro veterans, in large numbers, began to return to Southern communities. For example, by November 28, 1946, it was estimated that 20,000 Negro veterans had returned to New Orleans alone.

The impact of the Supreme Court's decision was particularly noticeable in Georgia by reason of the fact that, under Governor Ellis Arnall, Georgia had abolished the poll tax in 1943. Immediately following the decision in *Smith* v. *Allwright*, Primus E. King, a Negro of Columbia, Georgia, had attempted to vote in the Democratic primary of July 4, 1944, only to be turned away from the polls. He brought suit at once in the federal courts and his right to vote was upheld. Then, in February 1946, a special election was held in the Fifth Congressional District in Georgia and, in this election, Mrs. Helen Douglas Mankin, strongly supported by the Negroes of the district, came in ahead. The Bourbons immediately reintroduced the "county unit system" of voting, and in the July 1946 primary Mrs. Mankin was defeated.

The removal of the poll tax, the decision in the Primus King case, the election of Mrs. Mankin, and the registration of some 20,000 Negro voters in Atlanta, gave a special meaning to the July 1946 primary in which former Governor Eugene Talmadge sought to be elected, once again, to the office. Few campaigns of recent years in the South can match this one for bitterness and violence and the open incitation of racial antagonism. The Ku Klux Klan conducted numerous parades and meetings and engaged in many cross burnings and convocations. The real violence came, however, in the wake of Talmadge's victory.

Three days after the Democratic primary, five Negroes were lynched. One of them, Macio Snipes, a veteran, had been the only Negro to vote in Taylor County. Then, on July 20, 1946 — a date to be remembered — a mob of white men, unmasked, seized two Negro couples and killed them in broad daylight on a highway near Monroe, Georgia. "Three volleys of shots," reported the President's Committee on Civil Rights, "were fired as if by a squad of professional executioners. The coroner's report said that at least 60 bullets were found in the scarcely recognizable bodies." Although committed in a small rural county by members of an unmasked mob, this crime went unpunished and, for a long time, no investigation was made. The five Georgia lynchings, or executions, were clearly by way of retaliation against the Negroes of the state who had sent nearly 100,000 voters to the polls in the July primary. Later in the year, Columbians, Inc., launched the first fascist *Putsch* in America in Atlanta, which, like its famous Munich counterpart, was a strategic failure but a propaganda success.[32] All of these happenings took place, it should be emphasized, when the United States was still technically at war, the President's proclamation terminating hostilities not being issued until December 31, 1946.

When Negro veterans began to return to their homes in Mississippi early in 1946, they heard about "the new law," a phrase which the Negroes used to refer to *Smith* v. *All-wright*. The new law said that Negroes could vote in the Democratic primary. As though to confirm this happy news, the Mississippi legislature passed a law in April 1946 exempting *all* veterans, without distinction of color, from the payment of the poll tax for the requisite two years preceding the election of 1946. What clearer indication could have been given the Negro veterans that Mississippi had decided to acquiesce in the new law? Negroes had a special interest in voting in the Democratic primary that year, for Senator Theodore G. Bilbo, who had spent many hours vilifying Negro soldiers during the war, was a candidate for re-election. Like Talmadge in Georgia, Bilbo made a series of inflammatory speeches. In a speech in Jackson, on June 22, he appealed to "red-blooded Anglo-Saxons" to bar Negroes from the polls and said that "white men have the right to resort to any means at their command" to achieve this end.[33] This particular speech was prompted by the attempt of Elroy Fletcher, a Negro veteran with twenty-three months' service in the Pacific — a GI student at Jackson College — to register. For this offense, Fletcher was beaten and flogged with a heavy

[32] See Chapter IX, *A Mask for Privilege*.
[33] *New York Times*, June 23, 1946.

wire cable. On the eve of the primary election, a committee of leading white citizens in Greenwood called in the Negro leaders for a conference. The Negro delegation was given a list of Negro veterans and told to visit each one and to warn them not to vote. "They said five of us could vote but that there would be trouble if others tried to." Greenwood, the county seat of Laflore County, has a population of 14,384 whites, 38,970 Negroes. None of the Negro veterans voted.

The Mississippi election would have been pretty unpalatable at any time but it could hardly pass unnoticed so soon after the end of the war. So a Senate committee, under the benign chairmanship of Senator Allen J. Ellender of Louisiana, opened hearings in Mississippi on December 2, 1946. Although Bilbo was never seated, he won vindication by this committee. Despite certain intramural differences, the "whites" of Mississippi closed ranks and rallied in defense of the South's most notorious race-baiter. With the exception of a Roman Catholic priest and a rabbi, not a white man took the stand to find any fault with Bilbo's campaign of vituperation and abuse.[34] "Senator Bilbo," reported Carl Levin in the *New York Herald Tribune* (December 6, 1946), "was in fine fettle for his appearance at the hearing. Under the kleig lights of newsreel cameras, his face lighted up as the crowded room, jammed with his followers, reverberated with laughter or applause as he expounded his philosophy."

Nevertheless the committee — and all Mississippi — was amazed when nearly 150 black Mississippians crowded into the hearing room and demanded a right to be heard. "For the first time since Reconstruction," reported Mr. Levin, "Mississippi Negroes stood up as a group to fight their enemy." "Here in this seat of white supremacy," wrote Robert C. Williams in the *New York Post* of December 3, "something almost incredible is happening, which transcends the issue over the legality of Senator Bilbo's re-election. The Negro

[34] *Ibid.*, December 8, 1946, story by Harold B. Hinton.

is standing up for his rights. . . . He is being laughed at when he stammers or stumbles over his words, but the penetrating fact is that he is speaking his mind. Before he retreated in silence." The Negro was speaking his mind in many places in 1946, particularly the Negro veteran, and in places outside the South, this show of independence was meeting with violence: witness the burning of a Negro veteran's home in Redwood City, California, on December 6; of a riot in Philadelphia on September 29; and the first of a series of public housing riots in Chicago on December 7, 1946. Slight wonder, then, that Walter White should have told the annual meeting of the NAACP that "the year just ended has been one of the grimmest years in the history of the NAACP. Negroes in America have been disillusioned over the wave of lynchings, brutality, and official recession from all of the flamboyant promises of postwar democracy and decency." The only bright spot was "the flame of resistance" with which Negroes had greeted the counterattack of 1946.

It was the events of 1946, and particularly the Monroe lynchings, that prompted President Truman to issue Executive Order No. 9808, on December 5, 1946, establishing the Committee on Civil Rights. The strongest possible representations had been made to Mr. Truman following the Georgia lynchings. Not knowing just what to do and already worried about the 1948 election, the President did what is usually done under similar circumstances: he appointed a committee. "The historians of the next generation," reported Albert Anderson in an article for the Associated Negro Press on January 3, 1947, "will in all probability set 1946 down as the year when certain gains made in race relations in the South faced certain and dangerous setbacks. While they were mostly gains made temporarily as a result of the needs for unity in the nation during the war years, the swiftness with which the forces of reaction asserted themselves was definitely disappointing." It was the gathering of these forces, like a cloud on the horizon, that compelled the President to take action. If he had not appointed the Committee on Civil Rights, the wartime gains might have been nullified or reversed.

## 6. To Secure These Rights

In the wake of the disasters and reversals of 1946, the new year opened most inauspiciously with the national spotlight focused on South Carolina. On February 17, 1947, a Negro was removed from the jail in Greenville, viciously beaten, and finally shot to death in what came to be known as "the taxicab riot," since most of the rioters were cab drivers. With Negroes providing more than half the business for the local cab drivers, Negroes had only 5 of the more than 140 taxicabs in the city — a detail inadvertently revealed in the subsequent investigation. Twenty-eight defendants were arrested and placed on trial in this, the biggest lynching trial in the South's history. In this instance, a serious effort was made to secure a conviction: the trial judge was conspicuously fair and firm; the prosecution was conducted in a resolute manner; and yet, on the evening of May 21, the jury returned its verdict acquitting all defendants. With Negroes in the balcony looking down on the scene, a large crowd took over the courtroom as soon as the judge had retired to his chambers. There was great jubilation and merrymaking: speeches were made; jokes were cracked; and the defendants were toasted. Early the next morning, another Negro was taken from a jail by a lynch mob, this time in Jackson, North Carolina, but he finally managed to escape. Then, on July 11, eight Negro prisoners were killed by their white guards in a state prison camp at Glynn, Georgia, "while attempting to escape." These events, of course, merely stiffened the national determination to protect the civil rights of minorities; the celebration in the courthouse at Greenville was carefully noted — outside the South.

The South Carolina legislature had previously repealed all legislation bearing on primary elections — a hundred and fifty statutes in all — in response to the Governor's message stating that because of the decision in *Smith* v. *Allwright* it had become "absolutely necessary that we repeal all laws pertaining to primaries in order to maintain white supremacy in our Democratic primaries in South Carolina." This public conspiracy on the part of the governor and legislature of an American state to deprive citizens of their civil rights was upset by Federal Judge J. Waties Waring in a decision handed down on July 12, 1947. A native South Carolinian, Judge Waring suggested that it was time ". . . for South Carolina to rejoin the Union. It is time to fall in step with the other states and to adopt the American way of conducting elections." Although a substantial section of "white" opinion in South Carolina was quite willing to acquiesce in Judge Waring's decision, the Democratic Party in its convention in May 1948 adopted a new rule, requiring all voters to state under oath that they would "support the social, religious and educational separation of races" and oppose the federal "F.E.P.C. law"! This clumsy stratagem was promptly set aside by Judge Waring: "It would seem . . . that the action of the convention was a deliberate attempt to evade the apparent consequence of the Elmore case." In their running fight with Judge Waring, the South Carolina white supremacy advocates later adopted a law denying the right to vote to persons convicted of any of the following offenses, unless such disqualification had been removed by pardon, namely: burglary, arson, obtaining property under false pretenses, perjury, forgery, robbery, bribery, adultery, bigamy, wife-beating, house-breaking, receiving stolen goods, breach of trust, fornication, sodomy, incest, assault with intent to ravish, miscegenation, larceny and crimes against the election laws! Despite this legislation, it is estimated that between 50,000 and 60,000 Negroes voted in the Democratic primary in South

Carolina in the spring of 1950.[35] The immediate reaction to South Carolina's attempt to evade Judge Waring's first decision, however, was again to stiffen national determination to take a strong line with the South. Somewhat belatedly, the nation was reacting to the violence and disorders of 1946.

The pressures for action, rapidly mounting throughout 1947, were not entirely domestic in origin. On October 24, 1947, the NAACP filed formal charges with the United Nations over the discrimination against Negroes in the United States. To this sober, factual indictment, prepared by Dr. W. E. B. Du Bois, Earle Dickerson, William Ming, Leslie Perry, and others, there could only be one plea, namely, "guilty on all counts." The presentation of the indictment had been carefully and accurately timed. The United Nations was then debating charges of discrimination against Indians in South Africa and the issue of Negro discrimination in the United States was clearly of equal if not greater significance. Speaking in the name of 13,000,000 American Negroes, Dr. Du Bois said: "We number as many as the inhabitants of the Argentine or Czechoslovakia, or the whole of Scandinavia. . . . We are very nearly the size of Egypt, Rumania and Yugoslavia. We are larger than Canada, Saudi Arabia, Ethiopia, Hungary or the Netherlands. We have twice as many persons as Australia or Switzerland, and more than the whole Union of South Africa. We have more people than Portugal or Peru; twice as many as Greece and nearly as many as Turkey. We have more people by far than Belgium and half as many as Spain. In sheer numbers then we are a group which has a right to be heard." The Drafting Committee of the Commission on Human Rights was even then debating the form that the Declaration of Human Rights should take. Although the filing of the NAACP's charges attracted little attention in the American press, the impact in official circles was profound.

[35] *Ibid.*, April 14, 1950, story by W. H. Lawrence.

Three days after the charges had been filed at Lake Success, Attorney General Tom C. Clark, speaking in Boston, said that he felt "humiliated" that any group of American citizens should feel that it was necessary to seek a redress of grievances before the United Nations. He went on to say: "No act of accidental injustice, let alone those of calculation, will go unobserved by our enemies. Lip service to our ideals will be seen for the mockery that it is." Although the Commission on Human Rights, meeting in Geneva on December 4, 1947, voted down the Soviet proposal to investigate the charges filed by the NAACP, the filing of the petition had served a major purpose: Washington was deeply disturbed. Almost at the moment that Dr. Du Bois was presenting the petition, the press carried stories (November 28, 1947) that the Freedom Train, sponsored by Attorney General Clark, carrying the nation's treasured documents of human liberty, had been forced to by-pass a score or more of Southern communities that had refused to waive the Jim Crow ban. One could almost graph the mounting moral, political, and psychological pressures occasioned by these incidents.

It was at this critical period, late in October, 1947, that the Report of the President's Committee on Civil Rights was issued. The response to the report — "To Secure These Rights" — was astonishing: something like 1,000,000 copies were distributed and the general comment, editorial and otherwise, was enormous in extent and surprisingly favorable. Then, on December 11, 1947, came the report of the President's Commission on Higher Education, recommending the removal of all religious and racial barriers to learning and presenting an airtight case against quota systems and segregated schools.

The two documents, taken together, are of great historic importance. For the first time, the nation had taken a systematic inventory of civil rights, noting areas of relative strength, pointing out areas of weakness and regression. Of greater importance was the fact that the federal government had now clearly reversed its laissez-faire attitude toward the denial of civil rights to racial minorities. The existence of a positive obligation to secure these rights to racial minorities was now recognized for the first time since the Civil War. In historical terms, the issuance of the report on civil rights constituted a reversal of the fateful Compromise of 1876 by which the South, which had lost the war, forced a restoration of Bourbon supremacy.

To appreciate the importance of the report on civil rights, however, two additional factors must be kept in mind. In the first place, the report was not issued in a vacuum. The issuance of the report was, so to speak, the culmination to a period of great ferment and discussion, of great social change, and of intensive organizational activity which had transformed the character of the racial problem in the thinking of many people. For example, the 130 lynchings reported in 1900 aroused far less attention than the single lynching in Greenville, South Carolina, in 1947. As late as 1930 the volume of Negro protest was negligible; indeed it was not until 1938 that Negroes carried the question of their right to attend tax-supported professional schools to the courts and it was not until 1940 that they demanded, and won, the right to be paid the same salaries as white teachers, for the same services, in the public schools. But by 1947 the Negro minority was in a position not only to appreciate the importance of the report on civil rights but to exploit it.

In the second place, the report scotched, once and for all time, the defeatist notion that there was nothing much that could be done about the problem of racial discrimination. The political instincts of the average American citizen told him that this do-nothing defeatism was absurd but he wanted some official assurance, some indicated direction, a program in support of which opinion could be rallied. The report met this need; it was the nation's response to the challenge of the crisis year, 1946. By the spring of 1948, the public opinion polls were showing that civil rights had suddenly become a popular political issue.

About the report of the President's committee, and the idea for such a committee, there was little that was novel. In 1912 the newly formed NAACP had urged President Wilson to appoint such a committee. Oswald Garrison Villard, who presented the petition to the President on behalf of the NAACP, gave me the following account of what happened (in a personal letter of May 4, 1943): "Wilson . . . pretended to be much interested when I gave it to him, said he would give me an answer in due course and then refused to reply at all. When he was finally compelled to do so, he said he could not appoint it because he was a Democratic President from the South and the South would get the impression that he felt there was something to criticize in the attitude of the South on the Negro problem!" The idea for a commission on civil rights, the insistence on a positive federal approach to the problem, and virtually the entire program recommended by the committee were set forth in the first edition of *Brothers Under the Skin*. It was not the novelty but the extraordinary timeliness of the report that made it important. Issued on the eve of a Presidential election year, it could hardly have failed to provoke great political tensions.

Among other consequences, the issuance of the report committed the President and his administration to the protection of the civil rights of racial minorities. As though to symbolize this fact, Mr. Philip B. Perlman, the Solicitor General, submitted a history-making brief to the Supreme Court on December 6, 1947, in which he placed the government on record *against* restrictive covenants. Since then, the Solicitor General's office has consistently taken the position that government owes an affirmative duty to protect the civil rights of racial minorities and has filed five or more such briefs in important cases before the Supreme Court.

As 1947 was drawing to a close, a jury in Elizabethtown, New York, convicted three men of an aggravated assault on a Negro. The verdict was returned in a room of the Essex County Courthouse on one wall of which hangs a portrait of John Brown. For it was here that John Brown had settled in 1849 to help organize a colony of fugitive slaves and it was to Elizabethtown, too, that his body was returned for burial after the execution at Harpers Ferry in 1859. This incident, which would surely have gone unnoticed in another context, was widely reported in 1947. That such an incident could occur, in the land of the abolitionists, nearly a century after John Brown's burial, emphasized as no argument could emphasize the tardy response of the American conscience to the injustice of racial discrimination.

## 7. *The Election of 1948*

If 1947 was the year in which the rest of the nation began to respond to the postwar resurgence of bigotry in 1946, then 1948 was the year in which the South's challenge — it turned out to be a bluff — was met head on. On February 3, 1948, President Truman submitted his important Message on Civil Rights to the Congress in which he recommended a ten-point legislative program: a permanent Commission on Civil Rights; the strengthening of existing civil rights legislation; federal protection against lynching; more adequate protection of the right to vote; a Fair Employment Practices Commission; elimination of discrimination in interstate transportation; home rule and suffrage in the District of Columbia; statehood for Alaska and Hawaii; the removal of discriminatory bars in naturalization proceedings; and the settlement of the evacuation claims of Japanese-Americans. The program showed every evidence of hasty political improvisation on the eve of an election year but its importance was unmistakable.

On the night following the President's appearance before Congress, hooded night riders of the Ku Klux Klan marched through the streets of Swainsboro, Georgia, after thoughtfully notifying the wire services in advance, thus providing ample opportunity for full coverage and excellent photographs. If the Klan had acted at President Truman's instigation, the demonstration could not have been more effective in mobilizing sentiment behind the civil rights program. Indeed the verdict of future historians may well be that the Klan demonstration in Swainsboro, Georgia, on February 4 decided the 1948 Presidential election. At least one newspaper, the *Boston Post*, had a swift intuition of what had happened: "Americans may be generally divided into parties, but if they become convinced, spurred by Southern revolt, that Mr. Truman courageously placed his Americanism above political expediency, he might win in a landslide."

For President Truman to have run the hazard of a Southern revolt when a third party was already a certainty was an act of courage or desperation and was probably a combination of both. As it turned out, the President's sponsorship of a civil rights program was brilliant politics for it cast him in the heroic mold and won the nearly solid Negro vote in states whose vote in the Electoral College is decisive. In the South, too, the Negro vote had increased from an estimated 211,000 in 1940 to 645,000 in 1947 and to nearly 1,000,000 votes in 1948 — an extremely important safeguard against the consequences of a Bourbon revolt. On February 11, 1948, a hundred Negro leaders, in the face of great intimidation, met in Jackson, Mississippi, and cheered the President's civil rights program to the echo — on the eve of the statewide mass meeting called by Governor Fielding L. Wright to launch the Dixiecrat movement.

Actually the politics of the situation were much less desperate, from the President's point of view, than most observers realized. The Negroes were solidly behind the

President, North and South, and they held the balance of power in the key states. Of nearly equal importance was the fact that white opinion in the South was by no means united in opposition to President Truman. For example, on February 27, 300 delegates from 11 Southern states met in Atlanta under the auspices of the Southern Regional Council and in effect endorsed the civil rights program. A round-up of Southern editorial opinion in the *New York Times* of February 29 showed that many voters were anti-Truman but were still loyal to the Democratic Party. On March 3, the Texas Council of Church Women (white) endorsed the President's civil rights program without a dissenting vote. A public opinion poll, released at the same time, showed that 98 per cent of the Negroes in Texas publicly supported the President and endorsed the civil rights program and that practically one third of the whites also favored some form of civil rights legislation.[36]

The election of November 1948 is of major importance in the history of American race relations. The effects of a Southern revolt against civil rights legislation had been debated for years; they were now, and for the first time, officially demonstrated. The election proved two things: first, that the Solid South was no longer solid; and, second, that the Negro vote was worth more, in a close election, than the 127 Electoral College votes of 11 Southern States. The weakness of the Bourbon position, once revealed, robbed the South of its power to intimidate the national leadership of the Democratic Party. The election did *not* mean, however, that the situation in Congress had been changed. In 1948 the Democrats won 20 out of 32 governorships; elected a majority of 262 in the House to the Republicans' 171; and took 54 seats in the Senate to the 41 held by the Republicans. Nevertheless the Democrats defeated the President's civil rights program. When a record vote was finally obtained on a modified FEPC proposal

[36] *Kansas City Call*, March 26, 1948, article by J. W. Rice.

on February 23, 1949, a handful of Republican senators, working with their Southern colleagues, demonstrated that the balance of power in Congress had not been changed.

In retrospect it will be clearer than it is now that President Truman would hardly have acted as he did had it not been for the pressure of Henry Wallace's candidacy. Thirty-seven Negro candidates were sponsored by the Progressive Party and Mr. Wallace's constant prodding was certainly a factor in the issuance of the executive orders on July 26 creating the Committee on Equality of Treatment and Opportunity in the Armed Services and establishing a fair employment board in the Civil Service Commission. It can hardly be doubted, moreover, that political considerations played a part in the Supreme Court's decision handed down on May 3, 1948, in the case of *Shelley* v. *Kraemer*, holding that restrictive covenants could no longer be enforced in the courts. As important as Mr. Truman's sponsorship of a civil rights program was Mr. Wallace's tour of the Southern states: the first time a Presidential candidate had ever spoken directly to the issue of racial discrimination in the South. Edwin A. Lahey, who accompanied Mr. Wallace on this tour, reported from Jackson, Mississippi, on September 2, 1948, that ". . . the trip has dramatized the civil rights issue. . . . Every rotten egg and tomato thrown at the third party candidate, every obscene epithet hurled by race-hysterical Southerners, every attempt to enforce local laws of segregation, has seeped into headlines the world over, to give a picture of the civil rights issue that no number of fine speeches could portray." Almost before the conventions had adjourned, the National Citizens Council on Civil Rights, a powerful coalition of organizations, had been formed to press for enactment of the President's civil rights program and John Popham was reporting in the *New York Times* on "a spirited defense of Negro voting rights [in South Carolina] that is unparalleled in Southern annals."

The 1948 election has this historic meaning: the issue of racial discrimination has now become a national political issue for the first time since Reconstruction and will doubtless remain a major domestic issue until the whole pattern of public discrimination has been eliminated — everywhere in the United States. In the history books the election will also be catalogued as the first Presidential election in which the Negro minority participated significantly in every major region of the nation and in which the Negro vote was of crucial if not decisive importance. The election also dates the beginning of the end of the Solid South. For the ferment which the election touched off in the South indicates, clearly enough, that America's economic problem area No. 1 has been engulfed by a process of revolutionary socio-economic change.

## 8. *The Tardy Industrial Revolution*

Today, at the mid-point of the twentieth century, the South has been caught up in the same revolutionary industrial processes that, a century earlier, transformed the North. The revolution is most noticeable in the disintegration of the South's cotton economy. In the last twenty years, Southern cotton production has been priced out of the world market. As late as 1925, America dominated the world cotton market; today large competing areas have been developed in Mexico, Brazil, Egypt, India, China, Russia, Persia, Australia, Syria, and Central Africa. With American prices 50 to 60 per cent higher than the prices for competing grades of cotton grown elsewhere, cotton production has been shifting westward to the irrigated-mechanized cotton sections of the Southwest. At the same time, Southern farms have begun to expand in size; to become increasingly diversified; and the livestock industry is tending to shift from the West to the South as cotton moves from the South to the West. From 1940 to 1947, the

agricultural income of the South increased from $2,437,487-
000 to $7,818,968,000, with 60 per cent of this increase repre-
senting a greater productivity per acre.[37]

In the last eleven years, the South has gained 18,000 new industries employing about 1,000,000 persons and adding about
$6,000,000,000 to the region's annual income. Since 1920
the nation's kilowatt-hour production has increased 638 per
cent; the South's increase has been 1342 per cent, or more
than double the gain by the country as a whole. Important
industrial gains have been scored in the last decade in the
pulp and paper industry; furniture manufacturing; rayon;
the chemical and petroleum industries; aluminum and many
other industries. In the last five years, 5000 new businesses
have been established in the Tennessee Valley alone. In the
span of a generation — reckoned at 33 years — per capita in-
comes have risen from $56 to $891 in Alabama; from $110 to
$1137 in Florida; from $112 to $1002 in Louisiana; from $56
to $758 in Mississippi; from $63 to $930 in North Carolina;
from $84 to $856 in South Carolina; from $82 to $955 in Tennessee; and, in Virginia, from $107 to $1159. Describing these
and other changes, Bem Price concludes that "there is a ter-
rific ferment in the South today. . . . Beneath a pyramid of
tensions lie industrial and economic changes which, when
viewed as a whole, are nearly staggering." [38]

These underlying economic and industrial changes have
doomed the Jim Crow South. However bitterly regressive
elements may conduct rear-guard delaying actions, they cannot reverse the tide of change which has now engulfed the
entire region. For history has finally caught up with the
South: it is now experiencing, a century later, the impact of
the industrial revolution. As this process of change has un-
folded, Negroes have been moving ahead in the South:
slowly, patiently, but with massive strength. In a decade

[37] *New York Times*, July 15, 1950, story by John N. Popham.
[38] *San Francisco Chronicle*, series of articles, June 18, 19, 20, 21, 22, 1950.

the gulf which formerly divided the political outlook of Northern from Southern Negroes has narrowed to the vanishing point. In the early days of the New Deal, the NAACP had 6 branches in South Carolina; today it has 85 branches, with a membership of 14,000 — the largest membership for any Southern state. Today Negroes are voting in sizable numbers in every Southern state with the exception of Mississippi and they will soon be voting there.

The population shifts precipitated by the industrial revolution in the South are of major importance. During the war, more than 1,000,000 Southerners, including 600,000 Negroes, shifted from rural to urban residences within the South and the Negro exodus from the region still continues. Already it is estimated that Georgia, South Carolina, Alabama, and Mississippi will lose one representative each in the 1951 reapportionment as the West Coast gains perhaps 11 seats. At this rate, the veto power of the Southern contingent in Congress will soon be at an end. More than anything else, it is this process of revolutionary change within the South which has created what might be called the permanent crisis in race relations — that is, a crisis which will continue, without abatement, until the entire pattern of public discrimination has been wiped out.

The manner in which the issue of segregated schools has evolved in the last decade shows that the pressures for change are now constant and unremitting and that partial concessions only intensify these pressures. On December 12, 1937, the Supreme Court in the case of *Gaines* v. *Canada* ordered the University of Missouri to establish, within the state, a law school for Negroes or to admit qualified Negroes to the state university. Since then the barriers have been tumbling at the higher or graduate levels: in Maryland, Kentucky, West Virginia, Arkansas, Texas, Delaware, Florida, North Carolina, Missouri, and Oklahoma. It will be noted that most of these victories have been won in the border states and the states of the Southwest, which means that the area of the Deep South — the Jim Crow South — is shrinking. Within this area, the states began to set up, in 1947, a regional education system to escape from the implications of a series of Supreme Court decisions, but the decisions of the court in the G. W. McLaurin case (from Oklahoma) and Herman Marion Sweatt case (from Texas), handed down on June 5, 1950, clearly undercut the idea of a regional Jim Crow system of higher education.

In the argument of the Sipuel case, which involved the right of Ada Lois Sipuel to attend the Law School of the University of Oklahoma, the doom of Jim Crow in American education was clearly foreshadowed. The case was argued on January 9, 1948, shortly before the President sent his Civil Rights Message to Congress. Acting in an unprecedented manner, the Supreme Court decided the case *four days* after argument was concluded and directed that the mandate should issue forthwith (the usual procedure is to delay issuing the mandate for a period of twenty-five days). The decision, moreover, was unanimous. Pushing beyond the frontiers of the Gaines case, the court said that Oklahoma must provide a legal education for Miss Sipuel *"as soon as* it does for applicants of any other group" (emphasis added).

In the recent Sweatt and McLaurin cases, the court has now gone beyond the Sipuel case. Again in a unanimous decision, the court has pointed out that it could not "find substantial equality in the educational opportunities offered white and Negro law students by the state" (Texas had established a separate law school for Negroes). "In terms of number of faculty, variety of courses, and opportunity for specialization, size of the student body, scope of the library, availability of law review and similar activities, the University of Texas Law School is superior." For the first time, also, the court ventured beyond a narrow consideration of "separate but equal" and pointed out that the test of equality cannot be considered in a vacuum.

In the same vein, the court, again in a unanimous decision, ruled that the University of Oklahoma's segregation of McLaurin, a Negro admitted to the university for studies looking toward a doctorate in education, in the classrooms, cafeteria, and library of the university, was discriminatory. In these decisions, and in the Henderson case, decided the same day, the court has greatly weakened, if it has not directly overruled, the "separate but equal" doctrine of *Plessy* v. *Ferguson.* The immediate effect of the decisions, however, has been to quicken the pace of social change. A case is now on its way to the Supreme Court involving segregation in the elementary and high schools, for which there is already a precedent in the form of a Circuit Court decision holding that segregated schools violate the Fourteenth Amendment. It may take twenty years to complete the mopping-up operation now in process, but it is already quite clear that segregation, as a social policy, is doomed in American race relations.

## 9. The Conscience of the Church

As the ferment over human rights began to spread, it was inevitable that the conscience of the Church should finally be disturbed. Prior to 1940, the churches had been "concerned" over racial discrimination but there is little evidence to indicate that they had taken significant positions or even examined the discriminations practiced in religious institutions.

The most significant indication that a new wind is now blowing in Protestant circles on the subject of discrimination is to be found in the official statement on "The Church and Race," approved by the Federal Council of Churches at a special meeting in Columbus, Ohio, on March 5, 1946. The most remarkable aspect of this document, aside from its

analysis of the evils of segregation, is the frank admission that
the Protestant churches are probably the most rigidly segregated institutions in American life. Less than 1 per cent of the
"white" congregations have Negro members and less than
one half of 1 per cent of the Negro Protestants are included
in white congregations. The report also points out that
Negroes are frequently segregated in church hospitals, in
theological seminaries, and in church schools and colleges. At
a later meeting, held in Cincinnati on December 3, 1948, the
Federal Council adopted a declaration on human rights which
is the most comprehensive document of its kind to be issued
by the Protestant churches in the United States.[39]

Despite this new orientation, there is still much evidence to
indicate that the Protestant church groups will be among the
last institutions in American life to abandon segregation.
Many church schools, including Texas Christian University,
Phillips University, the College of the Bible, Cincinnati Bible
School, Culver-Stockton College, Lynchburg College, Christian College, William Woods College, Atlanta Christian, and
many others, still find it "necessary and mandatory to keep
their doors closed to the Negro student, thus making education not available in the area of greatest need." [40] On January 29, 1949, William Jewell College denied the application
of a Negro Baptist minister for admission to this Baptist institution. "The school always had a policy established and
Negroes have never been admitted," explained Dr. Walter
Pope Binns, "and the school sees no need for changing the
practice." Of fifty-five colleges queried by the Methodist
Conference on Christian Education, only twenty-seven accepted Negro students. Three out of seven junior colleges,
one out of four schools of theology, and three out of seven-
teen universities — all denominational schools — also drew
the color line. At the Baptist World Alliance, held in Copen-

[39] *New York Times*, December 4, 1948, story by George Dugan.
[40] AP dispatch, San Francisco, September 29, 1948.

hagen in 1947, American Negro delegates threatened to withdraw unless the Southern delegates ceased demanding separate accommodations!

Nevertheless the Protestant churches, for the first time since the Civil War, are beginning to rally church opinion against racial discrimination. The United Council of Church Women has issued a statement pointing out that there is nothing unethical or immoral in intermarriage; the Presbyterian Church in the United States (Southern) has urged its members to join in the fight against "the injustice and tyranny of religious and racial discrimination in the South"; and at a meeting of Southern churchwomen in Atlanta on September 10, 1949, a plan was worked out by which white Southern churchwomen would accompany Negroes to the polls in an effort to prevent intimidation. Indicative of this new trend in Protestant churches was the stirring address of Bishop G. Bromley Oxnam in Atlanta on October 4, 1949. "Class and race and nation are concepts too small to unite mankind," he said. "We must have a larger concept, one of a world family in which all men are brothers. All men are brothers, whether we like it or not, and the church has to put an end to the business of segregation and injustice."

An important factor in the changing attitude of the Protestant groups toward racial discrimination has been the new interest shown in racial minorities by the Catholic Church. On February 11, 1944, the Reverend Claude Herman Heithaus, S. J., speaking before the student body of St. Louis University at mass, made a blistering attack on segregated schools. "Ignorance," he said, "is the school of race prejudice, and provincialism is its tutor. Its memory is stuffed with lies and its wind is warped by emotionalism. Pride is its book and snobbery is its pen. It blinds the intellect and it hardens the heart. Its wisdom is wonderful and fearful, for it never learns what is true, and it never forgets what is false." It was this sermon which opened the doors of St. Louis University to

Negroes. Once the doors were opened, moreover, Archbishop Joseph E. Ritter decided to admit Negroes to the parochial schools of the diocese and backed up the decision with an announcement, read at all masses throughout the archdiocese, that Roman Catholics protesting the admission of Negro children to parochial schools would be excommunicated if they persisted in such action. Racial barriers are being rapidly removed in Catholic institutions and the Catholic Committee of the South is taking an increasingly strong stand against discrimination. It was the Catholic Interracial Council of Los Angeles that upset, for the first time, a miscegenation statute (in the Perez case decided by the California Supreme Court on October 2, 1948). Such actions as the cancellation by Archbishop Joseph Francis Rummel of the annual Roman Catholic observance of holy hour in New Orleans, in protest against discriminations in the city's parks, is merely one of many illustrations which might be cited of the new concern of the Catholic Church with problems of discrimination.

## 10. Popular Protest and Resistance

One of the most significant developments in race relations since 1943 has been the remarkable way in which individuals and groups have begun to protest discriminations that went unnoticed in prior years because no one cared to make an issue of them. When the Kiwanis Club of Ahoskie, North Carolina, in July 1947, refused to turn over a $3200 Cadillac, which a Negro had won as a raffle prize, such a storm of protest went up throughout the nation that the club was forced to reverse its decision. Almost certainly this decision would have gone unnoticed in 1940. The fact that Negro veterans were barred from seeing the play *Joan of Lorraine* in Washington in the fall of 1946 resulted in Actors' Equity Association issuing an unprecedented ultimatum to the National Theater to cease discrimination or face a boycott. "The time has come," read the public statement, "when Equity can no longer sit back impassively, trusting that evil will right itself." The recognition implicit in this statement is one of the "new facts" about race relations in the United States. On June 24, 1949, the American Association of University Women voted 2168 to 68 to accept Negro members and the Washington, D. C., chapter, which had declined Negro applications, withdrew. The issue was longstanding but it took an internal crisis to bring it to a decision. In October 1949, Jefferson Military College, of Natchez, Mississippi, where Jefferson Davis once studied, accepted a $50,000,000 grant of property subject to the condition that the school would teach "the true principles of Jeffersonian democracy and the Constitution, Christianity, and the superiority of the Anglo-Saxon and Latin American races." Such a storm of protest was provoked that the school was forced to reject the grant. In the wake of this incident, Lafayette College rejected a $140,000 bequest for scholarships for American-born students, "Jews and Catholics excepted." Selected at random, these incidents demonstrate how popular resistance to discrimination has mounted of recent years. The multiplication of such incidents, moreover, has been a powerful factor in changing public opinion.

One of the most significant of these "resistance movements" has been the protest against discriminations in the college fraternity system. The protest began at Amherst in April 1946, when the local chapter of Delta Tau Delta, in defiance of its national officers, surrendered its charter after being refused permission to remove discriminatory barriers from its bylaws. A year later, the Amherst local of Phi Kappa Psi pledged a Negro and refused to withdraw the pledge in response to an ultimatum from the national organization. The fact that the decision of the parent body, suspending the charter of the Amherst local, happened to coincide with the release of the report of the President's Committee on Civil

Rights served to focus national attention on the college fraternity system.

Shortly after the decision of the Phi Kappa Psi board ousting the Amherst chapter, the National Interfraternity Conference met in New York and, after heated debate, refused to take action against discriminatory policies. Speaking in defense of discrimination, the president of the conference said: "I love the discriminating tongue, the discriminating eye, and the discriminating ear, and, above all, the discriminating mind and soul. The person for whom I can find no love and respect is the indiscriminate person. To be indiscriminate is to be common, to be vulgar."

Despite this lofty disapproval, the agitation against discrimination continued. A new nationwide interracial fraternity, Beta Sigma Tau, was formed in the spring of 1948, and the attention it received was a measure of the public's interest in the problem of discrimination. But when the National Interfraternity Conference met in New York on November 28, 1948, the delegates voted, once again, to defer action. At this meeting, the president asked for a show of hands from those who favored "intercolor fraternities and also consider intermarriage between races . . ." only to be interrupted by a delegate who shouted: "We're running fraternities; not families." Any number of college administrators spoke out in defense of discriminatory membership policies, hinting that the movement against them was inspired by Moscow directives.

Throughout 1949 the agitation mounted. At the University of Wisconsin an all-white fraternity pledged a Negro; girls from thirteen universities met at Lake Geneva, Wisconsin, to form Pi Beta Sigma, a new college sorority open to all races; over a thousand delegates to the National Student Association convention urged colleges to ban new student groups that discriminated on racial or religious grounds. Alpha Phi Alpha, the first all-Negro fraternity, formed in

1909, voted to admit white students, and Phi Sigma Delta, one of the largest Jewish fraternities, voted to open its membership to all races, creeds, and colors. The MIT chapter of Alpha Chi Sigma, a national chemistry fraternity, surrendered its charter in protest against a racial discrimination limiting membership to "non-Semitic members of the Caucasian race." With the protest spreading in this manner, the National Interfraternity Conference, meeting on November 26, 1949, finally reversed its prior position and, by a vote of 36 to 3, with 19 delegates not voting, urged all affiliated groups to remove restrictive membership clauses. While the final victory was not of shattering importance, being largely verbal, nevertheless the fact that a protest movement could muster so much support, so quickly, is a significant indication that American public opinion has begun to change on "the racial issue."

## 11. End of the Detour

When Berea College was formed in Kentucky in 1855, its charter began with these words: "God Hath Made of One Blood All Nations that Dwell Upon the Face of the Earth." In keeping with this spirit, Berea College trained Negro and white students together until forced to comply with an act of the Kentucky legislature which prohibited "the mingling of students of the white and colored races in the same school or college." The college contested this legislation, which was known as the Day Law, but the Supreme Court of the United States upheld its constitutionality. In the spring of 1950, the Kentucky legislature finally amended the law to provide that Negroes and whites might attend the same school if the governing authorities approved. Thus, after a detour of half a century, Berea College has been *permitted to return to its original policy* of equal treatment and fair play.

The incident points up the meaning of the developments

of the last eight years in American race relations: after a detour of more than fifty years, the nation has been gradually returning to the unfinished task of reconstruction. Forced to make the detour or departure from American tradition by the successful counterrevolution of the South, the nation was compelled to mark time until the South itself was finally swept into the mainstream of American life. Thus in the last eight years the conditions for the successful conclusion of the reconstruction of American society to eliminate racial discrimination have been achieved: the undermining of the South's cotton mono-culture; the nationalization, and now the internationalization, of "the racial question"; the restoration by the Supreme Court of the original meaning and intention of the Fourteenth Amendment; the destruction of the ideology of white supremacy; the social interpretation of human differences formerly explained in racial or biological terms; the coming-of-age, in social, economic, and political terms, of the racial minorities; and the occurrence of important and far-reaching changes in American society. These changes have brought the long detour to an end.

This does not mean, however, that we have solved the racial question: it merely means that we have redefined the problem. In the meantime, the racial question, which formerly flared up in periodic violence and occasional crises, has now passed into a phase of permanent crisis. The best evidence of this fact is the violence which in 1949 flared up in response to the gains scored in 1948. Shortly after the first of the year, the South experienced a renewal of "Klan fever." In the first four months of 1949, sixteen "Klan" assaults were reported in the area of Chattanooga; in April a mob kidnaped seven Negroes in Hooker, Georgia, and beat them "unmercifully with leather belts and switches" (*New York Times*, April 10, 1949); and Alabama was swept with a wave of Klan violence, resulting in scores of indictments for floggings and other offenses. The first lynching of the year occurred on May 30,

1949, at Irwinton, Georgia. Violence flared up, too, outside the South: in the Anacostia Park riot in Washington, D. C., on June 29; in the Fairgrounds Park riot in St. Louis on June 22; and in the Park Manor housing riot in Chicago in August.

Of special interest was the rioting, violence, and home-burning which occurred in Groveland, Florida, on July 19, 1949, where National Guardsmen were used to restore order. The Groveland riot is of special interest in two respects: this was, perhaps, the first motorized race riot; and, second, it was more highly "militarized" than any previous American race riot and showed careful planning and preparation. "The lawlessness in Lake County," to quote from the report of the Southern Regional Council, "went far beyond a spontaneous mob action . . . it resembled a military operation more than a sudden outburst of local citizens roused to vengeance." [41] Rioters were swiftly and efficiently transported from areas a hundred miles or more removed from Groveland and the local sheriff negotiated with the leaders of the mob as though they were "generals of an opposing army." Units of the mob "sped from place to place like panzer units."

By the end of the year, however, it was apparent that the resistance to mob violence in the South, while not sufficient to prevent violence, was enlisting an ever-larger number of Southern recruits. The KKK, for example, was everywhere under serious attack: by grand juries, ministers, educators, civic leaders, and some public officials, and anti-mask ordinances had been adopted in twenty-five or more communities. Here and there assailants of Negroes were being arrested and prosecuted and out of these prosecutions at least one important conviction has been achieved: the conviction of a Klansman of manslaughter in Pell City, Alabama, on July 1, 1950, by a jury. In the future gains similar to those scored in 1948 will continue to meet with the violence recorded in 1949

[41] "Mobile Violence," New South, August 1949, vol. 4, no. 8.

until the pattern of public discrimination has been removed.

Although the long detour is at an end, racial relations have now merged with the issue of which they are merely a specialized phase, namely, class relations. A close survey of the gains of the last eight years, impressive as they have been, will show that they are principally important for what they portend rather than for any basic changes which they have worked. The barriers are being lowered, but for individuals; the Negro masses have yet to break through these openings. For this to happen, great changes must take place in the American economy; for one thing there must be an enormous expansion of educational and job opportunities. It so happens also that the permanent crisis in race relations coincides with a crisis in the economy, which is likewise permanent, and because of this a disturbing movement has arisen, described in the final chapter, the prime purpose of which is to use the agitation for racial equality to prevent a merger of class and racial discontents. The year 1950 marks the end of the long detour but it also marks the beginning of the permanent crisis in race relations.

# CHAPTER I

## The Non-Vanishing Indian

ANY STUDY of racial minorities in the United States must start with the American Indian. Indeed any study of the contact, and conflict, between "white" and "colored" peoples would, in a sense, have to start from the same point. For it was in the Americas that modern colonialism really had its origin. The native culture of the American Indian, as Gilberto Freyre has pointed out, was "the first culture to be subtly and systematically degraded" in the great expansion of European civilization which began with the discovery of the New World.[1] By the same token, any discussion of race relations in the United States must necessarily return to the American Indian. Not until Europeans began to colonize America was there any realization of the magnitude of the problem which now confronts the entire world, namely, how should a "civilized" nation deal with so-called "backward" native peoples?

Today it is as difficult for most Americans to realize that transoceanic colonialism had its origin here as it is for them to believe that American "race prejudice" had its inception in the relationship between dominant colonial powers and their dependencies. To us "colonialism" means "the British in India," not white Americans in Georgia. Edmond Taylor makes a typically American confession when he writes that not until he had lived in India for many months did he realize, for the first time in his life, "that the relation between the thirteen million Negro citizens of America and the one hundred and twenty million white citizens was the most

[1] *The Masters and the Slaves*, by Gilberto Freyre, 1946, p. 109.

serious, the most difficult, and the most disgraceful colonial problem in the world." [2] Indians have been favorite figures in American folklore and mythology for so long that it is hard for us to realize that our patterns of "color reaction" and "color behavior" could have had their origin in the utterly novel problems that arose when European colonizing powers attempted to transplant their culture to America. Negro-white relationships may constitute the most disgraceful colonial problem in the world but the world's oldest colonial problem has to do with Indian-white relationships.

## 1. "A Loving People . . . without Covetousness"

At the time the American continent was discovered, there were probably not more than 850,000 Indians living in what is now the United States. These Indians were widely scattered and their tribal organizations were largely unrelated. By a curious quirk, also, the maximum density of the Indian population was to be found in the section of the West Coast that is now California, which had a density ratio about three or four times greater than the nation as a whole, and in the Rio Grande Valley. In short the geographical distribution of a sparse Indian population in North America, unlike the tropical portions of the continent, offered a unique opportunity for the transfer of a large European population without the necessity of having to mix its blood or culture with the natives. The United States, indeed, offered history's most unique opportunity for mass migration; in fact it was this vacuum which drew immigrants across the Atlantic in such volume.

Not 1 per cent of the immense area of agriculturally valuable topsoil, including virgin timber and mineral resources, of the land that is now the United States was used intensively

[2] *Richer by Asia*, by Edmond Taylor, 1947, p. 103.

by the indigenous Indian population.[3] To the Europeans it seemed, therefore, that the land was almost entirely unoccupied but the paradoxical fact is that the Indians, in terms of their technologies and cultures, were then making full use of the environment. Within the limitations of native technology, there was not much room for population expansion. The Europeans never understood this fact but it was an agonizing reality to the Indians.

Had there been a large compact native population along or near the Eastern seaboard, then some interacting adjustment leading to integration might have taken place, as it did in Brazil. But the major Indian concentrations were in Central and South America where European colonizing assumed an entirely different form. At the close of the Spanish colonial period, there were not more than 15,000 Spaniards in the Americas — less than one third of 1 per cent of the population of New Spain. The Spanish settlements, moreover, were largely brought about by single men, whereas the colonization of the United States was based on a mass migration of families. The Spaniards, therefore, had to make use of the native population. The kind of crops that could best be raised in the tropics was another determinant of a pattern of settlement based on a quite different system of race relations. The plantation system of the Southern states, based on cotton and slavery, was strikingly similar to the pattern of settlement in South America, which probably accounts for the interesting fact that there were as many Negroes in the United States by 1790 as there were Indians in all the United States in 1492. Slaves were useful and what is useful survives.

The chief colonizing power in South America, of course, was Portugal. The British of the period of discovery were a people who had attained a degree of ethnic and cultural homogeneity in the insular atmosphere of the British Isles but the Portuguese were a quite different people. "With

[3] Report of the Land Planning Committee, 1938.

respect to physical conditions of soil and temperature," as Freyre points out, "Portugal is Africa rather than Europe."[4] The basis of unity in Portugal was religious belief rather than cultural or ethnic homogeneity. Portugal was a blend of Europe and Africa and the Portuguese were a dark-skinned people. For years the Portuguese had had the experience, unique among European peoples, of being ruled by dark-skinned Moors who possessed a superior technology and more advanced culture (the experience, of course, involved the entire peninsula). Because of this experience little prejudice against intermarriage existed in Portugal. Furthermore Portugal was underpopulated, as a result of wars and famines, and had to make the maximum use of the limited manpower it possessed in undertaking far-flung colonizations. Since both Spain and Portugal encouraged intermarriage as a policy, not only with native Indians but with imported Negro slaves, it is slight wonder that there should be twice as many persons of African origin in Central and South America, including the Caribbean area, as there are in the United States, or that there should be 30,000,000 Indians living south of the Rio Grande.

Although the circumstances of settlement were very different north of the Rio Grande, it is important to note that here, too, there was *no prejudice at the outset*. Indeed quite the contrary was the case. "They are a loving people," wrote Columbus of the Indians, "without covetousness, and fit for anything. . . . They love their neighbors as themselves, and their speech is the sweetest and gentlest in the world."[5] To the Europeans, the Indians were the survivors of some prehistory Garden of Eden; to the Indians, the white men were gods to be served and revered. Despite the sense of utter strangeness on both sides — it is not often that a new world is discovered — there was no aversion whatever. "No sooner

[4] Freyre, *op. cit.*, p. 14.
[5] Quoted in *They Came Here First*, by D'Arcy McNickle, 1949, p. 121.

had the European leaped ashore," writes Gilberto Freyre, "than he found his feet slipping among the naked Indian women." [6]

Intermarriage did take place in the American colonies and might have been as common there as in Brazil had it not been for the social and cultural factors previously mentioned which resulted in two different types of settlement. The extent of intermarriage was determined not by the degree of initial aversion — there was none — but by social and cultural factors. For example, an Indian wife was an enormous asset to a French fur trader. She could teach him the language and customs of the tribe with which he had to deal, and through marriage with her he often became a member of this tribe. But Indian women had little utility in New England, a trading and farming colony settled by families. Indians knew a great deal about wild animals and trapping; they were not too advanced in agricultural skills. At a later date, however, these factors were completely ignored. Francis Walker, a fairly "liberal" Commissioner of Indian Affairs, once stated that he would prefer to see the Indians exterminated than to see an amalgamation of the two races!

Since the Anglo-European colonists on the Eastern seaboard did not have to adjust their culture to that of the Indians, there being little incentive for adjustment, they never bothered to understand Indians. The only way in which they could have learned about Indians, in any case, was by living with them, in the intimate association of family and social life. But the colonists were not only ignorant about Indian life; they were grossly deceived and misinformed. There were hundreds of tribes with different languages and cultures and these cultures, which were by no means of a uniform level, were quite differently orientated than those with which Europeans were familiar. Yet the colonists insisted on regarding all Indians as alike. They had not the slightest comprehension

[6] Freyre, *op. cit.*, p. 85.

of the antiquity, the deep-rootedness, and the integration of Indian cultures.

The basic difficulty in the initial contact, however, has been pointed out by D'Arcy McNickle, namely, that the Europeans consistently ascribed to the people they found here "the customs, beliefs, and institutions with which they were familiar." [7] Freyre puts the problem in somewhat different terms: the chief error consisted, in his view, in the conqueror's determination to impose *the whole* of his culture upon the native population, all in one piece, all at one time, without compromise or mitigation.[8] The colonists could never understand and were constantly chagrined by the Indian's stubborn rejection of certain values of their culture. The Indians, too, were the victims of "situational delusion," but as the weaker party they could not afford to be quite so intolerant or so blind. From this initial phase of contact one can conclude that, while the cultures conflicted at nearly every point, there was no race prejudice per se. Three hundred years of initial contact — the colonizing phase — are summarized in this fashion by McNickle: "They had traded. They had made presents to each other. They had profited from their contacts. *So long as they were not in direct competition* for a piece of earth, they were able to live together. But once they were in conflict, the Indians never had more than one choice: either they gave way, or they were destroyed." [9] There were friction and misunderstanding and conflict in this early period but the concept "race prejudice" can hardly be applied to this phase in the relationship between Indians and whites. Since the Eastern seaboard was not an area of Indian concentration, the colonists got a foothold there without much difficulty and the Indians withdrew to the West, resulting in a type of mutual adjustment or accom-

[7] McNickle, *op. cit.*, p. 118.
[8] Freyre, *op. cit.*, p. 107.
[9] McNickle, *op. cit.*, p. 218. Emphasis added.

modation. Racial prejudice is not a by-product of racial or cultural differences as such; it stems rather from conflict or competition and is essentially a social phenomenon.

## 2. Satanic Consolation

The American government which came into being with the adoption of the Constitution began its dealings with Indians by treating the various tribes as national entities or domestic dependent nations with whom treaties were to be negotiated for all land acquisitions. The new government had in effect inherited this policy from Spain, France, and Great Britain. The eagerness of these nations to draw the Indians into offensive and defensive alliances against their rivals had forced them to deal with the tribes on a basis of assumed equality and with a pretense of fairness. The policy, in short, was based on strategic considerations. Similarly the recognition that Indians had a possessory right to the lands they occupied was based on the necessity of building up legal titles and "claims" to lands already claimed by some rival power. From 1789 to 1871 treaty making was the cornerstone of American Indian policy.

We had already entered upon the purely military or imperialist phase of our relations with Indians, however, long before Congress prohibited the making of further treaties in 1871. In inducing Indians to withdraw to the West, we had created the fiction of an "impermeable barrier" — the phrase is McNickle's — beyond which the frontier was not to expand but no measures were taken to stem the tide of western migration. The advancing frontier thus became a zone of conflict and lawlessness in which Indian rights were ignored and in which a fierce competition over land and other resources took place. Out of this conflict came war; then race hatred; then more wars in which race hatred was a major dynamic. "War and hate," to quote William Christie Macleod, "made a vicious circle which all too frequently broke out into the most brutal massacres which ended once and for all any receptivity on the part of the European settlers to the idea of race amalgamation. Instead came the desire for extermination." [10] More important: it terminated for a century the Indians' desire for assimilation.

The imperialist or military phase might be said to date from the removal of the Cherokees, which was ordered on May 29, 1830, following word of certain gold discoveries in Georgia which turned out to be insignificant. Even earlier, in 1820, President Jackson had announced that he was dispensing with "the farce" of treating with Indians as sovereign powers. Thereafter the Indians were moved further west, across the Mississippi, but the discovery of gold in California in 1848, in Colorado in 1859, and in Montana in 1861, greatly accelerated the westward movement of population. The faster the frontier zone moved, the fiercer the conflict became. It was soon discovered, of course, that in forcing the Indians westward we had neglected to reserve a corridor to the Pacific. Directly across the path of the various trails leading to the lands of gold and silver were the Indians of the Great Plains.

The Plains Indian, as McNickle points out, was "a creature of the white man, a product of the conquest of the Americas." [11] By acquiring horses from the Spaniards, the Plains Indians had become extraordinarily mobile, thereby increasing both the area and the tempo of conflict with the whites. Many of the Plains tribes were renegades from "an older way of life" who had been driven onto the Plains by other Indians and had there become nomads. The life of these Indians had been quickly transformed by the introduction of the horse, the gun, the iron ax and knife, and above all by the introduction of trade. Merely by way of illustration,

---

[10] *The American Indian Frontier*, by William Christie Macleod, 1928.
[11] McNickle, *op. cit.*, p. 57.

McNickle points out that tepees became larger, the slaughter of buffalo increased, and authority within the tribe began to disintegrate. Here, then, was an early manifestation of a process which has since become painfully familiar: of a "colored" race taking over and brilliantly adapting the military techniques of the "white" race and, at the same time, becoming increasingly belligerent as a result of the undermining of their native culture and mounting pressure on their resources.

Once the Alleghenies had been penetrated, the advancing frontier became the front line in an undeclared war of extermination. "Every river valley and Indian trail," wrote Frederick Jackson Turner, "became a fissure in Indian society." Each of the successive frontiers which punctuated the history of national expansion was, as he wrote, "won by a series of Indian wars." Open hostility was almost continuous until the so-called Battle of Wounded Knee in 1890, which was not so much a battle as a premeditated massacre of several hundred defenseless Indians.[12] As long as this warfare lasted, the Indian never had a chance to know white society. "The constant jostling from pillar to post," writes Macleod, "and repeated pushing back from contact with the sources of civilization, was one of the facts which prevented the rapid acculturation of the natives. Peace and security are necessary for the absorption by one people of the more advanced culture of another." [13]

Out of this conflict, the peculiar social blindness known as "racial prejudice" developed. Beeson, an early emigrant to Oregon, wrote in his journal that ". . . it was customary [for the settlers] to speak of the Indian man as a buck; of the woman as a squaw; until, at length, in the general acceptance of the terms, they ceased to recognize the rights of humanity in those to whom they were so applied. By a very

[12] See Report of the Acting Secretary of the Interior on HR 2535, dated April 28, 1937.
[13] Macleod, *op. cit.*

natural and easy transition, from being spoken of as brutes, they came to be thought of as game to be shot, or as vermin to be destroyed. . . . The domineering spirit grew by what it fed on, until, excited to madness by these recurring scenes of blood, men became utterly regardless of justice, even towards those of their race." Oregon settlers felt little compunction when they saw Indian women being clubbed to death and Indian babies being dashed against tree trunks. One early-day emigrant wrote that it was necessary to get rid of the Indian women, as well as the men, and also to eliminate the children who were the "seeds of increase." One of the first debates in the Colorado legislature was over a measure offering bounties for the "destruction of Indians and Skunks." The history of the conflict is implicit in General Phil Sheridan's remark at Fort Cobb, Indian Territory, in January 1869: "The only good Indians I ever saw were dead."

Fear and anxiety were unquestionably factors in the formation of this fixation about Indians — fear of the unknown perils of the wilderness and of its equally unknown, and therefore fearsome, inhabitants. D. H. Lawrence caught this feeling perfectly when he pointed out that "whiteness" had become not a symbol, but an obsession with American writers. In the Morse code of the unconscious, "white" became synonymous with Christian, with American, and with most of the values we respected. To this day Indians and Negroes are excluded from the images which many Americans conjure up when they think of home, and country, and flag. By tacit agreement, European immigrants became absorbed in "the melting pot"; Indians and Negroes became "problems." Out of the conflicts of this early domestic imperialism, hostility to race mixture became, as Dr. E. V. Stonequist has observed, "a ground pattern of American social organization."

Obscured by lapse of time, these deep-seated sources of prejudice have been covered over with layers of rationalization. Over a period of time, popular attitudes toward Indians came to reflect a curious fusion of personal greed and public spirit. "The avowed feeling," writes Macleod, "that the function of Indian policy was after all merely to keep the Indian at peace pending his gradual dying off from more insidious causes than the sword and bullet" became a national dogma. "Getting rid of the Indian" was paraphrased as "opening up the country for settlement." The belief that Indians were doomed to extinction was a perfect example of social wishful thinking, prompting one Mallery to comment in 1888 on "the satanic consolation of the convenient extinction doctrine." Senator Casserly of California, in a comment resurrected by McNickle, gave exact expression to the reality of this phase of Indian-white relationships: "Their [the Indians'] misfortune is not that they are red men; not that they are semicivilized, not that they are a dwindling race; not that they are a weak race. Their misfortune is that they hold great bodies of rich lands, which have aroused the cupidity of powerful corporations and powerful individuals."

It is indeed strange that we should have so largely forgotten the key role which this phase of our domestic imperialism played in the creation of a national psychosis on the subject of race. It is equally strange that we should have failed to correlate the curious interlocking destinies of Indians and Negroes in American society. For example, one of the main props of the treaty-making policy was the desire to use Indians as an unofficial, and unpaid, constabulary to keep Negro slaves from escaping to the West. For a time, we were quite willing to give Indians additional lands in the West because their occupancy of these lands completed the encirclement of Negroes on Southern plantations. An important motivation, also, in the ouster of the Cherokees was the fear that they might free the few slaves they owned or provide a refuge for escaping slaves. At the same time, Indians were careful to note how we treated Negro slaves. In the formation of national policy, we consistently failed to correlate our experience with Indians and Negroes. The Negroes had their champions in the Abolitionists, few of whom were at all interested in Indians, while being an Indian rights advocate came to be a profession practiced by those who showed little interest in Negroes. Putting these minorities in separate compartments of the national mind made it possible for us to think of "the Indian problem" and "the Negro problem" without ever thinking of "the racial problem."

It is important to note, also, that the Indian was thoroughly isolated during the purely military phase of our domestic imperialism not only from Negroes, who might have been natural allies, but from other subject peoples. Had the conquest taken place on the world stage, it might have aroused widespread condemnation. But since we had previously eliminated our rivals on the continent (they were themselves bent on plunder in other parts of the world by then), no one gave heed to the eloquent resistance of the Indian who, being unable to communicate his protest, had to act it out. Taking place within American society, Indian warfare became a purely domestic concern which was almost wholly unmitigated by currents of world opinion. The Indians, as de Tocqueville noted, "were isolated in their own country, and their race only constituted a little colony of troublesome strangers in the midst of a numerous and dominant people." They were surrounded; we were triumphant. The relationship of Negroes to whites was that of slaves to their masters; Indians were a thoroughly defeated, a suppressed nationality. Slaves learn from their masters; the defeated despise their conquerors.

### 3. Beans and Blankets: The Cultural Attack

Interrupted by the Civil War, the military conquest of the Indians was largely completed by 1880. It had been a costly and time-consuming but, on the whole, an enormously profit-able undertaking. As imperialist adventures are priced, this was a cheap one. We had succeeded in driving most of the Indians into the least usable, if scenically most beautiful, parts of the West and we had acquired a vast domain for exploita-tion. In California Indians originally owned 75,000,000 acres; we promised them — by treaty — 8,619,000 acres; and finally settled with them, after repudiating the treaties, for 624,000 acres. But in carrying out the military conquest we had at least shown some restraint in not interfering with the internal affairs of the tribes.

During the course of the military conquest, however, large numbers of Indians had been concentrated, for convenience in surveillance, upon so-called reservations. A reservation, someone said, was "a government almshouse where an incon-siderable number of Indians are insufficiently fed and scantily clothed at an expense wholly disproportionate to the benefits conferred." Having acquired most of the Indian Territory, it no longer seemed dignified for us to continue the warfare; it now became cheaper "to feed them than to fight them." By dispensing with the policy of making treaties with the tribes, however, an impasse had been created in the exploita-tion of the remaining Indian lands. Here then was the situa-tion: the frontiersman was impatient to possess the remaining Indian holdings and to get rid of the Indians; but the Indians, disarmed and in custody, refused to part with title to their tribally owned lands.

By 1880, also, a strong public opinion had developed in favor of some measure of reform in Indian affairs. To con-tinue the reservation policy of providing the Indian with beans and a blanket, it was said, would rob him of initiative and self-confidence. Since Indian societies were doomed to extinction in any case, the quicker this end was achieved the better for all concerned. Assimilation would be greatly accel-erated, so the argument ran, if the Indian's tribal government were disbanded; if his culture and religion were destroyed and his iniquitous system of communal land ownership broken up. These factors were supposedly all that was standing in the way of the complete absorption of the Indian into the main current of American life.

Those who sought a reform in Indian policy also believed that unless some method could be devised to bring about a swift distribution of the remaining Indian lands, frontier aggressiveness might force a resumption of warfare. They also feared — and with good reason — that unless the remaining lands were quietly distributed, the frontier population might take possession by force of arms and the Indians would receive nothing.[14] By finally adopting the concepts of this school of thought, Congress was able to break the deadlock on Indian affairs which had been reached by 1880.

Although it had laudable stated objectives, the policy that Congress now adopted had the effect of undermining Indian social organization and disrupting Indian cultural patterns. "To smother, to exterminate the entirety of the Indian heritage," writes John Collier, "became the central purpose in Indian affairs. Extermination was applied beyond the tribe and its government to the local community governments out of which the tribes were compounded, and beyond the local governments to the family. . . . As tribe and local community crumbled under the pressures, remote authority had of necessity to be extended past the group to the individual, and this authority was applied horizontally and exhaustively. . . . Invidious absolutism and yet benevolent: invidious toward all that constituted Indianhood, toward every instrument for moulding or implementing personality, while yet benevolent toward the *individual* Indian. And through its benevolence, the far more subtly destroying. Always, through so many mediums, the Indian was told that as a race he was

[14] See *Pratt: The Red Man's Moses*, 1935, by Elaine Goodale Eastman, where this point of view is sympathetically outlined.

doomed by social inferiority or impracticability. Always he was challenged to build a new personality out of no cultural heritage at all." [15]

The cultural attack was primarily directed against the system of tribal land ownership which was the basis of Indian life and culture. The principal instrumentality used, in this phase of the campaign, was the General Allotment Act of 1887. The passage of this act — which was universally opposed by the Indians — was hailed as "franchise day" by the reformers. Even such a distinguished Indianist as Francis E. Leupp referred to the act as "the Emancipation Proclamation of the red man." In general the act provided that every Indian, regardless of his wishes, should eventually receive a piece of reservation land to hold in fee simple. At the same time the Indian would be given the same property rights and responsibilities as the white man. This would make for the creation, among Indians, of that spirit of selfishness which, according to Senator Henry L. Dawes, one of the sponsors of the act, was the main motivation of white civilization. It would make the Indian a go-getter and rugged individualist who would no longer need the protection of a government bureau. It would also scatter the Indians among their white neighbors, making it possible for them to learn our folkways by imitation and example.

To give the Indian some protection against sharp practices, however, he was not to be permitted to alienate his allotment for a period of twenty-five years. But it was not long after the act was passed until the prohibition against alienation was nullified by a series of amendments. And since the Indians were a dying race, there was no need to provide for their descendants. Therefore the remaining reservation lands, after the general allotment had been made, were to be purchased by the government at \$1.25 an acre and thrown open to

[15] "Indians Come Alive," by John Collier, *Atlantic Monthly*, September 1942; see also *The Indians of the Americas*, by John Collier, 1947.

settlement. In the ordering of this distribution, as Mr. Collier observes, "by a process of natural selection, the whites saw to it that they got the best and richest of the Indians' lands." The motivation behind this program was, as Mr. Ward Shephard has said, "partly greed, but it was also partly sentimental reliance on one of those easy formulas for salvation. The formula was that by giving each Indian a homestead you could automatically do a number of desirable things: you could give him certain means of self-support, you could make him civilized and respectable by the magic of making him a property owner, and then you also could quite properly, having done these things, take away the surplus land that he didn't really need."

The economic consequences of the allotment policy were, to put it mildly, disastrous. At the time the act was passed, the Indians had around 138,000,000 acres of land. In 1933 this had been reduced to 52,000,000 acres, fully half of which was desert or semidesert in character. In other words, under the act the Indians lost upwards of 86,000,000 acres of land. Over 60,000,000 acres of the so-called surplus land were largely disposed of after 1887. Indians were induced to sell their individual allotments almost as rapidly as the limitations on alienation expired or were removed. As applied to timber and grazing lands, which must be managed in large blocks, the policy was economically suicidal.

Even in the sale of their individual allotments, the Indians were swindled, defrauded, and grossly imposed upon. Because of the restrictions on alienation (which also applied to alienation by will), the allotted lands became hopelessly ensnarled in legal complications (some 6,000,000 acres are still in heirship status). So complicated did the titles become that Congress authorized the Indian Bureau to sell or lease these lands. In the process of leasing them, gross mismanagement occurred. Out of some 37,000,000 acres of grazing land, it is estimated that 50 per cent of the carrying capacity has been lost through overgrazing and consequent erosion. Since the management policy was premised upon the necessity of getting an immediate cash income, which was doled out to the Indians, virtually none of the income was spent on capital improvements. The folly of the allotment measure must be considered also in light of the fact that the Indian was placed in possession of a tract of land without adequate capital, or even the means of raising capital, with which he might develop it. Nor were adequate means taken to provide him with the necessary machinery and equipment or the technical guidance essential to successful farming.

The cultural consequences of the allotment policy were, however, more disastrous than the economic. The economic, tribal, and social organization of the Indian tribes was rapidly undermined. In weakening Indian social organization, the allotment policy nearly destroyed the only foundation upon which a transformed Indian society might have been built. Far from making a go-getter of the Indian, it destroyed his initiative and self-confidence. By shattering the foundation of his culture it robbed the Indian of the drive that comes from believing in the future of one's society and nation. It was the culminating humiliation of a century of defeat and reversals. And, as Mr. Macleod has pointed out, "it is not easy to comprehend or to measure the spiritual bitterness of continuous moral and physical defeat." As a matter of fact this sense of social and cultural defeat is the poison which kills so-called primitive peoples on contact with technologically more advanced societies. "What kills off primitive peoples," writes Freyre, "is the loss . . . of their will to live, the loss of any interest in their own values, once their environment has been altered and the equilibrium of their lives has been broken by civilized man." [16] W. H. R. Rivers once pointed out that the Melanesians were dying of "banzo," of melancholy.

[16] Freyre, *op. cit.*, p. 181.

Allotment, moreover, was only one prong of a many-sided cultural attack. Not only must the Indian be assimilated overnight, but his children must be liberated from the baneful influence of family, tribe, and culture. Children between the ages of six and eighteen were "snatched" from their parents and kept in boarding schools which, in many cases, were far removed from where the parents lived. Here they were often kept from four to eight years consecutively, including vacations. Indian educational policy seemed to be pointed toward the destruction of family life and the liquidation of Indian culture. As late as 1931, only a few Indian schools carried instruction into the junior grades; and until 1929 the use of the Indian languages, as well as Indian dress and hair styles, was forbidden.

But the cultural attack had still other fronts. "The rooting-out process," writes Mr. Collier, "penetrated likewise into the deeper spiritual strata of Indian culture. The Indian languages were systematically suppressed in the Indian schools; the religious ceremonies, the poetry, music, and traditions were discouraged or suppressed; the precious and beautiful ancient arts and crafts were allowed to decline and in many cases to completely disappear. . . . Indian schools were illegally used for the practically forced proselytism of Indian children, regardless of the consent of their parents."

Such a prolonged cultural attack naturally took a frightful toll of Indian life, health, and well-being. By 1923 Indians had declined in numbers from the pre-Columbian estimate of 850,000 to around 220,000. They had lost at least two thirds of all their land in area and about four fifths in value. "Outside the boundaries of Russia, India, or China," wrote Dr. Haven Emerson, "I know of no nation, race or tribe of human beings which exhibit such tragic neglect of the most elementary protection against sickness and death as is to be found among American Indians." It was not until 1924 that a Division of Health was created in the Indian Bureau. Tuberculosis, trachoma, infant mortality, syphilis were the scourges of reservations described in 1931 as "germ-ridden cess-pools of sickness and disease." During the period when "forced assimilation" was the dominant theme in Indian policy, say from 1880 to 1929, little attempt was made to apply scientific information and knowledge in the administration of Indian affairs. "It was a startling thing in the early 1920's," writes Oliver La Farge, "to see how utterly the Indian Bureau remained insulated against all this, to see how it continued to exist and work not even in the nineteenth but in the eighteenth century." [17]

The outstanding evil of this policy of forced assimilation, however, was neither corruption nor incompetence; it was the lack of integrity in administering a national trust which stemmed from a failure to believe in the Indian's capacity to govern himself and to manage his own affairs. This denigration of the Indian was carried to the point where Congress, after 1871, arrogantly asserted the right to interfere with the purely internal affairs of the tribes, touching on such issues as language, religion, laws, customs, and even parent-child relationships. Up to this point, we had "fought" rather than "bossed" the Indian; now we proposed to make him over to our liking and taste. The effect of all this, of course, was to deny personal, social, and cultural freedom to the Indian; or, as McNickle puts it, "freedom to grow with experience." [18] Somehow we could not see that forced assimilation is a denial of the principle of self-government.

In large part the failure to trust the capacity of the Indian for self-government was based on a woeful ignorance of the Indian's cultural contributions to American life. A passage from Allen Harper's monograph on American Indians will indicate the extent of this contribution:

[17] *As Long as the Grass Shall Grow*, by Oliver La Farge.
[18] McNickle, *op. cit.*, p. 291.

As determined as they were to transplant intact the civilization of their homelands, the European settlers were, on their part, not slow in introducing modifications that gave a distinctly different *quality* to the life which they constructed in the New World. The Indian's contribution to their civilization in foodstuffs and drugs alone was phenomenal. It has been estimated that four sevenths of the total agricultural production of the United States consists of economic plants domesticated by the Indian and adopted by the white man. A writer has observed that "the extent of the debt to the Indian for his work of domestication is emphasized when we recall that the white man has not yet reduced to cultivation a single important staple during the four hundred years that he has dominated the New World." The white man appropriated the Indian's canoe, snowshoe, and toboggan; built his roads and canals over the Indian's trails; emulated the Indian's methods of warfare, fishing, and recreation; copied and adapted the Indian's clothes for life in the forest. The Indian passed immediately into the literature created in the New World; and, indeed, in far-off Europe, reports of him and his life inspired a number of writers to grow nostalgic in their enthusiasm for the primitive man. The Indian quickened and revitalized the imagination of the white man, caused him to reawaken an old instinct for the outdoors, and taught him how to live with the outdoors — one of the greatest of arts.[19]

On the other hand, the conceit which induced us to believe that we knew what was best for the Indian stemmed from a failure to recognize how profoundly our treatment of the Indian had handicapped the promise of American democracy. Merely to cite one illustration: the immense loot obtained in the spoliation of the Indian estate, as Angie Debo has shown, "exerted a powerful influence upon contemporary opinion and standards of conduct. The reaction of this process upon

[19] See *The Indians of the United States: Their Culture, Economy and Government*, monograph by Allan Harper, not published in English, but issued under the title of *Los Indios de los Estados Unidos* by the National Indian Institute, 1942, Department of the Interior, Washington, 73 pp. illus.

the ideals and standards of successive frontier communities is a factor in the formation of American character that should no longer be disregarded by the students of social institutions." [20] In point of time, the inception of the forced assimilation policy coincided with the failure of reconstruction in the South and the beginnings of modern-day white supremacy; but the 1870's also marked the beginnings of a savage assault upon the values of the democratic culture that stemmed from the Revolution of 1776. In denying democracy to the Indian and the Negro, the forward movement of American democracy was arrested and a long detour then had to be negotiated. The real test did not come until the 1870's for until then we had never seriously considered the acceptability of the Negro and the Indian as citizens. The moment they were considered and rejected, a strange dualism developed in the American tradition. For the truth is that we have since had two American traditions: one generous, and liberal, inclusive and democratic; the other narrow, bigoted, exclusive and authoritarian. The key to this dichotomy is to be found in the history of the Indian and Negro minorities.

## 4. *The Indian New Deal*

The beginnings of the New Deal in Indian affairs relate back to 1922, when the Pueblo Indians of New Mexico, to protest a scandalous attempt to rob them of their remaining lands, came together against a common enemy for the first time since 1690.[21] The stirrings of this protest led, in turn, to the Meriam Report of 1928 with its famous first sentence: "An overwhelming majority of the Indians are poor, even extremely poor, and they are not adjusted to the economic and social system of the dominant white civilization" — after four hundred years! The real turning point then came with the appoint-

---

[20] *And Still the Waters Run,* by Angie Debo, 1940, p. viii.
[21] McNickle, *op. cit.,* p. 288.

ment in 1929 of Charles J. Rhodes as Commissioner, and
J. Henry Scattergood as Assistant Commissioner of Indian
Affairs. Interestingly enough, both men were Quakers: it was
as though, to find nonaggressive administrators, we had been
forced to turn to a religious minority which, since the days of
William Penn, has understood the folly of coercion in dealing
with Indians. Officially the New Deal for Indians began, however, with the appointment of John Collier as Commissioner
in 1933.[22]

As Mr. Collier saw it, the New Deal for Indians had three
major objectives: economic rehabilitation of the Indian, principally but not exclusively upon the land; organization of the
Indian tribes for managing their own affairs; and civic and
cultural freedom and opportunity for the Indian. Underlying
these objectives was the simple principle, as Mr. Collier put it,
"of treating the Indians as normal human beings capable of
working out a normal adjustment to and a satisfying life within
the framework of American civilization, yet maintaining the
best of their own culture and racial idiosyncrasies." This principle goes back, in his thinking, to a central and universal
value: that the personality of the other, the different personality, group, or race, is dearer to the civilized man than anything
else. It is altogether possible that Mr. Collier derived this philosophy from the Indians themselves. Pleasant Porter, Chief
of the Creek Nation, told a senatorial committee in 1906 that
"the Indians haven't had time to grow up to that individuality
which is necessary to merge them with the American citizen.
The change came too soon for them . . . there is no life in
the people that have lost their institutions. Evolving a thing out
of itself is natural, transplanting it is a matter of dissolution, not

---

[22] See Chapter I, *The Indians of the Americas,* by John Collier, for an
interesting account of how Mr. Collier became involved in Indian affairs.
See, also, "United States Indian Administration as a Laboratory of
Ethnic Relations," by John Collier, *Social Research,* September 1945, vol. 12,
no. 3.

growth. There may be a few that will grow . . . but the growth will not be natural." [23]

Since land use is the essential problem of Indian economy (90 per cent of the Indians are rural), reform of land policies was the first concern of the Collier administration. By secretarial order, all further sale of Indian lands was prohibited. Then, under the Indian Reorganization Act of June 18, 1934 (approved by 74 per cent of the Indians by referenda), the further allotment of lands was terminated. Over 4,250,000 acres were added to the Indian land base. Excellent programs were instituted to prevent soil erosion, overgrazing, and the deterioration of arable lands. A revolving fund was established by which the Indian might acquire the necessary capital to become a successful farmer. The history of this fund eloquently demonstrates the Indian's capacity to manage his own affairs: over $12,000,000 has been loaned since 1935, with the losses, to the end of 1946, being only three tenths of 1 per cent. Co-operative marketing associations of all types were established and, through the Arts and Crafts Act of 1935, Indians were encouraged to develop their native arts.

Perhaps the most important phase of the Indian New Deal, however, consisted in the attempt to stimulate local self-government. The Indian Reorganization Act, characterized by D'Arcy McNickle as "the first action by white men in the New World to govern for the benefit of the Indian people," proclaimed the right of Indians to set up councils of their own choice; to raise and expend funds for public purposes; and, generally, asserted the right of self-government. Under this act, Indians were made equal partners in the administration of their affairs and the main function of the Indian Service became that of co-operative advice and technical guidance rather than despotic management. The importance of this act can hardly be exaggerated for, as McNickle points out, by 1934

[23] Quoted by Debo, *op. cit.*, p. 132.

Indians were "dying of legislatively induced anemia. . . . There was never a legislative body in the history of the world capable of supplying the power to think and the power to act in a people." [24]

Under Collier, too, the cultural attack upon the Indian was brought to an abrupt halt. The Service was instructed to respect "the fullest constitutional liberty in all matters pertaining to religion, conscience, and culture." The number of boarding schools was drastically reduced and efforts were made to develop bilingual educational programs. The employment of Indians in the Service itself increased from 30 per cent in 1933 to 59 per cent in 1935. Medical and hospital facilities were expanded and full use was made for the first time of social science research techniques.

Critics of the Indian New Deal charged — and still charge — that its policies were retrogressive; that Mr. Collier, influenced by the make-work programs of the Roosevelt administration, attempted to turn the clock back. But the Collier policies rested in the main on a sound and valid argument which has never been better stated than by McNickle: "Men are formed in society. Men also, as matured adults, mold society; but in the beginning the formation of the individual personality is accomplished by the world into which the individual is born. Indian societies are living organisms, having survived the gravest vicissitudes. When a Hopi Indian asks a white man to explain his behavior toward the Hopi people, he is not a single individual asking an impertinent question; he is an entire society and an entire history of a people asking for the explanation. It follows that the quickest way to reach and remake Indians is by working with them and through those very social forms which make the Indian world. This cannot be done if the Indian forms are wrecked before the Indians have found acceptable substitutes." [25]

[24] McNickle, *op. cit.*, p. 300.
[25] *Ibid.*, p. 295.

## 5. Since World War II

Convergent pressures and new social forces have currently combined to usher in still a new phase of Indian-white relationships. The first of the pressures, of course, is that of population on resources. Oliver La Farge sums up the situation in all its brutal determinism: "As their holdings stand today, the fullest exploitation of every acre by the most modern techniques would not suffice to keep all Indians eating." [26]

Consider, for example, the pressures which have developed on the Navajo reservation. There were only 8000 Navajos when the tribe was settled on the reservation in 1867; today there are 60,000. Although the reservation has been enlarged from 3,500,000 to 16,750,000 acres — an area larger than Massachusetts, Vermont, Connecticut, and Rhode Island combined — the terrain is so unproductive that the Navajos suffer from overcrowding even at a ratio of 300 acres for every member of the tribe! Overgrazing has sharpened the problem of subsistence for a people primarily dependent on sheep raising. It takes 30 acres of land on the reservation to support a sheep, 150 acres for a horse, 120 for a cow, and the amount of irrigable land is negligible. Dr. George Sanchez has estimated that the reservation cannot support more than 35,000 people.[27]

The plight of the Navajo has been spotlighted since 1947, largely because the isolationist press has sought to divert attention from the Marshall Plan. We should first "do something for the Navajo," so the argument ran, before we undertook to feed Europe. Out of the curious crosscurrents at work in Congress, there finally emerged a ten-year $88,570,000 rehabilitation program or "Little Marshall Plan" for the Navajos which President Truman approved on April 19, 1950. With less than 6000 of 22,000 Navajo children of school age enrolled in

[26] *New York Times Magazine*, April 30, 1950, p. 14.
[27] *The People: A Study of the Navajos*, by George I. Sanchez, U. S. Indian Service, March 1948.

reservation schools in 1949; with a tuberculosis rate of 380 per 100,000 (by comparison with 40 per 100,000 for the nation) and with the reservation having 2000 active cases of tuberculosis, it was about time that a large-scale aid-and-rehabilitation program was projected. But unfortunately the pressure of population on resources is merely one of a number of new pressures which are today noticeable in Indian affairs.

On July 15, 1948, the Arizona Supreme Court ruled that Indians are not persons "under guardianship" and therefore are eligible to vote. Then, on August 3, a federal court judge, in a suit brought by Miguel H. Trujillo, an Isleta Pueblo Indian who had served in the Marine Corps during the war, ruled that Indians could vote in New Mexico. These two decisions removed the final bars to the enfranchisement of the Indians, all of whom were made citizens of the United States in 1924. Prior to these decisions, however, Arizona and New Mexico had declined to include Indians in their social security appropriations.

One of the effects of the decisions, of course, has been to stimulate the search for off-reservation employment. Encouraged by this development, the Indian Bureau has opened field offices in Phoenix, Los Angeles, and Salt Lake City in an effort to place Indians more efficiently. It is currently estimated that 85 to 90 per cent of the employable Navajos now find some part-time work off the reservation each year. This means that something like $1,000,000 in unemployment insurance is now available in the winter months. From Arizona and New Mexico, Indians have been moving into metropolitan Los Angeles in quest of jobs. When interviewed, they have uniformly said that population pressures "back home" were responsible for their presence in Los Angeles. Many of them enter an urban labor market under definite handicaps; for example, of the 72,000 Indians on the Papago and Navajo reservations, probably not more than 20 per cent can read and write English.

Nevertheless the pull of good wages and the pressures back home combined to draw some 5000 Indian job-seekers to Los Angeles in 1950. Here, ironically, these "100 per cent Americans," whose native habitat is the Southwest, find themselves in the socially preposterous role of being the *most recent* "immigrant" group! [28]

Today Alaska and the states of the Intermountain West are coming of age economically. New development schemes are being projected; new plants of the Atomic Energy Commission's industrial empire are already in operation; and, as part of this development, the Western states have become increasingly restive about the enclaves of Indian land holdings. Throughout the Intermountain region it is almost impossible to project any development scheme without impinging, at some point, on Indian holdings. Out of this situation has emerged a new "concern" for the welfare of the Indian which masks, to a degree, a desire to bring the remaining reservation lands under state control.

Indicative of the new trend is the fact that representatives of fifteen Western states, meeting in Salt Lake City in May 1950, formed the Governors' Interstate Council on Indian Affairs. Ostensibly the council is pointed toward the earliest possible "assimilation" of Indians into "first-class citizenship." But the council seems to have another goal also, namely, to have Congress annul the treaties with the various tribes, thereby "freeing" the Indians for assimilation. The present Commissioner, Associate Commissioner, Chief Counsel, and two Assistant Commissioners of Indian Affairs, all former officials of the War Relocation Authority, are strong "assimilationists." In fact legislation is now pending in Congress, approved by these officials, which would not only end Indian wardship but would make possible a disintegration of the reservations as collective holdings. At the same time, the passage by Congress of the Tongass Act in 1947 has seriously

[28] Stories by Vern Partlow, *Los Angeles Daily News*, January 16, 17, 1950.

undermined Indian holdings in Alaska, indicating that the gains of the Indian New Deal are in jeopardy.[29]

Since the Indian New Deal, however, the status of Indians has rapidly changed from that of a suppressed nationality to a national racial minority. The true mark of minority status is invariably self-action looking toward eventual integration. Spearheaded by Indians in the Indian Service, the National Congress of American Indians began to take form in the spring of 1944. In April 1949, representatives of 125,000 Indians from eighteen Southwestern tribes met in Phoenix for the first regional conference of its kind to be held in the United States. In the past, non-Indians were constantly meeting to discuss "the Indian problem"; but here Indians were meeting to discuss such problems as hospitals located 150 miles from where most of the patients live; 1 doctor per 7000 Indians; and school facilities so limited that only a fourth of the Navajo children are enrolled. The report of the conference, indeed, reads like the report of any annual meeting of the NAACP.[30]

That Indians are verging on true minority status is also shown by many recent "incidents"; witness the Florence Begay incident in 1948. Florence Begay, a seventeen-year-old Navajo girl, was awarded a $2000 fellowship at Sarah Lawrence College. En route east, she was ordered to sit in the section reserved for nonwhites when the bus reached Amarillo, Texas. "I felt so discouraged," she said, "that I did not feel like going any further." So she turned back to Arizona and enrolled in the Arizona State College at Flagstaff. Eight years ago, this incident would have gone unnoticed; but in 1948 it aroused a storm of protest and attracted national attention. The 25,000 American Indians who served in World War II have been a powerful element in the transition to minority status.

[29] "Alaska's Nuremberg Laws," by Felix S. Cohen, *Commentary*, August 1948, p. 136.
[30] Story by Gladwin Hill, *New York Times*, April 6, 1949.

It is significant, therefore, that new pressures have been brought to bear upon what remains of Indian collective life at precisely the time that Indians, overcoming the last legal disabilities, are beginning to think of themselves as merely another minority in American life. No one can say how far, and how rapidly, this new phase will unfold; but it is clear that immense new "pressures" have been brought to bear on Indian group life. Will the respite from attack which Indians gained under the Collier regime, and the new resources and confidence they have acquired, coupled with the significant trend toward self-organization as a national minority, tide them over this next phase? Speaking as an official body, in the name of fifteen states, the Governors' Interstate Council on Indian Affairs will have great influence in Congress and may well succeed in forcing a too rapid "liquidation" of the Indian estate.

The Final Report on Indian Personality and Administration, a 60,000-word document presented to the Secretary of the Interior on December 31, 1947, by a team of social scientists, contains a word of caution on all schemes to step up the tempo of assimilation. The report points out that a hastily conceived rehabilitation of the Navajo economy might merely aggravate the existing psychological and cultural crisis; that a sense of haste has consistently blinded the Indian Service to the deeper aspects of the problem of acculturation; and that any scheme of rehabilitation to be successful with the Navajos — who present one of the thorniest acculturation problems — must be based on natural sociological groupings in the tribe. Oliver La Farge is doubtless right in pointing out that a "progressive policy which remains static, ends by becoming reactionary"; but what is a progressive policy? The real question is not about goals but about means and tempo. Now, as always, the great issue is this: Have the American people, at long last, achieved the social insight which will enable them to let American Indians, group by group, in their different and widely varying circumstances, decide what they want to do and the kind of life they want to lead? Have we the wisdom now to permit them to decide issues which, in the last analysis, they alone can decide? If the answer is yes, then it will mean that the American people have finally freed themselves from the illusion that one people can dominate another without limiting their own freedom in the process.

*     *     *

Today there are probably 425,000 Indians on the tribal rolls by comparison with a low of less than 250,000 in 1880, with some Indians living in every state of the Union. The trend toward extinction, arrested in the early 1920's, has now been reversed: the Indian population is currently increasing at the rate of about 1 per cent per year (2 per cent among the Navajos, Papagos, and Hopis of the Southwest). Indeed Indians are today the fastest growing minority in the United States and may increase to 700,000 or 800,000 by 1980.

# The Long-Suffering Chinese

THE FABLE reads that mysterious and inscrutable China, determined to live in isolation from the world, built an enormous wall to protect its empire from invaders. The Great Wall had its counterpart, however, in the vast hemispheric wall built by the Occidental world — comprised of legal statutes rather than bricks and stones — against the Chinese. The creation of this invisible hemispheric wall dates from the period when America, in its feverish rush to the West, reached the Pacific. Not until we had reached the Pacific did we make a sharp break with the American tradition of free migration and enact the first restrictive immigration measures. Here a new frontier was established: Europe, through American eyes, looked across the Pacific toward Asia. As Dr. Robert E. Park once observed: "It is as if we had said: Europe, of which after all America is a mere western projection, ends here. The Pacific Coast is our racial frontier."

The great wall against the Orient dates from 1882, with the passage of the Chinese Exclusion Act. Today, however, there is no land under either the British or the American flag where Chinese labor is admitted. Following the American or California precedent, Australia, Canada, and New Zealand legislated, at an early date, against Oriental immigration. Later the wall was extended from Tia Juana to Cape Horn, as Mexico, Guatemala, El Salvador, Nicaragua, Colombia, Ecuador, and Peru put up barriers against Chinese immigration. "European peoples around the Pacific," wrote Mr. Chester Rowell in

1926, "regard their borders as a racial frontier, which they are determined to maintain inviolate."

Throughout the whole Pacific area, the immigration dykes were built, sometimes only against the Chinese, but in other instances against all Oriental people. The United States, for example, first barred immigration from China, Japan, and the Philippine Islands and then extended the same prohibition to peoples from India, Siam, Indo-China, Java, Sumatra, Ceylon, Borneo, New Guinea, and the Celebes. These dykes, moreover, have taken the form of rigid legal prohibitions setting the people of Asia sharply apart from those of Europe and America. In each instance, also, the prohibition has been based directly, emphatically, and explicitly on so-called racial considerations, thereby creating a situation which was certain to provoke, sooner or later, strenuous countermeasures. In the Atlantic, the symbol of our policy was the Open Door; in the Pacific, the Yellow Peril. Now, in the middle of the twentieth century, we find ourselves excluded from a large section of Asia!

For years the movement of immigrants across the Atlantic was kept in a separate compartment from the similar movement across the Pacific. In the public mind, our "immigration problem," as such, was associated almost exclusively with the transatlantic migration, with Ellis Island, the Statue of Liberty, and the Melting Pot. Conversely, the transpacific movement was associated with an entirely different set of symbols: the Yellow Peril, the Chinese Must Go!, and Japanese Picture Brides. It was, as Dr. Edith Abbott pointed out, "an entirely different problem." Although the admission was not always made, the problem was "different" because the factor of race was involved. In time this difference in attitude crystallized into a dogmatic assumption that the yellow and brown races were "incapable of assimilation." Underlying the assumption, of course, was the unmistakable reality that we had refused to assimilate the Indian and the Negro.

The movement around the rim of the Pacific to set the European peoples apart from those of Asia had its origin in California. Here, in the words of Ching Chao Wu, "for the first time in the history of mankind, large numbers of Orientals and Occidentals, who had developed different racial characteristics and cultural traits during the long period of isolation, were thrown together to work out their destiny in the new land." Even today, a hundred years after the fact, it is impossible to appraise the full consequences of this fateful first meeting. Throughout the Pacific area and beginning in California, the exclusion movement has followed a definite course: from local agitation against a particular class or race of Asiatics to national movements directed against all Asiatics of every race and class; from economic arguments to cultural and biological arguments for restriction and exclusion. The pattern of the entire movement is implicit in the agitation against the Chinese in California. Just how, then, did the breach with our tradition of free migration occur? How was it possible for one state to force its views upon the nation and thereby to set in motion a chain of events of world-wide significance?

## 1. The Technique of Exclusion

The year 1876 marked a definite turning point in the history of anti-Chinese agitation in California. Up to this point, most of the barbarous and obnoxious anti-Chinese legislation adopted in California had been declared unconstitutional as being in violation of treaty provisions, the Fourteenth Amendment, or the federal civil rights statutes. The federal courts, as a matter of fact, were constantly preoccupied with California's outrageous "Hottentot" or race legislation in the period from 1860 to 1876. For the Chinese in California had wisely decided to defend their rights along strictly legal and constitutional lines. Compact social organization made it possible for them to raise the large sums necessary for test cases in the courts. It was these "coolies" from Asia, not the Indians or the Negroes, who made the first great tests of the Civil War amendments and the legislation which came with these amendments. American constitutional history was made in such far-reaching decisions as *United States* v. *Wong Kim Ark* and *Yick Wo* v. *Hopkins*. Yet, years later, K. K. Kawakami, seeking to dissociate the Japanese from the Chinese, said that the early Chinese were "slavish, utterly callous to the Occidental environment, and content with the inhuman treatment meted out to them." The fact is, as the court reports eloquently attest, that the Chinese in California conducted a magnificent fight for the extension of human freedom in America.

By 1876 the Californians had reached an impasse in their agitation against the Chinese. Not only had the federal courts made effective use of the Fourteenth Amendment in striking down a series of discriminatory measures, but in 1875 Congress had adopted a general civil rights act. Although the act was primarily aimed at overriding the Black Codes which the Southern states had adopted in an effort to circumvent the Fourteenth Amendment, it was also a blow at the attempt to Jim Crow the Chinese in California. It became necessary, therefore, to shift the campaign from the state to the national level; to move the debate, so to speak, from Sacramento to Washington. At the same time, the emphasis shifted from discriminatory legislation to immigration restriction for the civil rights act barred the way to exclusion-by-harassment. Thus it was that a measure suspending Chinese immigration for ten years was finally forced through Congress in 1882 after both Presidents Hayes and Arthur had vetoed similar measures.

The enactment of this measure — the first restriction imposed by Congress on immigration — represented a change in American foreign policy as well as a sharp break with American tradition. In the early treaties with China (1844 and 1858) nothing was said about the rights of Chinese residing in the United States; presumably they had the same status as other aliens. But after the Central Pacific had started work on the transcontinental rail line in 1863, and after the Pacific Mail Steamship Company had established the first transpacific service in 1867, the United States became intensely interested in opening up trade and commerce with China. These developments were largely responsible for the negotiation of the Burlingame Treaty of 1868 which was hailed in this country as opening a new era in the Pacific.

The Burlingame Treaty also marked the dividing line between two distinct and contradictory policies on the part of the United States toward the Chinese. Up to this point our efforts had been directed toward *compelling* the Chinese to admit Americans to China for the purpose of trade and commerce. In this contention we asserted the broad principle of free migration and the duty of international intercourse. The Burlingame Treaty, which carried out this principle, was reciprocal in its provisions. Article VII conferred on American citizens in China the "same privileges, immunities and exemptions" enjoyed by citizens of the most favored nation and other provisions gave Chinese subjects here the same protection. The only exception was a proviso that "nothing herein contained shall be held to confer naturalization upon citizens of the United States in China, nor upon the subjects of China in the United States." The reason this provision was included was obvious: Negro suffrage was then being hotly debated in Congress and the clause was inserted to expedite ratification of the treaty. The ink was hardly dry on the signatures to the treaty, however, before political pressure from California forced the government to negotiate an amendment providing that the United States might regulate, limit, or suspend Chinese immigration but "may not absolutely prohibit it." This amendment paved the way for the legislation of 1882 suspending Chinese immigration for ten years.

In the debate on the bill, Senator Hawley had pointed out that we, as a nation, had bombarded China for precisely the same privilege — namely, free migration — which we now sought to deny her. "Make the conditions what you please for immigration and for attaining citizenship," he pleaded; "but make them such that a man may overcome them; do not base them on the accidents of humanity." As finally passed — by a combination of Southern and Western votes — the act not only suspended immigration but contained an express prohibition against the naturalization of the Chinese. Naturalization had been restricted to "free white persons" since 1790 but the limiting phrase had not been construed until 1878. In that year, in a case involving a Chinese, a federal district court judge in California had ruled that the word "white" referred to a person of the Caucasian race. Actually the phrase "free white persons" was used to exclude slaves, regardless of their color, and Indians living in tribal organizations. It will be noted, for example, that not all *white* persons were eligible; only those who were *free* could apply. But with the adoption of the 1882 act the United States was formally committed to a policy of racial discrimination at variance with its traditions and principles as well as its prior policies. The measure also sanctioned state discriminations, since it denied the Chinese the protection of citizenship, and seriously undermined the philosophy upon which the federal civil rights legislation rested. Indeed one year later, in 1883, the Supreme Court declared the general civil rights act unconstitutional.

With the passage of the exclusion measure in 1882 and the Supreme Court's decision in the civil rights cases in 1883, the agitation against the Chinese reached a new pitch of intensity and violence throughout the Far West. In September 1885, a riot occurred at Rock Springs, Wyoming, in which 28 Chinese were murdered and property valued at $148,000 was destroyed. "Shortly afterward," writes Dr. E. C. Sandmeyer, "the entire west coast became inflamed almost simultaneously. Tacoma burned its Chinese quarter, and Seattle, Olympia, and Portland might have done the same but for quick official action. In California developments ranged from new ordinances of regulation to the burning of Chinese quarters and the expulsion of the inhabitants. Among the localities where these actions occurred were Pasadena, Santa Barbara, Santa Cruz, San Jose, Oakland, Cloverdale, Healdsburg, Red Bluff, Hollister, Merced, Yuba City, Petaluma, Redding, Anderson, Truckee, Lincoln, Sacramento, San Buenaventura, Napa, Gold Run, Sonoma, Vallejo, Placerville, Santa Rosa, Chico, Wheatland, Carson, Auburn, Nevada City, Dixon, and Los Angeles.[1]

These pogroms were so humiliating that the Chinese government promptly sought a modification of the treaty and an amendment was negotiated suspending all immigration for twenty years and providing indemnity for the loss of Chinese life and property. While this new treaty was being ratified in China, Congress abruptly passed the Scott Act of 1888 which slammed the doors to some 20,000 Chinese who had temporarily left the United States but who, at the time, had a perfect right of re-entry. Over a period of years the Chinese government filed protest after protest with the State Department against the enactment of this outrageously unfair measure without receiving even an acknowledgment of its notes. By this time our attitude toward China, as reflected in this legislation, was so brutally overbearing that many foreign offices assumed that we were trying to provoke a war.

Not content with this state of affairs, Congress then passed the notorious Geary Act of 1892 (again by a combination of Southern and Western votes). Continuing the suspension of immigration for another ten years, the bill denied bail to Chinese in habeas corpus proceedings and required certificates of residence from the Chinese in default of which they could be deported. The effect of the Geary Act, which was

[1] *The Anti-Chinese Movement in California,* by Elmer Clarence Sandmeyer, 1939, p. 97.

denounced by the Chinese Ambassador in Washington as being "in violation of every principle of justice, equity, reason and fair-dealing between two friendly powers," was to drive many Chinese from California and to terrify those who remained. In 1902 Congress indefinitely extended the prohibition against Chinese immigration and the denial to them of the privilege of naturalization. But further indignities were still in order. Despite strenuous protests from the Chinese government, Congress insisted on making the terms of the Immigration Act of 1924 barring aliens ineligible to citizenship specifically applicable to the Chinese, and at the same time made it impossible for American citizens of Chinese ancestry to bring their alien wives to this country. In 1926, 1928, and 1930, resident Chinese groups sought to have this latter provision modified, but to no purpose. At an even earlier date, also, we had projected our racially discriminatory immigration laws into the Pacific by barring Chinese immigration to Hawaii and the Philippine Islands.

The process by which the Chinese were excluded in response to pressure from California has been summarized by Mrs. Mary Roberts Coolidge as follows: "From suspension to restriction; from execution of treaty stipulations to flat prohibition of treaty compact, the movement went on until it culminated in the Geary Act, which reiterated and legalized the severer features of them all and added the requirement of registration. It was . . . progression from vinegar to vitriol." [2] It was also entirely in keeping with the history of our treaty dealings with the Indians. As a matter of fact, the exclusion of the Chinese squared perfectly with the policy of placing Indians on reservations and segregating Negroes by force of law. Modes of aggression which had been tried out against Indians and Negroes were easily transferred to the Chinese and a Californian on the Supreme Court had little difficulty in convincing his colleagues that it was as

[2] *Chinese Immigration*, by Mary Roberts Coolidge, 1909.

easy to breach a treaty with China as with the Indian tribes. "Experts in violence," as Felix S. Cohen has noted, "do not usually retire when a war has been won." [3] They look for new victims.

While China was as powerless to retaliate as the Indian tribes or the former Negro slaves, she did voice her resentment on more than one occasion. Mrs. Coolidge states, for example, that the exclusion of the Chinese and the indignities perpetrated in this country "undoubtedly contributed to the accumulated resentment which found expression in the Boxer Rebellion." Mr. Wu has gone further and stated that the Boxer Rebellion was the expression of a spirit which, if China had been stronger, would have resulted in the exclusion of all Americans from China. History has since proved that Mr. Wu was engaging in prophecy, not speculation.

## 2. The Politics of Exclusion

In retrospect one is intrigued by the question: How was it possible for a single West Coast state to force its racial views upon the national government and to shape, in effect, the foreign policy of the country? The brief if somewhat cryptic answer would be that the views of California were in fact the views of the nation since anti-Chinese prejudice can hardly be distinguished from the same prejudice against Indians and Negroes. But there is this difference: the measures which were adopted against the Chinese had international implications; they represented the first projection beyond the borders of this country of our domestic racism. Our dealings with Indians and Negroes had brought into being a set of conditioned reflexes which the Californians soon discovered were most responsive to racial propaganda. But the specific reasons for the success of California's agitation were these: the interrelations between the Negro and Chinese issues; the peculiar

[3] *Commentary*, August 1948, p. 137.

balance of political power within the nation; and the fact that both the Negro and the Chinese issue fused with a larger national capital-labor conflict.

"No small part of the persecution of the Chinaman," wrote Mrs. Coolidge, "was due to the fact that it was his misfortune to arrive in the United States at a period when the attention of the whole country was focused on the question of slavery." [4] Even so we started out to deal with the Chinese on a nondiscriminatory basis only to discover that this policy conflicted with our policy toward Indians and Negroes. Every issue affecting the Chinese cut across the whole complex of issues affecting the Negro. Without a single exception, the anti-Chinese measures were carried in Congress by a combination of Southern and Western votes. Southern Bourbons could not tolerate a policy in California that might have unsettling consequences in Alabama. Besides the more California became committed to a Jim Crow policy in relation to the Chinese, the greater became its obligation to support Southern racial policies in Congress. At one time, too, the South had shown a lively interest in the possibility of substituting Chinese coolie labor for Negro labor; without the sanctions of slavery it was feared that the Negro might be unmanageable. The proposal was seriously discussed in Memphis in 1869, and on several occasions Southern plantation owners visited California with this proposal in mind. Indeed the project was only abandoned when it became clear, after 1876, that the nation did not intend to abolish Negro servitude. Once the federal government surrendered to the South on the Negro issue, it was logically compelled to appease California on the subject of "coolie" labor.

The Chinese were directly related to the slave question in still another way. The great outward movement of coolie labor from China, in the years from 1845 to 1877, was a direct consequence of the discontinuance of slavery in the British

[4] Coolidge, *op. cit.*

Empire. During these years a traffic developed in coolie labor that rivaled "the palmiest days of the Middle Passage." Over 40,000 coolies were imported to Cuba alone, of whom it has been said that at least 80 per cent had been decoyed or kidnaped. By 1862 the movement had reached such proportions that the American government was forced to prohibit American ships from participating in the China-West Indies traffic. Wherever they were imported, the coolies were used to supplant Negro slaves in plantation areas and they might have been used for the same purpose in the United States if we had really freed the slaves. Had this been the case, the Southern representatives in Congress would almost certainly have voted against exclusion of Chinese immigration. On the other hand, the way in which coolies were used as substitutes for slaves in the West Indies served to alarm white labor in California.

The debate on the Naturalization Act of 1870 points up the relation between the Chinese question and the Negro question. This act extended the privilege of naturalization to "aliens of African nativity and persons of African descent" — an extension made unavoidable by the Emancipation Proclamation. During the debate, however, the question arose as to whether the same privilege should also be extended to the Chinese. "The very men," said Senator Carpenter, "who settled the question of Negro suffrage upon principle now hesitate to apply the principle . . . and interpose the very objections to the enfranchisement of the Chinaman that the Democrats urged against the enfranchisement of the Freedmen." Only in respect to nominal citizenship did we distinguish the two questions and this we did because the specific issue had, so to speak, been settled by the Civil War.

As a matter of fact, the Chinese and Negro had been intimately related in California long before 1876. "The antiforeign feeling in California," writes B. Schreike, "was unquestionably intensified by the presence of Southerners, who comprised nearly one-third of the population in the first decade of American rule." [5] A number of Southerners brought their slaves with them to California, where Indian peonage was as old as the first settlements. California enacted a fugitive-slave statute, refused to accept the testimony of Negroes in judicial proceedings until 1863, and rejected ratification of the Fifteenth Amendment. An early statute read that "no Black, or Mulatto person, or Indian shall be allowed to give evidence in favor of, or against a white man." Chief Justice Hugh C. Murray, a member of the American or Know-Nothing Party, described by the historian Bancroft as "immoral, venal, and thoroughly corrupt," construed this statute to include Chinese! While he may have been corrupt, he was certainly logical. "The same rule," he pointed out, "that would admit them [the Chinese] to testify, would admit them to all the equal rights of citizenship, and we might soon see them at the polls, in the jury box, upon the bench [!] and in our legislative halls." [6]

The national political situation in the post-Civil War decades was another factor which made it possible for California to blackmail the government on the Chinese question. During these decades, two Presidents were elected by minorities in popular votes and two more by majorities of less than twenty-five thousand. In these critical postwar decades, the control of both the Presidency and the two houses of Congress frequently shifted between the two major parties. The two major parties were parties of the North and the South; hence the Pacific Coast states came to be looked upon as holding the balance of power. [7] In effect both parties were compelled to appeal to the anti-Chinese sentiment in California. In 1880, six of seven California electors cast their voices for

[5] *Alien Americans*, by B. Schreike, 1936.
[6] Sandmeyer, *op. cit.*, p. 45.
[7] *Ibid.*, p. 111. See also Chapter X, in my book *California: the Great Exception*, 1949.

the Democratic Presidential nominee despite the fact that the state legislature was overwhelmingly Republican. The Republicans in Congress had not accepted the California "line" on the Chinese. Four years later, California was back in the Republican column because the Democrats had not been sufficiently "anti-Chinese." The reason for this peculiar national political situation is quite clear: the post-bellum Solid South had a measure of political power out of all relation to the percentage of its citizens who were permitted to vote. Not only were the Negroes excluded but, to ensure white supremacy, a one-party system had been established. Since it was useless for the South to campaign in the North, and vice versa, both regions campaigned in the West.

These same decades also marked an important period in the history of American labor. In the years from 1870 to 1890, a new industrial society was coming into being and the social stratification that came with this new dispensation created great misgivings and fears among working people. From coast to coast, this feeling of fear and hostility tended to be vented against minority groups. Just as workers once rioted against the use of machines, and destroyed the machines, so, in these decades, they tended to be hostile toward groups that *seemed* to threaten them with unfair competition; witness the attitude of the "poor white" toward the Negro. Hatred of the new social order fused with, and stimulated, a hatred of groups that could be identified as competitors.

In California the Chinese were mistakenly identified as the cause of the seemingly inexplicable economic distress which came at the end of the fabulous Gold Rush decades (1850–1870). Although the argument seemed plausible, there would have been a depression in California in the 1870's if the entire population had been made up of lineal descendants of George Washington. "White American" workingmen were pouring into the state: 59,000 in 1869; 150,000 in the period from 1873 to 1875. What with the completion of the Central

Pacific, the decline in placer mining, and the generally undeveloped economy of the state, there were simply not enough jobs. The rapidity with which the argument against the Chinese shifted from the economic to the biological, from "unfair competitor" to "incapable of assimilation," exposed the delusion on which it rested.[8]

On the other hand it seemed plausible to say — although the argument was equally fallacious — that the difficulty was purely racial and not economic. What Senator Morton had to say, on this score, made a great deal of sense:

If the Chinese in California were white people, *being in all other respects* what they are, I do not believe that the complaints and warfare against them would have existed to any considerable extent. Their difference in color, dress, manners, and religion have [sic], in my judgment, more to do with this hostility than their alleged vices *or any actual injury* to the white people of California. . . . Looking at the question broadly, and at the effect which Chinese labor has exerted in California, running through a period of twenty-five years, I am strongly of the opinion, that, *but for the presence* of the Chinese, California would not now have more than one-half or two-thirds of her present population; that Chinese labor has opened up many avenues and new industries for white labor, made many kinds of business possible, and laid the foundations of manufacturing interests that bid fair to rise to enormous proportions. . . .[9]

The latter part of this argument was clearly sound. It is to be doubted, indeed, if the Chinese were ever in *direct* competition with white Americans; their labor tended to complement rather than to supplant the labor of other groups. Actually there is good reason to believe that, by their presence, they tended to bolster up rather than to depress the wage standard of the white Americans which had been greatly in-

[8] See *Oriental Exclusion*, by R. D. McKenzie, 1927, p. 15.
[9] Sandmeyer, *op. cit.*, p. 88. Emphasis added.

creased by the abnormal conditions prevailing during the Gold Rush.[10]

To see the real source of conflict, one must cut back to the first contacts. The Chinese were "looked upon as a veritable god-send" when they first appeared in California, as, indeed, they were.[11] The difference in color, dress, manners, and religion, to which Senator Morton referred, was not then a source of conflict. With few exceptions, California *employers* consistently regarded the Chinese as a desirable, cheap, submissive, and efficient source of labor and looked upon these *differences* as fortunate traits precisely because they made assimilation difficult if not impossible.[12] In California the opposition to the Chinese was overwhelmingly a working-class opposition; hence its political potency and social power. Where two laboring groups are both being exploited but one more than the other, it often happens that the exploitation will generate conflict between the two exploited groups either because they fail to see the real source of the trouble or because the more powerful labor group finds it expedient to attack, not the exploiter, but the other victim. Out of this "false" conflict came the anti-Chinese agitation and out of this agitation came a racist ideology which survived in California for three generations.

The conflict was false, in economic terms, because it was extremely shortsighted and self-defeating. "The exclusion law," observes Mr. Wu, "which prevents aliens from coming in, cannot keep capital from going out. . . . If people are prevented from competing with one another in the same political region, their goods will still compete in the same world market." When the flow of Chinese labor was finally

[10] See, for example, Dr. Varden Fuller's study, to be found in Vol. 54, LaFollette Committee Transcript, p. 19, 823 *et seq.*

[11] Sandmeyer, *op. cit.*, pp. 11 and 14.

[12] *Ibid.*, p. 33. See also article by Dr. William S. Bernard on "The Law, the Mores, and the Oriental," *Rocky Mountain Law Review*, vol. X (1933), Nos. 2 and 3.

stopped, that of other groups, such as the Japanese and Filipino, was promptly stimulated. At the same time, American capital was seeking outlets throughout the Far East and in Central and South America, and in many instances was actually seeking out the so-called cheap labor areas. Had the California labor leaders elected to organize the Chinese, they could have worked out a strategy and policy which would have discouraged the importation of Oriental labor.

Today we are beginning to realize that the argument against "cheap coolie labor" is the counterpart of the argument that Western industrial technology should be monopolized by Western peoples. Both arguments are essentially isolationist. Having held back and sought to prevent the industrialization of the Far East, we now find ourselves in the position of sending, in dollar value, billions of industrial products to the Far East in the form of planes, and tanks, and guns. Today we complain that we have no spokesmen, no emissaries, to send to the Far East, who understand the peoples and speak their languages and who could explain "our" point of view to "them." Nor have we yet seen the light on this score. For example, on December 17, 1943, we repealed the Chinese exclusion acts and made resident Chinese aliens eligible for citizenship. But we then established a quota permitting the entry of 105 Chinese per year! This quota can be catalogued as a sociological joke for the number of Chinese leaving the United States each year will exceed the quota or, if not, the return of husbands marooned from their wives, and vice versa, will fill the quota easily. Of the quota figure, furthermore, 25 places must be reserved for resident Chinese who desire to leave the country and return under the quota. Repealing the exclusion laws was a good gesture but it was just that — a gesture.

### 3. Chinatown

The number of Chinese in the United States has declined from 107,500 in 1890 to 77,504 in 1940, of whom 30,868 were citizens. Driven from the mines and agriculture at an early date, they are today a highly urbanized minority: approximately 80 per cent live in the Chinatown ghettos of such cities as San Francisco, Los Angeles, New York, Chicago, Portland, Seattle, Boston, Philadelphia, Washington, Detroit, Baltimore, St. Louis, and Pittsburgh. The San Francisco Chinatown is the largest of these communities, containing 22 per cent of all the Chinese in the United States and 44 per cent of those living in California. In 1920 there were 694.5 Chinese males for every 100 Chinese females, a ratio of something like 7 to 1; in 1930 the figures were 59,802 males, 15,152 females. The unequal sex ratio is merely one of a number of factors indicating that, in the absence of some increase in the present quota, which is not even a replacement quota, the Chinese in the United States will decrease to the vanishing point.

The passage of the Exclusion Act of 1882 set in motion a process which, over a period of years, resulted in the present geographical distribution of the resident Chinese. In general the process has had three phases: a high degree of concentration in California and the other Western states from 1850 to 1880 (as late as 1870 nearly 99 per cent were concentrated west of the Rockies); a period of dispersal from 1880 to 1910, following the passage of the exclusion acts and the widespread anti-Chinese riots in the West in 1885; and, since 1910, a movement from smaller to larger cities and a new concentration in the major metropolitan centers.[13]

Over the years, too, marked occupational changes have

[13] "The Decline of Chinatown in the United States," by Rose Hum Lee, *American Journal of Sociology*, March 1949.

taken place among the resident Chinese. In 1860, some 34,933 Chinese worked in the mines in California but the number so employed dropped to 17,609 in 1870 and to 151 in 1920. At one time as many as 10,000 Chinese were employed in the construction of the Central Pacific rail line; today less than 488 are employed by the railroads. For a time the Chinese were widely employed in California in such industries as grain farming, fruit growing, and the drainage of tideland deltas. In 1886, for example, 30,000 Chinese worked as harvest hands in California; but by 1920 the number had dropped to 3617. At an early date, also, the Chinese were widely employed in California for various types of "women's work," principally cooking and washing. Rose Hum Lee points out that as long as there were two males for every female in the population of California, the Chinese had no employment problem; the appearance of American women contributed notably to the decrease in the number of Chinese, as did the emergence, in California, of a more stable economy. There was a time when the Chinese tried to gain a foothold in the service occupations, as porters, janitors, cooks, and domestics, but they tended to withdraw from these occupations, first, because they wanted to minimize competition in order to deflect racial aggression aimed at the Chinese community, and second, because more and more of them were being absorbed in Chinese-owned stores in the various Chinatowns.

In this occupational regrouping of the Chinese, one can see a general process at work. To maintain its dominance, a majority usually invokes three techniques against a minority: members of the minority are restricted, by various devices, to subordinate positions in the economy; restrictive legislation is used to erect barriers against the minority; and an effort is made to deny citizenship to the members of the minority. All of these techniques have been used against the Chinese. For a time they resisted the subordinating process but the backbone of this resistance was broken with the passage of the Geary Act in 1892. From then on, the Chinese withdrew from those jobs in which Americans competed and concentrated in those where no bitter voice was raised against them. By 1920, for example, 50 per cent were employed in restaurants and laundries. In 1870, some 2000 had been employed in general manufacturing but in 1920 only 100 were so employed. "The Chinese," writes Ching Chao Wu, "have succeeded where personal service is a factor in success. But they have failed in the region in which America is supreme — in occupations which involve the application of machinery. They have failed to gain a foothold in the occupations in which they have competed with, and so replaced, the native stocks." The moment the Chinese adopted a strategy of accommodation, the racial hatred of the majority turned to tolerant indifference and sentimental patronage. Oliver Cox, with obvious irony, describes the change in relationship in this manner: "In the end the Chinese on the Coast have been practically gypsyfied. 'The Chinaman was a good loser.' He has withdrawn from the struggle; he is no longer a significant threat to the standards of white labor. He may now be treated with a high degree of indifference or even amiability." [14]

But tolerance is not acceptance, and indifference is not integration. "The Chinese question" has long since lost its former urgency and sense of peril but the position of the resident Chinese has grown steadily worse. By retiring to their Chinatowns, the Chinese have been able to achieve a relationship with the majority which Mr. Wu describes as "symbiotic rather than social . . . cold, formal, and commercial." But nothing even approaching integration has taken place. The life of the resident Chinese, as Leong Gor Yun has pointed out, "is not an unhappy life — most of the time. But it is neither Chinese nor American: it is Chinatown. It is a life led by the Chinese in spite of, rather than with the

[14] Caste, Class & Race, by Oliver Cromwell Cox, 1948, p. 419.

co-operation of, the Americans among whom they breathe and somehow find their living." [15]

Since the passage of the exclusion acts, Chinese life in America has centered in that unique social community, Chinatown. The name of Chinatown, as well as its synthetic exoticism and set-apart character, attests the fact that the Chinese came to America with somewhat different objectives than the usual immigrants of the period. Products of an ancient highly integrated culture, they wanted to preserve their way of life in America until they could return in rich splendor to China. That so many of them were single men, culturally and racially quite sharply set apart from the people among whom they lived, only served to underscore this intention. Unable to acquire real property or to homestead, the early immigrants had to improvise, in their own nimble and quick-witted fashion, and to indulge in all sorts of makeshift occupations. They were, it was said, the great "gap fillers." Constantly retreating, constantly losing marginal occupations, they were in part driven into, and in part withdrew to, the area known as Chinatown. Rose Hum Lee has found that Chinatowns generally cannot survive in cities of less than 50,000 since it takes a city of approximately that size to provide sufficient patronage for the survival of the Chinese restaurant and hand laundry. Nowadays, however, steam laundries have forced Chinese laundrymen from the small city to the large city where a limited patronage can still be found for the meticulous hand work in which they specialize. At the same time, with the import-export trade being interrupted by the war, the Chinese-owned business has turned more and more from exotic importations to articles of home decoration, frozen and canned foods, and the bottling of spices, all handled American-style.

As the oldest and largest Chinese settlement in America, the San Francisco Chinatown is of particular interest. At the

[15] *Chinatown Inside Out,* by Leong Gor Yun, 1936.

height of the anti-Chinese fury in California, Chinatown was pointed to as conclusive evidence of the hideous character of the Chinese. "Foul, uncanny, vicious, and a menace to the community . . . a sliver of space seven blocks long and three wide," it was the super-slum of the West. Enforced segregation had resulted in great congestion and overcrowding which, in turn, had boosted property values. The Chinese, of course, were never the real beneficiaries of this unearned increment in property values; throughout the years most of the owners have belonged to the majority. An investigation in 1885 indicated that there were 14,552 bunks for single men in ten blocks of Chinatown. The fire of 1906 destroyed most of these old rookeries and the district was, to some extent, rebuilt. But it had to be rebuilt on the old site, since restrictive clauses in property deeds generally barred the use or occupation of property by Chinese outside the Chinatown ghetto. As families became more common, one-room units were taken over by entire families. Property in Chinatown became even more valuable than before the fire and rents rose rapidly. The problem of overcrowding and congestion was further aggravated during the depression, when many Chinese were driven into Chinatown from rural areas in search of employment or relief.

For years a legend prevailed in San Francisco that the blessed fire of 1906 had destroyed all that was ugly, sordid, and unhealthy about Chinatown.[16] But in point of fact, Chinatown is still a slum. Here is what the San Francisco Housing Authority had to say about the "quaintness" of Chinatown in 1941:

Expansion in Chinatown is limited. Fifteen thousand Chinese live in an area of five blocks by four blocks which is dedicated not primarily to residence but to shops, restaurants and institutions. Reports of the inconceivable conditions under which the

[16] See *Old Chinatown* by Arnold Genthe and Will Irwin, 1931; and *San Francisco's Chinatown*, by Charles Caldwell Dobie, 1936.

Chinese maintain themselves are not exaggerated. Of the 3830 dwelling units in Chinatown approximately 3000 are totally without heating equipment. In all Chinatown there are only 447 homes acceptable by the Survey standards, and *all* of them are in a high rental bracket. Buildings constructed after the fire to house single men on a bare existence basis — that is, containing tiny windowless rooms with hall toilets and kitchens and often no bath facilities anywhere — now house families . . . sometimes as many as ten to a room. Some in the very heart of San Francisco have neither gas for cooking nor electricity for light but use wood and kerosene.

They live crowded together above the shops and below the sidewalks. Their windows, if they have any, look out on streets that are noisy until the early hours of the morning. The children lack adequate homes; they play in the streets at night or sit with their mothers and fathers at the workshops until midnight. As a consequence of these living conditions, the Chinatown tuberculosis rate is *three times* that of the rest of the city. Though the Chinese cultural tradition has helped to maintain morale so far, there are now numerous indications of discouragement and disintegration.

Three of every five Chinese families are living in one or two rooms, rooms usually so small as to deserve the appellation "cubicles."

Approximately 81.9 per cent of the Chinese-occupied dwelling units in San Francisco have been pronounced substandard by contrast with 19.7 per cent for the rest of the population. Not only is the housing problem serious, but it is extremely difficult to correct. Property values in Chinatown, because of the congestion, are extremely high — a factor which has handicapped the Housing Authority in developing public housing projects in the area.

A recent survey of New York's Chinatown gives much the same picture of internal decay and disintegration. Between 15,000 and 20,000 Chinese live in the Chinatown that extends from Canal Street to within a few blocks of City

Hall. "Most of the buildings, which usually contain stores, restaurants and funeral parlors on the lower floors, are four to seven stories. Few, if any, have elevators, and 60 per cent are more than fifty years old. . . . The walls [describing one unit] were sooty and the floor was uncarpeted. The sleeping rooms were astonishingly small and ill-ventilated. They lacked windows. . . . Not all the places visited contained children. In two dark basement rooms two single middle-aged men lived. Some tenements seemed to be given entirely to dormitory-like use by groups of unmarried men."[17]

The color barrier has been, of course, the main stumbling block in the lives of the American-born Chinese. Up to the end of 1938, the Oriental Division of the United States Employment Service in San Francisco reported that 90 per cent of its placements were for service workers, chiefly in the culinary trades. The service has reported that, with few exceptions, most firms discriminate against the Chinese despite the fact that many of the American-born are well educated and have received special training. With the defense program well under way, Nate R. White reported that there were 5000 young Chinese in San Francisco for whom "there seems to be no future worthy of their skills." Instead of applying and using the skills for which they were trained, they were "washing dishes, carrying trays, ironing shirts, cutting meat, drying fish, and selling herbs."[18]

During the war, however, the employment situation showed marked improvement, as the Chinese began to find jobs as stenographers, timekeepers, welders, carpenters, shipyard workers, and in the aircraft industry. As more Chinese began to find work outside Chinatown, Chinese restaurants and hand laundries began to close their doors. The fact that China was our ally during the war, as well as the general wartime

[17] *New York Times*, June 15, 1950.
[18] "Crisis in Chinatown," by Nate R. White, *Christian Science Monitor*, February 1, 1941.

ferment on "the racial question," served to lower discriminatory barriers and to arouse new hopes in the resident
Chinese.[19] But these developments have only accelerated
the disintegration, the breaking-up, of Chinatown. Both external and internal pressures are forcing a dissolution of
Chinatown, long a symbol of the isolationism which we have
practiced toward the peoples of the Far East. Since the passage
of the exclusion acts, the resident Chinese have been the
victims of this policy but it may well be that we, the rest of
us, are destined to be the ultimate victims. Here, at any rate,
is a minority "problem" that we seem to have solved: within
another generation, the Chinatowns will probably have disappeared and the Chinese-Americans, cut off from replacements, will have "vanished" — that is, been absorbed into
the general population. Few ethnic groups have made a more
important contribution to the culture of California than the
Chinese, yet today one can see no visible evidences of this
contribution, with the exception of Chinatown itself. Just
as their cultural contributions have been absorbed without
leaving so much as a name place as a memorial, so the people
themselves seem destined to disappear as a minority.[20]

[19] See article by Rose Hum Lee, *Survey Graphic*, October 1942.
[20] See Chapter V, "Cathay in the South," in my book *Southern California
Country*, 1946.

# CHAPTER III

# The Forgotten Mexican

IN THE complex American ethnic system, the Mexican is clearly "the forgotten man." Far less is known about Mexican-Americans than about ethnic groups with only a fraction of their numerical significance. Numbering in excess of 2,500,000, the Spanish-speaking in the United States make up what Dr. George I. Sanchez has termed "an orphan group," a forgotten people. Still largely unorganized and incoherent, the Spanish-speaking constitute "the least known, the least sponsored, and the least vocal large minority group in the nation." [1] And in American life the rule seems to prevail that only those are given a hearing who speak for themselves. The Spanish-speaking have spoken out, not once but many times, but their voices have been unheard and their speeches have gone unheeded. Underlying the neglect of the Spanish-speaking is a curious paradox. The Spanish-speaking minority ranks second only to American Indians in historical priority, yet it happens to be the most recent immigrant group in American life. The group is so old that it has been forgotten and so new that it has not yet been discovered.

An ethnic group has been defined as a people living competitively in relationship of superordination or subordination with respect to some other people or peoples within the same area or region. In this sense there can be no doubt that the

[1] "The Default of Leadership," mimeographed copy of a paper read by Dr. George I. Sanchez, Fourth Regional Conference, Southwest Council on Education of Spanish-Speaking People, Albuquerque, January 23–25, 1950.

Spanish-speaking constitute a clearly delineated ethnic group. They are only clearly defined, however, within the system of which they are a part; what gives unity to the Spanish-speaking is the cleavage between "Anglo" and "Hispano" in the Southwest. Actually there is no more heterogeneous ethnic group in the United States. Nevertheless the cleavage between Anglos and Hispanos is so clearly etched that the diversity within the Spanish-speaking minority is forgotten; the reality is the cleavage or dichotomy between English-speaking and Spanish-speaking. Yet not all of the minority speak Spanish or the majority English. The sense of separateness is so pervasive, however, that Jews are regarded as "Anglos" in the Southwest and Erna Fergusson tells of the Negro in Albuquerque who, in conversation with an Anglo, referred, quite accurately, to "us Anglos." The point is, of course, that one ethnic group always implies the existence of another; the existence of an Anglo group is what makes it possible to speak of the "Spanish-speaking" as though the term denoted a compact group. The two terms are the head and the tail of a single coin, a single ethnic system; they define a relationship, not homogeneous entities. Just who, then, are the Spanish-speaking?

## 1. The Diversity of the Spanish-Speaking

Today an undetermined number of Spanish-speaking reside in the United States. The first attempt to estimate the size of this population was made in the taking of the 1930 census. Since this census defined as "Mexican" those persons "born in Mexico or having parents born in Mexico who are not definitely white, Negro, Indian or Japanese" — thereby excluding most of the Spanish-speaking of New Mexico — it was quite inaccurate. It did provide, however, a fairly accurate picture of the distribution of Mexicans. The total was given as 1,422,533 — the third largest "racial" group in the nation. Nine tenths of the Mexicans were found in five states: Texas,

California, Arizona, New Mexico, and Colorado — the states of the old Spanish borderlands. An enumeration in 1940, based on Spanish as the mother tongue, gave the total as 1,861,400 and placed 1,570,740 in the Southwest. The National Resources Planning Board estimated the Spanish-speaking population at "about 3,000,000" and placed 2,000,000 in the five states previously mentioned.[2] The difficulty with these and other estimates is that the Spanish-speaking are amazingly heterogeneous; hence any attempt to enumerate them by reference to a single norm, such as language, race, place of birth, or birthplace of parents, is bound to be misleading.

The 1930 census divided the Mexican population into these categories: first generation foreign-born, 616,998 (43.4 per cent of the total); native-born of foreign-born or mixed parentage, 541,197 (38 per cent); and native-born of native-born parents, 264,338 or 18.6 per cent. The estimate for this last category was wholly inadequate, there being approximately that number of "native born of native born" in New Mexico alone. The census accurately indicated, however, that this element is highly concentrated in the Southwest (about 95.6 per cent) and is to be found, for the most part, in New Mexico, Colorado, and Texas.

Today the Spanish-speaking population can be estimated, without pretense of statistical accuracy, as follows: Texas, 1,300,000; Arizona, 120,000; New Mexico, 250,000; California, 500,000; and Colorado around 90,000. The last four estimates are quite conservative. In the Southwest, the Spanish-speaking are concentrated within particular areas. For example, in Texas, 70 per cent are to be found in fifteen counties and about 50 per cent in five counties. In each of twenty-four counties extending from Santa Cruz in Arizona to Willacy in Texas, more than 50 per cent of the population is Spanish-speaking. In Texas there is a tier of predominantly Spanish-speaking counties, often two or three counties in

[2] *The Problems of a Changing Population*, 1938, p. 224.

depth, that is three fourths as large as the New England states combined.

In New Mexico the Spanish-speaking are concentrated in the Upper Valley of the Rio Grande and in the southern part of the state. In Colorado, the Spanish-speaking are to be found in the San Luis Valley, the southeastern corner of the state, in Denver, and in the northern sugar-beet counties. Seventy-eight per cent of the Spanish-speaking in California were to be found in 1920 in Southern California. Geographically, therefore, the Spanish-speaking are highly concentrated in the Southwest and within certain sections of the Southwest, namely, the old Spanish borderlands. Today the Spanish-speaking are predominantly urban, being more highly urbanized than the population of Mexico. The three largest urban settlements in the Southwest are: Los Angeles, around 385,000; El Paso, 58,291 (57 per cent of the population); and San Antonio, 82,373 (36 per cent). The Spanish-speaking have real numerical significance throughout the Southwest and are growing, in some areas, about five times as fast as the Anglo population.

Biologically the Spanish-speaking are a most diverse people. The number of Spaniards in the New World was never large and only a few thousand ever resided, at any time, in the borderlands. For example, Josiah Gregg estimated the number of Spaniards in New Mexico in 1846 as 1000 by comparison with 60,000 mixed-breeds. While the Spanish soldiers and colonists were supposed to live apart from the Indian settlements, the rule was never enforced and an entire Indian village would often abandon its seclusion and merge with the nearest Spanish settlement. As a matter of fact, the number of Spanish-born immigrants in the United States, at any time, has never been other than insignificant: 22,108 in 1910; 49,535 in 1930; and 109,407 in 1940. The Spanish-born, moreover, have always resided in the Eastern states; they have no relationship with the Spanish-speaking of the Southwest.

There are also around 30,000 Spanish-speaking in Florida: about 15,000 Cubans, 8500 Spanish-born, and small settlements of several thousand each of Minorcans. But these are mostly recent immigrants who have had virtually no contact with the great mass of the Spanish-speaking in the Southwest.

The first point to note about the Spanish-speaking of the Southwest, therefore, is that they came "north from Mexico": they are not European immigrants; they are of the Americas. With these people the Spanish heritage is of little biological significance and, aside from language and religion, of less cultural significance than the Indian and Mexican or mestizo heritage. Biologically the Spanish-speaking, as Dr. Sanchez has observed, range over all possible combinations of, first, their heterogeneous Spanish antecedents and, then, of the *mestizalje* resulting from the crossing of Spaniards and various indigenous peoples of Mexico and the Southwest.

Both the cultural inheritance and the historical experience of the Spanish-speaking are also quite diverse. Dating from 1598, some of the New Mexico villages are among the oldest settlements or colonies in the United States. In length of residence, the Spanish-speaking show great diversity: some are descendants of early New Mexico colonists; others are descendants of Sonorans who took part in the Gold Rush to California; while others have crossed the border in the last decade — or last month. A sharp rift exists between the "native-born of native-born parents," the Spanish-Colonials, and the immigrants who came after 1910 or 1920. Even the Spanish-Colonials, however, have a mixed set of historical antecedents. They make up three groups: the *nuevo mexicanos*, the *californios*, and the *texanos*.

The Spanish-speaking settlements of New Mexico are a century older than those of Texas and two centuries older than those in California. The New Mexico settlements were landlocked and severely isolated; while the California settlements had a sea route to Mexico and traded with New Eng-

land. The California settlements, moreover, were located in a
far more congenial and productive environment. The Spanish-
speaking settlements also differed in size. When the Treaty of
Guadalupe Hidalgo was signed on February 2, 1848 — by
which Mexico ceded to the United States the empire that is
the Southwest — there were approximately 75,000 Spanish-
speaking in the region: 7500 in California; about 1000 in Arizona; 60,000 in New Mexico; and perhaps 5000 in Texas. Even
the pattern or mode of settlement varied from one community
to the next: New Mexico was primarily made up of village
settlements, while the Texas and California settlements were
principally of the rancho type. These settlements, moreover,
made up "a broken border": they were widely separated;
there was little trade or communication between them; and,
in general, they were separately administered. The colonists,
therefore, never acquired a consciousness-of-kind and, to this
day, there is little exchange between the Spanish-speaking in
New Mexico and those in California — less, in fact, than between either area and points in Mexico. But, most important
of all, the settlements differed in their relations with Indians.
In 1848 there were about 180,000 Indians in the Southwest,
not including some 70,000 in California. The California Indians were extremely docile by comparison with those in
New Mexico, Arizona, and Texas. The Indians in these latter
settlements or territories were never conquered; on the contrary they were the masters, in a sense, of the Spanish-speaking.

No one knows, of course, the present size of the Spanish-
Colonial or "native-born of native-born" element. The census
of 1930 contains an estimate of 264,338 but the actual number is twice this estimate. The Spanish-Colonial element, whatever its size, is important for it has always functioned as a
buffer group between the Anglos and the more recent immigrants from Mexico. Moreover it is not a static element: it
expands with each generation. The Mexican immigrant is
likely to be "darker" and more Indian in ancestry and cul-

ture than the Spanish-Colonial. Indeed there is a sharp division between the two groups. To the native-born, the immigrant is a *cholo* or *chicamo;* to the immigrant, the native-born is a *pocho.*

What unites the Spanish-speaking, in addition to the fact that the Anglos set them apart, is their identification with the environment; they are an indigenous people in the Southwest. The land in which they live is an extension of the Mexican environment from which they came. Mary Austin once pointed out that the Spanish explorations north of the Rio Grande were virtually coterminous with "the cactus country": the Spanish went about as far, north and west and east, as the prickly pear, the gypsy of the cactus family, is to be found. Perhaps they stopped where they did because the environment had ceased to be familiar. In any case, the environment was quite similar to that of Mexico and, indeed, to that of Spain.[3] To this environment the colonists carried cultural practices and institutions which, being well adapted, struck deep roots and have survived through the years. As important as the factor of environmental similarity has been the historical fact that the Spanish-speaking have never been "immigrants" in the Southwest. They never sought admission to the Union; they were already here. Historically Mexicans have never emigrated to the Southwest: they have simply moved "North from Mexico." They did not ask to become citizens; they were made citizens by default, under pressure, and as a result of conquest. The status of the Spanish-speaking, moreover, has been affected, and often most adversely, by the state of relations between the United States and Mexico.

Living in a region which is geographically and historically a projection of their "homeland," and having struck deep roots in this region, the Spanish-speaking are not like the typical European immigrant minority in the United States.

[3] See my book *North from Mexico,* published by J. B. Lippincott Company, 1949, pp. 31-33.

They did not cross an ocean; they moved north across a mythical border. They were annexed by conquest and their cultural autonomy was guaranteed by a treaty. They resemble, therefore, certain suppressed national minorities in Europe, although a closer parallel would be the French-Canadians in the Province of Quebec. There is this all-important difference, however, that the border between the United States and Mexico is one of the most unreal borders in the world; it unites rather than separates the two peoples. The Spanish-speaking in the Southwest have never been cut off from replacements as were the Chinese and the Japanese. People have moved back and forth across the border for generations and the trails which lead north from Mexico are among the oldest in North America.

What the contact between Anglo and Hispano in the Southwest has always involved, therefore, is not so much a problem in individual acculturation as a problem in the adjustment or fusion of two cultures neither of which can ever hope to achieve a complete victory over the other in this region. The territory in which the Spanish-speaking live was rightly called a "borderland." Even the Anglo's numerical dominance has been consistently offset by the fact that the Hispano's culture, being better adapted, has shown remarkable survival value. In the Southwest, the three great cultures of the Americas meet: the Anglo-American, the Indian, and the Spanish-Mexican-mestizo.

Even linguistically the Spanish-speaking show remarkable diversities. Not all of them speak Spanish and those who do speak every conceivable variation of that language in terms, as Dr. Sanchez has noted, "of all phases of both quantity and quality." For some the language of the home is Spanish; for others English; for still others a vernacular that is neither the one nor the other but a combination of both. Most of the Spanish-speaking are Catholics but the degree of their attachment to Catholicism ranges from mere acquiescence and nominal affiliation to deep and conscious devotion. In many cases, moreover, the Catholicism to which they are attached carries the imprint, in form and ceremony, of Indian tribal rites. In a sense, too, the Catholic Church in the borderlands is still a "church in exile" — from Mexico. The Mexican Church was exceptional to begin with; it became more exceptional in exile. Nevertheless religion has been a factor, not so much in uniting the Spanish-speaking as in setting them apart from the Anglos of the Southwest who are mostly Protestant. What basically unites the Spanish-speaking — what makes them a clearly delineated ethnic group — is the generally similar character of Anglo-Hispano relationships throughout the borderlands. The manner in which these relationships emerged will make this clear.

## 2. A Pattern Emerges

Infrequent and fugitive as it was, contact between Anglos and Hispanos had been established in California, Arizona, and New Mexico for two decades prior to 1846. Despite the difference in culture, including the important difference in language and religion and that in racial inheritance, these first contacts did not result in antagonism or hostility. Throughout the preconquest period good relations prevailed and intermarriage was quite common. The fusion of blood and cultures was most noticeable in California, where any number of early Anglo-American settlers married Mexican women, became citizens of Mexico, joined the Catholic Church, hispanicized their surnames, and took over much of the culture of the Hispanos. California, however, was quite remote from the advancing frontier and the resident Anglo-Americans were a minority. In such circumstances, intermarriage was a form of polite, and doubtless pleasant, conquest.

In Texas on the other hand, the Mexican settlements were

directly in the path of the Anglo-American expansion. Unlike the rest of the borderlands, Texas was not separated from the concentrations of American population by mountain ranges and desert wastes; it invited invasion. In fact it was much easier to move from the nearest American settlements to Texas than to move from the Texas settlements to the centers of population in Mexico. Texas was 1200 miles from Mexico City; geographically it tilted toward the American zone of influence.

It was in Texas, therefore, that the conflict between Anglos and Hispanos had its inception. Under any circumstances, the first meeting of the two cultures would have presented high potentials for conflict. The language barrier, the difference in religious and political institutions, and a host of important cultural differences, made for acute misunderstandings. The initial contact, moreover, took place between representatives who were not a credit to either culture and who met in a zone of frontier lawlessness and violence. "Cultural differences," writes Dr. Samuel Harman Lowrie, "gave rise to misconceptions and misunderstandings, misunderstandings to distrust, distrust to antagonism, and antagonism on a very considerable number of points made conflict inevitable." [4] This statement, however, ignores the dynamic which made the misconceptions a source of conflict: the fact that the Spanish-speaking were in possession of a valuable territory which the Anglo-Americans were determined to possess.

Out of this conflict in Texas came the Mexican-American War which left, of course, a heritage of ill-will and antagonism. The Treaty of Guadalupe Hidalgo terminated formal hostilities but the source of conflict still remained. Conflict continued throughout the borderlands, now incorporated into the Union, varying only as circumstances varied and continuing into the present time. When the treaty was rati-

[4] *Cultural Conflict in Texas, 1821–1835*, by Dr. Samuel Harman Lowrie, 1932.

fied about 75,000 Spanish-speaking were living in the borderlands. Those who did not elect to withdraw to Mexico within a stated period became citizens of the United States by default. Only about 1500 withdrew; the others all became citizens, by default, of a nation whose language they could not speak and with whose institutions they were not familiar. It should be noted, also, that the treaty guaranteed the property rights and cultural autonomy of the Spanish-speaking. But in the absence of measures designed to assist acculturation, the guarantees were largely meaningless. Arizona and New Mexico, it might be noted, were denied statehood until 1912 and in New Mexico the development of an adequate public school system was long delayed.

The Mexican-American War of 1846 marked a conflict over control of the Southwest; the post-bellum period marked a competition for control of the resources of this region. Numerically, and in terms of power, the Spanish-speaking were at a great disadvantage in this competition. Not only were they a defeated people but they were hopelessly outnumbered. "In 1850," writes Lyle Saunders, "there were fewer than 400,000 people in the entire Southwest, of whom not more than 100,000 could have been Spanish-speaking. . . . In the ten-year period, 1850–1860, the population of the border states nearly tripled. Very few of the newcomers, however, were Spanish-speaking, so that where the Spanish-speaking group had been out-numbered about four to one in 1850, by 1860, they made up only about one-tenth of the total population of the Southwest." [5] Although the natural increase of the Hispanos was greater than that of the Anglos, the latter continued to migrate to the Southwest in larger numbers than the former.

[5] From a paper on "The Social History of Spanish-Speaking People in Southwestern United States Since 1846," by Lyle Saunders, Fourth Regional Conference, Southwest Council on Education of Spanish-Speaking People, Albuquerque, January 23–25, 1950.

But numbers alone do not measure the discrepancy in power. The Spanish-speaking in 1848 were largely descendants of families who had been in the borderlands for several generations and, in some cases, since the beginnings of settlement. Prior to the 1820's, these people had had little contact with the English-speaking world and, in terms of the culture of that world, were definitely backward and handicapped. It would be difficult to imagine an isolation more complete than that which prevailed in New Mexico from 1598 to 1800. Geographic isolation bred social and cultural isolation; isolated in space, New Mexico was also isolated in time. Contact with the Indians provided about the only opportunity for cultural innovation. In isolation, the culture of the people became highly integrated and relatively static. Intermarriage and social isolation also made for extremely cohesive family and social units. Since there was little commerce, there was not much incentive to develop the economy. For nearly three hundred years no new currents of life moved in this remote colony where "literacy" had as little meaning as "poverty." Just as there was nothing much to read, so there was nothing much to buy.

Lyle Saunders succinctly describes some of the more important features of the folk culture of the Spanish-speaking in the borderlands. "Most of them lived," he writes, "in scattered communities or on isolated farms and ranches. The rhythms of life were seasonal, as they had been for hundreds of years. Each community was largely self-sufficient; each individual possessed, in general, the same knowledge and skills as others in his age or sex group. The level of literacy was low, reading materials were scarce. Men learned and communicated by the spoken word. Formal education was limited to a small proportion of the population. Tools were few and simple. Travel was slow, difficult, and expensive, and most people were born, lived, and died in or near a single community. Social mobility was also difficult and most people remained all their lives on the social level into which they were born. Social change was slow. The relations between people were personal, and every person in a community knew every other person in all his social roles. Uniformity of knowledge, behavior, and belief was the rule." [6] Whatever the merits of this culture — for example its remarkable survival value — it was obviously backward by comparison with the Anglo-American culture of the period if measured in terms of competitive power, ability to manipulate the environment, and skill in the exploitation of resources.

For a time, however, special circumstances protected the Spanish-speaking. The discovery of gold in California drew the tide of western migration through and beyond the Southwest. It also shifted the westward traffic to the northern routes and provided a market for the products of the Hispanos. The most important safeguard, however, was the nature of the environment, which, throughout most of the region, placed a severe limitation on the size of the population that could be supported. For example the average density of population in New Mexico today — a hundred years after the conquest — is only five persons per square mile, about one ninth the density of the nation as a whole. To this day, the Spanish-speaking make up slightly less than half of New Mexico's population.

But with the coming of the rail lines in the 1870's and 1880's the isolation of the Southwest was at an end and a new economic empire began to emerge in the borderlands. Even before this happened, the Hispanos had been engulfed in Southern California, in Arizona, and in Texas; but the pressures did not become intense in New Mexico — the bastion of the Spanish-speaking — until after the coming of the railroads. It should be noted, also, that not all elements of the Spanish-speaking felt the Anglo-American competition with equal intensity. The small native upper class, the *ricos* of New Mexico and the *gente de razon* of California, had something to offer their

[6] Saunders, *op. cit.*, pp. 1–2.

conquerors, namely, control of the masses of the Spanish-speaking and partnerships in various enterprises. Naturally they fared much better than the *cholos*. Better educated than the *pobres*, and lighter in color, they were protected also by ties of marriage with the Anglos. With the coming of the railroads, however, this earlier "intimacy in isolation" came to an end, even in New Mexico.[7]

Out of, first, conflict over control of the Southwest, and, later, competition in the exploitation of its resources came the present-day pattern of relations between Anglos and Hispanos. Out of this competition-and-conflict, too, came the invincible stereotypes which each group has developed about the other: the Anglos being "gringos" to the Spanish-speaking; the Spanish-speaking being "greasers" to the Anglos. After 1870 the discrepancy in power between the two groups became so great that the Hispanic element would have been wholly submerged but for an ironic development, namely, the economic expansion of the Southwest which created a growing demand for cheap labor and thereby set in motion a new stream of migration north from Mexico. Later, with the revolution in Mexico, this stream became a torrent: over 1,000,000 immigrants surged across the border between 1900 and 1930. Thus the Hispanos not only received a vast army of recruits but were jarred out of their defeatism by the new revolutionary currents in Mexican life, including a new pride in the Mexican-Indian as distinguished from the Spanish or fantasy heritage.

This second invasion of the borderlands from Mexico, however, created new conflicts. It brought the industrially untutored Mexican worker into sharp conflict with large-scale farming and industrial interests in the Southwest. Out of this conflict came some of the first strikes and organizing campaigns in the region. But of greater importance was the fact that the American labor movement elected to discriminate

[7] *North from Mexico*, p. 297.

against the Mexican in an effort to protect living and working conditions and thereby created a breach in the solidarity of labor which has continued to the present time. The strategy of American labor was, first, to exclude the Mexican if possible; and failing this to subordinate him by forcing him into undesirable jobs and by creating an ethnic wage differential for the same jobs. At the same time the use of Mexican labor — not Mexican labor per se — seriously undermined the position of the small farmer in Texas and the resentments of this element were promptly directed not at the forces transforming rural society in Texas, but at the Mexican. In this confused struggle, the Mexican sought to disrupt the scheme by which his subordination was being brought about, but he was defeated. The struggle lasted over two decades. It was conducted under highly unfavorable odds and circumstances and the Mexican's defeat represented, in effect, his second defeat in the borderlands. The defeat arrested the Mexican's interest in acculturation and at the same time it increased the arrogance of the Anglos.

To compete successfully the Mexican's acculturation should have been greatly accelerated but special circumstances actually retarded the process. Of these circumstances the more important were the failure of the American labor movement to organize the Mexicans; the migratory employment in which so many Mexicans were involved, with the accompanying movement back and forth across the border; the isolated employment of Mexicans in desert mines and desert sections of the rail lines; the segregation of Mexicans in particular industries and occupations; the fact that the Mexican's acculturation took place, for the most part, in rural rather than in urban societies (at least in the first decades); the existence of a buffer group which minimized the necessity, for example, of learning English; the nature of the Southwest's "raw materials" economy; and the fact that the Southwest, in many areas, was but one step removed from the lawlessness and violence of the frontier and was accordingly bothered by the various insecurities that seem to go with cultural immaturity and social disorganization. There was also, as Dr. Sanchez has pointed out, a feeling on the part of the Spanish-speaking of "apathy, fatalism, loss of the will to do," which left them defenseless against the crudest exploitations: "to get their land, to get their vote, to get their labor and the product of their farms and ranches." [8]

At the same time the continued, rapid expansion of the Southwest's economy brought into being a set of conditions which made the further exploitation of Mexican labor, in new forms, entirely feasible and immensely profitable. Eventually the agitation against "cheap Mexican labor" forced a nominal closing of the border. In 1924 a Border Patrol was established and by 1929 the immigration laws were being enforced, after a fashion, along the border. Then came the depression which resulted in the repatriation of thousands of destitute Mexican nationals and their American-born children. For a brief period these developments, and the influx of some 350,000 so-called Okies and Arkies into California, arrested and even reversed the northward tide of Mexican labor.

But with World War II still another chapter in the long history of Mexican labor in the Southwest was started. Since we were at war and Mexico was our ally, it became necessary to mask the exploitation of Mexican labor with rhetorical formalities. Accordingly an agreement was negotiated between the two countries governing the importation of Mexican nationals for certain restricted types of employment, principally in agriculture and on the railroads of the Southwest. The conditions originally stipulated were intelligent and at first the agreement was reasonably well enforced. But it was not long before the importation program had been disintegrated by the pressures for unrestricted exploitation. The wartime importation of *braceros*, moreover, set in motion once

[8] Sanchez, *op. cit.*, p. 3.

again the earlier currents of migration. The number of Mexican nationals recruited for agricultural employment jumped from 4203 in 1942 to 120,000 in 1946. Once the wartime manpower shortages abated, the old agitation of American labor against "cheap Mexican labor" was resumed and brakes were imposed on the recruitment of Mexican nationals. But the brakes did not work for, now as always, the employers of the Southwest were determined to exploit Mexican labor, if not legally, then illegally.

From 1946 on the number of "wetbacks," or illegal entrants, steadily increased. Three elements make up the wetback invasion: legally imported Mexican nationals who have jumped their contracts or overstayed the period of their recruitment; former legally imported nationals who have received a taste of American "high" wages and keep returning to the States; and still other Mexican workers drawn north by stories of better working conditions and the pressures created by changes in the economy of Mexico. In 1947 the Immigration Service deported 207,000 Mexican wetbacks; and in 1948 and 1949 the number deported was even greater.[9]

In the spring of 1950, wetbacks were streaming across the border into California at the rate of 21,000 *a month* and, despite heavy monthly deportations, a more or less permanent pool of wetback labor, numbering 60,000 or more, had come into being.[10] In Texas the wetback pool was even larger, numbering 100,000 to 500,000 workers, depending on the season. With one Immigration Inspector for approximately every forty miles of border, Mexicans simply cannot be kept out of the border states once the attractions on this side of the border, and the compulsions on the other side, reach a certain intensity. With farm workers in the Federal District of Mexico receiving 3.50 pesos a day — a little over 50 cents in American

[9] *Wetbacks*, a report prepared by George I. Sanchez and Lyle Saunders for the Advisory Committee, Study of Spanish-Speaking People, University of Texas, June 12, 1949, p. 2.

[10] *Los Angeles Times*, May 3, 1950.

money — it is apparent that even a low wage rate, by American standards, of 45 cents an hour is a powerful magnet for Mexican workers.

The fable, of course, is that Mexican workers are only imported because resident workers will not accept certain types of employment at the "prevailing rate." But the truth of the matter has always been that the availability of "cheap Mexican labor" is what has determined the prevailing rate. Hart Stilwell describes the effect of the wetback invasion on the status of resident Mexican-Americans in Texas as follows: "Many of the gains made by Texas-Mexicans during the war have been lost as a result of the recent influx of wetbacks. And these people have brought new problems, some of which are of a baffling nature. If an equal number of fair-skinned, English-speaking people — say around 300,000 — living in a culture equivalent to that of the Mexican immigrant in his homeland were suddenly dumped into Texas, the social and economic and political upheaval would not be solved for years. Add to that the two additional complications of language and color differences, and you have a situation that appears almost hopeless. In fact, there is little prospect that the Mexican in Texas will ever achieve anything approximating economic and social equality until conditions in Mexico change for the better." [11] Here, again, most Americans fail to see that imperialism can be of two types: the type that carries its exploitative processes to remote native cultures and the type which draws non-industrial peoples to it by the promise or hope of a higher standard of living. The latter type is usually less brutal than the former but it is essentially a domestic imperialism.

### 3. *"The Malady Suggests the Cure"*

Although a wide variation in conditions may be found among the heterogeneous Spanish-speaking in the long stretch

[11] "The Wetback Tide," by Hart Stilwell, *Common Ground,* Summer 1949, p. 11.

of territory from Los Angeles to Brownsville, nevertheless the bond that unites the people is the similarity of conditions imposed upon them by the pattern of Anglo-Hispano relations. The extent to which the Spanish-speaking have been submerged in the general population may be measured in various specific fields — and indeed such precise statistical measurements have been made [12] — but the following generalized description by Lyle Saunders will serve to demonstrate the social consequences of domestic imperialism in the border states:

Everywhere . . . there is poverty. Not all Spanish-speaking are poor, but in general more of them are poor than is true for any other group. . . . Everywhere there are slum conditions in both rural and urban areas, and while not all Spanish-speaking people live in slums, more of them do than would be expected by chance and more of them do proportionately than any other population group. Everywhere there is poor sanitation, and again it seems to be the Spanish-speaking who live under conditions of improper sanitation in greater numbers and greater proportion than any other group. Everywhere the Spanish-speaking are found in the poorest paid, least skilled occupations in greater proportions than they are in the total population. Everywhere there are problems of education, but here again it is the Spanish-speaking group mainly whose children come to school late in the season, attend irregularly, and leave early. Everywhere, too, there is segregation or separation — sometimes voluntary, sometimes enforced — which insures that the Spanish-speaking people will work and play and live largely with other Spanish-speaking people while the Anglos associate mainly with other Anglos. Only rarely does one find a situation or a community in which there is not a separation of the two groups in almost all areas of living. If one were to attempt to characterize the condition of the Spanish-speaking Texans, he would be forced to say that, in general, and for nearly any index of socio-economic status that might be devised, the Spanish-speaking people are found to

[12] *The Social Areas of Los Angeles*, by Eshref Shevky and Marilyn Williams, 1949, p. 73.

occupy a less desirable position than the Anglos or the population as a whole.[13]

In this description the objective of social dominance is aptly summed up in the phrase, "a less desirable position." For it is precisely the "more desirable positions" that the majority wants; that it has carefully staked out for its members; and that it intends to hold for its exclusive, or as nearly exclusive as possible, benefit. The motive force is advantage or power; the end result — subordination of the minority.

Nowadays the Spanish-speaking have begun to challenge this century-old pattern of dominance with a new effectiveness and power. Within the last quarter century, the Southwest has become urbanized; once almost wholly rural, the Spanish-speaking are now predominantly urban. With urbanization, a Spanish-speaking middle class has begun to emerge although it is still small and not well organized. New types of leaders have also come forward: graduates of American colleges and universities; Mexican-American GIs (over 375,000 served in World War II); and products of the American trade-union movement. The self-organization of the Spanish-speaking, which might be said to date from the formation of the League of Latin-American Citizens in Texas in 1927, is still rudimentary but it is developing rapidly and significant social victories have already been scored; witness the decision in the Westminster School case in California, in August 1947, outlawing segregated schools for Mexican youngsters and the decision in the Delgado case (June 15, 1948) restraining the segregation of Mexican-Americans in the Texas schools.[14]

[13] Mimeographed copy of address by Lyle Saunders, National Convention, League of United Latin American Citizens, San Antonio, June 11, 1949, pp. 7–8.
[14] See "The Segregation of Mexican-American School Children in Southern California," by W. Henry Cooke, *School and Society*, June 5, 1948. Also *Westminster School District et al* v. *Mendez*, 161 Fed. Rep. (Second Series), p. 774, and decision by Judge Ben. H. Rice, Jr., in *Delgado* v. *Bastrop Inde-*

These developments, and similar trends, indicate that the status of Mexican-Americans is changing from that of a suppressed nationality group to a self-conscious national minority. To date, however, Mexican-Americans have not achieved anything like the social and political power of American Negroes. There are 1,300,000 citizens of Mexican descent in Texas — more than 20 per cent of the total white population — and they are a clear majority in many counties. Yet Dr. Sanchez could report in 1950 that "you will not find a single person with a Spanish name employed in the capitol building in Austin." At the same time, of course, Texas-Mexican students constitute less than 2 per cent of the enrollment at the state university and the death rate for tuberculosis in San Antonio is three times as great among Mexicans as among Negroes and whites. But beginnings are being made and these efforts to achieve self-organization are paying dividends: Mexican-Americans have been elected to office in Denver; to the state legislature in Arizona; and in 1949 the City of Los Angeles, in which Mexican-Americans are the largest minority, elected a Mexican-American to the City Council for the first time since one José Mascerel served in that body in 1881.

Special considerations help to explain what would appear to be the political backwardness of the Mexican-American and these special factors are most clearly outlined in New Mexico — the heart of the borderlands. As the oldest and most populous Spanish settlement, New Mexico's economic subjugation presented some special problems to the Anglo-Americans. For example, at the time of the conquest virtually all of the 61,525 people then living in New Mexico were Spanish-speaking. By 1860 the population had increased to 87,034, but 79,249 were native-born; by 1870, the population

---

*pendent School District*, No. 388 Civil, District Court of the United States, Western District of Texas.

was 91,784, but 83,175 were native-born. Thus for the first two decades after the conquest the population remained about 90 per cent Spanish-speaking.

In such a situation, the "natives" had to be handled with tact and delicacy. The political problem was solved, however, by a twofold stratagem. First of all, New Mexico was kept in territorial status for sixty-three years, thereby reserving the appointive power in the Anglo-Americans and giving them a veto power until such time as the Anglo-Americans had begun to achieve numerical parity with the Spanish-speaking. But there was still the problem of the territorial legislature and the territorial delegate in Congress — the elective positions. To cope with this problem, the Anglo-Americans cultivated the good will and active collaboration of the Quisling-like native upper class with whom they were allied by ties of marriage and of trade. Thus there developed the famous "don system" of New Mexico politics in which the *haciendado* was said to have voted his sheep as well as his peons. For years the dons controlled the legislature for the primary benefit of their Anglo-American partners and the lower-class Spanish-speaking were appeased with minor government patronage and the types of jobs and favors which the patrons could bestow. Essentially the same technique was used in California and Texas. The effect, of course, was to accentuate the apathy and to arrest the political maturity of the Spanish-speaking lower classes who were subject to a dual dominance: of their own "leaders" as well as of the Anglo-Americans.

The fact is that the Spanish-speaking have been betrayed not once but many times by their own leaders. But the key to this apparent gullibility is to be found in the familiar way in which the religious-and-language division tends to correspond with basic socio-economic cleavages, with the correspondence never being quite exact. From time to time, of course, exceptional leaders like J. Francisco Chavez and

Octaviano Larrazolo have emerged; but in general the leadership has been inadequate largely because it has been recruited from the "buffer" group — the native-born of native-born parents. The primary interest of this group has always been, not in improving the lot of the underprivileged, but in mediating between the Anglos and the recent immigrants from Mexico. Out of this mediating role certain advantages have accrued to the buffer group.

Dr. Sanchez describes a reality rather than making a charge when he writes that "political leadership here [New Mexico] as in Texas gives every evidence of being either completely unaware of, or completely indifferent to, the need to discover ways and means of accelerating the acculturation of the state's Spanish-speaking population. . . . At best this leadership [of the Spanish-speaking] does an unimaginative, pedestrian job . . . at worst . . . that leadership sees in political position simply an opportunity for selfish gain, for personal enrichment, and for a freedom of behavior that will not stand the light of moral judgment." [15]

One reason, of course, for the political frustration of the Spanish-speaking, and for their equivocal leadership, has been the absence of a Spanish-speaking middle class. But a middle class never exists in a vacuum; it cannot function in a nearly self-sufficient barter economy. Thus the backwardness of New Mexico's economic development has been a primary factor in the arrested political maturity of the Spanish-speaking. The Anglo-American bosses of New Mexico — such, for example, as the notorious "Santa Fe ring" of yesteryear — were not interested in the development of the state's resources but in their exploitation. Hence the economic problem of the state has always been, in large part, an aspect of the basic political problem, and vice versa. [16] In the 1920's and 1930's,

[15] See reference Note 1, above.
[16] See chapter on New Mexico politics, *Rocky Mountain Politics*, Albuquerque, 1940.

however, the village-farm economy of the Spanish-speaking, with its emphasis on self-sufficiency and its hopelessly retarded technology, began to give every evidence of social sickness and the disintegration has since continued unabated. It was at about this time, as one might expect, that the "touchiness" of the Spanish-speaking became acute and the Hispanos began to show signs of a new political awareness. The use, for example, of such terms as Spanish-American, Spanish-Colonial, and Latin-American dates from this period.[17]

The mounting pressure of the competition offered the Spanish-speaking by the Anglo-American farm families in the eastern part of New Mexico has been a factor in the growing self-consciousness of the former. The first Anglo-American settlers in New Mexico were scouts, Indian traders, territorial officials, lawyers, and merchants; a large influx of farm families did not take place until after 1880. In recent years, however, eastern New Mexico (which is culturally of Texas) has been steadily encroaching on "Spanish" New Mexico, economically, socially, and politically. Texas "folkways" have begun to appear in the former strongholds of the Spanish-speaking and the resentment of the latter has been growing. As long as the Spanish-speaking were a majority — and they were until recently — the Anglo-American strategy had to be based on tact and manipulation. This strategy seemed to invest the Spanish-speaking with political power but the real power was never theirs. It was this situation, indeed, that made the phrase "New Mexico politics" synonymous with the widespread corruption and defeatism that always accompany a frustration of democratic processes.

Nowadays the Spanish-speaking are beginning to be outvoted by the Anglos, who show a marked reluctance to vote for Spanish-speaking candidates. "Thus," writes R. L. Chambers, "political leaders who feel obligated to have Spanish-

[17] *North from Mexico*, p. 78.

speaking officials in state government must resort to padding of the ballot and other devices to win elections for the Spanish-speaking minority. Once these officials lose control — and they are gradually disappearing — then the 280,000 Spanish-speaking New Mexicans will be left with only a small voice in state affairs. A Spanish-speaking man, considered New Mexico's leading politician, explains how tickets are made up: 'You have to divide the ticket geographically as well as racially. All the big officials have to be Anglos. You let the Spanish-speaking people get lieutenant governor, secretary of state, state auditor, and a few lower offices. A senator and a congressman can be Spanish-speaking. But no more than one.' The politicians are not afraid of the Spanish-speaking vote going against them, for the state administration controls at least 7000 state jobs and hands out patronage to many Spanish-speaking New Mexicans who need jobs badly and are expected to vote accordingly. The pressure on the Spanish-speaking voter, therefore, is twofold. Pressure comes from the state administration to vote as the machine wants, as well as from the ever-increasing number of Anglo voters who, by their increasing numbers, are gradually making the vote of the native New Mexican meaningless." [18]

What these recent developments in New Mexico politics signify is that the economy of the Spanish-speaking villages is being disrupted and the anomalous situation in which a national and regional minority happened to be a majority in one state is coming to an end. The exceptionalism of New Mexico is almost a thing of the past. In the long run, the liquidation of the provincialism of New Mexico politics may well facilitate the acculturation of the Spanish-speaking. It is almost certain to bring new leaders to the fore and to equate the situation in New Mexico with that in Texas, Colorado, Ari-

[18] "Discrimination in New Mexico," by R. L. Chambers. Mimeographed copy of paper read at Fourth Regional Conference, Southwest Council on Education of Spanish-Speaking People, Albuquerque, January 23-25, 1950.

zona, and California, thereby making for a region-wide movement toward political self-organization. The Spanish-speaking, however, still suffer from a lack of self-expression; they have not yet reached the point which the Negro minority achieved in cultural expression in the middle 1920's. This is not to imply, of course, that the Spanish-speaking are comparatively, much less inherently, backward; there is nothing about their position in the American ethnic system which cannot be explained in terms of their history and experience. "What happened to the Spanish-speaking people," as Allen Harper has pointed out, "was inevitable in the circumstances."

The past explains the present but it does not determine the future. Great changes have taken place in the last few years, not in the status of the Spanish-speaking, but in people's thinking about "the Mexican problem." A hundred years after the Mexican-American War of 1846, the conditions now exist which can make for a new understanding and acceptance. At long last, the facts have been collected and sifted out and arranged; the relationships have now been thoroughly explored; and the techniques and social institutions now exist to hasten the process of acculturation. At the same time, the isolation of the old Spanish borderlands has ended forever: New Mexico is now the center of the industrial empire being conjured into existence by the Atomic Energy Commission. And, as Dr. Sanchez has insisted, "the maladies suggest the cure: if people are hungry, let us go out and see that they eat; if they are sick, let us strive to make them well; if they are ignorant and benighted, let us take enlightenment to them."

\*        \*        \*

Only two residents of Los Angeles, it is said, have ever won the Congressional Medal of Honor. One of them was infantry private David Gonzales, who died on the island of Luzon at the age of twenty-one while rescuing three of his countrymen. When his body was returned for burial, reporters visited the Gonzales home in Pacoima, in the San Fernando Valley. The house was in disrepair and title had passed to the city — at a tax sale. The mother of Gonzales and his seven brothers and sisters were faced with eviction. "There was a half pot of beans in the house. Eight and a half slices of bread, an eighth of a bag of flour and one tin of coffee. There was not a penny among them and no prospects of money." Income from Gonzales's insurance took care of his widow and son, but for the family there was nothing. The "neglect," of course, had to be grandly remedied. So the burial of Private David Gonzales became a political festival. The Mayor was on hand; High Mass was sung in the Church of the Guardian Angel; the American Legion provided a guard of honor; the City Council passed a resolution; and "food baskets" were delivered. Ceremonies will not, however, remedy the real neglect; the maladies suggest the cure.

# CHAPTER IV

# *The Hostage Japanese*

"No QUESTION of our time," wrote Frederick McCormick in *The Menace of Japan* (1917), "can vie in importance with that of the contact of alien races and systems on the Pacific Slope. It is, more than anything else, an indication of the swift development of the Pacific." The principal area of contact was in California. In Hawaii people came together but systems did not collide; competition took place but under circumstances in which the Anglo-Americans were an alien minority for many years. The tensions that developed in California represented sharp and basic conflicts and the pattern of relationships that emerged there foreshadowed the emergence of a similar pattern in Oregon and Washington, in Alaska and Peru. Indeed the course of events in California from an early date was widely and correctly interpreted as foreshadowing a future conflict between the United States and Japan.

## *1. The Time and the Place*

Although Commodore Perry liked to think of his expedition to Japan as being the completion of the voyage of Columbus, it merely represented the resumption of an early relationship. As traders in the South Pacific, the Japanese had come in contact with the Spaniards from the New World in the latter part of the sixteenth century. Japanese embassies had proceeded to Mexico in 1610 to study the conditions of trade. The *Mayflower* had not yet arrived and the back door to the

North American continent was wide open; but the Japanese withdrew in 1638 to a seclusion that prevailed until Perry's visit in 1854. Japanese castaways, however, had reached our shores before diplomatic relations were established between Japan and the United States. Commodore Perry's interpreter owed his knowledge of Japanese to a castaway named Sentaro who was a member of the expedition.

The event that unlocked the doors of Japan was, of course, the discovery of gold in California. The letter that Perry carried to Japan stated that ". . . California produces about sixty millions of dollars in gold every year, besides silver, quicksilver, precious stones, and many other valuable articles" — new wealth which, as President Fillmore explained, we were eager to use as the basis of trade. The rapidly developing clipper trade also made it imperative that our ships put in at Japanese ports for repairs and provisions. In fact the discovery of gold in California and the opening of Japan to Occidental influences were historically simultaneous and closely related events.[1]

Historically Japan had been opposed to the emigration of its people; from 1638 to 1854 emigration had been punishable by death. In the same period, also, the building of oceangoing boats had been forbidden by imperial decree to make certain that Japan preserved her policy of isolation. The policy was finally reversed at the behest of the Hawaiian Sugar Planters Association in 1884 and the Japanese began to migrate, first to Hawaii, and later to Canada, the United States, and South America. By 1890 there were 2039 Japanese in the United States and by 1900 the number had increased to 24,236 and by 1910 to 72,157. The first Japanese immigrants in California came by way of Hawaii, but after a few years many came directly from Japan.

It is doubtful if any immigrant group ever settled in America under more unfavorable international circumstances

[1] See *The Japanese Crisis*, by James A. B. Scherer, 1916.

than those which attended the settlement of the Japanese in California. Immigrants began to arrive in large numbers at precisely the moment when Japan began to loom large as a great power in the Pacific. Japanese immigration, therefore, came to be associated with the rise of Japanese nationalism. Rapidly developing a great-power complex, Japan was quick to resent discrimination against its nationals on the West Coast of the United States. To the Californians, on the other hand, these nationals appeared as the spearhead of an actual invasion and this uneasiness steadily increased as Japanese nationalism became more aggressive. Over a period of years, moreover, Japanese militarists cleverly exploited the discrimination against Japanese immigrants in California for domestic political purposes.

If Japanese immigration was badly timed, its direction was still more unfortunate. Out of 126,947 Japanese in the United States in 1940, 112,353 resided in Oregon, Washington, and California (99.6 per cent of the total). Of those on the West Coast, 93,717, or 73.8 per cent, resided in California; in fact the concentration of Japanese in California, and within one area of the state (Los Angeles County), had steadily increased over a period of years. In 1900 California was primarily rural; its institutions were newly formed and hastily conceived; its social heritage was largely that of a mining frontier; and its population exhibited many evidences of the insecurity which seems to beset marginal or peripheral areas of settlement. "Where there is a rapidly expanding population," writes Dr. Forrest E. LaViolette, "with no established social organization for distributing economic gain, the struggle for political control, for economic power, and for social prestige soon gives rise to individual feelings of not getting one's share, of having to watch carefully 'the other fellow' and other groups." [2] Paradoxically it is the peripheral frontier province,

---

[2] *The Canadian Japanese and World War II*, by Forrest E. LaViolette, Toronto, 1948.

not the established and crowded center of population, that seems to be most susceptible to the disease of xenophobia.

Almost from the moment of their arrival, the Japanese were caught in the crossfire of previous anti-Oriental agitations. Racial myths and ideologies dating from earlier agitations were quickly extended to them. "The forces," writes Ruth E. McKee, "that had accomplished the exclusion of the Chinese had developed legends, techniques, and arguments which with little editing could be turned against the Japanese. Politicians and pressure groups had served their apprenticeship in the anti-Chinese crusade. By the turn of the century these veterans were ready to launch a new offensive." [3] And no sooner had the Japanese arrived in California than the first tensions appeared in the relations between Japan and the United States. From 1900 to 1941, Japanese immigrants in California were in effect hostages or pawns in a great-power competition for the dominance of the Pacific, a vast area of which California was but a province.

Although agitation against the Japanese dated almost from the moment of their arrival — the first anti-Japanese mass meeting was held in San Francisco on May 7, 1900 — it should be noted that racial and cultural differences did not produce hostile attitudes in the first meetings between Japanese and Americans. Actually the Japanese castaways — the first Japanese to reach America — were "petted and exhibited and made much of." [4] A child castaway, Hikozo Hamada, became a protégé of the collector of customs at San Francisco and was presented to President Pierce who offered him an appointment to West Point. Under the name of Joseph Heco, Hamada acquired citizenship by naturalization on June 30, 1858 — proof that officials did not then regard Japanese blood as a bar

[3] *Wartime Exile: The Exclusion of the Japanese-Americans from the West Coast*, prepared by Ruth E. McKee for Department of Interior, Washington, D. C., at p. 10.

[4] McKee, *op. cit.*, p. 4.

to naturalization. The friendly reception given these first Japanese arrivals completely belies the notion that racial and cultural differences are in themselves a source of conflict. The plain fact is that when they began to arrive in California in significant numbers, the Japanese were quickly drawn into a vacuum which then existed in the labor market. As long as they filled this vacuum, they were welcomed even by the racists; the trouble began when these perverse Oriental immigrants began to act like other immigrants and sought to improve their lot.

## 2. Years of the Yellow Peril

The California-Japanese War began on February 23, 1905 — on the eve of the siege of Mukden — when the *San Francisco Chronicle* published the first of a sensational series of articles on the Japanese in California. It should be noted, however, that the hostile sentiment which these articles reflected was not entirely restricted to California: all America began to be apprehensive about Japan after the Russo-Japanese War. With the appearance of the *Chronicle* articles, which were widely interpreted as the opening blast in a general campaign, both houses of the California legislature unanimously adopted a resolution urging Congress to exclude the Japanese. By this time, the Chinese had already been excluded so that the anti-Oriental sentiment could be shifted exclusively to the Japanese. "The Chinese," the *Chronicle* had observed, "are faithful laborers and do not buy land. The Japanese are unfaithful laborers and do buy land." At the outset, however, Californians were by no means united in their opposition to Japanese immigration. The large farmers welcomed Japanese immigration; the businessmen generally approved of it; and the agitation stemmed pretty largely from the trade-unions and the chronic anti-Oriental elements.[5]

[5] See my book *Prejudice*, 1945, p. 19.

In the fall of 1906, the San Francisco Board of Education — the city administration was then controlled by the Union Labor Party — suddenly decided to enforce an ordinance, adopted the previous year, calling for the segregation of Oriental children in a separate school. At that time there were only 93 Japanese children of school age in San Francisco, which had a school population of 25,000. Indeed the sponsors of the action never bothered to conceal the fact that their real intention was to launch an agitation which would culminate in the exclusion of further Japanese immigration. A minor motivation was also to be found in the desire of Mayor Eugene E. Schmitz to divert public attention from his notoriously corrupt administration; he was indicted almost simultaneously with the decision of the School Board to enforce the ordinance.

In the context of events, the School Board's action was highly, and intentionally, provocative. Japan had just emerged victorious from the Russo-Japanese War and, a few months earlier, had contributed handsomely to the relief of San Francisco in the wake of the earthquake and fire of April 18. Word of the School Board's action touched off a wave of resentment in Japan. Protests were promptly lodged in Washington and President Theodore Roosevelt, denouncing the ordinance as "a wicked absurdity," ordered the Attorney General to bring suit in the courts to enjoin its enforcement. The suit never came to trial, however, for on March 14, 1907, President Roosevelt stopped further Japanese immigration from Mexico, Canada, and Hawaii by executive order and, at the same time, negotiated the Gentlemen's Agreement. Appeased by these actions, the San Francisco School Board agreed not to enforce the ordinance.

Discussion of the School Board "incident" in Congress revealed how closely the Japanese question was related to the Negro question. By and large, Southern senators and congressmen were in complete sympathy with their California colleagues.[6] Said a Mississippi statesman: "I stand with the State of California in opposition to mixed schools. I stand with Californians in favor of the proposition that we want a homogeneous and assimilable population of white people in the Republic." As a matter of fact, President Roosevelt was forced to back down on the suits to enjoin enforcement of the San Francisco ordinance because he discovered, first, that Congress would not support him; and, second, that the Supreme Court's decisions nullifying the Civil War amendments to the Constitution had made it impossible for the federal government to protect the rights not only of Japanese aliens but of Japanese citizens in California.[7]

The ink was hardly dry on the signatures to the Gentlemen's Agreement when the California racists began screaming about one major loophole: the importation of so-called Japanese "picture brides." Women constituted only 4 per cent of the resident Japanese population in 1900; but, since women could enter as picture brides under the Gentlemen's Agreement, the number rapidly increased after 1907. As the sex ratio came into some sort of balance — women made up 34 per cent of the population by 1920 — the number of native-born Japanese children naturally increased, a circumstance which filled the Californians with fear and foreboding. Seeing that the *status quo* achieved by the Gentlemen's Agreement was being threatened, the resident Japanese voluntarily petitioned the Japanese government to deny further passports to Japanese women. And in February 1920, Japan actually stopped the issuance of such passports, but Congress, influenced by the postwar race riots and the rise of the Ku Klux Klan, went ahead and adopted the Exclusionary Immigration Act of 1924 which barred further Japanese immigration. The adoption of this legislation was widely interpreted in Japan as a piece of warlike provocation and, coming as it did when

[6] *Ibid.*, p. 29.
[7] *Ibid.*, pp. 29, 30.

Japan was still suffering from the Tokyo earthquake and fire, it was deeply and enduringly resented.

From 1900 to 1907 the agitation against the Japanese had been largely sponsored and directed by organized labor and had been aimed at driving the immigrants from the cities and towns. By 1910 this objective had been virtually achieved. The next phase in the agitation consisted of an effort to drive the Japanese from the land as a necessary precondition to driving them from California, and of course to excluding further immigration. As part of this strategy, the California legislature adopted an Alien Land Act in 1913 over the protests and pleas of Secretary of State Bryan, who had come to Sacramento to urge a policy of caution and moderation. As the first official discrimination against the Japanese in California, the act touched off a wave of popular protest in Japan.[8]

During World War I, anti-Japanese agitation abated somewhat: there was a serious labor shortage in California and the Japanese were our allies. But the moment the Treaty of Versailles was signed, a new wave of anti-Japanese agitation, in part provoked by Japanese aggression in Korea, Siberia, China, and Shantung, engulfed the state. In 1920 a new and far more severe Alien Land Act was adopted as an initiative measure by a popular vote of 668,483 to 222,085, and similar acts were soon adopted in Washington, Oregon, Arizona, Colorado, Delaware, Nebraska, Texas, Idaho, and New Mexico. The Alien Land Act was made to turn upon the interpretation of the key phrase, "aliens ineligible to citizenship." That the phrase included Japanese was confirmed by the decision of the Supreme Court in the famous Ozawa case, decided on November 13, 1922. This interpretation in turn led to the use of the same phrase in the Exclusionary Immigration Act of 1924, the passage of which brought the United States and Japan to the brink of war. With immigration suspended, there was a lull in the agitation for nearly a

[8] *Ibid.*, p. 46.

decade, but with the Sino-Japanese War in 1937 the old fault-line began to be disturbed once again and, with the attack on Pearl Harbor, the Japanese minority was removed by the military from the West Coast — which had been the goal of the anti-Japanese forces for nearly forty years.

During this long agitation, a sharply etched Japanese stereotype had been given wide currency. It was from the School Board incident that Wallace Irwin received the inspiration for his popular fiction about Hashimura Togo — *Letters of a Japanese Schoolboy* (1909). In these letters, first published in *Collier's*, the "Jap" stereotype was first clearly outlined: the buck-toothed, bespectacled, wordy, arrogant, dishonest trickster who later became a well-known figure in the comic strips and pulp magazines and motion pictures. Two novels were planned and used as part of the postwar campaign against the Japanese, namely, *Seed of the Sun* (1921) by Wallace Irwin and *The Pride of Palomar* (1921) by Peter B. Kyne. Serialized in mass circulation magazines, both novels were long in active demand, in book form, in California public libraries. Cornelius Vanderbilt, Jr., sent copies of the Kyne novel to a list of important Americans and published their responses in a pamphlet entitled, *The Verdict of Public Opinion on the Japanese-American Question*. The Kyne novel, incidentally, was based on a racist tract written by Montaville Flowers — *The Japanese Conquest of American Opinion* (1917) — and was dedicated to Mr. Flowers. "How about John Chinaman?" a character asks the hero of the Kyne novel. "Oh, a Chinaman is different. He's a regular fellow — he appreciates the sanity of our position . . . John Chinaman . . . realizes . . . that he is not assimilable with us, or we with him." It is interesting to note that Kyne's fixation about racial differences stemmed from an early interest in the work of Gregor Mendel; indeed he once wrote a Mendelian novel.[9]

[9] See "Cappy Ricks and the Monk in the Garden," by Dr. Carl Bode, in

"Trained hatreds," as Josiah Royce once observed, "are particularly pathetic and peculiarly deceitful." By 1920 the Californians had been thoroughly trained in hatred of the Japanese and other Oriental people. Charges advanced against the Chinese in 1876 — when the first congressional committee to inquire into Oriental immigration visited the Coast — were dogmatically repeated in every subsequent investigation and applied, almost ritualistically, to the Japanese. For seventy-five years, as Dr. Charles N. Reynolds has pointed out, the people of California "lived in an atmosphere of racial consciousness." Surveying the files of one small-town California newspaper, Dr. Reynolds found 2877 news items about the Japanese, totaling about 20,453 inches of space, most of which reflected "irritation verging on hostility." He also found that the "peaks" of anti-Japanese publicity correlated with election years. "The almost complete disappearance of unfavorable news in the breaks between high levels," he writes, "is eloquent proof of the fictitious character of the anti-Japanese movement." [10] When a majority is attempting to subordinate a trading as distinguished from a working minority — and the Japanese, like the Jews, are essentially a middle-class or trading minority — much more emphasis must be placed on agitation since the agility of the minority constantly threatens to upset the strategy of dominance.

Every disturbance in relations between Japan and the United States only further disturbed the relations between Japanese and non-Japanese in California; and, conversely, every "incident" in California only complicated the international situation. Thus, as Ruth Fowler has observed, "California residents gradually found opposition to the Japanese an ever-present issue, being applied to almost all their political, social, and economic problems . . . it colored every direct

PMLA, Publications of the Modern Language Association of America, March 1949, Vol. LXIV, No. 1, p. 59.

[10] "Oriental-White Relations in Santa Clara County," unpublished dissertation, Stanford University, 1927.

and indirect contact that they had with the Japanese." [11]
Caught in this continuous crossfire, the resident Japanese were
the first casualties on the mainland of the real war between
Japan and the United States which began on December 7,
1941. Viewing this forty-year agitation in retrospect, one
can only marvel at the remarkable advances which the Japanese had made.

### 3. Assimilation: California Style

The early Japanese immigrants to the West Coast were
young, unmarried men, in their best working years, who came
to this country not as religious or political refugees but as
hard-working immigrants anxious to better their condition.
The children of Japanese peasants, they were accustomed to
the intensive cultivation of exceedingly small farms; indeed
they might best be described as experts in miniature farming.
Those who came from urban areas were principally the sons
of shopkeepers. The Californians regarded Japanese immigration as a planned invasion or infiltration but it was actually
stimulated, more than anything else, by the rapid urbanization
of Japanese society.

Most of the immigrants had the equivalent of an eighth-
grade education. Showing from the outset a great eagerness
to adopt American ways, they quickly donned American-
made clothes; cut their hair like Americans; used American
furnishings and gadgets in their homes; and tried to act —
often to the point of caricature — like Americans. Many of
them even changed their religious affiliations; for example,
the churches were making converts to Christianity at the rate
of five hundred a year in California in 1914. There was no
crime problem among the Japanese; they paid their bills; and
they looked after those of their kind who were in need. The

[11] "Some Aspects of Public Opinion Concerning the Japanese in Santa
Clara County," unpublished dissertation, Stanford University, 1934.

California-born generation even showed evidence of biological adaptation: the children were taller, larger, and heavier than those born in Japan and the shape of their mouths, due to better dental care, was different. In short if rapidity of cultural assimilation is the test of good immigration stock, then the Japanese were model immigrants.

Only recently released from the rigid class demarcations of a feudal society, the Japanese immigrants tended to place a premium upon success in the struggle for position and status. "It is as though," writes Helen Mears, "while living in Japan, repressed in their small islands, crowded for space, fed on a limited diet, breathing a thick steamy vapor, they have become closed in on themselves like a bulb, the life-germ dormant, so that when they are freed from the special and peculiar conditions of their own land, taken out into the full sun and crisp air, given proper nourishment, they develop with astonishing swiftness." [12] But, as might be expected, it was precisely the remarkable adaptability of the Japanese — resembling a similar Jewish adaptability — which militated against them in California, where they were damned because they were too energetic, industrious, and adaptable. In part this superior adaptability reflects the extent to which the Japanese, like the Jews, were organized for co-operative action. "Precisely because of their historical traits of allegiance and organization," wrote Dr. R. E. Park, "the Japanese are capable of transforming their lives and practices more rapidly than any other group. . . . They are inclined to make more far-going concessions than other groups in order to overcome American prejudice and secure status here. . . . Whether we like them or not, no other foreign-language group is so completely and intelligently organized to control its members, and no other group has at all equaled them in the work of accommodating themselves to alien condi-

[12] *Year of The Wild Boar*, by Helen Mears, 1942.

tions." [13] Like the Jews, the Japanese were too well organized and too adaptable; their success constantly incited envy and hostility. Indeed the Japanese must have concluded that prejudice is essentially racial since, in all other respects, they had so completely demonstrated their capacity for assimilation.

The first major occupations of the Japanese in California were in railroad construction and maintenance; as migratory sugar-beet workers on large-scale farms; and in the hop fields. From these three basic employments, they gradually found their way into other types of seasonal work, principally in agriculture. In most cases, they began at somewhat lower wage rates than other groups (after all they were the most recent immigrants), but as more and more Japanese concentrated in a particular occupation, they were quick to organize and to demand higher wages. Although excluded from trade-unions, they had associations which functioned, in many respects, as collective bargaining agencies. Kept out of urban labor markets by the trade-unions, the Japanese concentrated in seasonal agricultural work, gradually taking over types of work formerly performed by Mexicans and Chinese.

Piece rates prevail in many seasonal agricultural operations and the Japanese, by reason of their skill, diligence, and organization, were often able to turn these rates to their advantage. Quite gradually, therefore, they began to leave farm employment, after a season or two, for tenant farming on shares, often for their former employers. The next step, of course, was the substitution of a cash rental which often became the down payment on the purchase price of a small acreage; for example, between 1910 and 1920 the acreage of Japanese-operated farms more than doubled. As the number of Japanese farmers increased, the number of Japanese employed on Japanese-owned farms also increased, thereby decreasing the availability of Japanese as general farm laborers on Caucasian-operated farms. Thus by 1920 the Japanese

[13] See *Prejudice*, p. 94.

had been written off as of no appreciable value as a source of farm labor for the American farmer. The general upward mobility of the Japanese — from laborer to tenant to owner — is what incited the opposition to them in rural areas. The Alien Land Acts of 1913 and 1920, however, put a serious brake on Japanese expansion in agriculture; both the number of Japanese-operated farms, and the acreage in such farms, showed a sharp decline after 1920. Excluded from farm ownership, the alien Japanese began to concentrate on contract gardening and the cultivation of small scattered units of land adjacent to urban communities — land that could be leased without arousing substantial opposition.

For the most part the Japanese made their own place in California agriculture. Even the *San Francisco Chronicle* conceded ". . . that the most striking feature of Japanese farming in California has been the development of successful orchards, vineyards, or gardens on land that was either completely out of use or employed for far less profitable enterprises." Japanese pioneered in the production of many crops; reclaimed desert and swamp lands; and converted cut-over timberlands in the Pacific North into prosperous berry farms. For example, the Japanese pioneered in the production of cotton and cantaloupes in Imperial Valley; first made a success of rice cultivation in the Sacramento Valley; and were the first to discover that the thermal belt on the west slope of the Sierras was ideally adapted to vineyards and orchards. In fact it was estimated in 1920 that 70 per cent of the lands which the Japanese then controlled were lands which they had reclaimed or lands on which they had introduced new crops.[14]

Penalized by exclusion from areas and crops which the Anglo-Americans had pre-empted, the Japanese made a highly profitable niche for themselves in the production of specialty produce crops which they raised, often on marginal lands,

[14] McKee, *op. cit.*, p. 66.

for the growing West Coast urban markets. In the growing of these crops, of course, they possessed a cultural advantage, but it was prejudice that drove them to the marginal lands. The fact that they succeeded in doing what others had failed to do or had never attempted only infuriated their detractors. For the Japanese to succeed to any degree was an affront; but for them to demonstrate a marked superiority as farmers to their lords and masters was insulting, insubordinate, and essentially subversive. Thanks to their skill and diligence, the Japanese greatly increased California's agricultural income; land values and rentals soared to new heights; and business generally was stimulated.

In fact the economic myths used in the Japanese agitation so frequently backfired that, after 1920, the argument shifted to racial or biological grounds. Once this had happened, the economic argument was used in reverse; that is, the advocates of exclusion self-righteously contended that they were arguing *against* their own economic interests. But the source of their prejudice, however, remained clearly economic. In the first place, the success of the Japanese had made it difficult, along with other factors, for the American "small farmer" to get a foothold in California agriculture or to compete with them in forms of farming with which he was not familiar. Also some of the largest landholding companies in the state were among the largest employers of Japanese farm laborers and tenants. Quite apart from these factors, however, the success of the Japanese in raising crops which had never previously been raised, often on lands formerly regarded as marginal, greatly incited the envy and covetousness of non-Japanese farmers. Considerations of this substantial order, rather than such sociological clichés as "dual citizenship," "language schools," and "clannishness," really motivated the hostility to the Japanese.

## 4. Little Tokyo

Although the Japanese scored some amazing economic successes in California, the majority finally succeeded in putting them in their place. Their place, of course, was Little Tokyo: a special niche in the economy within which they were contained by a skillful use of several strategic weapons. By the middle 1920's it was clearly apparent that containment had been achieved. The principal weapons used — the weapons that worked the greatest injury — were these: exclusion from the trade-union movement which in a strongly unionized city such as San Francisco — then the center of industry, trade, and commerce in California — really barred the way to most urban economic activities; the Alien Land Acts which imposed a serious check on agricultural expansion; the pattern of restrictive covenants (first developed in California) which, paralleling the denial to alien Japanese of the right to own agricultural lands, walled off the Japanese from other groups in urban areas; the denial of the right of citizenship-by-naturalization — a severe blow since it not only excluded the Japanese from many businesses and professions but made it impossible for them to use their economic power politically; and, lastly, the Exclusionary Immigration Act of 1924 which, by cutting off the source of replacements, doomed the Japanese to permanent minority status. Hedged in on all sides, the Japanese had been forced to carve out a special, largely noncompetitive, niche for themselves. Once they had retreated to this niche — actually they were driven into it — the agitation against them abated but it never wholly disappeared since there was always the possibility that, in the event of war, they might finally be ousted from this special niche. Just what, then, was the nature of this special niche in the economy?

By 1924 — that is, with the passage of the immigration act of that year — the main economic pattern of Japanese life on the West Coast had been clearly delineated. First and fore-most, the Japanese were concerned with the intensive produc-tion, on small holdings, and by the use of a large amount of unpaid family labor, of specialty produce crops for the large urban West Coast markets. By and large they had been successfully excluded from the more profitable side of the produce business, namely, shipment of California grown produce to out-of-state markets. In 1940 some 22,027 West Coast Japanese, or 43 per cent of those gainfully employed, were to be found in agriculture — for all practical purposes in the produce industry. Most of the farms were small but the total production was impressive. For example, in Cali-fornia the Japanese grew about 42 per cent of the produce crops, valued at around $35,000,000 annually. The small isolated character of many of their holdings — really urban lots held for future industrial use — prevented their being farmed successfully by large-scale mechanized methods; fur-thermore many labor operations in produce crops are difficult to mechanize. The American shipper-growers had the advan-tage of machines, a costly technology, and large amounts of capital; but these advantages were offset by Japanese skill, the use of unpaid family labor, and the control of wholesale and retail outlets.

In the distribution of truck produce the key functions are in the hands of the wholesaler.[15] From beginnings that dated back to 1901, the Japanese had secured an important foothold in the Los Angeles wholesale produce market. By 1930 the Japanese-controlled portion of the business of the City Mar-ket amounted to $16,000,000 annually and in 1934 had risen to $25,000,000 — in each instance roughly half of the total business of the market. The integration here was vertical: certain crops were largely or exclusively raised by Japanese; Japanese wholesalers distributed these crops and financed their production; and the Japanese wholesalers in turn dealt

[15] *Removal and Return,* by Leonard Broom and Ruth Riemer, 1949, p. 83.

with Japanese retailers. Many of the Japanese retailers were former farmers who had started to sell produce from roadside stands and who had learned, perhaps from the Japanese in the floral industry, techniques of display which made the average Japanese retail fruit-and-vegetable concession a thing of beauty. In Los Angeles alone, nearly 1000 Japanese-Americans worked in the wholesale end of the produce business and between 2100 and 2500 Japanese-Americans were to be found in the retail end. Thus the actual dependence of the Japanese upon one industry was much greater than the census figures revealed. "The most striking feature of the prewar system of produce distribution," writes Dr. Leonard Broom, "was the ethnic continuity of the channels of production and marketing." [16]

The West Coast ghettos or Little Tokyos were primarily set up to provide goods and services for those engaged in the produce industry, thereby further increasing the economic vulnerability of the Japanese. Refused service in beauty shops, barbershops, hotels, and restaurants run by Caucasians, the Japanese had been forced to develop their own service community. Little Tokyo, of course, also catered to a small tourist trade and, in the case of Japanese rooming houses and hotels, catered generally to a transient or "skid row" trade. The Japanese, however, had only the business which the non-Japanese did not want or, for special reasons, could not get; their businesses were strictly marginal. Virtually all Japanese businesses were small-scale, undercapitalized, dependent upon unpaid family labor, and operated out of structures which were at once homes and places of business. Dr. Broom points out that the Japanese, despite their remarkable early gains, had failed to achieve a large measure of power in the social structure. In 1941 the per capita income for all California civilians was $982; for the Japanese-Americans it was $671. The most impressive evidence of this economic "contain-

[16] *Ibid.*, p. 92.

ment," however, was the fact that there were few really wealthy Japanese; most of the Japanese were small farmers or petty merchants. Aside from the produce business, the major props of Little Tokyo's specialized economy were contract gardening (largely noncompetitive); commercial fishing and employment in fish canneries; and the floral and nursery industry. The fish and floral industries were competitive but the Japanese had a cultural advantage in these fields which enabled them to survive despite strong competition.

By 1920 the Japanese had outgrown this contained status and the American-born generation, just reaching maturity, was becoming highly restive and impatient. The economic base had been entirely outgrown and a kind of regression was clearly apparent. The Japanese shops were badly managed, offered inferior merchandise, and were old-fashioned and nepotistic. "With the increase of the Nisei in the labor force," writes Dr. Broom, "job competition . . . became increasingly severe and there was a sense of pressure that was often interpreted by the Nisei as deriving from the competition of other ethnic groups." [17] Chain stores and supermarkets were beginning to ease out the Japanese-American who owned the retail produce concessions. True, the Japanese had not been kept at the bottom of the heap, like the Chinese; but they had been contained within one major economic bastion, which was, in effect, their special creation and achievement. The economic crisis which impended in 1940 also coincided with a crisis in the shift of power from one generation to the next. Of 138,834 Japanese in the United States in 1930, 50.2 per cent were foreign-born; but of 126,947 Japanese in 1940, only 37.3 per cent were foreign-born.

External pressures do not alone account, of course, for the existence of Little Tokyo. The Japanese immigrants had a strong sense of the meaning of family, community, and nation

[17] *Ibid.,* p. 9⁷.

and their social solidarity had its counterpart in a highly integrated culture. It was this strong, traditional, in-group feeling which enabled them to develop their competitive strength within the American economy. For example, the traditional patterns of organization among the Japanese had much to do with their success in bringing about a vertical integration in the produce trade. Not only were the Japanese communities closely knit but they were also essentially petit bourgeois in composition. Thus the fact that only a single class interest was reflected in the community made for an unusual degree of internal solidarity. Within this world, however, a sharp cleavage had developed between Issei and Nisei. Such, in general, was the situation which prevailed in Little Tokyo immediately prior to December 7, 1941. Little Tokyo rested on a temporary and essentially precarious equilibrium. Almost any severe jolt would have disturbed this fragile *status quo* and the jolt which came with the war was more than severe — it was catastrophic.

## 5. *Guilt by Race*

The evacuation of Japanese-Americans from the Pacific Coast in the spring and summer of 1942 was an act without precedent in American history. It was the first time that the United States government condemned a large group of people to barbed-wire inclosures. It was the first event in which danger to the nation's welfare was determined by group characteristics rather than by individual guilt. It was the first program in which race alone determined whether an American would remain free or become incarcerated.

— MORTON GRODZINS in *Americans Betrayed*

Eight years have passed since General J. L. DeWitt, acting pursuant to authority which descended to him from Executive Order No. 9066 issued by President Roosevelt on February 19, 1942, ordered 110,000 persons of Japanese descent — men, women, and children, two thirds of them citizens of the United States — removed from the three West Coast states. Nothing quite like this had happened in American history since President Jackson had ordered the Indians removed from Georgia. Today, thanks to several recent studies, it is possible to see this unprecedented violation of American civil liberties in proper perspective.[18]

Mass evacuation had devious and multiple motivations but security considerations were surely not the decisive factors. So far as General DeWitt was concerned — and the immediate decision was his — his reasoning had the merit of simplicity and candor: "A Jap is a Jap. . . . It makes no difference whether he is an American citizen or not, he is still a Japanese. . . . The Japanese race is an enemy race and while many second and third generation Japanese born on United States soil, possessed of United States citizenship, have become 'Americanized,' the racial strains are undiluted." [19] As Justice William Denman, of the Ninth Circuit Court, has caustically observed, "the identity of this doctrine with that of the Hitler generals towards those having blood strains of a western Asiatic race as justifying the gas chambers of Dachau is unmistakable." [20] When the Army ordered mass evacuation, the High Command knew perfectly well that, wild stories to the contrary, not a single act of sabotage had been committed in Hawaii where 35 per cent of the population was of Japanese origin.[21] Indeed it was the absence of sabotage which General DeWitt found to be "a disturbing and confirming indication that such action will be taken"!

[18] See McKee, *op. cit.;* also *The Spoilage,* by Dr. Dorothy Swaine Thomas and Richard S. Nishimoto, 1946; *Americans From Japan,* by Bradford Smith, 1948; *Americans Betrayed,* by Morton Grodzins, 1949; and the various reports of the War Relocation Authority, Department of Interior. And see my volume, *Prejudice,* published in 1944.

[19] See *The Spoilage,* p. 20; Final Report, Western Defense Command, p. 34; House Naval Affairs Command Report, Part 3, pp. 739–740, 78th Cong., 1st Session.

[20] *Acheson* v. *Murakami,* No. 12,082, Ninth Circuit Court, August 26, 1949.

[21] Report of Robert L. Shivers, prepared for Territorial Emergency Service Committees, Honolulu, 1946.

Just as it would be wholly erroneous to say that prejudice against the Japanese on the West Coast as a "natural" by-product of racial and cultural differences, so it would be equally erroneous to assume that "the people" of the West Coast demanded the mass evacuation of the Japanese. Evacuation was demanded, not by the people at large, but by particular groups and for specific reasons. Prejudice, indeed, is essentially a group rather than an individual or a mass phenomenon. It could be easily demonstrated that the presence of the Japanese contributed to the economic and social well-being of the Californians. The Japanese were *not* in competition with Californians as such; they were in competition with *particular* Californians, or groups of Californians. Historically the relations between these groups and the Japanese largely determined the extent of the prejudice against the Japanese; those with a vague generalized prejudice seldom bother to spend money on "anti-Japanese" campaigns or to organize pogroms. They may provide the votes but others always provide the money and the organizing energy and so it was with mass evacuation.

The moment we were at war with Japan, certain pressure groups in California saw that "a golden opportunity" existed to cut the Japanese down to size. The Western Growers Protective Association, made up of growers who controlled approximately 85 per cent of the row-crop vegetables shipped from California, actively promoted the campaign to secure mass evacuation of the Japanese. The prewar division in the produce industry, it will be recalled, was between the Americans who controlled out-of-state shipments and the Japanese who controlled the local markets. In the Salinas and Imperial Valleys, however, a few Japanese had dared to enter the out-of-state field and were in active competition with American shipper-growers. Furthermore the out-of-state shippers had long eyed the local industry with unconcealed covetousness and, with a war on and prices soaring, they were determined to take over the Japanese-controlled sector of the industry. And this is precisely what they did — with the aid of the military, the American Legion, the Native Sons of the Golden West, and sundry "patriotic" groups.

The activities of the Western Growers Protective Association, and such allies as the Grower-Shipper Vegetable Association, the Associated Farmers, and the California Farm Bureau, are carefully detailed and elaborately documented in Mr. Grodzins's admirable study.[22] Just how important this pressure was in bringing about mass evacuation must be appraised in light of the fact that the produce business was the mainstay of the Japanese economy in California. The Japanese did not have important economic allies or interlocking interests or diversified power relations. Economically they occupied a position which was — to an alarming degree — exposed and vulnerable since it was so thoroughly isolated.

On the other hand, the Caucasians in the produce industry had important allies and used and mobilized these allies with great skill. For example, it was the Los Angeles Chamber of Commerce which: (a) brought West Coast congressmen together for the first time to consider the evacuation of the Japanese; (b) prepared the first resolution demanding evacuation, which the West Coast delegation adopted as its own; (c) consistently needled the West Coast congressional delegation and supplied this delegation with material for propaganda and demagoguery; and (d) mobilized pressure from other groups to the same end. An executive of the Los Angeles Chamber of Commerce reported: "The Chamber does the work, the congressmen do the talking. . . . On the Japanese problem . . . the Chamber got the congressmen together not only prior to evacuation in order to get the movement underway but also more recently to protest any

[22] *Americans Betrayed*, 1949, by Morton Grodzins, Chapter II, "Pressure Groups."

move to let the Japanese come back to the coast." [23] There were, of course, various additional pressures from such me-too "civic" groups as the American Legion; but these political auxiliaries merely followed the lead of the major economic pressure groups and did their bidding.

The result, of course, was to build up what Mr. Grodzins calls an impressive air or "façade of unanimity." How little this ballyhoo had to do with security is convincingly demonstrated by the fact that after total mass evacuation had been ordered — which presumably should have satisfied the security-conscious — a new campaign was promptly organized, by the same groups, to see to it that the Japanese were never permitted to return to the Coast! Equally telltale is the fact that the Japanese were not evacuated from the Hawaiian Islands. At the time of the attack on Pearl Harbor, there were approximately 120,000 citizens of Japanese descent and 40,000 Japanese aliens in Hawaii; yet only 980 aliens and citizens were actually interned — a fraction of 1 per cent of the total.[24]

Mr. Grodzins sums up the situation in these words:

Racial prejudice, economic self-interest, political profit, and patriotism were, in combination, a potent source of social action. . . . The veneer of national safety was thin; below its surface and visible at many points was the less marketable but more substantial framework of racial animosity, economic aggrandizement, and political fortune-hunting. While the total arguments in favor of evacuation were mobilized under the banner of national defense, the end result was in many cases completely divorced from the issue of safeguarding the Pacific Coast from its enemies. . . . What is fact and what people believe is fact are separate and distinguishable. Individuals act not on the basis of absolute "truth" but rather on what they believe to be truth. . . . In the case of the Japanese evacuation, the regional arguments were, in large part, factually false. Yet this neither diluted

[23] Grodzins, *op. cit.*, p. 35.
[24] See reference Note 21, above.

the strength with which they were believed nor . . . did it make the regional forces less important in shaping national policy.[25]

There is an irony about mass evacuation which has somehow escaped attention. The economic vulnerability of the Japanese on the West Coast made their removal possible and this vulnerability had been brought about largely by external pressures and discriminations. In Hawaii the Japanese were not nearly so vulnerable; indeed they were the mainstay of the economic life of the Islands and hence could not be evacuated. Thus if the West Coast Japanese had not been driven into a special niche in the economy, the tragedy of mass evacuation, and the frightening precedent which it established, might have been avoided. "Japanese-Americans," writes Mr. Grodzins, "were the immediate victims of the evacuation. But larger consequences are carried by the American people as a whole. Their legacy is the lasting one of precedent and constitutional sanctity for a policy of mass incarceration under military auspices. This is the most important result of the process by which the evacuation decision was made. That process betrayed all Americans." [26] To this judgment one can only add that mass evacuation was not the product of wartime hysteria; it was the logical end-product, the goal, of a strategy of dominance which began forty years earlier and which was closely related to a similar strategy of American dominance in the Pacific. The resident Japanese were always the hostages of this larger strategy much as Japan proper is today the hostage of the American empire.

## 6. The Return of the Natives

Despite a vicious campaign for permanent exclusion, the Japanese-Americans were finally released from the relocation centers and, after a further delay, were then permitted to

[25] Grodzins, op. cit., p. 177.
[26] Ibid., p. 374.

return to the West Coast. Superpatriots inveighed against them; race-baiters incited mob violence; and the pressure groups snarled their disapproval. But the Japanese returned and, despite some violence, successfully braved the tempest. By the time the ban was lifted elements of the general population had begun to feel ashamed of the part they had played in the betrayal of the Japanese and now sought to make amends. The superb military record made by Japanese-Americans in the war was an additional factor which even the most brazen race-baiters could hardly blink. On the whole, public acceptance of the returning Japanese hostages was friendlier than might have been expected and, since 1945, few manifestations of the old "yellow peril" agitation have occurred. Not all of the Japanese, however, have returned. Sixty thousand were reported to have returned by the end of 1947 but it is doubtful if many more have returned in the last three years. Chicago, which had a prewar Japanese population of around 390, now has around 20,000, and colonies have been established in cities such as Boston, New York, Philadelphia, Washington, Denver, Salt Lake City, Cleveland, Cincinnati, and such outposts as Idaho Falls, Idaho.

Although the reception of the returning Japanese-Americans has been better than might have been expected, it is perfectly clear that the evacuees have failed to regain their special niche in the economy. First of all, the property losses of the Japanese were enormous; estimates range from $350,000,000 to $500,000,000. A claims commission has been established but if the maximum allowance is made for every evacuee it will still not reimburse the Japanese by a wide margin. By and large, the Japanese have not been able to regain their position in the produce industry, either in the wholesale or in the retail or production ends. Dr. Broom has estimated that whereas 20 per cent of the Japanese prewar labor force were wage and salary workers employed by non-Japanese, today 70 per cent or more of the labor force are wage or salary employees of Caucasians.[27] In contract gardening, the floral and nursery industry, and one or two other lines, the Japanese have regained approximately their prewar position; but, according to Dr. Broom, "their actual share in the income of the region was far smaller than before the war and the number of instances in which they occupied positions of power and responsibility were greatly reduced. Their weakened position in the economic power structure was even more striking than their losses in income status. In a sense they have lost nearly a generation in their striving for economic security, but they have not returned in large numbers to the forms of manual labor in which they began a generation ago, and it seems improbable that they will."[28] Japanese-American farm holdings are approximately one fourth of what they were before the war. Much of the land they farmed was converted during the war to industrial uses or subdivided for residences. In other instances, their former holdings have been consolidated into larger units.

While the Japanese were in relocation centers, Negro migrants surged into the former Little Tokyos, many of which became Bronzevilles overnight. There has been considerable friction in these areas between Japanese and Negroes, for the nature of the situation pitches the two groups into active competition in a crowded and socially neurotic milieu. Today a kind of truce prevails but the relationships are far from satisfactory. Superficially San Francisco's Fillmore district is a cosmopolitan area; but actually its integration is weirdly unreal. "The two groups live close together," writes one observer, "yet their lives do not touch; their contacts are superficial. Strong economic and social forces keep their communities and their lives as distinct as though they were miles apart."[29]

[27] *Removal and Return*, p. 67.
[28] *Ibid.*, p. 68.
[29] See Section III, special supplement, *Pacific Citizen*, December 24, 1949, p. 17.

The breaking up of Little Tokyo and, more important, the ouster of the Japanese from the produce industry, have forced the younger generation to seek jobs in the larger community, principally as white-collar workers, emphasizing a trend that had begun before the war. In the long run it is possible that the younger generation may profit from this experience but, cut off from numerical replacements, they would now appear to be a vanishing minority in the same category as the resident Chinese. Today the average age of the Nisei is about twenty-eight and they have matured, perhaps beyond their years, as a result of the harsh experience in the relocation centers. Here and there discriminatory bars have been removed: the Supreme Court, in June 1948, invalidated a California statute which prohibited alien Japanese from obtaining commercial fishing licenses (the Takahashi case); the Ninth Circuit Court, in Judge Denman's memorable decision, has set aside certain renunciations of citizenship which were obtained in the relocation centers (*Acheson* v. *Murakami*, August 26, 1949); and, more recently, the District Court of Appeals, in California, has followed the lead of the United States Supreme Court in the Oyama case, and has held the Alien Land Act unconstitutional. Even before this decision, the people of California had voted 1,143,780 to 797,067 *not* to incorporate the Alien Land Act into the constitution.[30] The fact that the District Court of Appeals should have used certain sections of the United Nations Charter to upset the Alien Land Act has been widely interpreted as the beginning of a new development in judicial interpretation of discriminatory legislation.[31]

In retrospect it can be seen that both the Chinese and the Japanese sought to defeat the strategy of dominance which the majority invoked against them but, in the end, both were

[30] "California's Proposition 15," by Grace Cable Kerocher, *Common Ground*, Spring 1947, p. 27.
[31] See Arthur Krock's column, *New York Times*, May 23, 1950.

defeated and the majority got what it wanted, namely, undisputed social, economic, and political pre-eminence. Now, at the mid-point of the century, the alien generation among the Japanese is rapidly disappearing; the Nisei have been more widely distributed, both geographically and occupationally; and the final absorption of the Japanese would seem to be merely a matter of time, cut off, as they are, from numerical replacements. The majority won a sweeping victory; but the price was high.

According to the language guides provided American occupying personnel, the Korean word for "American" is *Me-Gook*. Over a period of time, after the American occupation began, the prefix was dropped, the meaning was reversed, and the Koreans became "gooks" — with all the ugly connotations of "nigger." During the war, the term was also widely used to refer to Pacific Island natives but it was generally intended to include all Asiatics. "I was stationed in Seoul," writes a GI in the Letter Column of the *New York Times* of August 2, 1950, "during the first year of Korean occupation. I remember how the Koreans went out of their way to be friendly when the first United States troops arrived. . . . I also recall how time and abuse changed those early sentiments. . . . I can think of other incidents I saw in Seoul: jeeps sideswiping civilians when they were slow to move out of the way; soldiers cursing civilians; disparaging remarks about Korean lethargy, backwardness, hygiene, sanitary facilities and women. Even then the attitude was rather widespread. Certainly it did plenty of damage. . . . 'Gook' and all it implies is typical of the attitude that is causing so much alarm among United States advisors in Tokyo." There can hardly be any doubt, now, as to the origin of this attitude. Now that we are seeking a foothold among the Asians, who do not relish being called "gooks," we find that they still remember how Orientals were excluded from the United States. Gook — and all that it implies — had its origin in a situation in which a Caucasian majority on the West Coast was determined to dominate Asiatic minorities for its own clear profit and advantage. Today the same attitude is perpetuated by a situation in which we seek to use a preponderance of power to dominate Asiatic peoples in Asia to our clear profit and advantage.

CHAPTER V

# Hawaii: Island Racial Frontier

HAWAII occupies a key position in the American system of race relations. Although we seem to have forgotten the fact, the annexation of Hawaii was intimately related to the racial question in the United States; in the strategy of annexation one can see, in retrospect, the shadow of a larger strategy. To understand our domestic system of race relations, one must study the extension of this system to the peculiar conditions which prevailed in Hawaii; there the system, in all its contradictions and ambiguities and paradoxes, is revealed with great clarity. Hawaii was also the laboratory in which the formula for American expansionism — the outward expression of our domestic racial imperialism — was first worked out. Nations that practice imperialism must also practice racism. It is only by maintaining an artificial distance between "the natives" and the proconsuls of empire that the social and economic dividends of imperialism can be maintained at a sufficiently lucrative rate to offset the risks and trouble, the inconvenience and the hazards of expansion. Where a nation makes the mistake of attempting to fraternize racially with the peoples it conquers, the imperial relation cannot long be maintained.

## 1. Imperialism without Colonies

As an imperialist power, our basic problem has always been that the Constitution of the United States does not sanction the distinction between "subjects" and "citizens." This was clearly pointed out by Senator George F. Hoar in the debate on the annexation of Hawaii. There is no place under the American Constitution, he emphasized, for "the colonial system of Europe, based . . . upon the fundamental idea that the people of immense areas of territory can be held as subjects, never to become citizens"; indeed the Revolution of 1776 voiced a classic protest against this proposition. To annex and govern native peoples without their consent was clearly unconstitutional; it had never occurred to the founding fathers that their descendants "would be beguiled from these sacred and awful verities [of human liberty] that they might strut about in the cast-off clothing of pinchbeck emperors and pewter kings." [1]

On the other hand, it was quite unthinkable that we should extend full citizenship to the dark-skinned natives of outlying territories while holding Negroes in chattel slavery. It was pointed out in the same Hawaiian debate that the Philippines were tenanted by "a heterogeneous compound of inefficient Oriental humanity," peoples that differed from us in race, language, and custom and were obviously "not suited to our institutions, nor ready for liberty as we understand it." Thus the dilemma was twofold: from the constitutional point of view it was unthinkable that we should govern a people without their consent and yet, from the racial point of view, we dared not add to the number of "colored" citizens. The dilemma was solved, as "the Negro problem" was solved, by upholding constitutional principles and at the same time continuing to govern without the consent of all the governed; in short the American dilemma was simply extended to our outlying territories and possessions. The post-bellum "solution" of the Negro problem provided the key to the solution of the problem of Hawaii which in turn established the precedent for Puerto Rico and the Philippines.

[1] *Expansionists of 1898: The Acquisition of Hawaii and The Spanish Islands*, by Julius W. Pratt, 1936, p. 347.

Two thousand nautical miles from San Francisco, Hawaii was still closer to the United States than to any other important body of land; the distance from Honolulu to San Francisco was actually less than the distance from San Francisco to Washington. On a global map, Hawaii was simply an offshore extension of the American frontier. Hawaii occupied a unique position not only as a detached, insular frontier but because its first settlers were neither miners nor trappers but missionaries. The drama of annexation really began with the arrival of the *Thaddeus,* containing the first New England missionaries, at Kailua on April 4, 1820; indeed Hawaii was our first and only mission frontier.

At the time of Captain Cook's second visit to the islands, in 1778, the native Hawaiian population was estimated at about 300,000. Although this estimate was doubtless too high, the population seems to have been fairly well stabilized at that time on the basis of a subsistence economy. Armed with Bibles and hymnals rather than guns and bullets, and being few in number and overflowing with the milk of human kindness, the missionaries showed not the slightest aversion to the native population despite the difference in race and culture. It will be noted, however, that the missionaries constituted only a tiny minority and that the natives held undisputed possession of island resources which even then must have impressed the New Englanders as being of immense potential value. On their part, of course, the natives showed not the slightest prejudice; they embraced the missionaries with laughter and song and by 1840 some 20,000 island converts were singing hymns.

The missionaries had hardly set foot ashore, however, before they became interested in the potential economic wealth of the islands. For example, the Reverend Richard Armstrong soon left a meager Mission pittance for a $3000-a-year sinecure with the Hawaiian government. A few years later he was listed as the owner of six hundred acres of land

and by 1849 he was declining a friend's offer to invest funds on the mainland with the notation that he owned 1800 acres, and other investments, which were yielding him 12½ per cent interest! [2] With the discovery of gold in California, Hawaiian land values jumped from $1 to $5 an acre; a lively trade developed between Honolulu and San Francisco; and the sugar plantation — the first crude sugar mill was erected in 1837 — came into its own. In 1863 the American Minister reported to Washington that, with one or two exceptions, all the sugar plantations were owned by Americans. Under these circumstances, of course, Americans in the islands continued to show a remarkable freedom from the virus of racial prejudice.

Once their investments had reached a certain point, however, the Americans in the islands became audibly dissatisfied with the "inefficient" native government. As long as they had constituted a tiny propertyless minority, the Americans had not feared the native majority but their fears grew as their investments mounted and they were soon demanding annexation. Negotiations for a treaty of annexation were opened in the 1850's but the project had to be abandoned at that time since the natives showed a marked hostility to a connection which "even in the United States was regarded as disastrous to their race." [3] Slavery still prevailed in the United States and the Hawaiians were vividly aware that the slaves were all members of a colored race. The native press consistently stressed the theme that annexation would mean virtual enslavement for the Hawaiians. The influx of American population from California and "the well-known character of the ruthless pioneer" gave dramatic emphasis to this argument.

The key to the failure of these first negotiations, however, was to be found in the attitude of Prince Alexander Liholiho. [4]

[2] *American Expansion in Hawaii, 1842–1898*, by Sylvester K. Stevens, 1945, p. 26.
[3] *Ibid.*, p. 73.          [4] *Ibid.*

Liholiho was convinced that only statehood would protect the rights of the natives and that statehood was impossible because of the struggle between the North and the South for the control of new territories. He understood that "the grant of such advanced status to a territorial acquisition would have been contrary to all precedent and, in the midst of the intense political struggle of the times, a threat even to the equilibrium of the Union." [5] How could the United States grant full citizenship to "colored" Hawaiians and continue to hold nearly 4,000,000 Negroes in slavery? The popular and able Liholiho had, moreover, a personal reason for opposing annexation. David L. Gregg reported that the Prince had "personally felt keenly the nature of the color line as drawn in the United States from experiences while travelling." [6] One can readily imagine the incidents which the dark-skinned Liholiho observed, and in which he was personally involved, in travels on the mainland in the 1850's.

During the Civil War the demand for Hawaiian sugar greatly increased, and at the same time the importance of the whaling industry decreased. By the end of the war, therefore, the dependence on the American market was nearly absolute. Afraid that Hawaiian sugar might be excluded from this market, the planters resumed negotiations for annexation only to be rebuffed again in 1867. This time the vote of "recently admitted Southern Senators" tipped the scales against annexation. [7] Certain Southern states, of course, were interested in the produce of cane sugar; but all of them were interested in the racial question. Just as the Southern Senators were reluctant to grant citizenship to the natives of the islands, so the Hawaiians were afraid of the color prejudice of the South. The prospects for annexation immediately improved, however, after the adoption of the Fifteenth Amend-

[5] *Ibid.*, p. 75.
[6] *Ibid.*, p. 73.
[7] *Ibid.*, p. 101.

ment which the Americans in the islands cited to the natives as assurance that they need not fear American race prejudice.[8] In 1875 a Treaty of Reciprocity was finally negotiated which went into effect in September 1876, as Sylvester K. Stevens has pointed out, "coincident with the beginnings of some shift in the attitude of the people of the United States toward matters of foreign policy."[9] It will be recalled that 1876 was also the year in which a famous bargain was struck by which Hayes was awarded the Presidency, to which Tilden had been elected, in consideration of a promise to withdraw the last federal troops from the Southern states and to abandon the effort to enforce the Fifteenth Amendment.[10] It was this bargain which cleared the way for the future annexation of the islands, for if Negroes could be constitutionally disfranchised in South Carolina, ways and means could be found to cope with the native Hawaiian majority in the islands. Thus, as Stevens observes, "the seeds of a more vigorous foreign policy and a tendency toward imperial expansion were sown."

The turning point in Hawaiian-American relations, the Reciprocity Treaty of 1876, brought about a kind of *de facto* annexation of the islands. Sugar exports jumped from 25 million pounds in 1875 to 250 million pounds in 1890. The demand for labor soared; the plantation system was rapidly expanded; and the American investment was greatly increased. The principal beneficiaries, of course, were the American sugar planters who by 1872 owned 25 of 32 island plantations. The Civil War amendments to the Constitution, which had been used as the bait to induce the Hawaiians to ratify the treaty, proved to be of as little protection to the Hawaiians as to the American Negroes. Long prior to formal annexation, the social system of Hawaii had come to resemble

[8] *Ibid.,* p. 110.
[9] *Ibid.,* p. 154.
[10] *Rutherford B. Hayes: Statesman of Reunion,* by H. J. Eckenrode, 1930, p. 219.

the social system of the Southern states. "The life of Hawaii shortly came to resemble," writes Stevens, "that of the ante-bellum South in the United States with a small and powerful planter aristocracy in full possession of economic and social privileges. . . . The natives came to occupy a lowly position in the social scale. . . . The attitude of the planters toward this more or less servile labor element came to resemble the Southern philosophy of slavery days toward the Negro in the United States." [11]

Due to the absence of a "poor white" element, however, the racial division in Hawaii so perfectly coincided with the class division that the natives could be subordinated to the Americans in the plantation system without any of the uglier manifestations of racial prejudice. Cited as an island of equality in the American system of racial inequality, Hawaii actually provides an illustration of the principle of inequality in its purest form, for the natives were completely subordinated to the Americans in the social system. A series of islands in mid-Pacific, with an impressive native majority, Hawaii had to be governed by manipulation rather than by a policy of coercion. As a native people with a unified culture the Hawaiians could be manipulated, whereas the Negroes, whose culture and social organization were disrupted in the process of enslavement and transplantation, had to be ruled by force. In Hawaii, therefore, the more unpleasant outward forms of racial discrimination were avoided as a matter of policy. There were never any riots or lynchings or "night riders" and intermarriage was approved since it provided a means by which native resources could be acquired and a limited labor force could be stabilized.

From the impact of the Reciprocity Treaty came the "Revolution of 1893" by which the sons and grandsons of the missionaries finally dispensed with the luxury of native kings and queens and established the Republic of Hawaii.

[11] Stevens, *op. cit.*, pp. 143, 144.

In setting up a government, the Americans sought the advice of John W. Burgess, the theoretician of American imperialism, on how best to keep control out of the hands of irresponsible elements, meaning Asiatic and Hawaiian elements. The constitutional convention consisted of 19 members of the provisional government (wholly controlled by the American minority) and 18 elected delegates! However, only those could vote who took an oath that they were opposed to the restoration of the native monarchy, a measure which in effect disfranchised the native Hawaiians *in toto*. The *Hawaiian Gazette* pointed up the problem in these words: "It must be distinctly understood that, beside ruling themselves, the whites must create a form of government through which they can rule natives, Chinese, Japanese, and Portuguese, in order to prevent being 'snowed under.' " [12] All that need be said on this score is that white supremacy was established in Hawaii with much less violence and more effectively than the "poor whites" re-established the same doctrine in the Southern states at almost precisely the same time.

The constitutional anomaly of Hawaii might have been avoided had it not been for the McKinley Tariff of 1890. By giving a bounty of two cents a pound to domestic sugar producers and removing duties on all raw sugar imported to the United States, the act gave a great advantage to Hawaii's competitors on the mainland and at the same time placed Hawaiian planters on a par with other importers. The consequences, of course, were disastrous: sugar prices fell from $100 to $60 a ton and the Hawaiian planters suffered a $12,000,000 depreciation. To get around the tariff, a treaty of annexation was signed on February 14, 1893, which President Harrison submitted to the Senate for ratification on the eve of his retirement. The treaty was promptly withdrawn, however, by Cleveland, who thought that the Hawaiian Queen had been rather summarily ousted and

[12] Quoted by Pratt, *op. cit.*, p. 190.

that, after all, the natives should have been consulted.

Withdrawal of the Hawaiian Treaty touched off a debate which continued almost uninterruptedly for seven years. It was this debate, as Dr. Julius W. Pratt has pointed out, which "focused public opinion for the first time upon the issues involved in the expansion policy" and which also brought out the peculiar characteristics of American imperialism.[13] At an earlier date, James G. Blaine had emphasized that the United States should pursue a policy of expansion by "economic and commercial assimilation" rather than by "the material annexation of colonies." Britain and the other European powers had developed a different system. Since theirs was largely an overseas imperialism, they had dominated native economies by conquering and ruling the natives. Blaine contended that experience had shown this to be an expensive, hazardous, and essentially self-defeating policy. What really mattered was not whose flag was flown over the natives but whose products they purchased. The colonial phase of American imperialism had been concealed by the fact that we had simply overrun the Indians and ruled the Negroes as domestic chattel slaves. Later a skillful use of the Monroe Doctrine had made it unnecessary for us to follow the less efficient British model of imperialism in this hemisphere. The real key to the difference in the two systems, however, was to be found in the fact that the United States as a large land power with an extraordinarily dynamic industrial economy could undersell its rivals in the colonies which they had conquered at great expense and from which, as hated conquerors, they were certain to be driven at some future date.

The contrast between the two types or systems of imperialism was clearly pointed out in the Hawaiian debate. "Colonies," writes Dr. Pratt, "were not only certain to bear a fruit of danger and expense; they were valueless from the commercial point of view. Did not the colonies of Great

Britain afford us one of the most valuable of our export markets?" [14] Even where tariffs were imposed, the colonizing power could not monopolize the trade of the colonies. Again and again it was pointed out that the European notion of the commercial value of conquests, navies, and political control was outmoded or, if not outmoded, it had no relevance to the American problem of expansion. For us a much better plan would be to let the natives think that they ruled themselves; the substance of trade and not the form of rule was what counted. Although other reasons were cited, it was this argument which finally prevailed in the Hawaiian debate. After considering every phase of the matter, it was decided that the Queen should not be restored but that Hawaii should not be annexed.

And there the Hawaiian issue might have rested but for Dewey's victory in Manila Bay and the fact that American business interests suddenly began to fear that American products might be excluded from Europe and the Far East. Even before these developments took place, however, an ideology of expansion had been worked out by such ingenious dialecticians as John Fiske, Josiah Strong, and John W. Burgess. The expansionist ideology was based directly upon the concept of racial superiority: it was not only the privilege but the duty of Anglo-Saxon and Teutonic peoples to rule over the inferior dark-skinned peoples of the tropic zones. Manifest Destiny demanded "an Anglo-Saxonized mankind." Just as we should be careful about attempting to transplant our institutions in the tropics — the tropics were unfavorable to democracy — so we should be careful not to extend the privileges of democracy to the dark-skinned peoples of the tropical lands who were incapable of democratic self-government. Burgess, the mentor of Theodore Roosevelt, insisted that "the Teutonic element, when dominant, should never surrender the balance of political power," and there can be no doubt

[14] *Ibid.*, p. 256.

that he had the Deep South in mind when he made this statement.[15] The racial ideology of expansion was enthusiastically accepted by all the church groups, with the exception of the Unitarians and the Quakers, because it provided a perfect rationale for missionary endeavors of the kind that had been so successful in Hawaii. The Protestants made use of the ideology in their support of the war against Spain since it tended to mask their real motivation, which was to make converts at the expense of Catholicism. On the other hand, the Catholics had to support the war against Spain to prove their patriotism. Manifest Destiny was a generally acceptable rationalization of our warlike intentions since it stemmed directly from the treatment of domestic racial minorities.

Although we were determined to fight Spain to clear the way for American expansion in the Caribbean and the Pacific, we might not have annexed Puerto Rico and the Philippines had it not been for the peculiar situation in Hawaii. "The case of Hawaii," writes Mr. Stevens, "in 1898 was entirely different from that of any of the Spanish colonies. . . . Hawaii had become an outpost in the Pacific which was the product of typical American frontier expansion generated during the era of agrarian imperialism. It was much in the same category as Texas, Oregon, and California. It was this basic difference in the status of Hawaii which made so ineffectual the arguments of the anti-imperialists from 1893 to 1898." [16] Besides Hawaii had to be annexed in order to checkmate Japan. "The annexation of Hawaii," as the *Hawaiian Star* observed, "is for the benefit of the Hawaiian, the Latin, and the Anglo-Saxon races of these islands. It is not and it does not pretend to be for the benefit of the Asiatics. It is meant as a bar to the Asiatics." [17] We could safely annex Hawaii, argued Senator Platt, because annexation did *not*

[15] *Ibid.*, p. 8.
[16] Stevens, *op. cit.*, p. 299.
[17] *Ibid.*, p. 288.

mean that we had to accept the products or the peoples of the islands. Since the natives were colored, we were under no obligation to confer statehood upon the islands or citizenship upon the natives; on the contrary it was our duty to rule in Hawaii as Anglo-Saxons ruled in Georgia. "We come," said Senator Nelson, "as ministering angels, not as despots," just as the missionaries had come to Hawaii in 1820, Bible in hand. The dynamic behind racial discrimination was the dynamic which prompted expansion; as defined by one Senator, this dynamic was "a lust for power and greed for land, veneered with the tawdriness of false humanity."

In this manner the dilemma which had bothered President Cleveland was adroitly resolved and Hawaii was annexed. Under the Organic Act, all persons who were citizens of the Republic of Hawaii became citizens of the United States; but despite the fact that Hawaiians comprised an absolute majority for the first two decades after annexation, the Anglo-Saxon minority continued to rule the islands. In the wake of the Hawaiian annexation came the famous McEnery resolution in which the American racial dilemma became embalmed in the foreign policy of the United States. The McEnery resolution recited that it was not our intention to incorporate the inhabitants of the Philippine Islands into citizenship or permanently to annex the islands as an integral part of the United States; "but that it is the intention of the United States to establish on said islands a government suitable to the wants and conditions of the inhabitants of said islands, to prepare them for local self-government, and in due time to make such disposition of said islands as will best promote the interests of the citizens of the United States and the inhabitants of said islands." It will be noted, as Dr. Pratt points out, that we placed our interests first. Actually we rejected the Filipinos as citizens not merely because of the color of their skins but because our policy was "economic assimilation," not "political conquest." "It was not the intrinsic value of the Philippines

or their trade that most impressed American writers. . . .
Rather, their importance appeared to lie in their position as
a gateway to the markets of Eastern Asia." [18] With Hawaii
it was different: the islands guarded the approach to the
West Coast and protected the sea lanes to the Far East.

## 2. Pity the Natives

Long before annexation, the native Hawaiians had suffered
a catastrophic racial and cultural defeat. In 1853 the native
Hawaiians numbered 71,019; in 1865, 58,765; in 1872, 51,000;
in 1890, 40,622; in 1940, 22,636. "Within a century and a
half following the visit of the first white men to the islands,"
writes Dr. Andrew W. Lind, "the native population had
diminished to about one tenth of its pre-European size; and
the first half of this era alone witnessed a decline of 72 per
cent." [19]

No effort whatever was made to protect native land tenure
as the British had done, for example, when Fiji became a
crown colony in 1874.[20] Most of the lands still owned in
whole or in part by Hawaiians — and these lands are not of
much importance — are administered by trust companies
(controlled by the Big Five) for fees which have been
described as exorbitant.[21] Today 90 per cent of the cultivated
lands are devoted to sugar cane and pineapples and approximately 65 per cent of the working population is employed,
in one way or another, in connection with these two crops.
Virtually no attempt has ever been made, under the Republic
or under American rule, to rehabilitate the native population.
According to Joseph Barber, the death rate among native
Hawaiians is twice as high as the national average; their birth
rate is well below the average; and their infant mortality rate

[18] Pratt, *op. cit.*, p. 267.
[19] *An Island Community*, by Andrew W. Lind, 1938, p. 94.
[20] See *Fijian Frontier*, by Laura Thompson, 1940.
[21] *Hawaii: Restless Rampart*, by Joseph Barber, Jr., 1941, p. 239.

is eight times the national average. For the most part, the natives have been pushed into marginal economic occupations. "Few dollars pass through their hands," writes Mr. Barber; "indeed they, more than any other island group, are responsible for the fact that the average per capita effective buying income of Hawaii is less than $275 — lower than all but three or four states in the Union." [22]

With the expansion of the plantation system, the demand for workers greatly increased and the constant importation of contract laborers placed the native Hawaiians at a hopeless competitive disadvantage. In 1850, non-Hawaiians constituted only 2 per cent of the population but the proportion increased to 10 per cent in 1872; to 45 per cent in 1884; to 86 per cent in 1930. From 1850 to 1930 the planters spent more than $20,000,000 in the importation of upwards of 400,000 workers. Numbers alone do not suggest the impact of this immigration on the native population. Prior to annexation, for example, plantation workers were held in semi-feudal bondage and could not breach their contracts of employment. Against the competition offered by this semi-slave labor, the native Hawaiians were at as great a disadvantage as the "poor whites" were in their competition with Negro slave labor prior to the Civil War.

The Chinese were the first to be imported to Hawaii. Prior to annexation, when the Chinese Exclusion Act became effective in Hawaii, some 46,000 Chinese workers had been imported of whom about 8000 were "refugees" from the anti-Oriental crusades in California. Today there are about 28,380 Chinese in the islands, 84.91 per cent of whom are American citizens. As rapidly as their labor contracts expired, the Chinese left the plantations and moved into the towns and cities where they became active in small retail trade, repeating the pattern of their employment in the Philippines, Singapore, and the Malay Peninsula. By 1939, only 674

[22] *Ibid.*, p. 237.

Chinese were to be found as plantation workers. There is, of course, a large Chinese-Hawaiian population since many of the Chinese, coming to the islands as single men, married Hawaiian women. Today about 71 per cent of the Chinese are concentrated in Honolulu. According to Dr. Lind about 74 per cent of all of Honolulu's Chinese were concentrated in 1866 in a restricted Chinatown area; seventy years later most of the Chinese in Honolulu were still living within an area, half a mile square, which included the old Chinatown. Over a comparable period of residence in San Francisco, the Chinese have not achieved a much wider or more typical geographical distribution. The Chinese were imported to Hawaii, for the most part, in the period from 1852 to 1900.

In an effort to recruit immigrants who were "racially cognate" with the Hawaiians, the sugar planters ranged far afield. From 1868 to 1885, they imported about 2400 South Sea Islanders but this labor source was soon abandoned as unsatisfactory. Then from 1878 to 1886, the planters imported some 17,500 Portuguese, principally dark-skinned immigrants from the Azores and Madeira. From 1906 to 1913 approximately 8000 Spaniards were imported, most of whom subsequently moved on to California. Once the Philippines and Puerto Rico were taken over by the United States, the planters were able to tap the very large labor pools in these outlying possessions which were not walled off by immigration restrictions. The Gentlemen's Agreement of 1907 and the Immigration Act of 1924 greatly stimulated the importation of Filipinos of whom more than 120,000 were imported from 1906 to 1930.

In recruiting labor the planters were guided by a sense of strategy as well as by mere opportunism and expediency. As William C. Smith has pointed out: "The planters guarded well their interests lest they lose control. When the large influx of Chinese in the early days of sugar production endangered the scheme, they brought Portuguese and Japanese to checkmate them; and later, when the Japanese became dangerously numerous, they relieved the tension by the importation of Koreans, Puerto Ricans, Spanish, and more Portuguese." [23] The planters' strategy was not merely to play one group against another but to maintain a permanent minority population in the islands, for the "assimilation" of the plantation workers would have been against the primary interests of the planters. In a plantation system, as Oliver Cox has demonstrated, the assimilated worker is either lost to the plantation owner or becomes intractable.[24] In Hawaii the working out of this strategy is most clearly revealed in the case of the Japanese.

The first Japanese who came to the islands were 147 workers who were kidnaped or "piratically stolen" in 1868. As a result of official protests, these workers were returned to Japan. The Reciprocity Treaty of 1876, which opened the islands to American capital, also led to the Hawaiian-Japanese Labor Convention of 1886, which, for the first time, lowered the barriers to Japanese emigration. The agreement, coming in the wake of the Chinese Exclusion Act of 1882, provided for the importation of Japanese contract laborers for a term of three years, at wages of nine dollars a month and a food allowance of six dollars per month. Under the terms of this agreement approximately 180,000 Japanese were imported to Hawaii. Thus it was, as Dr. Lind points out, "that the same events which opened wider doors for the importation of American capital and Japanese labor to Hawaii also brought to a clearer focus the role which each of these emerging powers was to play in the Pacific for decades to come." [25]

When further Japanese immigration to Hawaii was suspended in 1907, the resident Japanese entered strenuous protests. The restriction, they contended, left them at the mercy of their employers since it condemned them to the status of

---

[23] *Annals of the American Academy*, September 1942, p. 42.
[24] *Caste, Class & Race*, by Oliver C. Cox, 1948, p. 418.
[25] Lind, *op. cit.*, p. 15.

a permanent minority. The effect of restriction was to reduce Japanese purchasing power while, at the same time, the sugar interests were left free to engage in still further mass importations of workers who, being more recent immigrants, would be employed at wage levels which would undermine the status of the Japanese. In May 1909, 7000 Japanese workers walked out of the plantations on Oahu but the strike was broken and the planters then began to recruit Filipino labor on a large scale. In 1919 the Japanese called a second strike, this time in conjunction with the Filipino Laborers Association. The planters promptly evicted 12,000 strikers from plantation cottages and dormitories. The strike was finally broken when the Filipinos, under Pablo Manlapit, returned to work. The planters spent more than $12,000,000, in this strike, in breaking the resistance of the Japanese.

The 1940 census returned 153,539 Japanese for the islands, 37.31 per cent of the total population, of whom 116,584 were citizens (73.93 per cent of the total). Like the Chinese, the Japanese have largely left the plantations, but 13,460 were still so employed in 1939. Of the number originally imported to the islands, about 40,000 moved on to California as soon as their contracts of employment expired. To appreciate the position in which the Japanese found themselves after the disastrous strikes of 1909 and 1919, it is important to keep in mind that the economy of Hawaii was then, and is still largely, controlled by one of the tightest economic oligarchies in the world. The Big Five — American Factors, C. Brewer & Company, Ltd., Alexander & Baldwin, Castle and Cook, Ltd., and T. C. Davies & Co., Ltd. — act as factors for all but three of the sugar companies and have substantial stock holdings in these companies; together they control about 96 per cent of island sugar production.[26] In addition the Big Five have holdings in public utilities, docks, shipping companies, banks, hotels, department stores, the wholesale businesses; and their

[26] *Hawaii: A History,* by Ralph S. Kuykendall and A. Grove Day, 1948.

influence ramifies outward through a complex system of inter-locking directorates, trusteeships, and family holdings. Thus the insubordinate Japanese, who had been "evicted" from the plantations, found themselves in this predicament: they were being rapidly replaced as plantation workers and, at the same time, the oligarchy blocked their entry into general commer-cial activity or small-scale farming.

Hedged in on all sides, the Japanese turned to the small re-tail trade where they encountered little opposition. So far as the Big Five were concerned, as John Williams has pointed out, "the retail market was chicken feed anyhow, compared with the wholesale agencies. The Hawaiian capitalists sewed up every agency by interlocking directorates of practically every company in Hawaii. The capitalists weren't worried overmuch about the expanding Japanese retailers; after all, the capitalists were in Hawaii to make fortunes." [27] Prior to Pearl Harbor, the Japanese constituted 56 per cent of the servants and personal attendants; 53 per cent of the fishermen; 43 per cent of those in manufacturing and mechanical trades; 42 per cent of the tradesmen and storekeepers; and 23 per cent of the small truck farmers in the islands.[28] In a sense, therefore, the Japanese in Hawaii have come to occupy much the same position in relation to the Anglo-Americans that Japan now occupies in relation to the United States; the American strat-egy of racial dominance was successful both locally and nationally.

Similarly the Filipinos in Hawaii have come to occupy much the same position in relation to the *haoles* that the Philippine Islands occupy in the American economic system. Subsequent to 1906, about 120,000 Filipinos were brought to Hawaii; later some returned to the Philippines and others moved on to Cali-fornia. In 1940 there were about 52,810 Filipinos in Hawaii,

[27] See series of articles by John Williams, *PM*, August 3, 4, 5, 6, and 10, 1941; particularly August 10, 1941.
[28] Barber, *op. cit.*, p. 136.

of whom 16,201 were American citizens. Used as strike-breakers against the Japanese, the Filipinos were initiated into the economics of imperialism in 1924 when, again under the leadership of Pablo Manlapit, they struck most of the Hawaiian sugar plantations. The strike lasted eight months and was characterized by great violence; four policemen and sixteen strikers were killed and the National Guard was called out to maintain "law and order." But the strike was broken and for thirteen years "peace" prevailed on the plantations. Manlapit returned for a time in 1937 but was soon banished from the islands.

As the most recent immigrant group in the islands, the Filipinos make up, of course, the mainstay of the plantation labor force: 43,170 are listed as plantation employees. Although a large minority, the Filipinos have never formed a compact community in the islands, perhaps because their native culture lacks integration. "There is a lack," writes Roman R. Cariaga, "of any principle of organization among the Hawaiian Filipinos powerful enough to knit them together in larger wholes." [29] Tagalogs quarrel with Visayans and Visayans war with Illocanos. "Disputes occur between factions and their leaders. Often organizations with the same objectives compete, as it would seem, unnecessarily." Organizations spring up like mushrooms and disappear almost as quickly. "Being highly disorganized, the struggle for social position in the Filipino community is intense. When an individual rises, the others endeavor to pull him down." Mr. Cariaga sums up the Filipinos' problem in this way: "Hawaii for most Filipinos of the immigrant generation is at present a half-world, a mechanical existence as a means toward an end, money, which will bring social prestige upon return to the

---

[29] *The Filipinos in Hawaii*, by Roman R. Cariaga, 1937; also see *Filipino Plantation Workers in Hawaii*, by Edna Clark Wentworth, 1941; *Labor in the Territory of Hawaii*, by James H. Shoemaker, 1936; and report by Henry A. Rudin, for sixteen years Welfare Director of Waialua Plantation, in the *Voice of Labor*, August 17, 1936.

ancestral area" — a social prestige which is all the more seductive because of the Filipinos' failure to achieve prestige in Hawaii. At the same time, the dream of a triumphant return to the Philippines keeps the Filipinos in Hawaii since they dare not return unless it be in splendor. However a new generation of Hawaiian-born Filipinos is now emerging: in 1930 there were 11,217 Filipino children in the islands under fifteen years of age. As this generation reaches maturity, a new chapter is being written in the experience of the Filipinos in Hawaii.

In addition to the group mentioned, other "importees" have been brought to Hawaii. Between 1909 and 1912, the Bureau of Immigration of Hawaii, at a public expense of $178,000, imported 2056 Russians from Manchuria. There are also approximately 6707 Koreans, of whom 4355 are citizens, and a Puerto Rican population of 7639, all of whom are citizens. And lastly there are the important mixed blood groups: 20,507 Caucasian-Hawaiians, all of whom are citizens; and 20,360 Asiatic-Hawaiians, all of whom are also citizens. Then there are some 21,268 native Hawaiians. The Hawaiians and part-Hawaiians increased 26.4 per cent from 1930 to 1940: from 50,860 to 64,310. Through intermarriage with imported stocks the native Hawaiians have managed to survive and now seem to be increasing. The combined Caucasian population remained almost exactly one fifth of the total population for two decades prior to 1940 but the mixed blood groups have continued to expand. "The neo-Hawaiian amalgam of Polynesian and foreign stocks," notes Dr. Lind, "seems destined finally to inherit the earth."

## 3. Racial Aloha

The various races making up the population of the Hawaiian Islands are now in process of becoming one people.[30] The base of the population pyramid is made up nowadays, of course, of

[30] The American Empire, 1940, p. 393.

the mixed or hybrid groups who constitute a new American type. In this respect what is happening in Hawaii reflects what has been happening generally around the rim of the Pacific. Despite the barriers which have been raised, millions of Orientals have migrated from the lands of their birth to other lands in the Pacific; for example, nearly 10,000,000 Chinese are now living in Java, the Philippines, French Indo-China, and parts of Oceania. Around the rim of the Pacific, too, may be found a large Eurasian population. In these areas as in Hawaii the "mixed" or hybrid groups may well come to be the means by which larger groups are linked together.

Wherever buffer groups of this kind are to be found — that is, where there have been no official bars to intermarriage — the uglier aspects of majority dominance are likely to be minimized and, in the long run, majority domination is likely to disintegrate. Intermarriage has never been barred in Hawaii and the official mores tend to be the mores of racial equality.[31] Historically the absence of taboos on intermarriage is an aspect of the insular position of Hawaii: the remoteness of the islands from the principal sources of labor supply made intermarriage desirable as a matter of policy. With the native peoples in possession of rich resources which the small invading minority was determined to possess, intermarriage also became an important part of the strategy of dominance. And once a mixed or intermediate group had come into existence, it became increasingly difficult to erect the barriers to intermarriage which might have produced a caste system.

Hawaii is of great interest in the study of race relations for the primary reason that race relations there assume their "pure" form — namely, class relations. In Hawaii the race problem is a labor problem; and, conversely, the labor problem is a race problem.[32] The fusion of race and class is so perfect that there is no mistaking the class basis of so-called race

[31] *When Peoples Meet*, 1942, p. 257.
[32] *Fortune*, August 1940.

relations. One reason for Hawaii's "mores of equality" is simply that the economic dominance of the Caucasians is so clearcut and decisive that non-Caucasians do not directly compete with Caucasians. The Caucasians can tolerate intermarriage and a large degree of racial *aloha* since their dominance cannot be disputed. Had there been a "poor white" element in the islands, in direct competition with non-Caucasians, uglier techniques of dominance would almost certainly have been used. William C. Smith points up the exceptional aspect of the Hawaiian racial pattern when he writes that "in the paternalistic system of the sugar plantations, the workers, mostly Orientals, have occupied a position so inferior to that of *all* white men, that there has been no competition between the two groups." [33]

In the past, a kind of racial *aloha* could be tolerated in Hawaii because of the absence of a strong labor movement. For the absence of such a movement, there are many obvious explanations: most of the workers who were first recruited came to the island under contracts of employment which could be enforced in the courts; the insularity of Hawaii made it almost impossible to secure alternative employment; and the craft unions, never too strong, traditionally excluded Orientals. Underlying all these reasons, however, was the adamant opposition of the Big Five to all forms of trade-unionism so far as plantation workers were concerned. Thus where strikes occurred in the past they were usually organized on racial lines which, in the peculiarly clear social atmosphere of Hawaii, were quite unambiguously class lines. Language and culture differences among the plantation workers actually served to unite the various racial and culture groupings, as in the strike of Japanese workers against Caucasian plantation owners. At the same time, the tendency of industrial conflicts to fuse with racial demarcations tended to weaken labor's solidarity by

[33] *Americans in Process*, by William C. Smith, 1937, p. 114, emphasis added.

preventing a general unification of the labor movement.

"When race relations in Hawaii are examined with care," writes Mr. Smith, "a paradoxical situation becomes evident. It is a matter of tradition and principle that there is or should be no prejudice. That is a doctrine to which the leading spokesmen of the Territory subscribe, and practically all members of the community feel bound to maintain it. Race equality is visible on every hand — in the freedom of intermarriage, in the absence of legal segregation in school or in residential areas, and in the ease with which members of the different races mingle at various social functions. Beneath this apparently calm surface, however, are found inequality, discrimination, prejudice, cynicism, and bitterness. The plantation system, in spite of the doctrine of race equality, has manipulated the importation of laborers from the several sources so that a small group of white Americans are in control not only of the sugar industry but of all aspects of life in the Territory. Much is said about the educational opportunities in the islands, and the young people are urged to use them in order to become good Americans. They are told about the 'room at the top' that is open to all on an equal basis. The children go through the schools and even through the university looking forward to the days when they will play important roles in the further unfolding of the great American epic. . . . Many, however, are awakened quite rudely from their dreams when, with diplomas in hand, they seek employment. Then they find barriers, some of them very subtle, to be sure, while their Caucasian classmates, protected by vested rights, move unopposed into preferred positions. This disillusionment has brought mutation in the attitudes of many of the Hawaiian-born sons and daughters of Oriental ancestry, 'from one of unquestioning endorsement of the existing order to one of complete rejection of their former loyalties.' " [34]

[34] "Minority Groups in Hawaii," by William C. Smith, *Annals of the American Academy,* September 1942, p. 43.

The situation described by Mr. Smith prompted Mr. Walter Dillingham, one of the island nabobs, to observe some years ago, and with prophetic insight, that "our troubles are ahead of us." Sooner or later it was inevitable that a younger generation would emerge, made up of various racial elements but all products of unsegregated public schools, which would not be content with the status of their immigrant parents. World War II delayed this protest but with the younger Oriental groups now coming into direct competition with "whites" for the better paid jobs and professional opportunities, and also demanding better pay for their customary jobs, racial feeling has come to the surface.

On September 1, 1946, the International Longshoremen's and Warehousemen's Union called out some 28,000 workers on 33 plantations and tied up the island's economy in what amounted to a general strike. In this strike, the solidarity of non-Caucasians against Caucasians became the solidarity of labor against the employers of labor. With this backing the union won a sweeping victory: the perquisite system was abolished; the plantations agreed to pay $10,500,000 a year in wage increases in lieu of these facilities; and minimum wage rates of 70.5 cents an hour were established. In the wake of the strike, 35 of 51 CIO–PAC endorsed candidates were elected to public office in Hawaii. Thus the insularity which employers had so long used against labor was now turned to labor's advantage. Again in 1949 the heterogeneous elements making up the ILWU won a spectacular victory in the islands. In this viciously contested strike, the population divided sharply on racial and class lines. Indeed the demarcation was so clear-cut and precise that the union was accused of fomenting racial hatred by simply appealing to the workers on class lines.[35] The pretense that racial prejudice does not exist in the islands was dispelled overnight.

[35] See stories by Kyle Palmer, *Los Angeles Times*, July 17, 18, 19, 20, 1949, particularly story of July 19, 1949, "Race Hate Fanned in Hawaiian Strike."

The manner in which the racial issue has become the economic issue, and the latter the former, is clearly revealed in the struggle for statehood. In the past, the main objection to statehood was always premised on misgivings about "the racial composition" of the islands. In the new world situation, however, this objection can no longer be voiced with quite the same directness and candor that it was once voiced. After the 1946 strike, and more clearly after the 1949 strike, the objection to statehood shifted from a racial to an economic basis; Communism rather than Racism became the main issue. Today the unity of non-Caucasians against Caucasians in the islands suggests, in a limited way, the problem that America now faces throughout the Far East: an Oriental hostility that is economic, not racial, but which tends to find expression as race feeling. It should be noted, however, that statehood for Hawaii has been held up, of recent years, by the Southern contingent in Congress on racial grounds. "The Southern bloc opposes Hawaii and Alaska as states," reports the *Los Angeles Mirror* of October 14, 1950, "because it fears that new Senators would vote for civil rights legislation."

The question which Mr. Smith posed long before the 1946 strike is still the pertinent question about Hawaii:

Will the white man in Hawaii be able to rub the sugar out of his eyes so that he can see things as they are? Will he be able to change a surface friendliness and show of equality into something which is real and genuine? Can the white man of America learn from the recent experiences of the white man in Burma and in India?

# CHAPTER VI

## Puerto Ricans and Other Islanders

MAINLAND Americans can be divided into two groups: those who know that 2,100,000 American citizens reside in Puerto Rico; and those — perhaps a majority — who remain unaware of this fact fifty years after the war with Spain. Most of those who know of the existence of these island Americans have a feeling that the United States merely added another dimension to "the racial problem" when General Nelson A. Miles, who had just liquidated the Indian remnant at the Battle of Wounded Knee in 1890, decided to seize Puerto Rico to keep the Navy from monopolizing the headlines. It has never occurred, even to these knowing ones, that the seizure of Puerto Rico was an outgrowth of our domestic racial dilemma.

Puerto Rico, of course, was not in the public thought when the "popular sentimental crusade" was launched against Spain. Cuba was our main preoccupation, sentimental and strategic, and the seizure of Puerto Rico was merely an incident of guarding Cuba's independence. The seizure of Puerto Rico was a bloodless and innocent affair: the Puerto Ricans cheered lustily; the Americans were greeted as liberators; and — suddenly — we found ourselves in possession of a beautiful Caribbean island, about the size of Connecticut, with nearly a million inhabitants. Puerto Rico was an afterthought or by-product of the war with Spain; the war really stemmed from our long-standing interest in Cuba but this interest was intimately related to "the Negro problem" in the United States.

## 1. Cuba and the Golden Circle

In 1841 Negro slaves outnumbered "whites" in Cuba: 436,-
000 to 418,000, not counting 153,000 free Negroes. For years
the Spanish had kept the Creole sugar planters in line by re-
minding them that it was Cuba's destiny to be Spanish or
"African" but never Creole dominated. The Negroes, free and
slave, were more loyal to the Spanish, who had imported them,
than to the Creoles who had grown rich exploiting them. In
1823 Spain's Royal Minister had told the American diplomatic
representative: "The fear the Cubans have of negroes is the
best weapon Spain has to guarantee its domination in that
island." [1] And to keep Creoles intimidated, the Spanish kept
importing more and more Negroes. From an early date, therefore, the Creoles came to think that the annexation of Cuba
by the United States — because of the slave empire in the
South — would protect them against Negro domination and
the possible loss of their slaves. At the same time, "the fate of
slavery in Cuba was of intense concern to Americans because
it was thought to be intimately associated with the fate of that
institution in the United States." [2] In 1822 John Quincy Adams
noted in his diary the two principal dangers which Cuba presented to us: it might fall into the hands of the British or it
might be "revolutionized by the niggers." Noting the domestic
reverberations of an abortive Negro insurrection in Cuba in
1844, John C. Calhoun, who was then Secretary of State, concluded that a liberation movement in Cuba would instantly
imperil the institution of slavery in the United States.

From 1822 to 1844 the United States was simply "worried,"
in a vague way, about Cuba; but as the domestic tension over
slavery increased some bright minds of the Young American
Movement evolved the brilliant notion that the annexation of

[1] *The Crime of Cuba*, by Carleton Beals, 1933, p. 99.
[2] *American Interest in Cuba: 1848–1855*, by Basil Rauch, 1948, p. 35.

Cuba might be used as a means of "solving" the issue of slavery in the United States. Interestingly enough, the chief instigator of this theory was John L. O'Sullivan, the New York politician who first used the phrase "manifest destiny," in 1845. And it must be admitted that O'Sullivan had a clever argument: annexation of Cuba would appease the South since it would provide an outlet for the expansion of the plantation system and thereby secure the institution of slavery; it would also be acceptable to the North since it would relieve the tension over Kansas and Nebraska and divert the planters from the free-soil states; and, finally, it could be made morally acceptable to the Abolitionists by throwing in, as a sop to them, a promise that the slave trade between Africa and Cuba would be stopped.

For two decades O'Sullivan tried to sell this "solution" of the slave issue, and on several occasions he nearly succeeded. During these decades Cuba was a major political issue in this country; annexationist intrigue was rife; filibustering expeditions were organized with the implied backing of American Presidents; and in 1854 three American diplomats issued the famous Ostend Manifesto which was intended as a kind of "trial balloon" for O'Sullivan's proposal. The Southern planters consistently clamored for annexation since they had a mortal fear of "free negroism . . . an unsightly, putrifying plague-spot that will some day be wiped out with a vengeance." [3]

The real dynamic behind the South's imperialism, however, was not the fear of "free negroism" in Cuba: the slave system simply had to expand in order to survive. Slavery was based on cotton and cotton, it was said, "exhausted the soil." But it was actually slavery, not cotton, that exhausted the soil. As Eric Williams has demonstrated, Negro slave labor could only be maintained in subjection by systematic degradation and "by deliberate efforts to suppress its intelligence." Rotation

[3] *Ibid.*, p. 189.

of crops and diversified farming were, therefore, "alien to slave societies." [4] The cotton planter was a "land-killer" through necessity: he exploited the land because he exploited the slaves and to hold his slaves he had to have fertile lands to exploit. The greatest economic defect of slavery consisted precisely in the fact that it exhausted the soil. "Expansion," writes Williams, "is a necessity of slave societies."

Thus it was that by 1854, or earlier, a real crisis had arisen *within* the slave system since the possibilities of continental expansion had been nearly exhausted. Cotton could not be grown in Kansas or Nebraska, or — so it was then thought — in California or New Mexico; and in southern Texas the presence of cheap Mexican labor blocked the introduction of slave labor. At the same time the planters realized that they were caught in a race against falling cotton prices and rising slave costs. In 1800 slaves brought on the average around $300 and cotton sold for 25 cents a pound; but by 1845 the ratio was $600 for a slave, and 5 cents for a pound of cotton. The planters could not see that the fall in the price of cotton had been caused by increased production; as they saw it the cotton empire was threatened simply because it could not expand. Their solution was "a golden circle empire," based on slave labor and "military ideas," which would include the Southern states, Mexico, Central America, and Cuba.[5] And in the North there were those who agreed with Stephen A. Douglas that the South should be encouraged to expand in this direction as a means of keeping the Southern states in the Union.

It was in this manner that the United States first became interested in Cuba and that the first annexation schemes were projected. The real test came on the eve of the Civil War when President Buchanan tried to revive interest in O'Sullivan's scheme as a means of diverting public attention from the issue of slavery. But by then the public's attention was riveted

[4] *Capitalism & Slavery*, by Eric Williams, 1944, p. 7.
[5] Rauch, *op. cit.*, p. 207.

on the Lincoln-Douglas debates in which Cuba figured as a major gambit. Douglas, for example, insisted that the crisis could be resolved by permitting the South to expand in Cuba: "When we get Cuba we must take it as we find it, leaving the people to decide the issue of slavery." On the other hand, Lincoln insisted that the North could no longer compromise since any further yielding would only result in a demand that we annex Cuba as a condition to the South's remaining in the Union — a price which he was not willing to pay. The only way to settle the issue of slavery, he said, was to prohibit further territorial expansion. And with his election, the annexation plans were defeated — for the time being.

As a matter of fact we might never have become involved in a war with Spain if it had not been for the Compromise of 1876, that is, if we had really destroyed the plantation system in the South. When the "ten-year" revolution broke out in Cuba in 1868 — a revolution which had been stimulated by the Emancipation Proclamation — the same elements that later worked out the Compromise of 1876 quickly shied away from a revolution in which the Negro masses of Cuba participated. Almost every Latin-American country favored the revolutionists and gave them aid; but powerful business and economic interests in the United States supported the Spanish since they feared the consequences should the revolution succeed. And when the final war for Cuba's liberation began in 1895, these same interests shared the theory of the frightened Spaniards and the wealthy Creoles that the revolution was "a war of negroes against whites." [6] Later, when it came to setting up an occupation government in Cuba, we "turned chiefly to the Tories, the respectable Cubans," the people who had looked with apprehension upon a free Cuba. The Negro lodges and other cultural activities were promptly prohibited and we favored the white Creoles in every way, setting up social barriers to protect their privileges and making them partners in

[6] Beals, *op. cit.*, p. 95.

the economic exploitation of Cuban resources.[7] Henry Watterson expressed the dominant point of view when he said that, in Cuba, we wanted nothing to do with "riff-raff; injin, nigger, beggar-man, thief — 'both mongrel, puppy, whelp and hound, and cur of low degree,' " while General S. B. M. Young suddenly discovered that the real Cuban patriots were "a lot of degenerates, absolutely devoid of humor or gratitude . . . no more capable of self-government than the savage of Africa." And Governor General Leonard Wood pointed out that our mission in Cuba was to build up a republic "by Anglo-Saxons in a Latin country." The mischievous Platt amendment, by which we reserved the right to intervene in Cuba, was simply the counterpart of the Compromise of 1876. Carleton Beals, for example, has pointed out, and proved, that our policy in Cuba was "half hypocritical, half idealistic"; and that it "led us to found a pseudo-Republic, half free, half enslaved." But this might just as well have been said of our policy in the South. In short, we aborted the Cuban revolution as we aborted the social revolution which was implicit in the issues the Civil War was supposed to have settled.[8]

The relation of Cuba to "the Negro problem," however, is even closer than this brief outline implies. Why, for example, had the American people refused for nearly three decades to be swept into the current of a "war of liberation" against Spain only to succumb to this agitation in 1898? Walter Millis, Julius Pratt, and Carleton Beals are all agreed that popular feeling actually precipitated the war with Spain, whatever the underlying causes may have been. It should be noted that the earlier campaign to annex Cuba, which had been rejected by the American people, had been advocated as a means of consolidating the slave power; such an issue could not unite the American people despite the cleverness of the argument. But the subsequent campaign, projected as a means of helping

[7] *Ibid.*, p. 61.
[8] *Ibid.*, p. 115.

Cubans win their independence, promptly appealed to the American dedication to freedom and liberty. The liberation of Cuba seemed to be, as Mark Twain said, "the American game" — which he defined as freedom — but it turned out to be the path to empire.

## 2. Pride without Prejudice

When Columbus discovered the island of Puerto Rico it was inhabited by about 30,000 Indians, but fifty years later the Indians had largely disappeared. Had the Indians been more useful as slaves, they might have survived; but the Spaniards soon discovered that one Negro was worth four Indians, as a slave, and so they began to steal Negroes in Africa to work lands stolen from Indians in America.[9] Today a few Indian culture traits survive and there is doubtless a strain of Indian blood in the Puerto Rican peasantry; otherwise the Indian heritage has entirely disappeared.

Negro slaves were imported to Puerto Rico for three centuries, beginning in 1511, but the percentage of Negroes was never as high as in the Caribbean islands where the plantation system was dominant. Puerto Rico was really a white garrison, not a plantation; the plantation system developed relatively late and sugar did not dominate the island's economy until after the American conquest. In the Caribbean, as Eric Williams has pointed out, the rule has always been: "no sugar, no Negroes." Where the sugar plantation was dominant, as in the Virgin Islands, Haiti, and the British, French, and Netherlands possessions, there the Negroes were likely to be in a majority; but where the small tobacco farm prevailed, as it did to a degree in Puerto Rico, Cuba, and the Dominican Republic, the population was "lighter."[10]

Even so the percentage of Negroes and the degree of racial

[9] Williams, *op. cit.*, p. 9.
[10] "Race Relations in Puerto Rico and the Virgin Islands," by Eric Williams, *Foreign Affairs*, January 1945.

intermixture have always been higher in Puerto Rico than the natives care to admit. When slavery was abolished in 1873, some 29,229 slaves were freed but the "colored" population was then estimated at 250,000. As these figures indicate, slavery had already been largely abandoned; in fact the Puerto Rican slave owners had themselves petitioned for the abolition of slavery. In the absence of sugar plantations, slavery had little meaning and liberal "racial" attitudes prevailed. For example, mulatto children were admitted to "white" schools in Puerto Rico six years before the Declaration of Independence was signed, and slave revolts, common in many of the islands in the West Indies, were almost unknown in Puerto Rico. Slaves often escaped from St. Thomas island to Puerto Rico but few escaped from Puerto Rico to St. Thomas.

When the United States assumed control in Puerto Rico, the population was said to be about equally divided between Negroes and whites, but the 1940 census indicates that the whites made up 76.5 per cent, the Negroes 23.5 per cent, of the population. The implication of a sharp decrease in the Negro element after 1899 flies in the face of all the theoretical evidence and is contradicted by certain known facts.[11] For example, the 1940 census did not recognize the existence of a large mulatto population, yet in 1920 this element had been estimated to be six times greater than the Negro population. On the theoretical side, the refutation is equally clear. For four centuries, whites and Negroes had lived together on a small island under circumstances which favored intermixture. During the first century, there had been twice as many white males as females and, for a variety of reasons, Spanish culture did not place strong taboos on alliances between white men and Negro women. For example, there were never any formal bars to intermarriage; indeed the Church encouraged and sanctioned such marriages.

[11] "The Morality of Race Mixing in Puerto Rico," by Charles Rogler, *Social Forces*, October 1946.

The nature of the island's economy, moreover, strongly favored racial crossing. Poverty is a fine tonic for pride and prejudice and most Puerto Ricans have always been extremely poor. Where three fourths of a population is ill-fed, ill-clothed, and ill-housed, only a few people enjoy a status which is worth protecting by taboos against marriages with members of less privileged groups. Most mixed marriages have taken place in Puerto Rico among lower income groups and these groups have been so thoroughly isolated from the privileged groups, and they have been so numerous, that their relations with the dominant groups have been largely noncompetitive. Hence there has been little sentiment against intermarriage. Intermarriage has also been encouraged by the fact that from 15 to 20 per cent of the marriages have never been formalized. Where a large mixed group appears in a population, and such a group appeared in Puerto Rico at an early date, the subsequent tendency is to quadruple the chances of racial mixing and to improve the mulatto's chances of becoming "racially anonymous."

The existence of a large "mixed population" is what accounts for the absence of lynchings, riots, and racial violence in Puerto Rico. Cases of rape ascribed to race are almost unknown and there is little overt discrimination. Racial differences are generally ignored in shops, theaters, hotels, and public conveyances. Negroes are numerous in the teaching profession and colored youngsters attend the public schools on a base of equality. Legally sanctioned segregation does not exist in any form and the humiliation of Negroes by statute would be unthinkable. All in all, Mr. Luis Muñoz Marín was probably correct when he wrote, some years ago, that "the nearest approach to social equality . . . within the supposedly permanent territory of the United States" is to be found in Puerto Rico.[12] In fact Puerto Rico might be cited as a perfect illustration of the fact that social equality can coexist with racial dis-

[12] *Nation*, April 8, 1925.

crimination and prejudice. Indeed this is the real Puerto Rican paradox.

For despite many eloquent disclaimers, it is quite clear that racial prejudice does exist in Puerto Rico. Mr. Muñoz Marín, for example, points out that a few "discreet instances" of intermarriage can even be noted "in the highest social pinnacles." Would these marriages be few in number or discreetly noted if racial prejudice did not exist? In the course of a chapter devoted to the thesis that prejudice is virtually nonexistent in Puerto Rico, Vincenzo Petrullo notes that "as elsewhere, it happens that most Negroes in Puerto Rico are poor and live close to the soil." [13] Others have also noted a preponderance of Negroes in certain sections of the island and have called attention to the fact that most of Puerto Rico's slum dwellers are Negroes. Yet Negroes have lived on the island for centuries with no bars to intermarriage and little overt discrimination. Mr. Petrullo reveals the answer to the riddle — the Puerto Rican paradox — when he casually observes that "the whites being dominant, the colored element is ignored, much as we ignore the colored peoples in the States, except that the Puerto Ricans are considerably less color conscious."

Now is it really true that Puerto Ricans are less color conscious or is it that they are so intensely conscious of color that they affect no interest in skin color? Several students of race relations in Puerto Rico have pointed out that most Puerto Ricans are extremely reluctant to discuss any aspect of the race problem with Americans.[14] Yet Maxine Gordon found that the speech of Puerto Ricans reflects an awareness of minute variations in skin color: *grifo*, meaning persons of white skin with kinky hair of any color; *jabao*, meaning persons of white skin with blond kinky hair; and *prieto*, meaning "just plain black." On the other hand, "browns" can be *pardo* or

[13] *Puerto Rican Paradox*, by Vincenzo Petrullo, 1947, p. 17.
[14] "Culture Contacts in Puerto Rico," by E. B. Reuter, *American Journal of Sociology*, September 1946.

*moreno* or *trigueño*, indicating different shades. The country people designate as *aguacero* (hard rainfall) those who are very black; *lloviznas* (mild rainfall) those who are medium black; and *opaco* (cloudy) those who are *trigueños bastante oscuro* — that is, persons with kinky hair but not completely dark skin. Miss Gordon also found interesting evidence of the fact that Puerto Ricans are highly conscious of color in some of their popular songs, such as a song with the query: "You may be white, but what kind of white?" or another with the question: "And your grandmother, where is she?" [15]

In New York the Puerto Rican immigrant stresses his Spanish name, his knowledge of Latin-American music and the Spanish language, and his different food habits, all by way of distinguishing himself from the mainland "colored" (much in the way the New Mexico "Spanish Colonial" insists that he is different from the Mexican immigrant). As Miss Gordon points out, this racial ambivalence sets up a many-sided pattern of conflict: (1) between colored New Yorkers and colored Puerto Ricans in competition for white social and economic privileges; (2) between Puerto Ricans, white and colored, and white residents of the mainland who are inclined to regard all Puerto Ricans as colored; and (3) between white and colored Puerto Ricans since the former do not relish being identified with the latter. "The white Puerto Rican," writes Miss Gordon, "withdraws discreetly . . . from the Negro islander. . . . When he visits the mainland, the white Puerto Rican avoids the Puerto Rican 'Harlems' in New York or elsewhere. In the relative immunity of an unknown outsider, he may even divorce himself completely from his fellow *white* Puerto Ricans and identify himself as 'Spanish' or 'Latin,' both terms ambiguous to the average continental. . . . Since the white Puerto Rican is never sure of his status with continentals, he denies relationship to the Negro wherever he finds

[15] "Race Patterns and Prejudice in Puerto Rico," by Maxine W. Gordon, *American Sociological Review*, April 1949.

him: in Puerto Rico, on the continent, in the Caribbean, or elsewhere in Latin-America. More significantly, he denies any tinge of Negro blood he himself may knowingly but secretly possess." [16]

Here, then, is the Puerto Rican racial paradox: the Puerto Rican expresses his prejudice by denying its existence; and he denies its existence either because he can never be quite sure that he is white or because he knows that he is not. Puerto Rico, indeed, provides the proof that not even a large measure of intermarriage will wipe out the consciousness of color *where there is some reason* for this consciousness to survive, that is, some advantage to certain groups. Miss Gordon suggests the nature of this advantage when she refers to the courteous avoidance of racial issues in Puerto Rico as "maneuvers for status." The white Puerto Rican simply does not dare to discriminate overtly against black Puerto Ricans because of the complexities and ambiguities created by the presence of a large mixed group. In the Deep South, by rule of law, a drop of Negro blood is sufficient to mark a person as colored; but in Puerto Rico, as throughout Latin-America, the contrary rule prevails.

In Puerto Rico people dance around the racial issue and, like most dancers, they are extremely polite, but each of them is well aware that the issue is there, even if "unacknowledged and denied." Racial prejudice must be denied in Puerto Rico since the emergence of a pattern of overt discrimination would threaten nearly everyone's standing as "white." The whole complex of racial attitudes in Puerto Rico has been given a special name: "cryptomelanic" — that is, the fear of, and effort to hide, the color problem within one's self. Although this is a social or group phenomenon in Puerto Rico, it is often an acute individual problem in the United States, as with persons who are visibly colored but insist, and have even convinced themselves, that they are white. In both cases the attitude is

[16] *Ibid.*, p. 296.

neurotic. For example, E. B. Reuter noted in Puerto Rico "a common indisposition honestly to face and to admit the unpleasant realities of the social and economic order. The common assertion that there is no racial prejudice expresses a public policy rather than a private reality." [17]

### 3. Our First Colony

As our first colony, Puerto Rico has unique theoretical and historical interest in the field of American race relations. "The slices taken from Mexico," writes Mr. Muñoz Marín, "were empty or more American than Mexican in almost everything but political allegiance; the power exercised over the Philippines is explicitly temporary; Hawaii came as a motley of peoples dominated by an American business and planting group. In Puerto Rico, on the other hand, the Americans acquired for permanent use a rather well-rounded civilization — here for the first time the American people undertook to boss a foreign culture." [18] The difference is really of degree but psychologically it is important since the conscious recognition that a nation holds a colony implies certain obligations which are usually ignored in majority-minority relations. Having once suffered as colonials, we have always insisted that we were opposed to colonial systems and have never recognized, for example, "the Negro problem" as a form of domestic imperialism. In much the same way, we have failed to recognize the peculiar brand of American imperialism which, as Paul Blanshard has said, is "a policy of imperial preference without the imperial label," an imperialism in which currency systems, tariffs, and economic resources take the place of direct permanent political controls.[19] Puerto Rico has always "bothered" the American conscience because it has been so

[17] Reuter, *op. cit.,* p. 98.
[18] *Nation,* April 8, 1925.
[19] *Democracy and Empire in the Caribbean,* by Paul Blanshard, 1947, p. 202.

unmistakably a colony, a possession. "As a noncontiguous possession," writes Richard Pattee, "somewhat distant from the continental land area, Puerto Rico has all the salient features of a fully developed and unified nationality . . . the American colony that has grown up is small and cannot expand in terms of settlers. . . . Puerto Rico is a very different case from Hawaii with its numerous racial groups, the Canal Zone with its preponderantly military emphasis, or the Virgin Islands of limited population and possessed of few marked cultural characteristics. It is also interesting to observe that the situation of Puerto Rico bears little resemblance to that of the Spanish-speaking population of Arizona, New Mexico, or Texas, where isolation, cultural disintegration, and economic considerations have influenced the development of this racial element. . . . There is a compact unit [in Puerto Rico] that is to be found in none of the other areas subject to American rule." [20]

The culture of this colony whose management we took over in such a blundering, unprepared manner was dominantly Spanish "but with peculiar colonial modifications." [21] External communications and contacts had been largely restricted to a Spain which was feudal in composition and medieval in outlook and which became increasingly backward. Isolated by its geographic position and by its political ties from North European contacts, Puerto Rico was little influenced by the Industrial Revolution and its contacts with the United States were less significant than those between Cuba and the United States. The Spaniards owned all the real property and, as Reuter pointed out, "exercised a virtually unrestricted authority in all phases of island life"; Puerto Rico was medieval as well as Spanish in culture. The masses had few possessions and, because of the island's colony status, few economic oppor-

[20] "The Puerto Ricans," by Richard Pattee, *Annals of the American Academy*, September 1942, p. 49.
[21] Reuter, *op. cit.*, p. 94.

tunities. Although the people spoke a Spanish patois, they were largely illiterate and intensely insular: for four centuries the island had been ruled as a colonial dependency.

In many respects, the record of American rule in Puerto Rico is one in which we can take pride: from 1900 to 1925 the island experienced a remarkable economic expansion; many public improvements were installed; the death rate was cut by 50 per cent in half a decade; relatively efficient administrative and judicial systems were established; a sound currency was ordered; and the tempo of social change was amazingly accelerated. "More happened in the first two decades of American life," according to Reuter, "than in the first four centuries of Spanish occupation." Puerto Rico produced twenty times as much wealth in 1950 as in 1898 but about 90 per cent of its trade was with the United States. During the first forty years of American rule, trade with the United States increased tenfold while trade with all other countries increased by only a third. To be sure, the American government has spent more in the island than its present capitalized value — in 1942 the American subsidy was $57,000,000 or $30 per capita — but particular American interests have profited handsomely. In general the period from 1900 to 1925 was one of great optimism: the death rate fell, the birth rate rose, and the population increased from 953,000 to 2,100,000.

But by 1925 the period of expansion was over and, in the meantime, the population had doubled and continued to increase at the rate of about 30,000 a year; 2,000,000 Puerto Ricans were trying to survive on 2,000,000 acres, only half of which were arable. By 1930 the death rate from tuberculosis was reported "higher than in any other civilized country of which we have accurate record"; the infant mortality rate was approximately twice the national average; nearly 90 per cent of the rural population and about 40 per cent of the urban were suffering from hookworm; diarrhea and enteritis were responsible for about 35 per cent of all infant deaths; 40

per cent of the population were illiterate and 80 per cent were unable to speak English; and the population density per square mile was perhaps the highest effective density rate to be found anywhere. Known as "Uncle Sam's Sweatshop," Puerto Rico's annual average per capita income in the late 1920's was $111 — compared with $738 in the United States. With some exaggeration, Reuter could report in 1946 that about all Puerto Ricans had to show for forty years of American rule was three times as much squalor and misery as existed in 1899.

Faced with these unpleasant realities, we proceeded to invent the myth that Puerto Rico seethed with misery because it was "overpopulated"; thus the Puerto Ricans were made to shoulder a responsibility which was really ours. As John Collier has pointed out, the overpopulation theory prompted the conclusion that Puerto Rico's problem is insoluble, for if the birth rate cannot be forced down, and the death rate cannot be deliberately forced up, and large-scale migration is impractical, then what is the solution? [22] The notion that Puerto Rico's problems were due to the Puerto Rican's fondness for large families simply echoed the absentee sugar owners' contention that the economic difficulties of the island were due to the incontrovertible fact that there are more Puerto Ricans than the planters need to take care of their sugar cane. "The problem of colonialism will continue," writes Felix S. Cohen, "so long as Puerto Rican workers are prohibited by the act of Congress in which they have no vote from refining the sugar they grow. The problem . . . would continue even if Puerto Ricans should cease to love their wives, their children, and their country as passionately as they now do." [23]

But the graver consequences of American rule in Puerto Rico appear in those "enduring disharmonies" which, as Reuter observed, "lie at a different level." The conflict in cul-

[22] *America's Colonial Record*, by John Collier, Fabian Publications, Ltd., September 1947.
[23] *News Letter*, Institute of Ethnic Affairs, March 1948.

tures has precipitated in every Puerto Rican personal conflicts which find expression in a larger social disorganization. "The externals of American life were superimposed," wrote Reuter, "the essentials of Western culture have not been assimilated." While the long-range effect of the contact between the two cultures will doubtless be stimulating, the immediate consequence has been emotional dissatisfaction of a degree bordering on social neuroticism. "The state of mind," wrote Reuter, "is one of painful confusion. The Puerto Rican is often divided between his sentiments and his interests: economically, he turns to the United States; sentimentally, he turns to Spain and to Latin America." The more completely mainland influences have penetrated the island — in science, technology, commercial method, and political organization — the more the Puerto Ricans have resented our denial of the one gift at our disposal which we withheld: self-government, self-determination, self-definition. A subordinate people will always resent the culture of the dominant group — even in its beneficial aspects. Thus many of the unfortunate consequences which Reuter attributed to a "conflict of cultures" really should be laid at the door of colonial rule.

Puerto Rico was not a sugar plantation in 1899 but we rapidly converted it into one. Nowadays the sugar industry accounts for 60 per cent of the island's exports, employs 40 per cent of the working population, and accounts for 60 per cent of the freight handled.[24] Yet it is incontestable that the profits of sugar, which derive from the tariff, accrue to about 8000 sugar-cane entrepreneurs. What Fernando Ortiz has written about sugar in Cuba also applies to Puerto Rico: "Sugar goes out — and stays out. . . . Sugar has exercised an almost tyrannical pressure throughout our history, introducing a constant note of oppression and force, without contributing toward the creation of robust institutions such as education, government, and civic responsibility. . . . It was sugar that gave us

[24] *Foreign Affairs*, January 1945, pp. 308–317.

slavery." [25] This statement, however, might be somewhat improved or at least clarified by stating it in reverse: it was slavery that gave the Cubans sugar. The point about the plantation system, of course, is that it provided a means by which labor could be exploited; the sugar plantation, as nearly all historians have emphasized, was an early form of capitalistic enterprise.

How much, then, of the confusion and disorganization which Reuter and others have laid to "the conflict of cultures" was actually due to the fact that, in a wholly unequal power relationship, we asked the Puerto Ricans to assimilate American culture without giving them any real freedom of choice? What we denied them was political and economic freedom: political, because we ruled without their consent; economic, because they had to submit to American economic penetration. An economic survey of the island and its population had been made soon after we took charge in 1899 but the report was ignored. As Mr. Petrullo points out, we built roads which served a military purpose and extended the benefits of the tariff to sugar production and thereby enriched American investors; but we did little to develop local industry, or to reduce transportation costs, or to develop any plan which "might have eased the economic plight of the Puerto Rican people."

The story of Puerto Rico is the story of what happens when a people is denied self-government. Now why were we so hesitant about extending self-government? According to J. Fred Rippy, the expansionists of 1898 hesitated about incorporating Puerto Rico as a territory because "they recoiled from admitting alien races with divergent cultures to the privileges and responsibilities of American citizenship." That this was not the full explanation, however, is shown by the fact that we extended territorial rule in Hawaii but Hawaii, it will be noted, was thoroughly dominated and controlled by *a resident* Anglo-American planter dynasty. If anything the ratio of

[25] *Cuban Counterpoint*, by Fernando Ortiz, 1947, p. 69.

Caucasians to non-Caucasians was higher in Puerto Rico than in Hawaii, so it was not race per se that made the difference. Hawaii was underpopulated and the Americans were already in control of the economy. Being underpopulated, Hawaii could *import* alien workers, highly selected for efficiency, made up mostly of single men, all of which made for a much higher per capita income. Most of the aliens imported, moreover, were "ineligible" to American citizenship. There was this difference too: Hawaii and San Francisco were one thing so far as the growing, refining, and marketing of sugar were concerned. Sugar "goes out" in Hawaii but a larger part returns than in Puerto Rico. In 1940 Puerto Rico's exports were $57.25 per capita and her imports $49.40; for Hawaii the figures were, exports $258.18, imports $271.88. Puerto Rico owned 12.8 motor vehicles per 1000 population; Hawaii 131 per 1000. Sugar played a large part in both island economies but Hawaii had only 500,000 people to feed; it was an important point in transpacific commerce; its rich lived on the island; and it had territorial status. As a matter of fact, Hawaii recruited Puerto Rican labor for a time but because Puerto Rico, unlike Hawaii, had a large Negro population, the practice was soon abandoned.

Hawaii was an off-shore extension of the American frontier; Puerto Rico was an island we annexed without ever really possessing. It seemed logical, therefore, to grant territorial status to Hawaii but we could never quite make up our minds about Puerto Rico. Hence we elected to treat it neither as a colony nor as incorporated territory and to deny it autonomy as well as statehood. All citizens of the Republic of Hawaii became citizens of the United States after annexation; but it was not until World War I that, as part of a calculated bid for Puerto Rican loyalty, we conferred citizenship upon the Puerto Ricans. Thus we created a real anomaly: 2,100,000 American citizens without a voice in Congress — more accurately, without a vote. As the Supreme Court has said, Puerto

Rico "belongs to" but is not "a part of" the United States This was tantamount, of course, to saying that the Puerto Rican was to be regarded as possessing no right which the white American was bound to respect. That we made territories of Alaska and Hawaii, thus indicating that we eventually intended to make states of them, was also due, in part, to the fact that these outlying possessions were not acquired by war or conquest.

Just as "cultural conflict" in Puerto Rico has been aggravated by economic conflict, so both cultural and economic conflicts have been aggravated by American race prejudice. It is Paul Blanshard's belief that the virtues of American policy in the Caribbean have been largely canceled "by one cardinal American sin, racial discrimination." [26] There can hardly be any doubt that overt racial discrimination has begun to develop in Puerto Rico and that it stems from American rule. The sugar companies, the banks, the airlines, the shipping companies, and the large department stores are all said to practice discrimination in their employment policies. The fact that Puerto Rico adopted a Civil Rights Act in 1943 also indicates that discrimination has become a problem. In the past, legal discrimination has not existed in Puerto Rico for the major reason that racial differences have been subordinate to class differences. According to Mr. Muñoz Marín there are only two classes in Puerto Rico, those who wear neckties and those who don't (in the British West Indies they say "those who wear shoes and those who don't"). Nevertheless racial prejudice antedated the American occupation, exists today, and is now assuming overt expression.[27]

Reuter found, for example, that Puerto Rican cultural contacts resulted in a type of mental confusion and inconsistent personality structure which in turn found expression ". . . in an undefined and inchoate condition of discontent,

[26] Blanshard, *op. cit.*, p. 205.
[27] *Foreign Affairs*, January 1945, pp. 308–317.

in an inarticulate nostalgia often for an imaginary past, and in a sentimental concern that may become maudlin about traditional or sacred values that appear to be in danger of being displaced." At a later stage, he noted that this discontent tended to assume *social* forms, that is, "*a more or less typical pattern of minority behavior*" (emphasis added). In other words, the form of the colonial relationship has been *making* a minority of the Puerto Rican population. Eric Williams has reached much the same conclusion by pointing out that the future of race relations in the United States will largely determine the future of race relations in Puerto Rico.[28]

On July 4, 1950, thousands of Puerto Ricans assembled in San Juan to celebrate the signing by President Truman of a law which has been widely heralded as marking the end of fifty years of American colonial rule and as conferring "independence" on Puerto Rico. An examination of this law, however, will show that it is a most amazing document. It does *not* confer territorial status and much less does it confer independence; on the contrary it leaves the fundamental relation between the United States and Puerto Rico unchanged. All that the act does is to give the Puerto Ricans a chance to vote on whether they want a constitution *within the framework of the Organic Act* — that is, local self-government without statehood or independence or territorial status. The following procedure is outlined: Puerto Ricans will first vote on whether they want such a constitution; if a majority say yes, then a constitutional convention will be called. At this convention, the delegates may adopt a constitution to submit to Congress, but the constitution must provide for a Bill of Rights and a republican form of government, *and* it must be *within* the framework of the Organic Act. If Congress then approves this document, the Puerto Ricans will again vote to determine whether it shall be adopted or rejected. If all this happens, however, Puerto Ricans will have no more say about

[28] *Ibid.*

American-Puerto Rican relations than they now have, nor will they have a vote in Congress. To celebrate the adoption of this act as "Puerto Rican Independence" is rank self-deception.

## 4. The Puerto Rican Migrants

Immigration to the mainland from our overseas dependencies greatly increased following World War I, with the greatest net gain being from Puerto Rico, with Hawaii second and the Philippines third. Between 1920 and 1940 the number of Puerto Ricans in the United States doubled, thus creating, for the first time, a gradual realization that "although in a sense citizens of this country, the residents of our island possessions constitute a real racial problem." [29]

Given the economic plight of Puerto Rico, it is not surprising that Puerto Ricans should be interested in coming to the United States. But it has been pointed out that a wholesale emigration of half or a third of the people would not solve Puerto Rico's economic problem, even if such a movement were feasible. [30] The more advanced South American countries have not shown any tendency to encourage immigration from Puerto Rico, and conditions on the neighboring Caribbean islands are, if anything, worse than conditions in Puerto Rico. In 1900, about 5000 Puerto Ricans were recruited for employment in Hawaii but the Negro blood of these workers became a matter of some concern to the sugar planters and further recruitment was stopped. In 1926 some 1500 Puerto Ricans were recruited for employment in the cotton fields of Arizona — an experiment that had a disastrous finale. [31] So, with these avenues closed, the Puerto Ricans began to turn toward New York, and not by accident since many of them

[29] *Races and Ethnic Groups in American Life,* by T. J. Woofter, Jr., 1933.
[30] *The American Empire,* p. 63.
[31] See *Ill Fares the Land,* pp. 79–80.

were colored and feared "racial discrimination which might be encountered" in many areas of the United States.[32]

With foreign immigration curtailed by the Immigration Act of 1924, the needle trades of New York began to look about for new sources of sweatshop labor. An extensive trade was soon worked up with Puerto Rico, in which needlework was "contracted out" to small operators in San Juan, largely on a "homework" basis. A little later, workers began to migrate to New York City, having, of course, a perfect legal right of entry. The actual beginnings of the migration, however, date from 1919 when the insular legislature established an immigration bureau and arranged to send 130 Puerto Ricans to Brooklyn to work in a cordage factory. But the needle trades were primarily responsible for the large migration of the late 1920's: from 1921 to 1930 about 100,000 Puerto Ricans migrated to New York City.[33] More recent studies have estimated the number of Puerto Ricans in New York at between 160,000 and 200,000.[34]

The Puerto Rican migration has, of course, been selective: it has been made up largely of young workers (the median age is around 24.2 years), with a higher percentage of skills represented than among Puerto Ricans generally; with most of the migrants — perhaps 70 per cent — being drawn from the urban communities of San Juan and Ponce. About 43 per cent came before World War II, 22 per cent arrived during the war, and 35 per cent came in the postwar period. Many of the postwar migrants came to New York in so-called "bucket seat" planes at a fare of $72 from San Juan.[35] For the most part the migration has been made up of family groups, with about 4.4 persons per family. Like most immigrants, the Puerto Ricans have been extremely poor and have faced the usual

[32] *The Puerto Rican Migrant in New York City*, by Lawrence R. Chenault, 1938; Part I, Transcript Tolan Committee, p. 116.

[33] Chenault, *op. cit.*, also Tolan Committee Transcript, above.

[34] *New York Times*, June 16, 1948.

[35] *Ibid.*, June 1, August 3, 4, 8, and September 4, 1947.

immigrant problems, including the language handicap. Based on answers given by the immigrants, studies have shown the New York Puerto Ricans to be 63 per cent "white," 5 per cent Negro, 15 per cent mulatto, and 17 per cent *grifo*. These answers, of course, reflect the familiar Puerto Rican evasiveness on the score of racial origin; or, more accurately, their indifference to race and their intense color consciousness. As might be expected, studies made by Dr. Warren Brown have shown that Puerto Ricans in New York are confused and disturbed by racial discrimination.[36] And, as with other immigrant groups, "the Puerto Rican problem" has been greatly exaggerated and the usual folklore has appeared: Puerto Ricans are "highly emotional," prone to use knives, "greatly oversexed," rowdy and boisterous, clannish, hotheaded, diseased, and so on.

Although the Puerto Ricans in New York have doubtless improved their lot by migration, it is quite clear that migration is not an answer to Puerto Rico's problem, which is not overpopulation but colonial status. For example, the Puerto Rican Industrial Development Company has been able to find jobs for 7233 Puerto Ricans in the United States in the last six years but the average addition to the Puerto Rican labor force is something like 22,000 every three years. While Puerto Ricans are "a problem" as permanent residents of New York, they are hailed as "saviors of the crops" when they enter as migratory workers under contract. "Michigan's $14,000,000 Beet Crop Saved by Air Lift of Puerto Ricans," reads a headline in the *New York Times* of June 18, 1950, telling how 5050 workers had been flown in from San Juan to "block and thin" 140,000 acres of sugar beets — here, again, the Puerto Rican's fate is mixed up with sugar. Americans who saw newsreel pictures of the crash of an unchartered plane with a loss of 28 lives were not told that these 28 Puerto Ricans were en route to sugar beet fields in Michigan.

[36] *Ibid.*, November 19, 1949.

As a result of the Puerto Rican migration, nationalist campaigns for Puerto Rican independence have become very much a part of New York City politics. During the trial of Albizu Campos, the Puerto Rican nationalist, some 10,000 Puerto Ricans paraded in Harlem shouting "Free Puerto Rico!" and "Down with Yankee Imperialism!" And it has been said that the decision to let the Puerto Ricans vote on a constitution was in part intended to alienate Vito Marcantonio's Puerto Rican following in New York. But, by a strange perversity, the domestic and overseas phases of American imperialism are still not correlated. The American Negro resents the "colored" Puerto Rican's affectation of Spanish origin; while the "colored" Puerto Rican wants, if possible, to avoid the label of "Negro" in New York. By and large, there has never been much, if any, solidarity between Caribbean Negroes and American Negroes, for the former are more color conscious than race conscious, and the latter unfortunately share many of the prejudices of the white majority.

### 5. Silver and Gold

In the outlying territories and possessions of the United States, including Alaska, Puerto Rico, Hawaii, Samoa, Guam, the Virgin Islands, and the Panama Canal Zone, live upwards of 3,000,000 people — Caucasians, Negroes, Asians, Eskimos, Indians, Polynesians, and Micronesians — most of whom are citizens and over half of whom are "colored." World War II brought these peoples vividly to the attention of mainland citizens for the first time, revealing all the paradoxes and contradictions in our overseas imperialism.

Consider, for example, the anomaly that is the Canal Zone. The Canal Zone is an area ten miles wide, extending five miles on each side of the Canal, from deep water in the Atlantic to deep water in the Pacific, except for the city of Panama on the Pacific and the city of Colón on the Atlantic which are adjacent to the Canal Zone terminals of Balboa and Cristobal. The Canal Zone is something quite special in international law: it is not a territory, possession, colony, protectorate, servitude, mandate, trusteeship or condominium; in fact no one knows how to characterize the zone. Legally it is a kind of military reservation, governed by officials responsible to the Secretary of War; a strip of land over which the Republic of Panama reserves a residuary sovereignty. Whatever else it may be, the Canal Zone is an irritating exhibit of American Jim Crowism in the Caribbean, an exhibit that is all the more insulting by reason of the fact that the Canal was built by Caribbean Negroes and has since been maintained and improved by their labor. Since the Canal is not a territory, the residents have never had the right to vote on any aspect of their lives and only those born there of American parents are regarded as American citizens.

By a tradition extending back to the period of French activity in the Canal Zone, workers have always been divided into two categories: "gold" employees and "silver" employees, now known as "United States rate employees" and "local rate employees." The French brought the first wave of Caribbean Negroes to the Zone in the 1880's and paid them in "silver" which was the currency of the Caribbean; and at differential rates, since it would not do to pay them higher rates than those which prevailed in Panama. The United States failed to change the gold and silver classifications when it took over the Zone in 1904. Paul Blanshard lists three reasons for this failure: the Panama Canal was south of the Mason and Dixon line; there were then no Negro organizations in the United States of sufficient strength and influence to have reversed the ruling; and this, generally, was the period of the Vardamans, the Tillmans, and the Watsons. Whatever the reason, the government institutionalized the gold and silver categories and applied the dichotomy in organizing the social life of the Zone.

Gold employees are those engaged in the skilled trades and in the executive and supervisorial positions; they, of course, are white and most of them are citizens of the United States. The silver category is made up entirely of natives of the tropics, most of whom are Panamanians; they are employed as semiskilled and unskilled workers. For years "gold" and "silver" signs appeared over water fountains, bathrooms, post offices and other public places in the Canal Zone, but the signs were finally removed in 1947 — largely as a result of the invasion of the Canal Zone by a left-wing branch of the CIO Public Workers Union; and, at the same time, the "gold" designation was changed to "U. S. rate employees" and "silver" to "local rate employees." But the system was not changed in any degree.

A policy of racial segregation still prevails throughout the Canal Zone and the policy is rigidly enforced: in residential areas; by occupations; in recreational facilities and in the schools; and in all phases of social life. "Patterns of racial discrimination and social segregation," writes George W. Westerman, "have been official policies of the Canal Zone government from time immemorial." [37] The effect of these policies, of course, has been to stigmatize Panamanians as inferior in their own country. The discrimination, moreover, is comprehensive; it applies to rates of pay, housing, recreational facilities, schools, teachers and teacher salaries, time of payment (every two weeks for gold employees; every month for silver); subsistence schedules when working away from home ($2.25 for the gold, $1.20 for the silver); methods of promotion; types of jobs; sick leaves; retirement schemes; and pensions. By adhering to this policy, we have for forty years advertised the United States throughout the Caribbean as a mean and miserly exploiter of native labor.

The Jim Crow policies of the Canal Zone have also spread

[37] *A Study of Socio-Economic Conflicts on The Panama Canal Zone,* by George W. Westerman, December 1948.

anti-Negro feeling among the Panamanians, who resent our preference for English-speaking black workers from the islands of the Caribbean. The civilian population of the Zone varies from 50,000 to 60,000 workers. In December 1948, 25,848 civilian employees were listed as local rate or silver employees, and 8282 as U. S. rate or gold. It should be emphasized that the Jim Crow policy of the Canal Zone represents official United States policy; no issue of State rights is involved. The policy has real significance in the Caribbean where, as Paul Blanshard has pointed out, a basic causal connection obtains between color, class, and ownership. Neither the dilution of Negro blood through intermarriage nor the relative absence of racial discrimination can obscure the fact that the class system of the Caribbean is color determined: "dark" or black workers at the bottom; a brown or mulatto population in the middle ("the ham in the sandwich"); and white workers on top.

### 6. "White-minded Negroes"

The Virgin Islands — St. Thomas, St. Croix, and St. John — acquired from Denmark in 1917, have a land area of about 85,000 acres and 25,000 population. The population, which is about five sixths "colored," has declined about 50 per cent in the last century. The Virgin Island Negroes, of course, are English-speaking and they are all citizens of the United States. For some years the islands were governed by the Navy but in 1931 a civilian administration was established under the jurisdiction of the Department of Interior, and five years later the residents were given the right to elect local officials. The Virgin Islanders have a legal right of entry to the United States and quite a few have already migrated to the mainland, their positions being taken by Puerto Ricans.

The situation on St. Thomas Island, which has been carefully investigated by Albert A. Campbell,[38] may be taken as typical. St. Thomas is probably the world's most snobbish community: a place where nearly everyone looks down on someone else, with the population being divided into a variety of groups reluctant to associate together. Yet — here again the Caribbean paradox — there is little race prejudice, as such, in the Virgin Islands, including St. Thomas, and little racial discrimination! The answer to this puzzle is that St. Thomas, once the center of a lucrative slave trade, is still largely inhabited by slaves — slaves to custom and history and social delusions.

The Danes, of course, had a real problem with the Virgin Islands: how were they to govern a large Negro slave population on three tiny islands? Islands are prisons but they can also be fortresses and the Danes were aware of all the perils. It was obviously impractical to maintain a large resident white garrison; the islands were profitable but they were not that profitable. So the Danes solved the problem by setting up an ingenious system under which the Negroes obligingly policed themselves. The system, as might be expected, was based on the familiar divide-and-conquer formula. First of all, Negroes were divided into occupational classifications: those who worked in the fields and those who worked as house servants, and the latter became, if they were not originally, somewhat lighter in color than the former. Then Negroes were divided into those born in Africa, who were called "salt-heads" and formed a minority within the slave population, and the native-born. Finally there were the "free" Negroes, a carefully recruited elite, light-skinned, given preferred positions and encouraged to lord it over the others. The divisions just mentioned were largely customary but the Danes also divided the Negroes into two formal divisions or classes. The first division included the ranking officers of the Negro military, the junior

---

[38] *St. Thomas Negroes: A Study of Personality and Culture,* by Albert A. Campbell, Northwestern University, 1943.

Negro officers, and the noncommissioned officers and "free" Negroes. The second division embraced all the other Negroes, the slaves. In this manner the Danes created among the Negroes a morbid preoccupation with social status that penetrated down to the lowest elements in the slave population. And the Negroes, of course, came to associate status not with race but with color, even to the point of wanting to "marry light" and to work for "white" employers. By 1855 distinctions almost as wide as those between whites and Negroes in the Deep South could be observed between blacks and mulattoes, and between *sambos*, *griffs*, and *mustis*, so that no unity whatever existed among the Negroes. The Danes were careful, moreover, to keep the system fairly fluid; that is, they reserved the right to transfer a Negro from one classification to another. The spread of status, and privilege, among St. Thomas Negroes, from lowest to highest, was truly enormous: the entire population was minutely stratified. To call a person "colored" in this society was a mortal offense, since color more than race was a badge of status.

This grotesque social order has survived, almost unchanged, to the present time, despite the fact that the Danes were the first to prohibit the slave traffic (1803) and abolished slavery, as such, in 1848. Today St. Thomas has a population of 11,265: white 1785, Negro 9480. The "colored" population is still highly stratified. At the top are about 100 upper-class Negroes who live in luxury in hilltop homes which overlook the squalor of the Negro working-class quarters. These upper-class Negroes seldom marry "below their color" and even less often below their class. They not only avoid the Negro masses: they look down upon them with great contempt. Then there is a Negro middle class, made up of about 10 per cent of the Negro population, consisting of teachers, minor officials, craftsmen, and grocers. This element frequently uses occupational titles in salutations, as "Mr. Grocer Jones" and "Mr. Lawyer Brown." The middle class also associates color with class and has no enthusiasm whatever for Negro officials or for Negro ministers, preferring to "look up" to those who are lighter in skin color. For example, this element was quite critical when William Hastie was appointed Governor of the Virgin Islands — the first Negro to hold the office.

Below the middle-class Negroes, of course, are the Negro masses, the former slaves, who make up 90 per cent of the island's population. "Their class position," writes Dr. Campbell, "is almost as far removed from that of the privileged minority as were the positions of masters and slaves. Their class-race attitudes reflect the influence of their historical subordination in a highly status-conscious society." With them, "the admiration for all things white is accompanied by a contempt for all things colored." They have a strong awareness of color; little awareness of race; and are lacking in any feeling of solidarity with American Negroes. Some years ago, a small colony of French fishermen moved to St. Thomas from St. Barthelemy, and settled by themselves. *All* the Negroes look down upon these *chacas*, as they are called, and refuse to associate with them; but their attitude is based on class, not race, showing that their keen color consciousness is really class consciousness.

In the past there has been a great deal of social and economic discrimination on St. Thomas Island, based on color as it correlates with class; but there has been almost no racial prejudice or racial discrimination. With American rule, however, some emphasis has been placed on race. American officers in their swimming parties at the beach and their dances at the Grand Hotel have not hesitated to draw the color line, and certain hotels have now begun to cater to the prejudices of tourists, with dining rooms reserved "for tourists only." Most of the white residents look back rather nostalgically at the period when the Navy ruled: "St. Thomas was a charming place under the Navy." That race consciousness, as such, is emerging in the Virgin Islands as in Puerto Rico is shown by the fact that in September 1950 the legislative assembly of the Virgin Islands adopted a civil rights act. Jean Deveaux, reporting adoption of the act in a story in the *New York Times* of October 8, 1950, implies that increased American tourist trade led to its adoption.

### 7. The Pacific Islands

Guam, which we took from Spain in 1898, had a population in 1940 of 22,000, of whom some 21,000 were members of a native Indonesian stock known as Chamorros. Within a year, the United States Navy had succeeded in taking from the Guamanians most of the rights which they had formerly enjoyed under Spanish rule. Although the residents were mostly Roman Catholics, the Navy, traditionally strong on white, Southern, Protestant personnel, exiled all the priests except one and enacted a law prohibiting Roman Catholic religious processions; later the Apostolic Delegate was denied entry to the island.[39] For years a succession of Naval Governors, with a new governor being designated every eighteen months, enacted, repealed, amended, and re-enacted a crazy-quilt pattern of laws, including such items as measures prohibiting the ringing of church bells in the morning and whistling in the vicinity of the Naval Governor's palace. The Navy also prohibited the use of the Chamorro language in the government service or in the schools. According to Mr. Ickes, the Navy even gathered up and burned dictionaries of the Chamorro language and replaced Guamanian native police with Marines. Segregated schools were established for the natives, on whom taxes were levied that were not levied on the resident Navy personnel. However the Navy did prohibit land alienation and kept the white population at a minimum, which relieved some of the pressures on the native population. Although

[39] *News Letter,* Institute of Ethnic Affairs, June 1946.

promised "civil rights" under the Treaty of Paris, the Guamanians began petitioning for these rights in 1902 and the petitions have continued down to the present.

With large areas of Guam damaged by bombardment and not yet rebuilt, the Navy has proceeded to build an 18-hole, 6000-yard golf course with water hazards and sand traps for what Mr. Ickes calls its "class-conscious" officers. In Guam a native carpenter gets 43 cents an hour; a "continental American carpenter" gets $1.36 an hour. The Americans get annual and sick leave with pay, the Guamanians take leave without pay. The American workers get time and a half for overtime; the Guamanians get straight time. It now appears, however, that Guam will finally be given territorial status and a system of self-government similar to that of Alaska, Hawaii, and the Virgin Islands.[40] The Guamanians, most of whom are English-speaking and American in cultural outlook, do not desire statehood; but they do want local self-government. Since the war, something like $25,000,000 a year has been spent on military installations at Guam, converting the little island, twenty-five miles long, ten miles wide, into a tropical island fortress.

American Samoa, with a 1940 population of 12,908, came under American rule voluntarily in 1899, but on the basis of an express understanding that the residents would be given civil status and a rule of law. Yet, as Mr. Ickes points out, "from 1899 to and including today Samoan life has been lived under naval absolutism." [41] A sociable people, the Samoans like to conduct visitations from one village to another on special occasions; these visitations are called *malagas*. On March 8, 1927, the Naval Governor passed a law prohibiting further *malagas* without his approval — which is a fair sample of what military government means. Back in the 1920's, when the natives protested such high-handed action,

[40] *New York Times*, June 25, 1950.
[41] *News Letter*, Institute of Ethnic Affairs, June, 1946.

their leaders were charged with "conspiracy" and arrested. Samoa is what is termed a land of "indefinite political status": it is regarded as a territory; its natives owe allegiance to the American flag; yet it is governed by the United States Navy and might, for all practical purposes, be a battleship. Both in Guam and in Samoa we have made the mistake of assuming that honest, educated, practical Naval officers make good officials to govern native peoples; but there is a wealth of evidence to show that many of these officers have taken a patronizing and condescending, if not a prejudiced, attitude toward the natives.[42]

And since World War II the status of 121,000 people — Japanese, Okinawans, and Koreans — who inhabit the Marshall, Marianas, and Caroline archipelagoes has become a major policy issue. This is the region of Micronesia ("tiny islands"); further to the south is Melanesia ("black islands") and to the west is Polynesia ("many islands"). The natives of Micronesia are of two main types: the Chamorro, who are descendants of western islanders who intermarried with the Spanish and the Filipinos in the sixteenth century; and the *kanaka*, inhabitants of the Caroline and Marshall archipelagoes who did not come under European influence until a later period. Neglected as the natives have been by their various rulers — Spanish, German, Japanese, and American — the average literacy in the Marshalls is said to be that of the American fourth grade. No one knows, of course, what will be done with these islands and their inhabitants; the great issues are, trusteeship vs. annexation, civilian vs. military rule.[43]

[42] See "Americans as Governors of Natives in the Pacific," by John Useem, *Journal of Social Issues*, August 1946.

[43] *News Letter*, Institute of Ethnic Affairs, September 1946.

# CHAPTER VII

## *The Little Brown Brother*

... presently came the
Philippine temptation. It was
strong; it was too strong. ...
It was a pity; it was a great
pity, that error; that one grievous
error, that irrevocable error.
— MARK TWAIN

THE TEMPTATION to seize the Philippines came late in the Spanish-American War since neither Puerto Rico nor the Philippines were "in the range of public thought" when we declared war.[1] Cuba was the main focus of attention and with Cuba the famous Teller amendment ruled out the idea of annexation. The acquisition of Puerto Rico was easily rationalized: the Puerto Ricans regarded us as liberators. "The great difficulty," as Walter Millis has pointed out, "was, of course, the Philippines."[2] Even President McKinley recognized that the Philippines stood upon a different basis. There, unfortunately, Admiral Dewey had permitted Emilio Aguinaldo to proclaim a republic before the American land forces had arrived. It took three years and cost as much in life and effort as the whole war with Spain to suppress the Aguinaldo insurgents. Apart from the cost, however, the insurrection was embarrassing since it complicated the problem of annexation and the Philippines by then were recognized as the largest of "the large constructive opportunities" which the war had presented.

[1] *Emotional Currents in American History*, by J. H. Denison, 1932, p. 240.
[2] *The Martial Spirit*, by Walter Millis, 1931, p. 339.

President McKinley, however, managed to rise to the occasion: "It is none the less true . . . that, without any original thought of complete or even partial acquisition, the presence and success of our arms in Manila imposes upon us obligations . . ." What really tipped the scale was not this ingenious reasoning but the fact that our sense of "mission" was keener in the Philippines than in Cuba or Puerto Rico. For the Philippines were underpopulated and were inhabited not by Creoles or Spaniards, but by "the little brown brother." To this little brown brother we owed a greater obligation than to the Cubans or Puerto Ricans; and, besides, dark-skinned people fell within the scope of the Anglo-Saxon's mission and manifest destiny. Even so, there was a moment when the American people hesitated, when it seemed to be touch and go . . .

## 1. *"To the Person Sitting in Darkness"*

"A popular sentimental crusade," the Spanish-American War was nevertheless opposed by a strong coalition of divergent elements: Gold Democrats, Silver Democrats, Liberal Republicans, Mugwumps, Reformers, and Intellectuals.[3] The opposition, however, was directed not so much to the war as to any notion of territorial expansion arising out of the war. Hence "the Philippine temptation" provided the anti-imperialists with their strongest argument: Why should Cuba with 1,600,000 people have a right to freedom and self-government, and the 8,000,000 people who dwell in the Philippine Islands be denied the same right? The argument assumed dramatic form when, in February 1899, the Filipinos under Aguinaldo, bitterly disappointed by what they regarded as our rank betrayal, launched their rebellion. Now Americans could read,

[3] "The Anti-Imperialist Movement in the United States, 1898–1900," by Fred H. Harrington, *Mississippi Valley Historical Review*, Vol. XXII, pp. 211–230.

with keen embarrassment, of American atrocities in the Philippines which were in every respect as bad as those of the Spaniards in Cuba. With the opposition rapidly mounting, the Treaty with Spain was only forced through the Senate by the narrow margin of two votes, and the Bacon Resolution, which would have pledged independence to the Philippines, was defeated by the vote of Vice President Hobart. Indeed the opposition might have won if it had not been for certain weaknesses and limitations of the anti-imperialist movement.

For one thing, the whole case was made to turn on an abstract principle, the application of which was not altogether clear to the public. The principle was self-government but its application was not clear since Negroes were not self-governing nor were Chinese or Japanese or Indians. The opposition was limited to this abstract principle since the masses of the people were not directly involved. For example, several million American Negroes took no part in the anti-imperialist movement — a movement which said nothing about our domestic racial imperialism. Nor, with the exception of Gompers and one or two leaders, was the labor movement involved. The truth is, of course, that the rank and file of labor, at this time, was poisoned with racist views of one kind or another. As a matter of fact, so were some of the "anti-imperialist" leaders. For example, Gompers referred to the Filipinos as "a semi-barbaric population, almost primitive in their habits and customs," while Thomas B. Reed referred to them as "yellow-bellies" and "naked Sulus."

The anti-imperialist movement had another curious aspect which seems to have escaped attention. Puerto Rico and Cuba were regarded as being much closer to us, as indeed they were, than the Philippines; but the feeling was based on factors other than distance. Puerto Rico and Cuba were part of the Atlantic world; they were Western, Christian, and predominantly white. The Filipinos were Asiatic and dark-skinned. It seemed proper, therefore, to subject the little brown brother to a period of tutelage under white instructors.

No one had a keener realization of this aspect of the Philippine temptation than Mark Twain, who wrote a savage satire on the Business of Extending the Blessings of Civilization to Our Brother Who Sits in Darkness.[4] This business, he thought, was essentially self-defeating since the people sitting in Outer Darkness were becoming extremely shy about the blessings of White Christian Civilization, "and such darkness as is now left is really of but an indifferent quality and not dark enough for the game." Besides, as he pointed out, the Brother Sitting in Darkness was almost certain to say: "There is something curious about this — curious and unacceptable. There must be two Americas: one that sets the captive free, and one that takes a once-captive's new freedom away from him and picks a quarrel with him with nothing to found it on; then kills him to get his land." And Twain of course was right: there had been two Americas since 1876, one dedicated to freedom and self-government, the other reluctant to apply these ideals to non-Caucasians. This was the basic reason why, when the great test came, we could not resist "the Philippine temptation."

## 2. The Pinoy Arrive

The early American educators in the Philippines thought that it was their mission to give young Filipinos a sense of American ideals, history, and tradition. Great emphasis was placed on civics, oratory, and a kind of political hagiography. Young Filipinos were given prizes for bombastic orations modeled on the forensic style of Daniel Webster and Roscoe Conkling. American textbooks and teaching methods were used and, until 1940, all instruction was in English. Through the practice of extolling everything American and ignoring

[4] *North American Review*, February 1901.

the native culture, we succeeded in educating a generation of Filipinos away from the islands, so to speak, and encouraged this generation to look toward the United States. Many of them, quite naturally, wanted to come to this country.

The relative ease with which a superficial "Americanism" was imposed was due in part to a lack of integration in the native culture. Prior to the arrival of the Spaniards in 1521, the Filipinos had a primitive but distinct culture which had been stimulated by contact with the early traders and peoples from the neighboring islands. But long years of Spanish rule, and the increasingly severe dictation of secular affairs by the Church, had succeeded in confusing, unsettling, and disorganizing the native culture. This state of affairs, of course, was only compounded when we took over the islands in 1898. "The linguistic homogeneity that had been incorporated in the Spanish language," writes Carlos Bulosan, "was uprooted by the English language, and the weaker dialects of the people succumbed one after the other without any favorable effects upon either invading or invaded culture." After 1898 a generation was uprooted and transplanted in the hothouse of American civilization.

As an Oriental people, geographically and racially close to the great cultures of the East, yet Westernized to a large degree through familiarity with Western language, law, custom, and religion, the Filipinos were the hybrid orphans of the Far East. Since their attitude toward Western civilization was unlike that of other Oriental peoples, they readily adopted many phases of American culture although the adoption was probably mimetic. The ease with which this was done convinced us that we had performed miracles in the islands. According to the census of 1939, for example, 91 per cent of the Filipinos are "Christians" and 27 per cent speak some English. But beneath the veneer of American culture is a chaos of unintegrated native cultural growths. Fifty years after the American conquest, the Filipinos still speak some forty languages divided into eighty-seven dialects and their traditions and customs represent a selection and synthesis of primitive, native, Spanish, Chinese, and American cultures with many minor influences.

Virtually all of the Filipino immigrants who came to the United States prior to 1920 came as students or "fountain-pen boys." For the most part, they came to study in the liberal arts and showed a marked preference for rhetoric and law. By and large, they made a wholly favorable impression. Bright, courteous, and charming, many of them came from "the better families" of the islands. Liked as students and prized as house boys, Filipinos were exhibited on many American campuses, and at many religious conferences, as grateful and precocious wards of the American government. The census of 1920 reported the presence of some 5603 Filipinos in the United States. Most of these were students who had stayed on in this country as well as a fairly large number of mess boys who, after a period of enlistment in the Navy, had taken their discharges in American ports. Not until the late 1920's, however, were we aware of "a Filipino problem"; the first articles on resident Filipinos appeared in 1928. In May 1926 *Survey Graphic* had devoted an entire issue to Oriental immigration without mentioning the Filipinos.

The first Filipino immigration was voluntary but the post-1920 influx was artificially stimulated. Fearing that the Gentlemen's Agreement of 1907 would restrict the number of Japanese field hands, the Hawaiian Sugar Planters Association brought the first shipment of Filipinos to Hawaii in that year: 188 men, 20 women, and 2 youngsters. From 1907 to 1926, the planters imported upwards of 100,000 Filipinos to Hawaii and it was from this source that Filipinos were recruited, after 1920, for employment on the mainland. Since there were no legal restrictions on Philippine labor, the Hawaiian planters opened recruitment offices in Manila to speed up the traffic. Special lecturers, with motion pictures, were sent to the Philippines to induce the Filipinos to sign three-year contracts of employment in Hawaii. Steamship agents distributed handbills throughout the islands which gave glowing accounts of idyllic working conditions on Hawaiian plantations. Many of these ship brokers, as the steamship lines admitted, were "crooks — they misrepresent fact; they overcharge emigrants; and often they are pimps." [5] Supplemented by word-of-mouth rumor, the promotional campaign was so successful that the planters were able to discontinue the prepayment of transportation expenses in 1926 without checking the flow of Filipino labor to Hawaii. When the Japanese went on strike in 1920, however, the planters again recruited Filipinos and, after the passage of the Immigration Act of 1924, which barred Japanese immigration to Hawaii, another major effort was made to lure Filipinos to Hawaii. Between 1925 and 1929, some 45,000 Filipinos arrived in Hawaii.

After 1920 many Hawaiian Filipinos began to move to the mainland, although it might be more accurate to say they were moved. For the sensational strike which the Filipinos conducted in 1924 resulted in many of them being blacklisted in the labor records of the planters. During the 1920's, also, legislation was pending in Congress which threatened to cut off the supply of Mexican labor in California. The pendency of this legislation had the effect of stimulating the recruitment of Filipinos. From 1923 to 1929, Filipinos arrived in California at the rate of about 4177 a year. Of this influx, about 56 per cent came by way of Hawaii, 35 per cent came directly from the Philippines, and 9 per cent from Chinese and Japanese ports. In all, about 150,000 Filipinos left their homeland for Hawaii or the mainland between 1907 and 1930, and of this number about 52,810 remain in Hawaii and about 45,563 in the United States.

[5] *Filipino Immigration*, by Dr. Bruno Lasker, 1931, p. 217.

The Filipinos who came to the West Coast after 1920 were not students but workers in search of employment; over half of them came from the relatively backward provinces. Many were without formal education — spoke neither Spanish nor English, and lacked special skills. In California, unlike Hawaii, this second wave of immigration encountered sharp racial antagonism; the Filipinos inherited all the venom accumulated from earlier anti-Oriental agitations. Most of the immigrants were young — 84.3 per cent were under thirty — and they came without parents, wives, or children. From 1920 to 1930, some 1395 Filipino males entered California for every 100 Filipino females, giving an excess male population of 39,328. Thus as immigrants the Filipinos were severely handicapped in almost every respect. Indeed it was precisely these handicaps which made them desirable immigrants since the handicaps could be used to restrict Filipinos to some highly undesirable types of work. The fact is that there is scarcely a Filipino in Hawaii or California who did not leave the Philippines at the invitation, express or implied, of some employer. The "pull" factors were much more important in this migration than the "push" factors. The Philippines, of course, are underpopulated: in 1940 the density rate was something like 147 persons per square mile as compared with 488 per square mile in Japan and 822 in Java. Half of the land has been classified as potentially arable yet only 27 per cent was in cultivation in 1938. Immigrants were induced to leave more because of the attraction of all that was promised and the lack of immediate economic opportunities than because of any pressure of population on resources.

## 3. California Whirligig

Filipino immigrants were caught up in a weird California whirligig from the moment of their arrival in San Francisco. For years fly-by-night taxi drivers transported newly arrived

Filipinos from the Embarcadero to Stockton — one of the large Filipino concentrations. The taxi fare for a group of four or five Filipinos would be around $65 or $75, while the regular train or bus fare would have been about $2 per person. Taxi drivers, rooming-house operators, labor agents, and Filipino contractors — all were on the lookout for the Pinoy as they arrived in San Francisco full of curiosity about the land of Daniel Webster, Abraham Lincoln, and William Howard Taft.

Of 45,563 Filipinos in the United States in 1940, some 32,338 resided in California. From their arrival, the Filipinos have been concentrated in three general types of work: domestic and personal service; in the Alaska and West Coast fishing and fish-canning industry; and in certain specialized agricultural work, as in the asparagus and lettuce fields. In 1930 11,441 were to be found in domestic and personal service jobs, as bellboys, bus boys, hall boys, janitors, kitchen helpers, pantrymen, and dishwashers; while 4210 worked in the Alaska salmon fisheries on either "the long season" of seven months, commencing in April, or "the extra season" of about three months, commencing in June. The balance were in agriculture, working in crews under the direction of Filipino labor contractors and row bosses. For a time about 4000 worked in the merchant marine but most of these were discharged in 1937 as the result of an act of Congress requiring that 90 per cent of the crews should be American citizens. More recently they have begun to find employment as Pullman porters. Only 635 Filipinos were listed "in general trade" in 1930.

Those who have found urban employment, if only as domestics, have fared better than the others. In Los Angeles, where a sizable number reside, the Filipinos are to be found on Bunker Hill and in the cheap rooming houses and hotels along Temple Street. Restaurants and hotels in this district often carry signs reading: "This is a Filipino place." In the city and the country, Filipinos live in groups or clusters; dictated by economic necessity, the bunching also provides a measure of social protection. The "boys" patronize special night clubs and pool halls and sponsor an astonishing number of "sweetheart contests" and lotteries. Group ownership of cars, clothes, and musical instruments is quite common. Hedged in by numerous legal and extralegal restrictions, Filipinos lead a bizarre and fantastic existence. The prejudice against them may be measured by the statement by a San Francisco judge that they are "scarcely more than savages" and the denunciation of an official of the Los Angeles Chamber of Commerce that they are "the most worthless, unscrupulous, shiftless, diseased semi-barbarians that ever came to our shores."

Wherever Filipinos congregate, for seasonal work or between jobs, special tenderloin districts prey upon their loneliness and ostracism. There you will find the Filipino pool hall (a basic institution), the taxi dance halls, and the "Filipino Social Club" which is usually a blind for gambling. For years six major taxi-dance halls in Los Angeles, employing several hundred women, catered exclusively to the Filipino trade. Entertainment in some of these dance halls is about the costliest to be found in California: ten cents for a dance that lasts exactly one minute. It has been estimated that half of the annual earnings of Filipinos in California — and the total would run into the millions — is lost in gambling. In Stockton — "the Manila of the United States" — the "take" on Filipino gambling and prostitution has been estimated at $2,000,000 a year.[6]

Preyed upon by every variety of leech, kicked around by the police, the Filipinos have also been grossly imposed upon by their own countrymen. Racketeering Filipinos sell the Pinoy a bewildering variety of worthless merchandise as well

[6] *Proceedings of the First Official Filipino National Convention in America*, 1938, p. 82.

as tickets for raffles, picnics, lotteries, "sweetheart contests" and cockfights; and initiate them, for fancy fees, into a bizarre assortment of lodges, social clubs, and fraternal organizations (more than 103 Filipino organizations were counted some years ago in Los Angeles). In many communities, parasitic Japanese or Chinese settlements cater to the needs of the Pinoy. In Seattle, for example, more than two thirds of the Filipino arrests are made in or near the gambling resorts, dance halls, and pool rooms of Chinatown.[7] Despite these conditions, Filipinos have a good record for law observance — a fact demonstrated by the Wickersham Report.

Among Filipinos the disposition to gamble is a cultural trait with a specific historical reference. Slavery has had a long history in the Philippines, and it has not been entirely stamped out to this day. Slavery for debt or peonage is indigenous in the Philippines and where peonage prevails, there gambling is encouraged. The imposition of a monetary economy only furthered this tendency. "American large-scale employers of labor in the Philippines," writes Dr. Bruno Lasker, "at first thought it a good idea to attract and stabilize a sufficient labor force by providing cockpits along with dance halls and other attractions," and in both California and the Philippines "the pool table is almost indispensable to the Filipino labor contractor."[8] Various interests in Stockton, notorious for its corrupt municipal politics, encourage gambling as a means of stabilizing the Filipino labor force in the asparagus industry.

The labor force in California agriculture has long been noted for certain rigidities and stratifications.[9] Local social usage, for example, reserves certain jobs for certain racial or national groups; thus the Filipino is said to be the ideal worker in lettuce, asparagus, carrots, and sugar beets. Ac-

[7] *American Journal of Sociology*, May 1938.
[8] *Human Bondage in Southeast Asia*, by Dr. Bruno Lasker, 1950, p. 132.
[9] *The Agricultural Labor Force in the San Joaquin Valley*, U. S. Department of Agriculture, February 1950, p. 3.

cording to this usage, the Filipino, unlike other workers, is not bothered by the peat dust of the delta lands where asparagus is grown and, being smaller than most farm workers, can "stoop" with greater ease. In this manner, the Filipino has come to be earmarked, so to speak, for certain special labor operations. When these operations are examined, however, it will be found that they are of the type in which family labor cannot be utilized; children and women can pick peaches, apricots, and cherries, but they cannot cut asparagus. To cut asparagus, an army of single men is needed and, for greater efficiency, this army must be tied to the cutting of asparagus so that it will return year after year to the same work. Denied other types of work by prejudice, and always in debt to the Filipino labor contractor — usually for a gambling debt — the single Filipino makes the ideal asparagus cutter precisely because he can be, and is, ostracized. The basis of this ostracism is really not racial or cultural or social; it is economic. Instead of saying that Filipinos are set apart because they are "different," it would be more accurate to say that they are regarded as different because they cut asparagus. Actually "asparagus" has more to do with their status than "race" or "culture."

Furthermore the parceling out of the agricultural labor market to heterogeneous groups, divided by racial antagonism, has been proved to be an effective barrier to unionization.[10] Just as racial prejudice is an indispensable factor in the manipulation of this kind of labor market, so the way in which Filipinos, and other groups, are fitted into the market deprives them of effective opportunities for assimilation and keeps the prejudice against them alive. Filipinos have rebelled against this system time and again but they have never managed to escape.[11] In lettuce and asparagus, the Filipinos

[10] *Labor Unionism in American Agriculture,* by Stuart Jamieson, Bulletin No. 836, Department of Labor, 1945, p. 74.
[11] *Ibid.,* p. 178

work under Filipino contractors, in crews of ten to thirty workers, with every phase of the work being minutely stipulated in formal contracts, down to the size of the cutting knives to be used and the manner in which every operation is to be performed.[12]

Caught as they are in this California whirligig, it is not surprising that the Filipinos, unlike other minority groups, have not developed communities of any great social stability.[13] By and large they have not created permanent settlements or colonies for they live in bunkhouses, rooming houses, hotels, and labor camps. The "Little Manila" districts are just convenient service centers for them in the periods between jobs. Usually Little Manila is simply an appendage to some long-established Chinatown or Little Tokyo. While there are no Filipino communities as such on the West Coast there is *a* Filipino community in the sense that Filipinos are united by strong nationalist feeling which reflects the discrimination against them. To be a Filipino in Calfornia is to belong to a blood brotherhood, a freemasonry of the ostracized. Since most Filipinos, in Hawaii and the mainland, have married out of the group, the minority seems destined to disappear or vanish into larger minority clusters. Here, again, the lack of an integrated native culture facilitates the adoption of the ways and customs of other groups.

## 4. *"Legally Undesirable Heroes"*

Hardly had the Filipinos arrived in California when a third wave of anti-Oriental agitation swept through the state and the familiar demand for exclusion was sounded. Beginning in Yakima, Washington, on September 19, 1928, a series of violent anti-Filipino race riots occurred in various West Coast

[12] *Farm Labor Contractors in California,* Department of Industrial Relations, State of California, p. 89.
[13] See "The Filipinos," by Dr. Grayson Kirk, *Annals of the American Academy,* September 1942, p. 48.

communities. Riots were reported in Tulare, California, in October 1929; in Watsonville, in January 1930; in Stockton; in Hood River and Banks, Oregon; and in the Imperial Valley. And when a group of Filipino field workers migrated to Florida to work in the vegetable fields, riots were reported there in July 1932.[14] Even after Filipino immigration was barred, a few riots were reported, as in Lake County, California, in June 1939.[15] The West Coast riots, of course, had significant repercussions in the Philippines. When the body of Fermin Tobera, who was killed in one of the riots, was returned to Manila for burial, the press referred to Tobera as "a martyr of American intolerance," a National Humiliation Day was proclaimed, and 10,000 Filipinos attended the funeral service which was sponsored by the government.[16]

The anti-Filipino riots were part of the movement to exclude further Filipino immigration; indeed it would be hard to say whether the riots stimulated this movement or the movement stimulated the riots. As early as May, 1928, Congressman Richard Welch of California had introduced legislation to prohibit further immigration from the Philippines. But as long as the American flag flew over Manila, it was impossible — or difficult — to bar Filipino immigration. Hence those who sought to bar Filipino immigration suddenly became partisans of Philippine Independence! The labor leaders, who desired exclusion, now joined with certain economic groups who desired to erect a tariff wall against Philippine commodity imports, in demanding independence for the islands, knowing that only in this way could Filipinos and Philippine commodities be excluded.[17]

Prior to the passage of the Philippine Independence Act, the courts had ruled that natives of the islands had not become

[14] *New York Times*, July 24, 1932.
[15] *San Francisco Chronicle*, June 19, 1939.
[16] *The Filipino Immigrant in the United States*, by Honorante Mariano, 1933.
[17] Kirk, *op. cit.*, p. 46.

citizens of the United States by cession and that Congress had not extended citizenship by implication in any of the legislation affecting the Philippines. The possibility of citizenship by naturalization still remained but, in view of *Loyota* v. *United States*, 268 U. S. 402, and *Ozawa* v. *United States*, 260 U. S. 178, Filipinos were regarded as ineligible to citizenship. By a nice irony the act of March 24, 1934, which decreed independence for the Philippines, made it possible to bar Filipinos from the United States; in fact the act probably would not have been passed had it not been for this motivation. Prior to the passage of this act, Filipinos enjoyed a perfect right of legal entry to the United States since they were regarded, for many purposes, as "wards" of the government; when they traveled, for example, their passports were stamped "American citizen." Technically, however, the Filipino was neither an alien nor a citizen nor yet a ward; in the words of a Manila newspaper, the Filipino was a "legally undesirable hero." This uncertain status reflected our uncertain intention about the Philippines, but with the passage of the Philippines Independence Act it became possible to exclude Filipinos as aliens.

It cannot be too often repeated, as Dr. Serafin E. Macaraig has insisted, that "national policies of exclusion of non-assimilable races by powerful nations have been very influential in intensifying race conflicts." [18] For example, when it was first suggested that Filipinos might be excluded from the United States, the proposal provoked intense resentment in the Philippines. "It is unthinkable," said the *Manila Times*, "that the American flag should fly over the Philippines while the citizens who look to it for defense and support are barred from entering the United States." In fact we forced the Filipinos to accept exclusion only by making exclusion the price which they had to pay for independence. Agitation for exclusion unquestionably stimulated prejudice against

[18] *Introduction to Sociology*, by Serafin E. Macaraig, Manila, 1938.

Filipinos on the West Coast and against Americans in the Philippines.

Under the Philippines Independence Act, an immigration quota of 50 a year was fixed for the Filipinos, which, of course, was tantamount to exclusion. In fact this was the lowest quota provided for any nation, lower even than that allowed Monaco with a population of 2020! However the sugar planters in Hawaii managed to insert a provision which made it possible for them, under certain circumstances, to import additional Filipinos to Hawaii. At the same time, it became impossible for Filipinos legally resident in Hawaii to move on to the mainland, except in limited circumstances. This provision was also adopted at the request of the sugar planters in Hawaii. The effect, of course, was to hold Filipinos in Hawaii.

But exclusion did not satisfy the leaders of the anti-Filipino agitation in California: they wanted deportation. On July 11, 1935, President Roosevelt signed a bill which they had sponsored, known as the Repatriation Act. Under this act the government undertook to pay the transportation expenses of Filipinos who desired to return to the Philippines, but the act contained the provision that those who returned could not later re-enter the United States. As might be expected, the act was not applicable to Filipinos then in Hawaii. Passed in the depth of the depression, the act was intended as the means by which some 45,000 Filipinos might be lured back to the Philippines; but only 2190 actually returned.

Although Filipinos were required to register under the Alien Registration Act of 1940, some 16,000 were called up under the first draft; most of them, of course, were of draft age; and an all-Filipino battalion was formed.[19] In this manner, a fairly large number of resident Filipinos finally managed to become American citizens.

The contrast between the treatment of Filipinos in the

[19] *Asia*, October 1942, p. 562.

United States and the treatment of Americans in the Philippines provides an interesting measure of American race prejudice. In 1939 some 8639 Americans were living in the Philippines, enjoying all the rights and privileges of citizens. At that time, also, Americans were reported to hold investments in the islands of $258,000,000, including some 63,000,000 acres of land. While insisting on an unlimited right of entry for American capital and American citizens to the Philippines, we limited Filipino immigration to a quota of 50 a year and restricted the employment of Filipinos to a limited number of dead-end jobs. With the Philippines reported as the fifth largest market for American goods, Filipinos could migrate to almost any country of the world with greater ease, and in larger numbers, than to this country. The discrimination against Filipinos in the United States simply mirrors the relation between the United States and the Philippines.

During World War II it seemed likely that many of the disabilities from which resident Filipinos have long suffered might be removed. There was a new stirring of hope and freedom; we felt profoundly grateful to the Filipinos for their demonstrated loyalty; and, from Seattle to San Diego, the resident Filipinos looked forward to an emancipation from prejudice and discrimination. When Philippine Independence was proclaimed on July 4, 1946, it seemed as though this meant freedom for Filipinos everywhere — in Hawaii and on the mainland as well as in the Philippines. But just as we really did not grant independence to the Philippine Islands, so we failed to take advantage of the wartime ferment to improve the lot of 100,000 Filipinos in Hawaii and the mainland. What we did, of course, was to grant *political* independence while retaining vital economic controls.

During the fifty years that the United States ruled in the Philippines, many improvements were made: roads were built; cities were developed; schools were established; hospitals were constructed; and welfare services were provided. But since the national economy was already focused on exports, these improvements were primarily designed to improve things for the large industries, the mines, and the transportation and commercial interests which were entrenched in the islands. The export of Philippine raw materials was greatly stimulated by the reciprocal free trade arrangements of 1909 which had the effect of fastening the colonial bond on the islands. Little industrial progress was made and natural resources were poorly developed since the American money that went into the islands was invested, not to make consumer goods or industrial products, but to stimulate the production of sugar, hemp, and copra. Emphasis on exports only stimulated class divisions since most of the increased production fell to the owners of a few large plantations. "Considering the enormous advance in the islands' production of wealth," writes Dr. Lasker, "it cannot be held that the masses received back more than a fraction of what they contributed to it." [20] In 1941 High Commissioner Paul McNutt reported that although national income had increased fivefold under American rule, "neither a sizable independent middle class nor an influential public opinion has developed. The bulk of the newly created income has gone to the Government, to the landlords, and to urban areas, and has served little to ameliorate living conditions among the almost feudal peasantry and tenantry. . . . The gap between the mass population and the small governing class has broadened, and social unrest has reached serious proportions."

The truth about Philippine independence, as Senator Millard E. Tydings, author of the independence act, has admitted, is that we granted political independence while retaining the economic controls. First of all, we passed a Rehabilitation Act, the vital benefits of which were made conditional upon acceptance of the Philippine Trade Act. The Philippine Trade Act fixed absolute quotas on certain exports which were to

[20] See Note 8, above, p. 232.

come in duty free, pegged the peso to the dollar, made it well-nigh impossible for new industries to develop in the islands, and stipulated equal rights for Americans with Filipinos in the exploitation of Philippine resources. Since certain of these provisions were incompatible with the Philippine constitution, the Filipinos were forced to amend the constitution so that they could ratify the Philippine Trade Act so that they could have the benefits of the Rehabilitation Act! The so-called "parity" provision of the act, as Carolyn Freeland has pointed out, was one-way parity: economic equality in the Philippines for Americans — and Americans alone — and no economic equality for Filipinos in the United States.[21] In short we granted the Filipinos independence only to confront them with an ultimatum: legislate yourself into a colonial economic dependence upon the United States or else forgo the economic benefits of continued free trade.[22] An American businessman in the Philippines described the consequences of this policy to Dr. Claude A. Buss in this manner: "We are moving back toward the types of Spain, with the *illustrado* class dominated by a few scoundrels, and with the people in peonage. With a power-drunk oligarchy in power, the country can crash to pieces while the machine does as it pleases." [23] As though in answer to this prediction, the headlines now read: "Rural Pressures Strain Philippines" (*New York Times*, August 20, 1950); and "Philippines' Economy is Near a Breakdown," August 20, 1950 (*New York Times*). And with the "Huks" capitalizing on our mistakes, we may now be faced with the "necessity" of having to reoccupy the islands! As long as the United States holds the Philippines as an economic colonial dependency, some 18,000,000 Filipinos should be regarded as an American racial minority.

Failing to free the islands, we have failed to "free" the

[21] *News Letter*, Institute of Ethnic Affairs, April 1947.
[22] *News Letter*, Institute of Ethnic Affairs, January 1947, p. 5. See also *More Than Conquerors*, by Otto Tod Mallery, Chapter 17, 1947.
[23] *Fortune*, February 1949.

resident Filipinos. "Where is the heart of America?" asks Manuel Buaken. "I am one of many thousands of young men, born under the American flag, raised as loyal, idealistic Americans under your promises of equality for all, and enticed by glowing tales of educational opportunities. Once here we are met by exploiters, shunted into slums, greeted only by gamblers and prostitutes, taught only the worst in your civilization. America came to us with bright-winged promises of liberty, equality, fraternity. What has become of them?" [24] Today this is just as good a question in Manila as in Stockton, California.

\*          \*          \*

Closely related to the fate of the resident Filipinos is that of some 2405 Hindus — lonely representatives in America of the millions of India. In the period from 1900 to 1910, about 6000 Hindus, mostly single men from the Punjab, came to the West Coast, over half of whom later returned to India. Their presence promptly occasioned the familiar reflex action: Hindus were attacked in Bellingham, Washington, in September 1907; at Live Oak, California, in 1908; and in St. Johns, Oregon, in 1910. In 1910 the immigration authorities began to exclude Hindus by an administrative interpretation of existing statutes and on February 5, 1917, the "barred zone provision" of the immigration act of that year stopped further immigration.

Most of the Hindus came to California by way of British Columbia, working first in the lumber mills, then on the railroads, and finally in agriculture. In the course of a few years, some of them became successful California farmers, raising rice, vegetables, cotton, and other crops. But in March 1923, the Supreme Court ruled that Hindus were "ineligible to citizenship" and the ruling brought them immediately within the purview of California's Alien Land Act,

[24] *New Republic*, September 23, 1940.

so that the Hindus became farm workers, not farmers. The decision of the Supreme Court was "denounced as totally unjustifiable in the Punjab, where the people speak an Aryan language and claim to be of the white race." [25]

Like the Filipinos, the Hindus have been severely isolated in California. The Hindu cultural traits which most clearly measure the social distance between Hindus and other Californians are the very ones which the Hindus prize most highly: for example, long hair, beards, and turbans. Few in number and severely isolated, many Hindus have become extremely embittered and the bound volumes of the decisions of the California appellate courts are studded with records of their violent internecine quarrels and contentions. As a group they exhibit many of the traits of a neurotic. In a few areas, as in the Imperial Valley, Hindus have become small farmers and have married Mexican women. Since the children of these marriages will grow up in Mexican communities, the Hindu minority will vanish with the disappearance of the immigrant generation.

Small as this minority has always been, it has had an extraordinary influence. Through such spokesmen as Dhan Gopal Mukerji, Kedar Nath Das Gupta, and Taraknath Das, all of whom worked in the fields in California, this tiny minority has brought the race prejudice of America to the attention of India in the most significant manner. All Asia has been made aware of the fact that all Asiatic peoples — Chinese, Japanese, Filipinos, and Hindus — have been treated alike and have met the same fate — discrimination and exclusion — in California. The Hindu minority is small but it is large enough to indicate to all of India that Hindus are treated like other Asiatics in the United States.

[25] *Our Racial and National Minorities*, 1937, p. 453.

## CHAPTER VIII

# "The Negro Problem": A Case History

No DOMESTIC social issue has received more attention than "the Negro problem." However the problem is not as old as we think: it dates from the issuance of the Emancipation Proclamation in 1863. Indeed it was this act which created the Negro problem — that is, whether to acknowledge the Negro's emancipation, with all the implications, or to pretend that emancipation had some other meaning. Only in this sense has there ever been a Negro problem in the United States.

As a matter of fact, the attempt to relate prejudice to the specific nature of its object is a cunning projection of the prejudice of the dominant group; "cunning" because it passes as scientific curiosity. As long as the majority can pretend that the source of prejudice inheres in the nature of the victim, social action can be indefinitely postponed; there is always still another investigation which must be made. For example, it can hardly be denied that the Negro has been overstudied and overinvestigated; whereas all too little is known about the circumstances under which we came to have a Negro problem. This chapter, therefore, has been designed to provide a natural history of the Negro problem.

## 1. "The Habit Makes the Monk"

Historically, racial discrimination in the United States is an outgrowth of slavery, and slavery, by a strange paradox, was a by-product of the freedom implicit in the discovery of a largely uninhabited New World; slavery "was simply a way of recruiting labor for the purpose of exploiting the great natural resources of America." [1] Indentured servants and bondsmen vanished into the wilderness almost as soon as they arrived and there was no large native population to exploit. Specifically free labor could not be recruited in sufficient volume to meet the requirements in cotton and other plantation crops, nor could free labor be kept on the plantations. On the other hand, the economics of large-scale production on the plantation offset the inefficiency of slave labor. As the plantation system spread, the "poor whites" found themselves at a hopeless competitive disadvantage on their barren hilly acres. Their status, moreover, deteriorated in direct relation to the number of Negro slaves who were used as craftsmen and mechanics as well as field hands. As paradoxical as the fact that slavery stemmed from freedom was the fact that the cessation of the African slave trade, by enhancing the value of slaves, greatly intensified the problem of abolishing slavery.

The dynamic of gain and not any qualities of Negroes as Negroes produced the institution of slavery. Even bondage was not related to "race" as such; indentured white servants were more characteristic of Virginia than Negro slaves in the early eighteenth century. Rights were denied not on the basis of race but on the basis of power. On the eve of the nineteenth century, a tenth of the Negro population lived outside the slave system and these Negroes were recognized as having some of the rights of freedmen. In the United States, slavery was not an antecedent fact; it was a growth or rather an improvisation. Since slavery was not recognized under the common law, the system had to be evolved out of apprenticeship and vagrancy laws and through a gradual accumulation of precedents. The basic paradox and contradiction of racial discrimination in the United States is to be found in the fact that slavery was not a primordial fact but a later acquisition incon-

[1] *Caste, Class & Race*, by Oliver C. Cox, 1948, p. 332.

sistent with the stated purposes for which the Republic was formed.

"Slavery in America," writes Dr. W.E.B. Du Bois, "is a strange and contradictory story. It cannot be regarded as mainly either a theoretical problem of morals or a scientific problem of race. From either of these points of view, the rise of slavery in America is simply inexplicable. Looking at the facts frankly, slavery evidently was a matter of economics, a question of income and labor, rather than a problem of right and wrong, or of the physical differences in men. Once slavery began to be the source of vast income for men and nations, there followed a frantic search for moral and racial justifications. Such excuses were found and men did not inquire too carefully into either their logic or truth." [2] Myth, as Durkheim once said, imitates society, not nature. The myth of racial inequality did not arise until social institutions, such as slavery, had created unequal relations between men.

Neither a Negro nor a race problem existed under slavery. In the first place, the plantation system did not permit direct competition between Negroes and "poor whites": the large plantation holdings, embracing the best lands, kept the poor whites at a distance. The masters were not in competition with the slaves or the slaves with the masters; the master owned the slave and the slave "belonged to" the master. Ironically the Negro slave was a part, although a subordinate part, of the plantation system; the poor whites were the real minority or subordinate group. "Under slavery," writes Dr. E. Franklin Frazier, "whatever racial antagonisms there might have existed between masters and slaves were reduced to a minimum by the social controls regulating their relations." [3]

Nevertheless in the South, as in Brazil, it was slavery and

---

[2] Statement presented by the NAACP to the United Nations, October 23, 1947, p. 6.
[3] *The Negro in the United States*, by E. Franklin Frazier, 1949, p. 143.

the one-crop system which most deeply affected "the social plastics" of the region. Out of slavery came the myth of racial superiority and other mischievous self-deceptions and social delusions. Traits which to this day are pointed to as evidence of the Negro's inferiority are clearly not traits of the Negro but characteristics of all slaves. "At times," writes Gilberto Freyre, "what appears to be the influence of race is purely and simply that of the slave, of the social system of slavery, a reflection of the enormous capacity of that system for morally degrading masters and slaves alike. . . ." The Negro unlike the Indian could not escape from slavery; hence "it is . . . an absurdity to hold the Negro responsible for what was not his doing or the Indian's, but that of the social system in which they both functioned." [4] Had it not been for Negro slaves, Indian-white relations might have taken a quite different form; and, conversely, had it not been for the Indian, slavery might not have been enforceable. Slavery, not biological traits or cultural differences, was responsible for the hostility between Negroes, Indians, and whites. The origin of the beliefs upon which racial dominance rests is suggested in the adage quoted by Freyre: "The habit makes the monk." The social form determines the belief; not the belief the social form.

The misidentification of "traits" is illustrated in the matter of sexual morality. As Freyre has pointed out, slavery was opulent in vices since the economic interests of the masters sanctioned depravity. Wherever slavery has prevailed, it has produced the same consequences regardless of the "race" of the slaves. "White slaves" are not slaves because they are white; they are prostitutes because they are slaves. "It was not the Negro," writes Freyre, "who was the libertine, but the slave who was at the service of his idle master's economic interests and voluptuous pleasure. It was not 'the inferior race' that was the source of corruption, but the abuse of one

[4] *The Masters and the Slaves,* by Gilberto Freyre, 1946, p. 324.

race by another, an abuse that demanded a servile conformity
on the part of the Negro to the appetites of the all-powerful
lords of the land. Those appetites were stimulated by idleness, by 'a wealth acquired without labor' . . . by 'idleness'
or 'laziness' which means — by the economic structure of the
slave-holding regime itself."

Slavery clearly shaped the "social plastics" of the South.
For example, there was a close correlation between the number of Negro slaves and the degree to which Negroes were
completely subordinated and treated as a form of property.
The larger the investment in slaves, and the greater the
economic return from their labor, the more intensely the slave
myths were propagated and the tighter were the social controls. The belief in the Negro's "inferiority" is today most
widely held, and most passionately affirmed, in those areas
where the strongest incentives exist for the exploitation of
Negro labor. "Throughout the Cotton Belt," writes Frazier,
"race relations are characterized by the complete social subordination of the Negro." [5] The degree of the Negro's subordination varies with the acreage in cotton and in relation to
the existence of alternative employment opportunities.

Slavery, as Oliver Cox has pointed out, is not "a derivative
of human idiosyncrasy or wickedness, but rather . . . a
function of a peculiar type of economic order. . . . The
exploitation of native peoples, imperialism, is not a sin, not
essentially a problem of morals or of vice; it is a problem of
production and of competition for markets." [6] In this country,
slavery was an aspect of the relation between Europe and
America. Free labor poured into the United States in quest of
free land, and the force of this invasion would have rapidly
undercut slavery had the Industrial Revolution not created an
extraordinary opportunity for the further exploitation of
slave labor in the production of cotton. The more the wealth

[5] Frazier, *op. cit.*, p. 222.
[6] Cox, *op. cit.*, p. 336.

and power of the cotton states increased through the shipment of cotton to overseas markets, the more belligerent these
states became and the more strenuously they sought to expand into the free-soil states to the west. From the beginning,
therefore, race relations in the United States have been an
aspect of the relations between Europe and America and between European nations in a competition for world markets.

The means that nations use to exploit other nations are the
means by which one group within a nation exploits another.
"For the full profitable exploitation of a people," writes Cox,
"the dominant group must devise ways and means of limiting
that people's cultural assimilation. . . . Assimilation dimin-
ishes the exploitative possibilities." [7] Just as a form of cultural
and social parallelism between the dominant and the subordinate group is an essential aspect of the strategy of dominance,
so the industrially dominant nation seeks to maintain a
measure of "social distance" in its relations with so-called
"backward" peoples. This distance may create prejudice
and make for misunderstanding but it does not reflect initial
hostility or aversion. For example, statutes against intermarriage are not based on racial antipathy; if an attraction did
not exist, the statutes would not be necessary. As a matter of
fact the miscegenation statutes were adopted *after* a long history of sexual intimacy between white masters and Negro
women held as slaves.

Slave relations are not race relations although they strongly
influence the latter. The basic reason why "a Negro problem"
did not exist prior to the Civil War is to be found in Chief
Justice Taney's remark in the Dred Scott case that the Negro
was to be regarded as "having no rights which the white man
was bound to respect." This remark explains the basis of the
difference between slave relations and race relations. In one
sense, "racial conflict" does not arise under a slave system;

[7] *Ibid.*, p. 336.

the conflict is between two types of labor, one free and one slave, and not between free laborers some of whom are white and others colored.

## 2. The Discovery of a Dilemma

The discovery of America's racial problem or dilemma dates from the first movement of Union troops into slave territory. "It was only with the advance of the invading armies farther and farther into Southern fields," writes Dr. Paul Skeels Peirce, "that the significance of the Negro as an element in the contest became more exactly defined and more generally apparent." [8] First by the hundreds and later by the thousands, liberated Negro slaves came flocking to the federal army camps for support and protection. Once the Emancipation Proclamation was issued, of course, the problem became at once more urgent and more complicated. A few months later the government established the Bureau of Colored Troops in the War Department and the famous 54th and 55th Massachusetts Negro regiments were formed. These decisions created the Negro problem. "A race problem developed for the first time," writes Dr. Charles S. Johnson, "when the fixed social position of the Negro slave was changed by his emancipation."

As the war continued, various petitions from the Freedmen's Aid Societies finally forced the government to give serious consideration to the problem of what was to be done with 4,100,000 propertyless, largely illiterate former slaves. The administration, Lincoln included, at first toyed with the idea of colonizing the former slaves in Africa or South America — a fantasy which betrays underlying prejudice. Indeed it was only after two years of debate that a bill was finally passed on March 3, 1865, creating the Freedmen's Bureau in the War Department. In freeing the slaves, as

[8] *The Freedmen's Bureau*, by Dr. Paul Skeels Peirce, 1904.

Charles Beard observed, the nation had created "a large and anomalous class in the American social order — a mass of emancipated slaves long destined to wander in a hazy realm between bondage and freedom." The haziness of this realm, however, reflected the haziness of the majority's intentions.

For a war-weary nation, the problems thus created were of extraordinary magnitude. Negroes were wandering about in droves: landless, confused, hungry, and full of terrifying uncertainties. The school problem alone was of staggering proportions: of 4,100,000 slaves, some 1,700,000 were of school age. Nor was it a matter of expanding existing institutions to meet new needs: there were no institutions on which to build. In the South, as Dr. Maurice R. Davie has pointed out, "the war had left a stricken upper class possessing nothing but lands and a servile population possessing naught except the labor of their hands." [9] Actually the former slaves were in a worse position than before the war since the basis of their monopoly of certain skilled labor positions had been destroyed and they now faced the competition of the poor whites. Such was the scope of the problem which the Freedmen's Bureau was asked to solve — without adequate funds, precedents, directives, or a clearly formulated policy.

All things considered, the Freedmen's Bureau did a remarkable job in the brief period it was in existence (March 3, 1865, to June 30, 1872). The year the Bureau was abolished it was operating 2677 day and night schools, with 3300 teachers (most of whom it had trained) and 149,581 pupils. In establishing such institutions as Howard and Fisk Universities, Hampton Institute, and St. Augustine Normal School, the Bureau inaugurated a system of professional, normal, and industrial training that was of great value to Negroes. In one year alone, the Bureau trained over 2000 teachers, half of whom were Negroes, and, in many areas of the South, it laid the foundation for what later became a system of tax-sup-

[9] *Negroes in American Society*, by Maurice R. Davie, 1949, p. 63.

ported public schools. The Bureau also provided institutions for the care of the sick and infirm, the insane and the crippled; the aged and the deaf-and-dumb. It established an excellent medical-aid program for Negroes; founded hospitals; and built asylums. Some medical aid was furnished to at least 1,000,000 Negroes. It also aided orphans and the destitute and transported 30,000 "displaced" freedmen to their former homes.

The Bureau also sought to adjust the former slave to a system of free labor. For example, it sought to intervene between the former slave and the plantation owner for the purpose of negotiating an equitable labor contract. Not less than 50,000 such contracts were prepared which contained minimum guarantees as to food, fuel, shelter, and payment of a fixed money wage. In many cases, agents of the Bureau appeared in court on behalf of Negro claimants. In Maryland and Virginia, agents of the Bureau forced the release of hundreds of Negro children who had been "farmed out" to employers as apprentices. While this attempt to provide a shield for the protection of Negroes was not too successful, nevertheless the Bureau "imparted a conception — inadequate and distorted though it may have been — of his [the Negro's] civil rights as a freedman." [10] It encouraged the Negro to vote; protected his right to vote; and, as its enemies charged, probably told him how to vote.

In response to a congressional mandate to provide every freedman with "forty acres and a mule," the Bureau set about the task of distributing abandoned and confiscated lands to former slaves. This, of course, was the crux of the problem; without a measure of economic independence the Negro was certain to be reimprisoned in a system of thinly disguised slavery. But the Bureau never had more than 800,000 acres at its disposal; in fact only two tenths of 1 per cent of the land in the rebel states was ever held by the Bureau. If all

[10] Peirce, *op. cit.*

these lands had been available, the Bureau could not have given even one acre to every freedman, let alone a mule and the means by which the land might be worked. As a matter of fact, most of the lands were quickly repossessed by the former owners in the wake of wholesale amnesties and the Negroes were promptly dispossessed. With the collapse of this program, the brave venture of the Freedmen's Bureau came to an unhappy end.

In the meantime, of course, the Southern states had boldly enacted the Black Codes which stripped the freed Negro population of all but the barest provision for civil rights — marriage, ownership of property, and the right to appear in court. The Radical Republicans promptly met this aggression by placing ten Southern states under military rule, and by enacting the Civil Rights Act and the 14th Amendment. It now seemed as though Congress intended to carry the "unfinished business" of the Civil War to a conclusion and to end the American dilemma. The determination of Congress was still strong when it passed the Civil Rights Act after the Southern states had rejected the 14th Amendment.

But reconstruction, which appeared to be heroic, was based on a realistic appraisal of a novel aspect of the dilemma which had come with victory. Negroes, of course, were overwhelmingly concentrated in the South. If the Negro was now to be counted as a full person for the purpose of determining representation in Congress, instead of three fifths of a person, the North would have fought the Civil War only to vest political control in the South. This, then, was the real dilemma. To offset the threat of Southern dominance, the Republicans proceeded to disfranchise a large portion of the South's white population through the invocation of military rule. At the same time, federal agents "voted" Negroes in large blocs. The haste with which certain Western states were admitted to the Union in the postwar period shows how desperate were the Republicans and how precarious their control had be-

come. For example, the constitution of Nevada was tele-
graphed to Washington so that the Republican majority
might hastily admit the state, and in similar manner Montana,
Idaho, and Washington were invested with statehood to in-
sure the ascendancy of the Republican Party. The political
objective of reconstruction, therefore, was to maintain Republican ascendancy by force until such time as a clear
Republican majority could be built up in the Western
states.

Even so reconstruction might have been carried through
to its logical conclusion but for a number of developments
of far-reaching importance. In 1873 came a panic which
shook the structure of the national economy from top to
bottom and a depression which lasted for five years. The
depression made the Northern industrialists ponder the long-
range implications of emancipation and reconstruction. "If
victory meant full economic freedom for labor in the South,
white and black," writes Dr. Du Bois, "if it meant land and
education, and eventually votes, then the slave empire was
doomed, and the profits of Northern industry built on the
Southern slave foundation would also be seriously curtailed.
Northern industry had a stake in the cotton kingdom and in
the cheap slave labor that supported it. It had expanded war
industries during the fighting, encouraged by government
subsidy and eventually protected by a huge tariff rampart.
When war profits declined there was still prospect of tre-
mendous postwar profits on cotton and other products of
Southern agriculture. Therefore, what the North wanted was
not freedom and higher wage for black labor, but its control
under such forms of law as would keep it cheap. . . . The
moral protest of abolitionists must be appeased but profitable
industry was determined to control wages and government." [11]

The problem of political control, however, was greatly

[11] See Note 2 above.

complicated in the postwar period. There was the usual post-war reaction "against the government"; the depression of 1873 had created wide unrest; a war-expanded American industry was still not in a position to compete for world markets; the Liberal Republicans were appalled by the corruption of the Grant administration; and the Democrats had won important victories in 1874. To build a more or less perpetual Republican majority it was necessary, first of all, to use the revenues from the tariff system to pay Northern veterans a pension; pensions and the tariff were "as inseparable as Gold Dust twins." By 1875 the government was giving Northern veterans $29 million annually and this sum jumped to $60 million in 1879; to $89 million in 1889; and to $159 million in 1893. Pensions helped to provide purchasing power in the North for the products of Northern industry, and Northern industrial production was in turn based on Southern agriculture and cheap Negro labor. At the same time, pensions meant votes. "The Grand Army of the Republic," writes Dr. Walter Prescott Webb, "was powerful at the polls, where it won a far larger percentage of victories than it won against the armies of Lee. No politician dared deny a lifelong subsidy which was paid impartially to the pauper and to the million-aire." [12] Finally there was the West: a new raw-materials empire, rich in mineral wealth, offering an excellent market for the products of Northern industry. The rapid admission of Western territories as states would wed these states to the Republican Party. The presence of many Union veterans in the West, the control of territorial governments by the appointive power, the manipulation of laws governing the public domain, the granting of homesteads to veterans, and liberal appropriations for Western river-and-harbor and other public improvements, as well as the use of "pork barrel" legislation generally, helped to build up Republican majorities in the West.

[12] *Divided We Stand,* by Walter Prescott Webb, 1947, p. 19.

Indeed Louis M. Hacker explains "reconstruction" perfectly by suggesting that the real reconstruction was in the North, not the South. By 1875 the Republicans had a firm hold on the key states of Ohio, Indiana, Michigan, and Wisconsin, and the threat of a South-West alliance had been averted. The Civil War, as Dr. Hacker points out, had done its work too well: "it had destroyed a political opposition based upon a class interest" — the kind of opposition to industrial capitalism which the landed aristocracies had presented in Europe.[13] The Republicans, however, could see that a new class opposition might arise; hence they were disposed to strike a bargain with the planter dynasty. Instead of resolving the Emancipation dilemma, they seized upon it as a means by which the appearance of democracy could be used to frustrate the democratic process. This great opportunity arose in 1876 — the year in which Congress sent its first committee of inquiry on "the Chinese problem" to California; in which the Reciprocity Treaty with Hawaii went into effect; and in which the first investigation into the new Rockefeller oil monopoly was launched.

### 3. Resolution of the Dilemma

"In 1876," writes Dr. Du Bois, "the democratic process of government was crippled throughout the whole nation."[14] Many factors were responsible for this impairment: the emotional letdown after the war; the dispersive effect of the wild rush to the West which drew in its wake the first wholesale European immigration; the confusion produced by the rapid rise of a new social system; and, above all, the vicious counterattack in the South from 1868 to 1871. Reconstruction was a prolonged race riot: over 5000 people were killed

---

[13] *The Triumph of American Capitalism*, by Louis M. Hacker, 1940, p. 383.
[14] See Note 2 above.

and the custom of lynching, which dates from this period, rapidly became institutionalized.[15] The Ku Klux Klan and the "rifle clubs" not only forced Negroes but also many poor whites to "cross Jordan" — that is, to shift to the Democratic Party. By 1876 all the Southern states with the exception of South Carolina, Louisiana, and Florida were under "white rule"; in the latter states federal troops were still stationed.

But to appreciate the precise sense in which democratic processes were impaired in 1876, it must be kept in mind that large masses of disfranchised Negroes and poor whites were used *as the basis* on which the South's representation in Congress was computed. It would have been profoundly undemocratic if the Bourbons had simply excluded Negroes and some poor whites from the polls; but the Bourbons counted these elements for the purpose of determining representation but refused to count their votes. This was more than a denial of democracy; it was a perversion of democratic processes.

The use of force to suppress the rebellion had also weakened democracy. National unity was no longer based on consent. "The Union endured," writes H. J. Eckenrode, "and there was the hope that the stitches by which the almost severed sections had been sewn together would heal in time, though the cicatrices were still raw." In this weakened condition, American democracy was confronted with the rise of an industrial system which posed a host of new social and economic problems. "In 1876," to quote Eckenrode, "the results of war, violence, and unconstitutional rule had become painfully evident. Far more apparent were the consequences of the great and sudden industrial expansion, the conversion of the United States from a primitive, loose-jointed agricultural country into a nation of mills and factories; the rise of modern finance; the beginnings of stock speculation; the creation of an immense railway system, the intoxication and corruption of a novel era, a new page in

[15] Davie, *op. cit.*, p. 54.

history. The world has had many deities. The seventies in America witnessed the orgiastic welcome to a new god — Machinery." [16] And with the machine, of course, had come "machine politics."

By 1876 the Bourbons were also ready for a deal. They had largely won the battle of reconstruction by the use of wholesale terror but they were thinking of the future and they greatly feared the possibility of a political coalition between poor whites and Negroes. "To divide the leveling host" it was necessary to separate the underprivileged whites from the Negroes.[17] The way to do this, of course, was *to create* "a race problem." The mind of the poor-white South had been poisoned against the Negro by the competition of slave labor. It was not difficult, therefore, to incite the poor whites against the Negroes by offering them as bait many of the jobs formerly filled by Negroes. For example, there were 100,000 Negro mechanics as compared with 20,000 white mechanics at the close of the war; but between 1865 and 1890 the Negroes were largely driven from these and other jobs. The effect, of course, was to convert the poor whites into a kind of underpaid, unofficial guerrilla constabulary which policed the Negro population and kept it, as a labor force, cheap and docile. Nevertheless the Bourbons had one abiding fear: that the North might intervene, once again, in an effort to protect the civil rights of the Negro.

With the "New South" and the "Reconstructed North" ready to bargain, the election of 1876 provided the last scene in the Civil War drama. The Democrats were odds-on favorites: they had an able candidate in Tilden; they had won important victories in 1874; and resentment against the corruption of the Grant administration was widespread. However, the Republicans still controlled the electoral machinery

[16] *Rutherford B. Hayes: Statesman of Reunion* by H. J. Eckenrode, 1930, p. 111.
[17] Hacker, *op. cit.*, p. 381.

in South Carolina, Louisiana, and Florida. The returns indicated, of course, that Tilden had won; but the Republicans, knowing that they controlled the three key Southern states, refused to concede the election. After a long deadlock, the famous "Bargain of 1876" — really of 1877 — was reached: the Republicans agreed not to interfere with the election of Democrats to state office in South Carolina, Louisiana, and Florida and to withdraw the troops from these states; and the Bourbons agreed to give Hayes the Presidency which Tilden had won. The agreement was even reduced to writing — like a contract. "On the one hand," writes Dr. Eckenrode, "Tilden was sold by the Southerners; on the other, the negro [*sic*] was sold by Hayes' representatives." Both parties knew that the bargain implied the nullification of the Civil War amendments to the extent that the Negro would thereafter be "eliminated from politics."

There was, indeed, a nice symmetry about the Bargain which resolved the emancipation dilemma. To appease the Abolitionists, the Negro's citizenship was affirmed. Each Negro would now be counted as a full person for the purpose of determining congressional representation but, at the same time, Negroes would simply not be permitted to vote. Thus a large bloc of votes, both in Congress and in the Electoral College, would not be subject to democratic control. In this manner, the Bourbon element would be free to manipulate "the racial problem" and thereby to divide its potential opposition. As Dr. Du Bois points out, the consequences were of far-reaching importance: "the disfranchisement of the American Negro makes the functioning of all democracy in the nation difficult; and as democracy fails to function in the leading democracy in the world, it fails in the world." Out of the racism of this period came the dynamics for the American overseas imperialism of the turn of the century: the dilemma was simply projected on a world-wide basis.

It should be noted, however, that the American people did

not make nor did they approve the Bargain of 1876. The majority that had elected Tilden believed that the decision which awarded the Presidency to Hayes was morally wrong.[18] Strange as it may seem, Tilden could probably not have withdrawn the federal troops if only because the Republicans would have been certain to make political capital of the fact.

Dr. Eckenrode's answer to the question of who won the Civil War provides a biased but illuminating answer to the related question of who profited by the Bargain of 1876: "All that had been accomplished was the exchange of one set of masters for another. The industrialists, far more cruel and relentless than the planters had ever been, now ruled the country and ruled it like hereditary lords. The United States had made an immense industrial advance in the Civil War period but the condition of the toilers was little bettered. Great factories, in which herds of 'hands' labored much harder than slaves toiled, had taken the place of the small establishments of primitive America in which the owner worked side by side with his men." Having paid off the native-American element with pensions and homesteads and preferred jobs in industry and government, Northern industrialists could use the South's racism to separate native-born and foreign-born in the North much as poor whites and Negroes were separated in the South.

The real meaning of the Bargain of 1876 was revealed the following year when the railroad workers precipitated the first acute labor crisis in American history. "Class hatred," writes Denis Tilden Lynch, "was a new note in American life where all men were equal before the law." [19] The South was still in the turmoil of reconstruction; anti-Chinese sand-lot rioters ruled in San Francisco; and 100,000 railroad strikers and 4,000,000 unemployed surged in the streets of Northern cities. At a cabinet meeting on July 22, 1877, the adminis-

[18] Eckenrode, *op. cit.*, p. 230.
[19] *The Wild Seventies*, by Denis Tilden Lynch, 1941.

tration considered placing several states under martial law. For a moment the nation seemed to hover on the brink of a new civil war — a war of class against class — but the storm subsided.

## 4. In the Wake of the Bargain

The Bargain of 1876 did not immediately restore the Bourbons to full power. "The road to reunion" had first to be paved with the sacrifice of the rights which the Civil War amendments had conferred upon Negroes. The first task, therefore, was to convince the Supreme Court to carry out, in judicial terms, the bargain which the legislators had negotiated. Reference to a few Supreme Court decisions will indicate how expeditiously and smoothly the legal phases of "operation reunion" were concluded. In the Cruikshank case (1876), the Civil Rights cases (1883), the Harris case (1889), and *Plessy* v. *Ferguson* (1890), the Supreme Court nullified the Civil War amendments so far as Negroes were concerned and placed the Bill of Rights outside the protection of the 14th Amendment. The effect of these decisions, as Justice Harlan pointed out in a memorable dissenting opinion, was "to permit the seeds of race hate to be planted under the sanction of law."

These decisions made it possible for the South *to legislate* the Negro's subordinate status; that is, to enforce this status by law. Discrimination was not limited to a denial of suffrage: through residential segregation, segregation in institutions and places of public accommodation, in schools, employment, and all walks of life, the Negro was forced into a subordinate world by techniques of dominance which have since been used in other areas, as in South Africa. The notion that this legislation "followed" or "reflected" the mores is far wide of the mark; it *made* the present-day mores of the South. The strategy was perfectly clear: through enforced segregation the Negro was to be denied, so far as possible, the opportunity for assimilating the culture of the dominant group, thereby perpetuating his subordinate status. "Segregation," as Leslie S. Perry has pointed out, "is the vehicle of unrestrained and undisguised white domination." [20] Segregation creates more prejudice than it reflects; it is an artifact, not a natural growth or organism. In the period from 1876 to 1937, about the only area in which the Negro was successful before the Supreme Court was in cases involving criminal trials and procedures and these cases, it will be noted, did not imply an extension of rights to Negroes.

"The year 1876," wrote George S. Merriam, "marked the disappearance of the Negro problem as the central feature of national politics." [21] It also marked the disappearance of all serious concern with the problem of racial discrimination. From 1870 to 1900, the outside assistance furnished by Northern foundations and missionary societies, according to Dr. Charles S. Johnson, constituted "the sole constructive influence from without a south that was itself poor, disorganized, and reactionary." With the exception of a proposal to safeguard federal elections and a proposal to grant federal subsidies for education, no important federal legislation aimed at the Negro problem in the South was even proposed between 1876 and 1906. [22] And congressional inaction, of course, was widely interpreted as equivalent to a declaration that discrimination by states and local communities was permissible. [23] It is quite erroneous, therefore, to believe that the pattern of racial discrimination which developed in this period was never sanctioned by the federal government; on the contrary, it was a direct product of federal policy if not of federal action.

Since the only hope of effective remedial action consisted

[20] See Note 2 above.
[21] *The Negro and the Nation*, by George S. Merriam, 1906.
[22] *Ibid.*
[23] See *The Legal Status of the Negro*, by Charles S. Mangum, Jr., 1940.

in the possibility of federal intervention, the national decision to sanction discrimination necessarily led to the dogma of the insolubility of "the Negro problem." The dogma rationalized the decision. "The race question," wrote John Moffatt Mecklin in 1914, "belongs to this class of essentially insoluble problems." "Relations between American Negroes and American whites," wrote Scott Nearing in 1929, "occupy a frontier of conflict which is beyond the pale of organized society." "I have been forcibly impressed," wrote William P. Pickett in 1909, "by the constant repetition of the thought that the problem is in its essential character insoluble." "No matter which way we turn in the north or in the south," wrote André Siegfried in 1927, "there seems to be no solution." There could be no solution since we had decided not to solve the problem. Even the social theory of the period supported this decision with "scientific" rationalizations.[24]

"Constitutional disfranchisement," which began in the 1890's, was intended to place the fruits of the Bargain of 1876 beyond reach of legislative interference. It was not accomplished, however, without significant protest: witness the sharp increase in lynchings and the violence which marked the Populist campaigns in the South. The Wilmington, North Carolina, race riot of 1898, in the opinion of Dr. E. Franklin Frazier, marked the triumph of the constitutional phase of the South's counterrevolution. The riot stemmed directly from the gains which the Populist Party had scored in the 1896 elections by a limited fusion of Populist-Republican, and poor white and Negro votes, in some Southern communities. The triumph of the counterrevolution in 1898 coincided with the beginnings of American overseas expansion. Once the seal of constitutional approval had been placed on the Bargain of 1876, we were ready to extend "white suprem-

[24] See "Sociological Theory and Race Relations," by E. Franklin Frazier, *American Sociological Review*, June 1947.

acy," which was almost synonymous with "manifest destiny," to the islands of the Pacific. Even before the Wilmington riot, however, Booker T. Washington's famous speech in Atlanta in 1895 had given white America the comforting assurance that Negroes, for the time being at least, would accept a subordinate status.

Despite the fact, however, that discrimination had been given constitutional sanction, Bourbon rule rested on essentially insecure and shifting foundations. For, after all, the Civil War had made some changes. "There *had* been a revolution," wrote Ray Stannard Baker; "society *had* been overturned." On a limited scale, new opportunities had been created for Negroes and the type of leadership which Booker T. Washington symbolized had been quick to take advantage of these openings. As the losses of the war were regained and new industries came to the South, Negroes began to accumulate property and here and there a new Negro middle class began to emerge. But the revolution which had created these opportunities for Negroes had also created new opportunities for the poor whites. Thus in the 1890's the competition for jobs and land between poor whites and Negroes reached a new pitch of intensity and class antagonism developed within the dominant white group. "Wherever the whites divided as Democrats and Populists," writes Dr. Paul Buck, "the rival factions courted the colored vote and some of the turbulence of Reconstruction came back." [25] Noting an upsurge of "racial feeling" half a century after the Civil War, many Americans concluded that "the Negro problem" was really insoluble.

The movement for "constitutional disfranchisement" in the 1890's reflected the Bourbons' concern that the poor whites as well as the Negroes were getting out of hand. The immediate cause, however, was the introduction by Senator Henry Cabot Lodge of legislation aimed at protecting federal elec-

[25] *The Road to Reunion*, by Dr. Paul Buck, 1937.

tions (as a Republican, Senator Lodge was anxious to stimulate a Democratic-Populist division). Commencing in Mississippi in 1890, the South began systematically to disfranchise the Negro: through grandfather clauses, literacy tests, poll taxes, and other devices. Prior to the appearance of the Populist Party, terror had sufficed to keep the Negro from the polls; but it was now necessary to place his disqualification beyond the reach of federal intervention and at the same time to minimize the political power of the poor whites. For similar reasons, Jim Crowism had to be placed on an official basis: between 1881 and 1907 a system of segregation was enacted in every Southern state. Although these measures were carried into effect by such leaders of the poor whites as Tillman, Vardaman, and Watson, they actually represented a betrayal of this element; for example, the poll tax probably disfranchised as many "poor whites" as Negroes.

The poor whites, however, were given some concessions — at the expense of the Negroes. The poor whites wanted better social services and more schools and these demands were met, to some extent, by simply diverting funds to segregated white schools. Since states normally appropriate school funds to each county on the basis of the number of children of school age, a large Negro school population could be used as a means of securing an increased state appropriation. Hence, as Leslie S. Perry has pointed out, "the larger the proportion of Negro children in a county, the smaller is the per capita expenditure on their education and the greater the expenditure for the white children." [26]

The new *system of discrimination* that emerged in the South in the 1890's did more than codify existing Jim Crow customs: it greatly increased the scope, variety, and complexity of these customs. As George S. Merriam noted, "there developed a new or a newly apparent aggression upon the weaker race." Not only were devastating inroads made on

[26] See Note 2 above.

the new employment opportunities which Negroes had won, but segregation was used to widen the gulf between the races. "The tendency has been," wrote Merriam in 1906, "to a wider separation. Once the inmates of mansion and cabin knew each other's way. Now they are almost unacquainted." "A slow but widespread process of race separation in all parts of the country," wrote Mr. Mecklin in 1914, "is gradually divorcing the Negro from the white man's world." Not only did the gulf seem to be widening but the myths of the Negro's inferiority became increasingly dogmatic. "I am just as much opposed to Booker Washington as a voter," said Senator James K. Vardaman, "with all his Anglo-Saxon re-enforcements, as I am to the cocoanut-headed, chocolate-colored, typical little coon . . . who blacks my shoes every morning." Here the pretense that Negroes were being denied certain rights merely until they had acquired social poise and an education was entirely abandoned.

Dating from the Atlanta race riot of 1906, the new aggression forced many Americans to realize that the Negro problem had grown in magnitude as the old social order had disappeared in the South. "With the passing of the generation of whose life it [slavery] was an accepted fact, both black and white, the relations which it slowly evolved are passing also" — so wrote Dr. A. H. Stone in 1907. "Not only will there be race friction," he continued, "but it will increase as the weaker race increases its demands for the equality which it is denied." This development in American race relations correlated with a somewhat similar world-wide development. About this time, Captain H. A. Wilson, traveling in Africa, noted that the natives in remote areas had somehow heard a vague report that a yellow nation (Japan) had defeated a white nation (Russia). "There can be no doubt," wrote Dr. Stone, "in the mind of any man who carefully reads American Negro journals that their rejoicing over the Japanese victory sounded a very different note from that of

White America. . . . It was a clear cry of exultation over the defeat of a white race by a dark one."

### 5. "Up from Slavery"

By forcing the Negro into a separate and segregated world, the whites forced him to form social organizations of his own and to attempt a "national liberation" movement rather similar to that which many colonial peoples have organized; that is, a movement to shake off discrimination. The Negro's struggle to achieve real minority status might be said to date from 1896 when Dr. Du Bois inaugurated the Atlanta University Studies of the Negro: "the first attempt to study in a scientific spirit the problems of the Negro in American life." [27] Previously the Negro's status had been so characterized by various "badges of servitude" that it resembled slave status more than the status of a minority. The difference was indicated by the fact that Dr. Du Bois proposed to study the problems *of* the Negro, not "the Negro problem." The same trend was strikingly apparent in the Niagara Falls conference of 1905 — also initiated by Dr. Du Bois — which led to a meeting the next year at the scene of John Brown's raid at Harpers Ferry, and to the ringing declaration: "We shall not be satisfied with less than our full manhood rights." Out of this movement came, of course, the National Association for the Advancement of Colored People.

In the period from 1900 to 1940, such social processes as migration, urbanization, and industrialization worked enormous changes in the structure of "the Negro problem." From 1900 to 1930, some 2,250,000 Negroes left farms and small villages in the South for the cities of the South; and the number of counties in "the black belt" declined from 286 in 1900 to 180 in 1940. In the period from 1910 to 1920, an estimated 500,000 Negroes moved from Southern areas to Northern in-

[27] *The Negro in the United States*, by E. Franklin Frazier, 1949, p. 503.

dustrial centers and another 500,000 moved north after the war. In 1900 only 22.7 per cent of American Negroes lived in urban areas but by 1940 the percentage had increased to 48.6. Eighty-nine per cent of the Negroes in the North, two thirds of those in the border states, and 36.4 per cent of those in the South, now live in urban areas. Prior to World War I, Negroes constituted an industrial reserve upon which employers could draw in times of labor shortage, or strikes, but by 1929 they had become an integral part of the labor force in nearly every important industry. In 1930 they made up 22.7 per cent of the building laborers; 16.2 per cent of the unskilled workers in steel; and 25 per cent of the unskilled workers in the meat-packing industry. At the same time, illiteracy dropped from 81.4 per cent in 1870 to 16.3 per cent in 1930. The growth of Negro settlements in urban areas was accompanied, of course, by the establishment of more Negro businesses and the creation of new professional opportunities. With occupational differentiation, socio-economic classes began to emerge in the Negro world and the new Negro middle class began to win political recognition. After 1917 Negroes appeared in the legislatures of such states as Michigan, Illinois, Missouri, New Jersey, California, New York, Pennsylvania, Kansas, Ohio, and West Virginia, and as councilmen and judges in many cities.

The migration of Negroes and the expansion of the activities of the federal government after World War I brought the government into a new relation with Negroes. "Race relations," as T. J. Woofter, Jr., observed in 1925, "have become more national and less sectional because, in its expansion, the federal government has come into contact with the Negro in new ways. The use of Negro troops, aid to the Negro farmer, application of the various funds appropriated for education and public health, the relation of the Negro to the labor problems of the nation, and the influence of the presence of large numbers of Negroes on the immigration policy are all concrete instances of the growth, altogether apart from party politics, of a national attitude to replace the old sectional view of race contacts." [28] The postwar movement of Negroes to the North was, for example, both a cause and an effect of the Exclusionary Immigration Act of 1924.

As much as anything else, perhaps, it was World War I, and the frightful postwar race riots, that changed American race relations by making race relations a national concern. Herbert J. Seligmann, for example, noted that World War I had not so much improved the position of the Negro as it had increased his strategic importance in the national scene. Far from harmonizing the two races, the war had created a situation in which the problem of living together in the same society "was made immensely more urgent and more menacing." [29] The postwar riots indicated that "the south's color psychosis" had spread throughout the nation. The Ku Klux Klan was strong in Western states such as Oregon and Colorado, and in Indiana, and lynchings were reported in Delaware, Pennsylvania, Ohio, Indiana, Illinois, Colorado, and Kansas.

The nationalization of the race problem — striking evidence that Negroes were emerging as a real minority — brought the problem back, once again, to Congress. In 1919 and 1920 resolutions were introduced calling for an investigation of lynchings and in 1918 a Division of Negro Economics was created in the Department of Labor. At about the same time, also, the Supreme Court took cognizance of the new strategic position of the Negro by reinvesting the "due process clause" with some of the original meaning which the court had denied it in the 1870's and 1880's. Beginning with *Moore* v. *Dempsey* in 1923, a new trend was noted in the court's decisions affecting Negroes which has been explained as reflecting "the shifting of the social outlook of some of the justices." But the change

[28] *The Basis of Racial Adjustment*, by T. J. Woofter, Jr., 1925.
[29] *The Negro Faces America*, by Herbert J. Seligmann, 1920.

also reflected the fact that Negroes now had the resources and the leadership to battle for their rights and the social organization, as in the NAACP, to fight effectively.

Just as the Supreme Court was forced to shift its social outlook, so such racists as Madison Grant, Lothrop Stoddard, and Dr. C. C. Josey began to spin new theories and myths as they correlated the rise of Negroes with "a rising tide of color" in the world. And if one compares two special studies of "the Negro problem" prepared by the American Academy of Political and Social Science, one in 1913, and one in 1928, it can be readily seen that social theorists were also being forced to change their outlook on the problem. The editor of the 1928 volume pointed out that "since that time [1913] students of race as well as laymen have had to discard or even reverse many of their theories concerning 'trends' and 'solutions' of Negro development and 'problems.'" As Negroes verged on minority status, the Negro problem began to give way to various specific problems faced by Negroes. Social theorists also began to see, for the first time, how the myth of *a Negro problem* had confused earlier investigators. "For years the Negro," writes Robert L. Sutherland, "has been a problem in Sunday school quarterlies, textbooks, and public addresses, but an understanding of the full and intricate nature of the problem has seldom been attempted. Typically, these approaches have lumped all twelve million Negroes — black, brown, and light yellow, rich and poor, good and bad — together as a homogeneous group deserving the white man's sympathy, contempt, or assistance." [30]

With World War II, American Negroes emerged into full minority status and their objective became not equal status but complete integration. The Second World War, like the First, greatly enhanced the Negro's strategic significance. Since 1940 it has been perfectly clear that Negroes hold a pivotal position in American politics, in the balance not only

[30] *Color, Class and Personality*, by Robert L. Sutherland, 1942, p. xiv.

between regions and parties but between classes. The tendency of Negroes, during the depression, to turn to left-wing political movements underscored the meaning of this change. The same significance was apparent in the manner in which Franklin D. Roosevelt shifted the Negro vote from the Republican to the Democratic column. The meaning of this new strategic power might be put this way: just as the Bourbons were forced to make concessions to poor whites in the 1890's, so concessions must now be made to Negroes, and for the same reason — to prevent a trend to the left.

By one of the major ironies of American race relations, reaction has found the technique to delay the radicalization of Negro protest in the concept of civil rights. The term "civil rights," by usage dating from the original federal Civil Rights Act, relates to the right of persons to equal accommodation in places of public amusement, entertainment, and convenience.[31] In its origin, therefore, the term is to be distinguished from "civil liberties," which guarantee certain individual rights from encroachment by government. It will be noted that President Truman appointed a Committee on Civil Rights, not on civil liberties.

Since 1947 this distinction has been steadily sharpened so that today "civil rights" has come to mean those civil liberties which a benevolent government grants, more or less as a favor, to racial minorities; while "civil liberties" proper relate to those rights which individuals must assert against government. With subtle but unmistakable emphasis, Negroes have been offered a bargain: civil rights for a repudiation of radical protest. The intent of the bargain, of course, is to keep the racial and economic crises in separate air-tight compartments. Yet, as the Jewish minority has discovered, civil rights do not guarantee full equality when the basis of inequality is to be found in unequal competitive power. For example, it is significant that despite all the gains they have made American Negroes "have

[31] Davie, *op. cit.*, p. 288.

failed to develop business enterprises commensurate with their achievements in other phases of American civilization." [32] Studies have shown that while Negro enterprises constitute almost half of all businesses in Negro neighborhoods in Chicago, they receive less than a tenth of all money spent by Negroes in these areas.[33] Certain businesses in which Negroes have generally succeeded, such as mortuaries and certain types of insurance, represent fields which "white" business abandoned and Negro businessmen occupied by default.

The strategic importance of American Negroes has also been greatly enhanced since World War II as part of the changing relation of America to the rest of the world and of the relation of American Negroes to other racial groups. Before the outbreak of World War II, one third of the area and one third of the population of the world were under colonial rule. These 700,000,000 colonial people might be considered as a special minority problem, since they are colored peoples ruled by whites who suffer from various disabilities and discriminations which also affect domestic minorities. As Dr. James G. Leyburn has pointed out, "modern minority problems, with the exception of those in Europe, had their original in the spreading abroad of Europeans after the discoveries of Columbus" [34] so that there is historical warrant for relating colonialism to the problem of racial minorities. That 5246 Englishmen rule some 22,000,000 natives in Nigeria does not destroy the parallel between the status of Nigerians and a domestic minority; for the essence of minority status is not to be found in the numerical ratio between two groups but in the discrepancy in power. In each case, the test is whether government rests on the consent of the governed.

It is against this background of world colonialism that the enhanced strategic importance of the Negro minority must

---

[32] Frazier, *op. cit.*, p. 409.
[33] *Ibid.*, p. 406.
[34] *World Minority Problems*, by James G. Leyburn, 1947, p. 15.

be measured. For the world colonial problem has passed into a new phase with World War II and the changes which have come in its wake. The number of people under colonial rule has been reduced to perhaps 200,000,000 and the pressure for freedom within these remaining colonial areas has rapidly gathered fresh momentum. Discrimination against racial minorities in the United States is today intimately related to international politics and American foreign policy and one may confidently expect the lot of our domestic racial minorities to improve as colored peoples in other areas emerge from colonial status.

The treatment of American minorities, however, is basically of deepest concern to American citizens and for a reason that has been well stated by Felix S. Cohen. "Here in America," he writes, "the treatment of minorities has always been the best index of liberal civilization. Advances of inventions in our commerce, industry, science, or government begin as unorthodox ideas, and have flourished on this soil because America was par excellence a land where men could differ from their neighbors and find tolerance. American prosperity, not less than American inventiveness and American freedom, are profoundly threatened by an upsurge of intolerance. And of all forms of intolerance that directed against a racial minority is the most terrible, because there is no escape from one's race. . . . And yet, terrible as is the fact of racial oppression to an oppressed minority, it is, in the long run, more terrible to the dominant society of the oppressor. For the fact remains that while racial intolerance has seldom destroyed its intended victim, it has almost always, in the end, destroyed the society in which it flourished. . . . For the rights of each of us in a democracy can be no stronger than the rights of our weakest minority." [35]

[35] *Commentary*, August 1948, p. 143.

# CHAPTER IX

## The Jewish Minority and Anti-Semitism

IN MOST BOOKS on minorities, the Jewish minority and the problem of anti-Semitism have usually been regarded as special issues requiring separate consideration. For years the tendency has been to view the Jews as a highly specialized — "a peculiar" — minority, with unique references and implications. And it must be conceded that it is difficult to relate the problems of the Jewish minority to those, say, of certain racial minorities. It was for this reason that I omitted any consideration of the Jewish minority in the original edition of *Brothers Under the Skin*. I have now decided, however, to include a chapter on the Jewish minority and anti-Semitism precisely because the difficulties mentioned can be used to throw an interesting light on important phases of minority status.

One of these difficulties has to do with nomenclature. In the past, the tendency has been to classify minorities as racial, ethnic, religious, or cultural, and then to engage in lengthy and essentially inconclusive arguments about whether a particular group belongs in one classification or another. In similar fashion, both Jews and non-Jews have argued endlessly, and inconclusively, about the proper designation of the Jews — whether they are a cultural, religious, or a "sociologically racial" minority.[1] Curiously enough, even Jewish sociologists have written of the Jewish minority in terms which, by characterizing the minority as racial, have reflected the racist ideology against which Jews have bitterly contended.

The fact is that the tendency to classify minorities in terms

[1] *The Nature of Human Nature*, by Ellsworth Faris, p. 341.

of "traits," racial or cultural, is misleading for it diverts attention from the *relationships* between minority and majority and also suggests that minority status is to be explained in terms of the minority's distinguished traits or characteristics. Yet the "light" Negro, the "assimilated" Jew, and the "Spanish" Mexican have all discovered that there is more to minority status than the sum of the various "differences" which distinguish the minority from the majority. Actually the tendency to classify minorities in this fashion is a carry-over of the racist thinking of the last century which consistently sought out differences rather than similarities between groups.

This does not mean, of course, that all classifications of minorities are futile; it merely means that we have been classifying minorities in terms of unrealistic and irrelevant norms. Instead of classifying minorities by "traits," it would be much more realistic to classify the different schemes or techniques by which one group subordinates another. Minorities should not be held up as "exhibits"; on the contrary, we should study the relationships between majority and minority. To the extent that linguistic, religious, cultural, or racial differences are a factor in the scheme of subordination, then these differences are relevant to a classification of minorities; otherwise they are more likely to confuse than to clarify the issues.

For a number of reasons the Jewish minority differs from the so-called "racial" minorities but the factor of race itself is the least important of these reasons. For example, the long history of Jewish persecution, which has made the Jews traditional scapegoats in the Western World, and the peculiar historical relationship between Judaism and Christianity, are more important factors than race per se. But the age-old cry that the Jews killed Christ complicates, it is not a cause of, modern anti-Semitism. Jews are a "peculiar" minority because they have a unique history and experience. Although there is no Jewish problem as such, the Jewish minority has many special problems, of which anti-Semitism is, by all odds, the most important. Similarly, anti-Semitism differs from the "race-baiting" of Negroes and is, indeed, a most peculiar social disease. Negroes and Mexicans are oppressed; Jews are excluded. Clubs, guest ranches, and swank resorts do not bother to specify that Negro patronage is not accepted but Jews are excluded by name. The fact that the discrimination practiced against Jews, as well as their problems, has certain special characteristics should indicate to us that there is something peculiar about the relationship between the Jewish minority and the majority and such is clearly the case.

Jews belong to a special group of minorities that might best be called "trading" minorities. The majority does not hold Negroes and Mexicans at a distance; it subordinates them — directly, blatantly, unapologetically. But the majority seeks to contain Jews. The difference is reflected, also, in the stereotype of the two groups. The Negro is lazy, shiftless, irresponsible, dirty, and so on, whereas the Jew is clever, cunning, extremely ambitious, too intelligent for his own good, and so on. In both cases, the stereotyping process is the same but it is used for different purposes, with a different strategy in mind, and it reflects a different relationship. Negroes are a "working" minority; Jews are a "trading" minority. The difference is also reflected in the public-opinion polls which have shown that very few people believe that Negroes have "too much" social, economic, or political power; whereas a large number believe that Jews possess a degree of power which is somehow "menacing."

Trading minorities, of which Jews are the classic type, are not as common or nearly as numerous as working minorities, but they include many minorities in addition to Jews. The list would include, for example, the Parsees of Hindu society and the Armenian Gregorian Monophysites in the world of Islam (both mentioned by Toynbee); the overseas Chinese in many countries (if the Japanese had not conquered Malaya, it was said, the Chinese traders would have taken over); the Indians in Kenya; certain Mohammedan groups in Central Asia; Quakers and Huguenots (at least historically); and, in the United States, Armenians, Japanese-Americans, Syrians, and Greek-Americans. In a rather farfetched sense, one might even say that the Yankee peddlers of the pre-Civil War period belong in the same classification or typology of "marginal trading people." [2] The working minority is visibly subordinate; the trading minority is marginal rather than subordinate. The majority senses both types as competitors but the basis of the rivalry is different.

To state the issue in this way is to recognize immediately that the difference between racial minorities and the Jewish minority is a difference in degree and not in kind; that competition for place, prestige, power, and position is the source of conflict in both cases; and that though the basis of the competition may be different, the majority's strategy is the same, namely, dominance. Indeed part of the trouble with our thinking about such issues as anti-Semitism is that the Jewish minority has for too long been regarded as a special case. The Jewish experience in America, which recapitulates their experience elsewhere but with important variations, provides an excellent illustration of the nature of marginal trading minorities.

## 1. The Jews and America

A Jewish writer once observed that "anti-Semitism in America should be like the snakes of Ireland: there shouldn't be any." As a matter of fact, the stain of anti-Semitism was not there — originally. Certainly the official record — the conduct of the American government toward the Jewish minority — is virtually stainless. Historians are generally agreed that the emancipation of the Jews in Europe was more apparent than real; the medieval heritage of anti-Semitism simply could not

[2] *Jews in a Gentile World*, by Graeber and Britt, 1942, p. 389.

be obliterated overnight with the stroke of a pen. But this tradition really never existed in the United States and certainly not in its European form. It was here that the Jewish question first lost its medieval theological overtones and became, almost from the outset, a secular question. As Hugo Valentin has observed, the Declaration of Independence really marks the beginning of Jewish Emancipation since the United States was the first modern state to order a complete separation of Church and State and to adopt an unconditional guarantee of freedom of religious worship. Just because anti-Semitism in America has been largely of the private rather than the public or governmental variety, we have been blind to the fact that much the same type of exclusion has come to prevail here that was known in Europe, with the important difference, of course, that anti-Semitism has never been officially sanctioned or enforced as a state policy, which is merely another way of saying that we have a tradition of equality in the United States which was lacking in Europe. How, then, did the stain develop?

In 1776 there were only about 1000 Jews among approximately 3,000,000 American colonials. For the most part, these were Sephardic Jews who had come to the United States by way of Holland and South America and who had found, on the whole, a friendly reception here. To be sure, there was prejudice against them and statutory discriminations were to be found in a few states, but Arnold and Caroline Rose describe the general situation well when they write that "they [the Jews] were not oppressed any more than the Catholics or Quakers. . . . The discrimination was social and economic, but did not extend to the legal or political spheres." [3] Furthermore the status of Jews rapidly improved with the strong democratic currents that came after the Revolution of 1776.

By 1880 there were approximately 250,000 Jews in the United States. The increase was made up, almost entirely, of

[3] *America Divided*, by Arnold and Caroline Rose, 1948, p. 37.

German-Jews who came to this country in large numbers following the reaction which swept over Europe in the wake of the Napoleonic Wars. In point of time, the German-Jewish immigration was intermediate; that is, it fell between the "old" and the "new" immigration. It was made up, also, of people who, having known legal equality in Germany, adjusted rapidly to American conditions. In manners and appearance, in education and culture, German-Jewish immigrants were not sharply set apart from the native population. Even their religious practices were soon brought into substantial alignment and conformity with American practice. Swept immediately into the current of westward expansion, the German-Jews were carried far from the ports of entry and became widely and sparsely distributed. In the rapidly growing communities of the Middle West, the Far West, and the South, they found, and made the most of, extraordinary economic opportunities. In such communities as Cincinnati, Chicago, Louisville, St. Paul, Dallas, San Francisco, and Los Angeles, German-Jewish "first families" won high status based on priority of settlement and the wealth and distinction which they had achieved. Merely to mention such names as Straus, Rosenwald, Seligman, Warburg, Schiff, Morgenthau, Sloss, Sutro, and Lubin, is to suggest the remarkable upward mobility of the German-Jews.

The great post-1880 migration of Jews to the United States stemmed from the countries of eastern Europe. Set in motion by pogroms and officially inspired anti-Semitism, some 1,467,-266 Jewish immigrants, from Russia, Rumania, and Austria alone, arrived in the period between 1880 and 1910: an average of something like 48,908 per year. In every respect, these immigrants were more sharply set apart from the native population than the German-Jews. In appearance and manner, custom and speech, and in religious observances, they were far more "conspicuous" than their coreligionists. Having experienced extreme persecution, the Ashkenazic Jews of middle Europe were inclined to be orthodox in religion and radical in politics. In terms of the stereotype, they were "more Jewish" than the Sephardic or German-Jews.

But what principally distinguished them was the fact that they were desperately poor — 40 per cent arrived with less than thirty dollars — and that they were much closer to the realities of the ghetto than the German-Jews. With many of them, pogroms, ritual murder trials, and official anti-Semitic bars were not far-off memories but vivid recent experiences. They were also relatively late comers. The German-Jews, who had settled here fifty years earlier under far more favorable circumstances, naturally tended to look down upon their "unprepossessing coreligionists" and, as one Jewish historian puts it, to regard them "as a grotesque species of ill-bred savages." Indeed the word "kike" is said to have been first applied to Russian-Jews by German-Jews in the United States.[4] The great bulk of American-Jews today are, of course, of east European origin. The fact that approximately one third of the present-day Jewish population is foreign-born serves as a reminder, also, that, as a group, Jews are fairly recent immigrants.

Judged by objective criteria, few more desirable immigrant groups ever came to America than the east European Jews. With the possible exception of the Irish, they showed the least inclination of all immigrant groups to return to Europe. They brought their families with them; they were slightly more literate than the average immigrants of the period; and they were an urban people of many skills, trades, and talents. By 1880, however, a definite pattern of urban immigrant settlement had been established and into this "slum" complex the Jews were inexorably drawn. The year 1880, which divides the "old" from the "new" immigration, also marks a turning point in the American economy: free lands were rapidly disappearing and the first trusts and monopolies were being

[4] Article by Dr. Wm. M. Kephart, *Social Forces*, Vol. 29, p. 153.

formed. Many east European Jews, however, started out directly in the trades, rather than in the familiar immigrant pattern of the unskilled or semi-skilled occupations, and from their earnings they were able to send their children to college. Generally speaking, they showed a greater upward social mobility than other east European immigrants who arrived at about the same time. The tide of Jewish immigration from eastern Europe continued at full flood until World War I, paused momentarily, and was then resumed only to be brought to an abrupt halt by the Exclusionary Immigration Act of 1924, which carried, of course, unmistakable overtones of anti-Semitism.

Taking advantage of the cleavages in American Jewry, the native racists cleverly divided American-Jews into three categories: the Sephardic Jews of the pre-1840 period ("Superior to other representatives of Israel"); the German-Jews, junior to the Sephardic Jews in time and prestige, occasionally elected "to one of the most exclusive city clubs — although here, it must be admitted, progress is more difficult"; and, finally, the "Polish" or "Russian" Jews, to whom the European Jewish stereotype was first applied. For example, the first appearance of the stereotyped, caricatured Jew on the American stage dates from the 1870's.[5] The divisions, of course, were real, but they were given completely misleading rationalization. Since they were being placed in polite and special categories, neither the Sephardic nor the German-Jews were inclined to challenge the rationalization. On the other hand, the rationalization made it possible for some native Americans to give vent to a latent anti-Semitism while at the same time denying the existence of any bias. Officially there was no anti-Semitism in America; if any prejudice existed, it was merely a justifiable antipathy to the "undesirable" Polish or Russian Jew.

The rationalization concealed but it could not obliterate an

[5] See "Minority Caricatures on the American Stage," by Dr. Harold E. Adams in *Studies in the Science of Society*, 1937.

emerging pattern of discrimination. In one community after another, German-Jews had risen rapidly, and to high stations, but they had not gone quite to the top, nor, to this day, has room been made for them at this exalted level. Standing at the top rung of the ladder, barring the way, were the tycoons of the period: Vanderbilt, Huntington, Hill, Harriman, Rockefeller, Gould, Carnegie, Morgan, Armour, and the others, of whom only Gould, as Henry Adams pointed out, "showed a trace of Jewish origin." Here was no effete European aristocracy anxious to acquire injections of new wealth by intermarriage with a rising social element. On the contrary, here was a money-crazed elite, untrained in the uses of wealth and social power, arrogant, ruthless, and domineering. To the German-Jews, this element seemed to say: Beyond this line you cannot go. It was here, in the upper reaches of the society, that the doors were first slammed and the invitations first withdrawn.

Hoffman Nickerson, who has never liked the Jews, nevertheless states the fact accurately when he writes that the upper classes in America forced the Jew to renounce "his hope of concealing his separateness in order to rise within non-Jewish societies. . . . Had the American rich accepted social relations and intermarriage with the Jews to the same extent as the French or the British rich, the comparative looseness and fluidity of our social structure might well have bogged us down badly in the hopeless blind alley of assimilationism." [6] Fortunately, from Nickerson's point of view, we had "no class of poor nobles or gentlefolk open to the temptation of marriage with rich Jews and able on their side to obtain a measure of social recognition for their Jewish partners." This was much the same view expressed by Hilaire Belloc, who, like Nickerson, is no partisan of the Jews. There had been scarcely a trace of anti-Semitism in the United States, he wrote, through

---

[6] *The American Rich,* 1930, by Hoffman Nickerson; see also, by the same author, *Arms and Policy* (1945) and *The New Slavery* (1947).

the early and middle nineteenth century. When it did appear, it took the form of "a certain social prejudice among the wealthier classes in the East." [7]

There had, of course, been earlier expressions of prejudice but they had not been deeply significant. But when the Grand Union Hotel at Saratoga Springs noisily refused accommodations to Joseph Seligman and his family, in the summer of 1877, the significance of the discrimination was unmistakable, for Seligman was one of the best known and most widely respected German-Jews in the United States, a man of culture and refinement. Henry Ward Beecher preached a famous sermon on the Saratoga Springs incident in which, after denouncing the discrimination, he had insisted that the affair was as a slight breath, a white frost, a "momentary flash of insult," painful and annoying to be sure, but like the bite of a mosquito to a man in his whole armor. But apparently the "bite" was more serious than he realized for in 1893 the son of Jesse Seligman, brother of Joseph, was blackballed by the Union League Club, of which his father had been one of the founders and a former vice president.

A decade after the Saratoga Springs incident, Alice Hyneman Rhine wrote an article on "Race Prejudice at Summer Resorts" in which she pointed out (my emphasis): "This prejudice, in its *outward* expression at least, is a *new* feature in the New World. *Only within the present decade* has there been an anti-Jewish sentiment *openly* displayed in the United States." [8] From Saratoga Springs, the discrimination had spread throughout the Catskills and Adirondacks and had become an accepted social practice. The German-Jews minimized the importance of this spreading stain of discrimination but it was nevertheless deeply significant for it symbolized the fact that, beyond a certain point, the Jews would not be accepted; at this point an invisible curtain had been lowered. No one would

[7] *The Jews,* by Hilaire Belloc, 1922, pp. 201–203.
[8] *Forum,* July 1887.

admit — neither Jew nor Gentile — that the curtain was there for, as Ludwig Lewisohn pointed out, the official script said that there was no anti-Semitism in America. But it was there, all the same, and it could be "seen," so to speak, in the absence of Jews in the upper reaches of the society.

In this earlier period, an occasional German-Jew had been admitted to the inner sanctums of social life to which the elite are accustomed to withdraw, the better to consolidate their social power. But the position of these lonely exceptions became increasingly embarrassing as time went on and no further Jews were admitted. And, a little later, specific barriers began to be raised against Jewish applications. Harris Newmark, one of the pioneer merchants of Los Angeles, had been admitted to the city's most exclusive club. But his memoirs contain this rather unhappy comment: ". . . several Los Angeles clubs were organized in the early era of sympathy, tolerance and good feeling, when the individual was appreciated at his true worth and before the advent of men whose bigotry has sown intolerance and discord, and has made a mockery of both religion and professed ideals." [9] Other German-Jews must have felt a similar bitterness when they saw this "early era of sympathy" pushed aside by what Veblen called "a gradually advancing wave of sentiment favoring quasi-predatory business habits, insistence on status, anthropomorphism, and conservatism generally." [10]

The first indications that anti-Jewish discrimination, which had theretofore been exclusively social, had begun to assume economic implications were noted around 1910. Dr. A. L. Severson, in a study of help-wanted ads in the Chicago press, found that there had been no discriminatory ads in the period from 1872 to 1911. Beginning in 1911, however, ads specifying "Christians only" or "Gentiles only" began to appear with increasing frequency, and a decade later had reached signifi-

[9] *Sixty Years in Southern California*, by Harris Newmark, 1916, p. 383.
[10] *The Theory of the Leisure Class*, by Thorstein Veblen.

cant proportions.[11] The appearance of this pattern of economic discrimination, at this time, indicated that two things were happening: the second generation east European Jews were beginning to enter the clerical labor market in significant numbers, and Jewish immigrants, in large numbers, were moving out of the needle trades in New York into other trades and occupations. "In the tailor shop," wrote S. M. Melamed, "the Jewish working man competed with no one else. But when he leaves the shop and invades the field of the retailer, the peddler, the promoter or the real estate man, he will tread upon somebody's corn." [12]

A number of events around this time, including the formation of the Anti-Defamation League in 1913, a spate of articles on discrimination, and the calling of numerous conferences on employment problems, as well as many "incidents," all serve to indicate that the cold social exclusion of the earlier period had come to be paralleled by an aggressive anti-Semitism with economic and political implications. The explosion which destroyed the illusion that anti-Semitism did not exist in the United States was the Leo Frank case in Georgia in 1913. Then, in the postwar period, came the Russian Revolution and the attempt to define "Bolshevism" as a blend of Jewishness and Communism, which was, of course, a theme in the violent anti-Semitic campaign launched by Henry Ford in 1920. Just as the upper class leaders of American Jewry had erroneously minimized the significance of the Frank case, so these same elements were quite confident that Ford's apology of 1927 had brought the unhappy postwar developments to a close. But, with the depression and the rise of European fascism, the earlier political agitation was resumed on a bold and greatly expanded scale, rising to a crescendo of violence and verbal obscenity in the years 1939 and 1940. By 1940 there could be no doubt, even in the high "hush-hush" circles of Jewish life,

[11] *American Journal of Sociology*, January 1939.
[12] *Jewish Experiences in America*, p. 121.

that anti-Semitism had somehow taken root in American life, not as a noxious European importation, but as an aspect of the growth of the American economy. The stain was there: it might spread; it might disappear in time; but it could no longer be blinked.

## 2. *In the Middle of the Middle*

"What is remarkable about Jews in America," wrote the editors of *Fortune* in a survey published in 1936, "is not their industrial power but their curious industrial distribution, their tendency to crowd together in particular squares of the checkerboard." [13] The findings of the survey showed clearly, if inadequately, the general distribution of Jews in the American economy: their negligible influence in insurance and finance; their almost complete absence from the domain of heavy industry, including coal, auto, rubber, chemical, shipping, transportation, shipbuilding, petroleum, aviation, railroads, and other industries; and their similar absence, in any significant way, from the important private-utilities field and lumbering, agriculture, mining, dairy farming, food processing, the manufacture of heavy machinery, and so on. The survey brought out, of course, the existence of a measure of Jewish influence in the light industries field and in a few new industries (such as radio and motion pictures), and in certain industries, such as the liquor industry, to which a social stigma once attached. Although the survey spoke eloquently of the real Jewish position in the American economy, it failed to note certain important qualitative aspects of Jewish business: its marginal character in relation to non-Jewish firms in the same field; the fact that so much of it is "nepotistic, speculative, and otherwise old-fashioned in comparison with the cartelized, impersonal industrial corpora-

[13] *Jews in America*, 1936.

tions"; [14] the heavy risk factor; and the fact that so many of the businesses with which Jews are identified are of a character that fails to invest ownership with social power and prestige.

The same crowding on the checkerboard may also be noted in the professions in which Jews are concentrated in the self-employed categories and largely absent in the professions directly related to American industry — such, for example, as engineering. The percentage of Jews gainfully employed in the professions is well above the national average and is highly concentrated in medicine and law, which together account for one third (in San Francisco) and two thirds (in Boston) of all Jews in the professions.[15] In a study made in Ohio, for example, it was shown that the number of Jews in the professions of medicine, law, dentistry, and pharmacy was approximately in balance with the ratio of Jews in the general population, but that the number in teaching, engineering, architecture, and certain other professions was below the ratio of Jews in the general population.[16]

No amount of sophistry and rationalization can disguise the fact that the occupational distribution of Jews shows certain striking differences from that of the general population. The concentration in retail trade is, perhaps, the most striking difference: 43 per cent of the Jews in Passaic and 60 per cent of those in Pittsburgh are engaged in retail trade by comparison with a figure of 16.7 per cent for the country as a whole. About 38 per cent of the Jewish group is to be found in the self-employed category by comparison with 19 per cent in the general population.[17] The trading group, among Jews, is

[14] See the article by David Riesman, *Public Opinion Quarterly*, Spring 1942, p. 41.

[15] "How Many Jews in America?" by Sophia M. Robison, *Commentary*, August 1949, p. 185.

[16] "Jews in the Liberal Professions in Ohio," by L. J. Levinger, *Journal of Jewish Social Studies* II, 1940, p. 429.

[17] Robison, *op. cit.*, p. 190.

almost three times larger than the national average; the Jewish professional group is, on the whole, about twice the national average; while the proportion of gainfully employed Jews in the skilled occupations is nowhere near that in the total population. Claiming 17.5 per cent of all gainfully employed Americans, agriculture claims only about 1 per cent of the gainfully employed Jews. "Even if we were to classify the white collar workers among the proletariat," writes Lestchinsky, "the wage earning element among Jews would still be only half as large as among the American population in general. Seventy per cent of the economically active population in the country are wage-earners; among Jews this group constitutes only about forty per cent. Furthermore, while seventy per cent of all wage workers among non-Jews are engaged in physical work and only about thirty per cent in clerical office work, this proportion is reversed among Jews. Since Jewish white collar workers are mostly connected with mercantile rather than with industrial enterprises, it is not surprising that they are actually and psychologically closer to the middle class. A large part of them eventually leave the proletarian status altogether, the women after marriage and the men through setting up in some business independently." [18]

Jews are not only a predominantly middle class group: they are in the middle of the middle class. The nub of the matter, as Lestchinsky has pointed out, is that the Jews ". . . have quite naturally taken . . . a redundant position between the Anglo-Saxon and the other ethnic groups." They tend to occupy the in-between positions, the positions "left over by the British-Americans and other dominant groups." [19] It so happened that heavy Jewish immigration from eastern Europe coincided with heavy non-Jewish immigration from the same

[18] "The Position of the Jews in the Economic Life of America," by Jacob Lestchinsky in *Jews in a Gentile World*, 1942, pp. 402–416. See, also, to the same general effect, "What Sociology Knows About American Jews," by Nathan Glazer, *Commentary*, March 1950, pp. 275–284.
[19] *Ibid.*

source, and for generations Jews had discharged the functions of a middle class in relation to the peasants of central and southeastern Europe. It was quite natural, therefore, that they should discharge the same function, for the same groups, here. They were experienced with urban living and a complex money economy and they had little difficulty with language since most of them were literate and many were already trilingual. It is not surprising, therefore, that Dr. W. Lloyd Warner should report that the Jews of Yankee City had climbed the status ladder faster than any other ethnic group, including groups that had been in the city for one or two generations longer.[20]

In terms of the relevant historical and cultural factors, there is nothing "abnormal" about American Jews; they have distributed themselves in ways which have been entirely normal and understandable. This admission, however, should not be permitted to conceal the fact that there is something highly abnormal about the Jewish position in the economy. For the fact is that throughout their tragic experience, Jews have been *excluded* from certain economic categories, and this forced exclusion cannot be ignored in any attempt to explain their peculiar distribution on the occupational checkerboard. Historically the exclusion was due to many factors: Jews could not be tillers of the soil because land tenure was related to feudal obligations and the absence of "free" lands; Jews could not become soldiers because military service was part of feudal tenure which had its semireligious aspects; as "strangers" in the medieval world Jews were perforce required to live in cities; and, in cities, most of the trades were hereditary and to practice one of the technical trades guild membership was necessary. About the only trades the Jews could practice were those within their own community and for this community; that is, they had to be butchers, because of their dietary laws,

[20] *The Social System of Ethnic Groups,* by W. Lloyd Warner, 1945, p. 203.

and tailors, since certain laws had to be observed in the making of clothes. Thus, by a process of elimination, moneylending and, later, foreign trade became their occupational norms, moneylending because Christians could not charge interest, foreign trade because of the Church's doctrine about the "just price." [21] Jews were moneylenders, indeed, because they were the only people, during the Middle Ages, who were permitted to engage in moneylending. Their experience, therefore, contains a blending of coercive and permissive factors; of accident and design; but the pattern, once established, has tended to be self-repeating.

Although the traditional Jewish economic position was largely due to historical factors, it was out of this relationship that the antagonisms were generated which, sooner or later, always resulted in expulsion or exclusion. The source of the enmity was to be found in the economic relationship, as of borrower towards lender; but, as Louis Boudin has pointed out, "when an evil practice can be personalized either in the form of a particular foreign element, or by 'foreigners' generally, the hatred becomes concentrated and easily assumes violent form." [22] When the Italians were the principal money-lenders in England, they, too, were hated by many borrowers, notably by borrowers of small means who had to pay high rates of interest. "A barbarian," writes Toynbee, "cannot bear to see a resident alien living a life apart and making a profit by transacting business which the barbarian lacks the skill to transact himself" — or, one might add, the means or the right.[23] Thus one country after another penalized the Jews during periods when they were indispensable only to expel them as soon as a native middle class had been developed. Welcomed as commercial pioneers, they were evicted or ex-

[21] "Recent Developments in Economic Theory and The Resurgence of Anti-Semitism," by Louis B. Boudin, *ORT Economic Review*, June 1947, pp. 3–33.

[22] *Ibid.*

[23] *A Study of History*, by Arnold J. Toynbee, 1947, p. 136.

cluded as soon as their services had ceased to be indispensable.

In general, this pattern has been repeated in America, as the *Fortune* survey shows, but with important differences. Jews have assumed their traditional economic roles but not in relation to the entire population for here a native middle class had already come into being. Here they have not been expelled: they have simply been kept in their corner, in their special niche in the economy. Anti-Semitism in America stems from the peculiar position of Jews in the economy and takes two characteristic forms: discrimination against the Jewish business as such; and various attempts to minimize Jewish competition by restricting Jews to certain businesses and professions.

It will be said, of course, that the Jewish position in the economy is a "natural" outcome of certain accidents of history. For example, as relatively late comers, Jews have faced special handicaps in the field of heavy industry. Heavy industry, moreover, is a field in which they lack traditional skills. In finance and insurance, too, the established family fortunes had, in many cases, already been made and the control of these fortunes implied control of the financial and insurance empires. The fact that Jews had socially inherited skills in some fields and not in others also helps to explain their economic distribution. But factors of this kind do not add up to an entirely satisfactory explanation of an admittedly abnormal economic distribution. Too often the marginal position which Jews so frequently occupy is clearly the badge of some prior exclusion. For example: excluded from insurance, Jews have gone into the insurance brokerage business; excluded from iron and steel, they have bought and sold scrap; excluded from the auto industry, they have gone into the used car business. Nor has it been *every* new industry in which they have been able to get a foothold. Indeed about the only new industries in which they have succeeded have been those which the dominant groups originally ignored, such as motion pictures. In

such new industries as advertising, petroleum, and the manufacture of chemicals, they have not been able to make much
headway.

Just as the accidents of history do not provide an entirely
satisfactory account of the Jewish place in the American
economy, so it is quite impossible to explain this position in
terms of the psychological traits of Jews or in terms of any
inherent qualities. To say that Jews have succeeded in business, as one Jewish historian has done, because they are "active
and restless" does not say enough; why are they active and
restless? The basic explanation is clearly social. "A body social,
a group or class," writes Toynbee, "which is socially penalized
either by accident or by its own act or by the act of other
members of the society in which it lives" is able to respond to
the challenge of being handicapped in or altogether excluded
from "certain fields of activity by concentrating its energies
on other fields and excelling in these." [24] Veblen, of course,
offered much the same explanation for the existence of certain
special skills among Jews and of certain socially conditioned
qualities.[25]

Paul H. Emden's description of how the Quakers came to
be an important element in the economic life of London fits
the Jews as aptly as though it had been said of them:

Exposed to long persecution for their religion's sake and accustomed to look upon harsh treatment as a tribulation without
offering — or indeed being able to offer — any great resistance,
they went through a hard school for many generations and
learnt calm and prudence. Prejudice on the part of others excluded them from the liberal professions, even from sport, and
their own objections to taking an oath which was in conflict with
their convictions rendered them incapable of holding even the
most unimportant office. . . . In view of their pariah position,
the inherited gifts and the education of their children were con-

[24] *Ibid.*
[25] *Political Science Quarterly*, March 1919, "The Intellectual Pre-eminence
of Jews in Modern Europe," by Thorstein Veblen.

centrated solely on religion and business; nothing could keep them from the practices of their faith, and no prospective profit, however high, could influence them when hour of the Sabbath called to worship. The same high standard which ruled their private and intimate family life governed their business transactions, and their principles precluded expensive tastes. They were intelligent, diligent, and above all — for this is the inheritance of a persecuted sect — cautious. The habit of always having to be prepared for anything compelled them to exercise the greatest possible prudence, and consequently to be constantly solvent, a quality indispensable in a manager of other people's money. Inculcated self-restraint and discretion turned them into reliable advisors on financial secrets and good merchants. In constant activity they were ever on the lookout for new possibilities of extending their business; they did not wait for the customer to come to them; they sought him out or sent to him, and in this way, by stages, the fraternity of commercial travellers came into being. Trade, commerce, industry and traffic received new ideas from them, and they found large sums for the purpose of carrying them into practice. . . . For children to marry outside the faith was not a very frequent occurrence; any one so doing deliberately excluded himself from close communion and inter-marriage prevented the dissolution of great wealth. In this way vast fortunes were made solely by accumulation.[26]

It can be seen that essentially what is involved here is a self-generating, self-repeating cycle: discrimination leads to the development of certain compensating skills and understandings which in turn make for a degree of success which immediately incites envy, leading, once again, to exclusion. In Europe, Jews were tolerated as long as their services were indispensable; the moment this ceased to be the case, they were excluded: from Portugal, from Holland, from England. And so they moved eastward, from country to country, becoming perforce more "Jewish" as they were pushed eastward until, in the Pale of Settlement, "their martyrdom reached its cli-

[26] *Money Powers of Europe*, by Paul H. Emden, 1938, p. 186.

max." Then, in the disruptive wake of social change, they began to retreat westward, with some landing in Germany, France, and England, but the great bulk of the refugees were shunted further westward across the Atlantic. Here their experience has been repeated, but with a difference, for it has been repeated symbolically rather than literally; and with important variations. "Here," as James Parkes has written, "the old battle of assimilation and nationalism is being fought out within a new framework. European Jewry was asked in the Nineteenth Century to assimilate to an already existing non-Jewish culture and way of life, and the assimilation was primarily that of surrendering what was characteristically Jewish and accepting what was characteristically non-Jewish, even Christian. The position in America is different; for the whole continent is simultaneously assimilating the significance of its own existence, and the task to which Jews are called within that assimilation can be creation rather than renunciation; for one of the things to be assimilated in a new tolerance and equality is the variety of national traditions of which the continent is the repository and the expression." [27]

No one knows just how many Jews live in the United States today, but with the liquidation of 6,000,000 Jews in Europe during World War II, America and Palestine have become the twin pivots of Jewish life in the world. The *Universal Jewish Encyclopedia* gives the American Jewish population for 1942 as 4,975,000 or about 3.78 per cent of the total population; but this is only an approximation and the actual figure may not exceed 4,000,000. Jews may be found in every state, and in Hawaii, Alaska, Puerto Rico, and the Canal Zone, but more than half of all the Jews in the United States live in New York, most of them in the City of New York. The thirteen cities with more than 40,000 Jews contain five sevenths of the estimated Jewish population but they make up only one seventh of the total population. The concentration of Jews in large

[27] *The Jewish Problem in the Modern World*, by James Parkes, 1946.

metropolitan areas is shown by the fact that five cities of more than a million population — New York, Chicago, Philadelphia, Los Angeles, and Detroit — account for six eighths of the Jewish population but only one eighth of the total population. It was in America that the Jews acquired the economic power, the confidence, and the political skill which largely brought about the creation of the new state of Israel.

### 3. The Malaise of Henry Adams

Those who like to believe that anti-Semitism in the United States is merely a European importation picked up and fostered by native "crackpots" — and the list of those holding this view would include some of the leaders of American Jewry — overlook the fact that anti-Semitism is clearly a social growth. Long before Hitler's name was known in America, unmistakable manifestations of the anti-Semitic sickness could be detected in significant sectors of American life. Consider, for example, the revealing case history provided by Henry Adams.

Anti-Semitism was surely not part of the social inheritance of Henry Adams. John Adams reflected the prevailing attitude toward Jews in post-revolutionary America when he wrote of them: "They are the most glorious Nation that ever inhabited this Earth. The Romans and their Empire were but a Bauble in comparison of the Jews. They have given Religion to three quarters of the Globe and have influenced the affairs of Mankind more, and more happily, than any other nation ancient or modern." [28] And to the extent that anti-Semitism can be said to be implicit in the Christian tradition, then Adams's skepticism should have guaranteed immunity from this source. Actually the key to Adams's anti-Semitism is to be found in the manner in which the rise of industrial capital-

[28] *Danger in Discord*, by Oscar and Mary F. Handlin, 1948, p. 10.

ism created in him a feeling of profound alienation from the society of which he was a part.

The education of Henry Adams, as he himself had written, had ceased in 1871; the balance of profit or loss for the twenty years that followed was "exceedingly obscure." Nothing had turned out in America quite as Adams wanted it to turn out and his disappointment was bitter and acute. Above all, he resented the new industrial society that came into being in the post-Civil War decades. Adams wrote understandingly, and with deep appreciation, of the America of 1800–1860; but, as Dr. Edward N. Saveth has pointed out, he loathed the degradation that came with "industrialism, the reign of the money-changers, Grantism, and corruption in high places." [29] From this America, Adams felt profoundly alienated, and the Jew, somehow, became the symbol of "the restless, grasping, speculative" world which had replaced the older America that he knew and revered and from which he stemmed.

In 1868 Adams returned to the United States after serving as his father's assistant in the American Embassy in London during the Civil War. He took an instant dislike to the America he discovered upon his return. "Not a Polish Jew fresh from Warsaw or Cracow," he wrote, "not a furtive Yacoob or Ysaac still reeking of the Ghetto, snarling a weird Yiddish to the officers of the Customs — but had a keener instinct, an intenser energy, and a freer hand than he — American of Americans with Heaven knew how many Puritans and Patriots behind him. . . ." Although he knew few Jews and had hardly any Jewish friends, the Jew nevertheless became for him the symbol of his own alienation; a symptom of his acute maladjustment to society; and the embodiment of the economic type. "I wish I were a Jew," he once said, "which seems to me the only career suitable to the time."

[29] See the chapter "Henry Adams' Norman Ancestors" in *American Historians and European Immigrants*, by Edward N. Saveth, 1948. All references to the writings of Henry Adams in this section have been taken from this brilliant analysis.

Although his acquaintance with Jews was negligible, Adams's writings abound with value-judgments about Jews. The Jew was an exploiter, not a creator of art; he cornered the bric-a-brac market and forced prices up. "Anything these Jews touch," he wrote, "is in some strange way vulgarized." Bad taste in furniture, painting, and interior decoration, he promptly branded as "typically Jew." He even showed some of the symptoms of the characteristic paranoia of the anti-Semite. For example, he feared that the *North American Review* might fall into Jewish hands! To Adams, as Dr. Saveth notes, the Jew was "a dread harbinger of socio-economic change"; a symbol that somehow stirred the apprehensions of those who belonged, like Adams, to the entrenched privileged orders. In the psychic economy of Henry Adams, the Jew was, indeed, a highly ambiguous symbol: of alienation; of the capitalistic corruption of civilization; of social change; of radicalism; of the degradation of taste.

Both Henry and Brooks Adams shared one of the anti-Semites' favorite distinctions: between "finance" capital, which was "evil," that is, Jewish, and "industrial capital," which was somehow non-Jewish and therefore "good." The distinction, of course, has always enabled the victims of the industrial transformation of society — the psychic as well as the economic victims — to attack "capital" without attacking capitalism. Opposed to finance capital, Adams could not bring himself to join forces with the trade-unions and the Populists in opposition to McKinley nor could he feel any sympathy toward Debs and organized labor. The most sophisticated of American historians, Adams could nevertheless write, as he did in 1896, that "we are in the hands of the Jews; they can do what they please with our values"! He actually believed that Jewish bankers had conspired to prevent the free coinage of silver.

In his view, of course, the Jews ruled England and Germany and France as well as the United States. He was pleased to note ". . . how emphatically the army, through the court-martial, set its foot on the Jews and smashed the Dreyfus intrigue into a pancake." In 1893 he wrote to a friend: "In the coming rows you will know where to find me. Probably I shall be helping the London mob to pull up Harcourt and Rothschild on a lamppost in Piccadilly." Both the Boer War and the Dreyfus case were, of course, the doings of Jews. "The Jews," he wrote, "make me creep." And, again: "I have been preaching, like John the Baptist, the downfall of the Jews, and have figured it up in parallel columns." "The mere sight of a Jew," writes Dr. Saveth, "was enough to set him off. Aboard ship, on a Chicago elevated train, in Madrid, London, Paris, Washington, Vienna, their presence was obnoxious to him." Four years before his death, he felt that the battle with the Jew had been lost. "The atmosphere really has become a Jew atmosphere. . . . We are still in power, after a fashion. Our sway over what we call society is undisputed . . . yet we somehow seem to be more Jewish every day."

As I pointed out in *A Mask for Privilege*, John Jay Chapman shared to the fullest extent the views of his friend Henry Adams about the Jews. The case histories of Adams and Chapman — the finest representatives of the older pre-Civil War cultural tradition — is of major clinical importance to the study of anti-Semitism. For these case histories confirm the finding of Dr. T. W. Adorno that the Jew's "alienness seems to provide the handiest formula for dealing with the alienation of society. Charging the Jews with all existing evils seems to penetrate the darkness of reality like a searchlight and to allow for quick and all-comprising orientation." [30] Adams and Chapman, remittance men, supported by industrial dividends, nevertheless "blamed" the Jews for a transformation of American society of which these scholarly Americans were indirect beneficiaries. It is impossible to ponder the meaning of the envy, the malaise, of Henry Adams without realizing that

[30] *The Authoritarian Personality*, by T. W. Adorno et al., 1950, p. 618.

anti-Semitism is integrally related to the phenomenon of "alienation" in modern society.

### 4. "A Most Peculiar Disease"

In most majority-minority situations, the latent dislike of "different" or "foreign" groups tends to fuse with social and economic cleavages. For example, the rise of the "racist" ideology in the latter part of the last century coincided with the emergence of sharp class differences; the sharpness with which racial differences were stressed tended to rationalize the increasing sharpness with which class lines were being drawn. The energies that fanned these latent dislikes into overt patterns of discrimination were clearly social in origin, as witness the fact that the "peaks" of anti-Semitism correlate closely with periods of social, economic, and political dislocation.

Anti-Semitism, however, differs from other forms of minority-baiting in at least two respects. For a variety of reasons, the Jew makes the best of all possible scapegoats. He is the perfect target for all displaced aggressions. For one thing, the Jewish stereotype is the most ancient, pervasive, rigid, and best-known of stereotypes; it is part of the culture and imagery, the vocabulary and folklore, of the Western World. The Jew, also, is the perfect Imaginary Foe. He is foreign, "alien," distinctive, widely dispersed, without a country (for centuries); and he suffers from a compounding of all the disabilities of minority status. The Jew is history's stand-in for the Devil, the Bad Man, the Evil One. In short, the Jew, for many reasons, is psychologically the perfect target.[31]

But the economic position of the Jew — his function in the economy — also makes him the perfect sociological scapegoat for the peculiar frustrations and aggressions which are engendered by the class conflicts of an industrial society. The

[31] *Ibid.*, p. 638.

economic position of the Jew, into which he is partly driven
and in part retreats, makes it appear *as if* Jews were responsible
for conflicts of which they are clearly victims. This illusion of
responsibility makes the Jew a perfect political target. Dr.
Paul W. Massing, in his study of political anti-Semitism in
Imperial Germany, has shown what an amazingly versatile
weapon anti-Semitism can be in the disputes and conflicts of
modern industrial societies.[32] Consider, for example, the political "uses" which were made of anti-Semitism in Germany: it
was used to unite Protestant and Catholic conservatism; it was
the ideological bridge over which the lower middle classes
were drawn back into the camp of reaction; it was also used
to attack the parties of the left, and so forth. To the conservative *Junker,* the liberal or radical Jew was a source of annoy-
ance; to the peasant the Jewish cattle dealer, peddler, and mid-
dleman appeared as the Capitalist Exploiter; to the urban
middle class the Jew was the Arch Rival, the Unfair Competitor, the satirical Misfit Bourgeois.[33] Above all, anti-Semitism is
a screen or background on which the disaffected can project
an unconscious revolt against a burdensome civilization. "The
rich," wrote Herman Bahr, "take to morphium and hashish.
Those who cannot afford them become anti-Semites. Anti-
Semitism is the morphine of the small people. . . . Since they
cannot attain to the ecstasy of love, they seek the ecstasy of
hatred. . . . It matters little who it is they hate. The Jew is
just convenient. . . . If there were no Jews the anti-Semites
would have to invent them."[34]

Critics of the point of view that modern anti-Semitism has
a close relation to the conflicts of an industrial society harp on
the fact that Jews were persecuted centuries before the rise of
industrialism. But there is a clearly recognized distinction between "anti-Judaism" and anti-Semitism; between what has

[32] *Rehearsal for Destruction,* by Paul W. Massing, 1949.
[33] Adorno, *op. cit.,* p. 638.
[34] Quoted by Massing, *op. cit.,* p. 99.

been called medieval or "classical" anti-Semitism and the modern or "racial" variety which dates from the coining, in 1873, by the German anti-Semite Wilhelm Marr, of the expression "anti-Semitism." It is generally recognized that this new rationalization of anti-Judaism found expression in the form of a racial ideology largely because the rise of industrialism had created so many new economic opportunities that there was a real danger that the Jews, at long last, might escape from their fateful economic position. Modern anti-Semitism, so-called, aimed at arresting this tendency and, since this was its primary social purpose, it became the perfect political magnet to attract reactionary and regressive elements.

Although the distinction between medieval and modern anti-Semitism is important, economic envy was also the dynamic force behind medieval anti-Semitism. The Jews were never persecuted, it was said, unless the king was in need of funds. The sociology of the Jewish moneylender provides the key to an understanding of medieval anti-Semitism. Excluded from many forms of economic activity, Jews had acquired experience in the handling of funds and their wide geographical distribution made them ideal "international" bankers. To win tolerance or asylum, they were usually forced to agree to be the king's financiers and the exactions he levied on them — in connection with a status which was always precarious — made them diligent tax collectors and moneylenders, thereby drawing on them a fire which should have been directed at the king. The king was never opposed to anti-Semitism; the fact that it existed, and that it could be stimulated if need arose, made it possible for him to keep "his Jews" — and the Jews were often referred to as personal chattels of the king — properly terrorized. At the same time, the populace often enough had good reason to hate, not the Jews, but the role which certain Jews were forced to play. A better illustration of hatred arising from false definition of a social situation could scarcely be imagined. Ideologically, anti-Semitism is rooted in confusion and self-deception as to the real cause of social evils.

Today when one attempts to specify the major disabilities which prevail against Jews in American society, it becomes immediately apparent that "anti-Semitism" is still their major problem. With other minorities, notably Negroes, the weight of specific issues, such as housing and employment, is the overwhelming reality of minority status. But housing is not a major problem with Jews (although there is a special Jewish housing problem) nor is employment (although there is much discrimination against Jews in employment). Recognizing this difference, Oliver C. Cox has tried to make a distinction between social intolerance (anti-Semitism) and race prejudice.[35] But the distinction is not in the quality of the prejudice but between two different types of majority-minority relationships.

The real problem of the Jews is the insecurity, the ever-present, floating anxiety which comes from the knowledge that anti-Semitism has risen to plague them in America; that it is still "there" — lurking somewhere in the environment; latent today but capable of becoming virulently active to-morrow; indefinable but as real as any affliction could possibly be. As a "marginal trading minority," Jews have escaped, by and large, from the more obvious minority disabilities; but anti-Semitism still clouds their lives. The awareness of this danger is like living with an ever-present knowledge that some "faceless" enemy is stalking one, waiting for a chance to strike, certain to take advantage of any opening, likely to appear in the most unexpected sources. Indeed one of the most irritating and baffling qualities about this "enemy" is that Jews, in many cases, can never be quite sure whether it was anti-Semitism that drove the client or customer away, that caused the door to be slammed in their face, or that prompted "the kids next door" to shun their youngsters. Long

[35] *Caste, Class & Race*, by Oliver C. Cox, 1948, p. 392.

experience has taught them, moreover, that there is little they can do to appease or deflect this enemy; it is like fighting a phantom. Jewish "traits" have not produced this hatred; the hatred is largely responsible for the traits. The source of the hatred is not to be found in the object of the hatred but in the personality of the anti-Semite; in the relationship between Jew and non-Jew; and in the advantages, real or imagined, which the dominant groups gain by holding the Jew at arm's length.

The reality of anti-Semitism in America might be suggested by the life history of an imaginary Jew, Sam Epstein. Of immigrant parents, Sam has known the spur of poverty and discrimination; he is a product, so to speak, of "the impact of penalization." Like his parents, he has had to work a little harder than most people merely in order to survive. The gap in experience between Sam and his parents, coupled with the powerful attractions and compulsions in American life, has gradually drawn him away from the Jewish community. He has never ceased, however, to think of himself as a Jew because he has never been permitted to forget this fact. Nor would it make any difference, in this respect, if he were to change his name or submit to facial surgery or join the Ethical Culture Society. By the time he is forty-five or fifty, he has made a modest fortune but he begins to feel, however vaguely, that he has somehow been cheated; that he has not been given the forms of recognition which would normally go with the degree of success he has achieved. At about this time, he joins a Jewish golf club, which may be, and often is, the most luxurious in the community but which never ceases to be labeled "Jewish." At this juncture in his career, also, he is rediscovered by the Jewish community or, as is often the case, he turns toward the community in an effort to win there the status and recognition which have been denied him in the larger community. Soon his name appears in the "year-book" as among the large donors to various Jewish charities, and before long he is one of the leaders of the Jewish community. Now he will become gradually "more Jewish" and may even come to believe that it is improper for his children to have a Christmas tree. The world into which he has now in part retreated, in part been driven, and in part consciously sought out, is rich in meaning; it has real warmth of feeling; it offers profound satisfactions. There is nothing "wrong" with this world except that it is a little suffocating, a little too closed-in, a little too highly organized. But it is a world which can only be understood by realizing that it is an island surrounded by a vague but unmistakable ocean of anti-Semitism.

Since it is impossible, in our American world, to keep the Jews in a ghetto, we keep them in this world apart, this invisible ghetto. For as long as they are kept there, they can be identified; and as long as they can be identified, a certain competitive advantage flows to the non-Jewish groups. Jews have a perfect intuitive understanding of this social reality. They will laughingly refer to some handsome apartment hotel as a "ghetto," realizing that its occupants — despite their wealth, their success, their property — are still the victims of a subtle ghettoization. The best way to suggest this reality is to point to the obvious fact that the ranking Jewish society matron of any American community is outranked by her opposite number in the dominant group; that the outstanding Jewish civic leader is invariably topped, in terms of prestige, by his opposite number; and that the largest Jewish fortune is never quite as large as the largest non-Jewish fortune. Although the relationship has its ludicrous aspects, it is full of intense frustration, anxiety, insecurity, and real peril. Jews may not suffer from the same disabilities as other minorities — indeed many of them do not suffer at all in this sense — but the disabilities are there, all the same, and even those who do not suffer are usually "anxious." These disabilities, all of which are subsumed in the disease of anti-Semitism, exist as a direct consequence of the strategy by which dominant elements hope to maximize social, economic, and political power in society. The feelings upon which anti-Semitism feeds are profoundly complex but anti-Semitism itself is clearly a technique of social dominance; it is a mask for privilege.

CHAPTER X

# Beyond Civil Rights

Habits are maintained so long
as they bring rewards.
— Poor Richard

*Brothers Under the Skin* was one of the first American
books on race relations to stress the importance of an affirmative federal policy on racial discrimination; that is, the implementation and protection of the civil rights of all citizens
of the United States regardless of race, color, or creed. It is
no longer necessary, however, to repeat the argument supporting this position. The report of the President's Committee on Civil Rights grants the argument, echoes its major
contentions, stresses the same factors, and adopts the same
conclusions. What had to be proved in 1943 is today generally
conceded, namely, that racial discrimination is a national
problem; that the federal government can no longer ignore
the fact of discrimination; and that well-recognized techniques exist by which civil rights can be protected. Now,
however, the argument must be carried forward to a recognition of the fact that social equality and equal civil rights
can coexist with a system of discrimination. Extension
of the earlier argument becomes only the more urgent
by reason of the fact that so many Americans have come
to think of a civil rights program not as a means to an
end, but as a definitive and final solution to "the racial
problem."

## 1. Wanted: A Point of View

In the last decade a wealth of energy and good will, supported by a very large outlay of funds, has gone into a nationwide effort to improve race relations in the United States. For the most part, however, this effort has not been informed by any feeling for the difference between strategy and tactics. Certain values have been offered, in an offhand way, as ultimate objectives: equality, the dignity of the individual, freedom from discrimination. Nor is this vagueness about objectives accidental; it arises from a failure to grasp the fact that discrimination is not a "natural" fault of society but an aspect of the way a particular society is organized. What the civic unity movement needs, therefore, is a point of view about the business at hand. It is all very well to open up department store tearooms to Negro patronage, but too much emphasis on this type of activity can create the illusion that discrimination is merely a form of social bad manners to be corrected by a course in racial etiquette.

In the civic unity movement in the last eight years so many different points of view have been urged that no clear point of view emerges. "Point of view" has the same importance to social movements that "policy" has for government; without a generally accepted point of view, it becomes impossible to relate means to ends, tactics to strategy. In the absence of a point of view *about discrimination,* prejudice becomes confused with discrimination; race with class; "cultural conflicts" with social conflicts; and "cultural differences" with economic relationships. At the same time — and this is what really matters — "civic unity" becomes a bright green island in an azure sea, an abstract social goal or daydream, unrelated to the larger social forces which make up the continents or land masses. A realistic point of view would sort the various determinants of race relations into categories marked "primary" and "secondary," "causes" and "consequences." What the civic unity movement needs, above all, is a feeling for the dynamics of discrimination, the energy or motive force that converts latent antagonism into overt patterns of discrimination. To identify this force, however, certain points of view about race relations must be distinguished.

In the last decade, a vast effort has been made to publicize the facts about "race" and racial differences. In pamphlets, motion pictures, cartoons, animated films, posters, books, and lectures, certain points have been endlessly repeated: there are no pure races; populations differ biologically in only a petty inventory of superficial differences; races cannot be ranged as "inferior," "mediocre," "superior," and so forth. Most of this activity has had real educational value but the point of view underlying it has been stressed in a manner that distorts the meaning of race relations. Racial myths can be deflated in a manner that creates the illusion that discrimination is simply based on an unfortunate misunderstanding about race; clear up this misunderstanding and all will be well. Unfortunately the evidence indicates that a real look at racial differences does not necessarily correct biased views.[1]

The findings of anthropologists about "race" are of immense interest and importance but race has very little to do with race relations. Racial differences are of little importance per se, nor is it these differences which really divide people; racial differences do not necessarily result in conflict. Nor is there any evidence to support the once-popular view that inherited biological antipathies separate races or that a "white" group is "instinctively" repelled by a "black" or vice versa. It is the situation or relationship in which one racial group knows or confronts the other that determines attitudes and behavior. Race does have a relevance to race relations but it is social, not biological. What people think about racial differences *is* important in race relations and race is also impor-

[1] *The Authoritarian Personality*, by T. W. Adorno et al., 1950, p. 617.

tant as a badge of difference, a means by which individuals can be identified at sight as members of a group assigned an inferior status. But an exact, even an encyclopedic, knowledge about race and racial differences will throw little light on the strategies which are invoked when groups compete, on unequal terms, for place, power, and position.

As a concept "prejudice" is as deceptive and as ambiguous as "race." Prejudice, like race, has only a marginal relevance to race relations. Race relations are not based on prejudice; prejudice is a by-product of race relations — as influenced by other factors. Current psychological theories of race relations, however, are almost exclusively concerned with prejudice, which is discussed as though it were the cause of discrimination. Valid in fields to which they relate, these theories are also valuable aids to an understanding of race relations but they are not directly concerned with race relations. For example, it is known that certain social groups have a special susceptibility to anti-Semitic propaganda, but it is also known that all members of such groups are not anti-Semites nor do they become anti-Semites nor are they equally susceptible. Common observations of this order are often pointed to as though they disposed completely of all theories of discrimination based on group competition. To know why some members of a group known to have a general susceptibility become anti-Semites and some do not, one must turn, of course, from sociology to psychology and psychoanalysis. But in terms of what matters — in terms of human lives and the safety of society — it is more important to note the observed and verifiable fact that certain groups have this susceptibility than it is to become wide-eyed with wonder over the discovery that exceptions exist or that variations can be noted.

Psychological theories of prejudice, offered as theories of race relations, exploit individual exceptions in a manner that detracts attention from the rule. Such questions as Why is this brother prejudiced and that one without prejudice? are raised in a manner that implies that group competition has nothing to do with discrimination. Now, to know why an individual is prejudiced — or why he is without prejudice — he must be analyzed from several different points of view. For example: (1) What is this individual like as a biological entity (that is, age, sex, intelligent quotient, state of health, crippled or handsome, and so forth)? (2) Just who is this individual and what are his social identifications (that is, race, nationality, cultural and religious background, class position, occupation, income, and all similar factors)? (3) What are the salient characteristics of the society and culture of which he is a part and what is the position in time — in history — of this society and culture? (That is, being a member of the middle class may have quite different meanings, depending on whether one is German or Jewish, whether the time is 1870 or 1935, and whether the place is Iowa or Munich.) (4) What is the history of this particular individual (that is, the history of his family and parental relations, of his social and emotional experience — was he a veteran and, if so, was he wounded? — and his economic history as well — did he strike oil or was he caught in a depression)? All of these and other factors — I have no doubt — would have to be analyzed before the question could be answered.

Although this type of analysis relates to another field of interest — the psychological theory of prejudice — it does have a relevance to race relations: it explains the variable and exceptional; it is indispensable to individual therapy and educational theory; it accounts for the success or failure of certain types of racial propaganda; and it illuminates many other phases of race relations. But it is addressed to the individual problem of prejudice, not to the social problem of discrimination. To make a theory of the function of prejudice in the psychic economy of the individual do double duty as a theory of group discrimination is to confuse different, if related, levels of meaning. Case histories of every German would have failed to explain what happened to the Jews in Germany between 1918 and 1939. The clearest delineation of the personality types most susceptible to anti-Semitism will not explain why Jewish dentists find it almost impossible to practice dentistry in certain Western states. In the same way, concepts of social psychology are relevant to an understanding of race relations, but they do not explain the strategies by which certain groups maintain their dominance over other groups.

All of this could be passed over as merely of academic interest were it not for the fact that by failing to note the limitations of widely prevalent theories of race relations the civic unity movement has dissipated its energies and resources and raised false hopes of easy victories. In fact the civic unity movement is today in danger of being shunted into a dead end; it is being diverted from central issues to marginal concerns, from the reality of race relations to the minutiae of prejudice. To hold a course, the civic unity movement must have a point of view, not merely about prejudice and race, but about race relations as "strategies" or maneuvers by which privileged social groups maintain their dominance.

## 2. Strategies of Dominance

Modern racism dates from the overseas expansion of European peoples which began with the discovery of the New World. The shortage of labor gave rise to slavery and slavery in turn led to racism. "Slavery was not born of racism," writes Eric Williams, "racism was the consequence of slavery." [2] Not only were Negro slaves "the strength and sinews of this western world," but, once launched, the slave trade became immensely profitable and laid the foundation, in accumulated wealth, for the subsequent industrial revolution in England.

[2] *Capitalism & Slavery*, by Eric Williams, 1944, p. 7.

The use of Negro slaves in the growing of certain strategic crops in the West Indies gave an enormous advantage to the nations which could use a monopoly of these crops to corner the trade in other items. The magic of sugar, for example, has always consisted in its great strategic trade value; the nation that could offer sugar in trade was the nation with which other nations wanted to trade. Not only did the traffic in slaves make for the accumulation of huge capital reserves but it greatly stimulated — it was the basis of — the famous triangular trade, commodities for slaves, slaves for sugar, and sugar for commodities, which largely made it possible for England to become the first great industrial power. The value of the slave-sugar traffic may be indicated by the fact that little Barbados, with 166 square miles of territory, was worth more to British capitalism than New England, New York, and Pennsylvania combined.[3]

The rise of industry stimulated a migration of peoples since many industrial sites were selected by reason of their proximity to the sources of power. If one looks at the rise of industry from the point of view of the industrial working population then it is quite apparent, as Dr. Everett C. Hughes has pointed out, that "in no considerable industrial region of the world has an indigenous population supplied the whole working force."[4] Even in its early beginnings in the sixteenth and seventeenth centuries, capitalism required readily exploitable labor reserves. In western Europe, these reserves were *driven* toward the industrial centers by the dispossession and pauperization of peasants and handicraft workers and by such stratagems as the acts of enclosure. In this early recruitment, however, "exploiters and exploited were alike white," and usually of the same language, religion, and culture, so that no occasion arose for the development of strategies of

[3] *Ibid.*, p. 54.
[4] "Queries Concerning Industry and Society Growing out of Study of Ethnic Relations in Industry," by Everett C. Hughes, *American Sociological Review*, April 1949, p. 211.

dominance based on racial and ethnic differences. But with the overseas expansion of industry, and with the movement of industry into so-called "backward" areas in the mother country, industrial stratification began to be correlated with racial and ethnic status.

Dr. Hughes has pointed out that, so far as the labor force is concerned, industrial regions can be divided into two general classes: (1) those in which industry is built around a nucleus of *native* labor, drawn from the immediate area, with the technical and skilled personnel being recruited from this element; and (2) those in which industry is located in outlying or overseas areas, or remote nonindustrial areas in the same country, into which the skilled workers and technical personnel must be imported along with the machinery and equipment from the mother country or the major center of industry. Industry, as Dr. Hughes notes, is a great "divider" as well as a "mixer" of peoples. It brings people together for production but it also sorts them into various categories based upon the kind of work they do. In the meeting of races which came with the overseas expansion of European peoples, it so happened that the races were always unlike in culture and in no respect do cultures differ more significantly "than in the skills, work habits and goals which they instil into the individual." [5] With industry being the monopoly, so to speak, of one race or group, inequality was implicit in the recruitment of nonindustrial peoples for industrial employment.

Since industry is based on a division of labor, any assignment of workers to tasks implies *some* discrimination or selection. In the rise of industry this was particularly true since those who did the hiring had to choose from peoples who were not alike ethnically. Initial assignments thus implied ethnic choice or discrimination. At the same time, also, industry was not slow to realize that one way to keep a labor force exploitable is to keep it divided. However the segrega-

[5] *Ibid.*, p. 212.

tion of workers into various classifications on the basis of race or ethnic origin did not originally imply conscious discrimination since it often happened that the most "unlike" racial and cultural groups were those with the least industrial experience or the least wage-labor experience. On the basis of efficiency alone, these workers might well have been assigned to the lowest positions in the industrial hierarchy. The strategic value of this arrangement was an afterthought, a by-product of a situation. But industry came to assume, whether planned or not, the form of an ethnic hierarchy.

The ideology of industry has always stressed industry's indifference to persons; efficiency is the goal and the most efficient worker gets the job, theoretically. On the other hand, the ideology of capitalism has always been saturated with the folklore of racial and ethnic differences: Mexicans can't handle machines; Poles can do this job but not that; and so forth. If these legends or myths are examined, it will be found that they usually arose after a particular racial or ethnic group had been assigned to the task in the performance of which it is supposed to have a natural aptitude. Thus the myth served to keep each group anchored to its allotted task in the industrial hierarchy. For example, the myth that white men could not work in the tropics was based upon the determination of white men to get other men to work for them in the tropics. George Whitefield, the famous revivalist, urged the repeal of the initial prohibition against slavery in Georgia on the ground that "it is plain to demonstration that hot countries cannot be cultivated without negroes." [6] The fact that only Negroes performed certain tasks prompted the belief, of course, that only Negroes could perform these tasks. To a later generation, therefore, experience and observation seemed to confirm the folklore about Negroes. In this manner, over a period of years, there came into being a vast body of lore and opinion about various racial and ethnic groups and their alleged apti-

[6] Williams, op. cit., p. 43.

tudes and shortcomings which not only influenced foremen and supervisors in making selections for jobs but came to have a powerful influence on the expectations of workers.

Once an equation is established between ethnic status and job status, the equation tends to be self-perpetuating since the ethnic group assigned to a particular job status will seek to monopolize that type of work for its members. Orvis Collins has shown how these status-structures function in a particular New England factory.[7] In this factory, known as "Somerset" and established in 1890, Collins noted that ethnic identification was one of the important factors which determined appointments and assignments: "large areas of the plant hierarchy are almost completely occupied by members of one ethnic group." In fact the correlation between ethnic identification and status was so exact, and had prevailed for so many years, that workers had come to accept it and to rely upon it. Appointments made in defiance of the system provoked resistance. In the hierarchy of this plant, the managerial, executive, and white-collar jobs were held by Yankees; the foremen and supervisors were Irish; and the unskilled or common laborers were "miscellaneous." Family names served as badges of identification; if your name was O'Brien you were ethnically eligible to become a foreman. Management no longer consciously defended the system; it defended itself; it had become part of the social structure of the factory. Although the system was obliquely ridiculed, as in the endless "jokes" which factory employees told about the various ethnic groups involved, this ridicule actually defended the system by recognizing, and accepting, its existence. In one instance, a new position was created in the factory which might have been classified as supervisorial or managerial. A real fight ensued over this job until the owners made it clear

[7] "Ethnic Behavior in Industry: Sponsorship and Rejection in a New England Factory," by Orvis Collins, *American Journal of Sociology*, January 1946.

that they intended to regard it as managerial. Once this decision was made, the workers acquiesced in the appointment of a Yankee to the job.

The rise of racial and ethnic hierarchies in industry brings about a similar stratification outside the factory or plant. For example, where industrial expansion takes place, the mill town becomes a small city: real estate values rise; the population increases; country people are drawn to the city; and new economic opportunities of many kinds are created. Where such an industrial expansion takes place within a mother country, natives "on the ground," on the scene when the expansion begins, usually are the ones to profit by these subsidiary opportunities. The expansion of industry will push them to the top of the social structure of the town much as the same process will push their counterparts to the top positions within the industrial hierarchy. Once in particular status positions, they will defend the hierarchy of which they are a part by defending their position in this hierarchy. Upward mobility in the social structure of factory and town is determined by "co-optation": new recruits are tapped for advancement by those of similar racial and ethnic identifications.

Industry, however, must continue to draw new recruits for the low order positions; that is, it must keep the reservoir of exploitable labor — the labor reserve — at a certain level. Known to the workers, this policy is keenly resented by them. Traditionally this resentment has taken the form of exclusionist trade-union policies and has found expression in fiercely worded chauvinistic statements. At various times, the American labor movement has bitterly opposed the introduction of Negroes, Mexicans, and other groups into particular industries and into particular jobs within these industries. But to call this "race prejudice" is to misidentify the source of the feeling. Poor whites from the hill country of West Virginia, Kentucky, and Tennessee, known as "crickets" and "hilligans," have aroused much the same opposition although they belong to the dominant racial majority.

Where an industrial order arises within a mother country, industry is interested in the recruitment of workers; that is, in drawing workers to the factory and the factory town. Under these circumstances, industry will favor policies of labor mobility, including the utmost freedom of migration. The strongest advocates of an "open door" immigration policy were, of course, precisely those elements which profited most handsomely by a "closed door" policy on commodity imports. Where labor must be recruited within a common labor market, industry will favor a margin of upward mobility, the better to encourage new recruits to enter industry. And, for much the same reason, the general social structure of such an industrial area will be of the open-end variety.

But where industry invades an area — where industry goes to the workers — as where a plant is established in a colonial area, a different set of policies will prevail. In such cases, as in the flight of Northern textile concerns to Southern labor markets, a new kind of community comes into being: "the company town." The same is true, also, where industry must be located near raw materials, as in the case of mines and smelters. The company town is a colonial institution, the industrial counterpart of the plantation. Here ingress and egress are made difficult and strict control is maintained over the town and all economic opportunities in the town, all as part of a determination to corral and to hold a supply of labor. In such situations, wage differentials are established for different ethnic groups even for the same types of work, the better to hold skilled workers to the job.

Where industry is established in an overseas colonial area, personnel is imported from the mother country for the top executive, managerial, and white-collar positions. But since mother-country personnel cannot be imported or will not migrate in sufficient volume to make up the new middle class, some mobile group in this area, with experience in middle-class functions, will generally move in to monopolize the new economic opportunities created by the expansion of industry. An example may be found in the way the overseas Chinese have filled the function of a middle class in many areas of southeast Asia. In colonial areas, industry is usually in favor of strong governmental controls over the labor force; whereas in mother countries, industry is violently opposed to "regimentation." Colonial areas call for strong controls since the owners of industry belong to different racial and ethnic groups than those with which the workers are identified. Correlation between ethnic status and job is likely to be more obvious in colonial areas and in backward regions than in mother countries or old-established centers of industry.

Even in mother countries, however, the history of industry is the history of the attempt to find new sources of readily exploitable labor. To retard the assimilation of newly recruited workers, industry has fostered policies of "cultural parallelism" by which the assimilation of the latest batch of recruits is made difficult. Generally speaking, the exploitability of a group can be measured by the degree to which it has not been assimilated. Thus the racist cry, "incapable of assimilation," is not so much an accusation as the echo of a pre-determined policy. It means: "This worker is *not* to be assimilated." In every industry area, in colonies, backward regions, or old centers of industry, the presence of such unassimilated groups provides industry with a hidden social subsidy; that is, industry is able to employ certain workers for less than what would otherwise be the prevailing wage for certain jobs. The universality of this practice is such as to raise in Dr. Hughes's mind the question of "whether industry can maintain the level of profit which it has come to expect when all such hidden subsidy has wasted away and the population must be kept from industrial income even when not working for industry." [8]

That more people do not more clearly see this aspect of an industrial social order in a profit economy is due to the fact that their attention is riveted on the particular plant or industrial community in which they live. In some cases, the particular plant or community may have "assimilated" all workers; a point may have been reached at which everyone, from janitor to boss, speaks the same language, with the same accent, and attends the same church. Cases of this kind are rare but they do exist. However, in such cases the plant never stands alone: it is always part of a larger industrial system; it is always related to some raw material or "colonial" area, which may be overseas or may be located in some backward or disadvantaged region but which is economically a part of the same industrial system. In such cases, therefore, the labor subsidy is hidden or concealed in a remote segment of the industrial process. Those who owned and those who worked in the first sugar refineries in Bristol had probably never seen a sugar plantation in the West Indies; yet the plantation, and its Negro slaves, were as much a part of the refinery as any item of machinery or equipment.

Both in colonies and in mother countries, in older centers of industry and in backward areas, the owner groups have learned to use strategies of dominance. Just where the lines are drawn in any particular plant or community will vary in relation to many factors: the location of the plant; whether it is old or new; the kind of industry, and so forth. Variations in the strategy are not important; what is important is the organization of industry, and of industrial communities, as ethnic hierarchies. There is no uniformity in the hierarchies but the system is uniformly hierarchical.

As Dr. Hughes points out, the existence of strategies of dominance accounts for the "intermediate" types to be found

[8] Hughes, *op. cit.*, p. 217.

in many industries and that familiar figure, "the straw boss."
Intermediate ethnic groups usually stand between the owners
and managers and the lower-level working population. Their
occupational or social intermediacy correlates with an ethnic
or racial intermediacy: they are like both major groups but
not identified with either. It is this quality which makes them
ideal foremen, supervisors, and straw bosses. Once cast in such
a role, a group quickly acquires a vested interest in "intermediacy." The presence of such groups is one of the strongest
bulwarks to the social and economic power of the owning
class and the strategy of dominance usually calls for a kid-
glove handling of the members of such a group. For example,
they are usually presented in the folklore as "popular" or
"likable" types. But the popularity of the foreman is an aspect
of his job, which is to please both management and workers.

Does industry, asks Dr. Hughes, really favor ambition and,
if so, under all circumstances, for all groups, and with equal
emphasis? Actually industry's attitude, as he points out, is
highly ambivalent; it wants some workers to be ambitious
but not too ambitious; while with other groups the less ambition the better. Most industries have what Dr. Hughes calls
"the thank God for" people: the plodders and diggers who
are not too ambitious and whose advancement in the industrial hierarchy is retarded by special myths and rationalizations. The rationalization that these groups are lazy, shiftless,
dirty, have too many children, drink too much, are improvi-
dent, and so forth, is used to justify their retention in a
particular niche in the hierarchy. The rationalization not only
makes it possible to justify the practice but it becomes what
Dr. Robert K. Merton has called "a self-fulfilling prophecy." [9]
For if the rationalization is repeated long enough, people come
to accept it and to act in reliance upon it. If enough people
believe that "Mexicans can't handle machines," Mexicans will
find it difficult to get jobs handling machines; and the fact

[9] *Antioch Review,* Summer, 1948.

that no one sees Mexicans handling machines will re-enforce the rationalization. Thus, as Dr. Hughes points out, "there grows up a body of belief about the special working qualities of various ethnic groups. These stereotypes, which may or may not correspond to the facts, act to limit the vision of those who select help and who initiate sponsorship."[10]

## 3. A Strategy in Operation

In order to understand "strategies of dominance," one must examine certain strategies in operation. Of the various case histories available for illustration, none is more illuminating than that of the French-Canadians in the province of Quebec since here the strategy is based on a reversal of the usual majority-minority relation.[11]

The French, of course, preceded the British in the settlement of Quebec. Numerically dominant, they are more homogeneous than the English-Canadians, who came later and have always remained a small minority in the province. Despite the fact that the French-Canadians are the majority element, however, they are socially, psychologically, and culturally a "minority," suffering from every disability associated with minority status. Just how, then, does a minority "boss" a majority?

When the British finally drove the French from Canada, the French-Canadians in Quebec were left behind as a national cultural element destined to be a minority in Canada but a majority in their native province. With the French-Canadians, high birth rates were encouraged as a means of preventing the British from overrunning the province. At first the British started to deal with "the French-Canadian problem" in the immemorial manner — by driving the French from certain

[10] Hughes, *op. cit.*, p. 220.
[11] See *French Canada in Transition*, by Everett C. Hughes, 1943. Also *French Canada*, by Stanley B. Ryerson, 1944.

marginal areas by force, as with the Acadians, and in other areas by attempting to coerce cultural uniformity. The American Revolution, however, brought about a modification of this strategy. The British then decided to grant the French-Canadians cultural autonomy but, at the same time, to align the leaders of feudal Quebec with them by agreeing to recognize and protect their feudal privileges.

Retarded by the feudal structure of their society, the French-Canadians had to take a back seat while the British pioneered in most forms of capitalist enterprise. The loyalty of the French-Canadian to his culture, his language, and his religion was systematically exploited by the British in alliance with those of the same French language, culture, and religion who were the beneficiaries of the feudal structure of Quebec. To have fought to overthrow this feudal structure, including the vast seigneurial grants to large landowners and the Church, the French-Canadian would have been compelled to fight against his own leaders and might, thereby, have jeopardized the grant of cultural autonomy. Besides, it was difficult for the French-Canadian to see the stock certificates which the beneficiaries of French-Canadian feudalism owned in British corporations. Caught in an impossible position, the French-Canadian tended to blame all the evils of his society on the British and to develop a set of typical "minority" attitudes.

If one looks not at population statistics but at economic power, it is clear that French-Canadians are in point of fact *an economic minority*. The owners of industry in Quebec are not lineal descendants of the French-Canadians who owned small-scale enterprises when the British took over; on the contrary, they are Britishers, and the descendants of Britishers, who came in at a later date. By reason of the retarded economic development and outlook of French-Canadians, the British were able to seize the industrial initiative and to create points of industrial activity to which the French-

Canadians were drawn from rural areas. Wherever the British established a center of industry, they brought in British personnel for the top managerial, skilled, and technical positions. Of the 768 directors of the 83 largest corporations with headquarters in Quebec, only 93 are French-Canadians. Similarly of 10,694 firms in Montreal rated as those of greatest "estimated pecuniary strength," virtually all are English-owned. Heavy industry is monopolized by the English and wherever the English control an industry, English-Canadians dominate the top positions. The French are numerous in the retail side of business but the British control the wholesale firms. In all professions related directly to industry, as in engineering, architecture, and accounting, the British predominate. The French are concentrated in the self-employed profession but the large law firms, of course, are British.

In short the English in Quebec are more than an ethnic minority: they hold "majority" power and have the attitudes of a majority. The whole situation is summed up in one statement by Dr. Hughes: "On the economic side, the French-Canadian city culture has become stabilized about an earlier phase of capitalism." Because of this, the French-Canadian intellectuals tend to idealize the past; to scorn modern industry and science; to make much of values which probably never existed; and to indulge in mass movements which, in their contradictory programs, reflect in perfect fashion the contradictory position of the French-Canadians in the economy of Quebec.

In the study of one particular industrial community, Dr. Hughes was able to trace out English-French relationships in great detail. The British, for example, held *all* positions of great authority in the city's major industries and performed *all* functions requiring technical training of a high order. Only a tiny minority in the plants and in the community, the British and English-Canadians held a tight grip on the top-level positions. On the other hand, local business, the service trades and the professions remained in the hands of the French, who made up 90 per cent of the population. In all the industrial plants, the French constituted a vast majority of all employees but it was a rare occurrence, indeed, when a French-Canadian was able to penetrate the line separating supervisorial and managerial positions from "common labor." In essence, the British dominated what might be called the "general staff" positions and held all "straight line" positions above the rank of foreman. Industry was run by a British "fraternity." This fact was well known to the French and created among them a morbid consciousness of "minority" status. As might be expected, the British had developed an elaborate folklore to justify their refusal to admit French-Canadians to their fraternity.[12] Clerical positions in the British-owned industries were usually filled with English-Canadian personnel since it was from this element that recruits were drawn for the better positions.

The industrial hierarchy, as might be expected, was reflected in the social hierarchy of the community. The English were at some pains to maintain their top social position by seeing to it that few — only two to be exact — of their group worked in business under French employers. Throughout Quebec, in fact, Dr. Hughes noted the all-important fact that "generally speaking, English do not work under French authority."[13] Although some French worked under English employers in nonindustrial concerns, this was of rare occurrence since the economy had been stabilized on a division of function which allotted the nonindustrial businesses to the indigenous majority. In the nonindustrial sector of the economy, French fought it out with French, thus creating divisions within the French-Canadian ethnic group which made it impossible for them to achieve significant unity on major

[12] *French Canada in Transition, supra,* p. 55.
[13] *Ibid.,* p. 73.

issues. Since the French were so great a majority, the British were excluded from local government and, indeed, rarely bothered to vote; but this in no manner disturbed their dominant position.

In this instance, the use of language had important strategic implications. Many of the French were bilingual; but few of the British had bothered to learn French. The French salesman and professional man had to know English as did the French industrial employee, since English was the technical language of industry. In the same way, the English matron did not have to learn French but the French maid had to learn English. The group with the purchasing power can always make its wishes known to a subordinate group without learning its language. The boss does not need to learn the language of his employees; they learn his language. In other words, "if they [the English] were to speak French in these relationships — except in a joking or patronizing spirit, as is occasionally done — they would be in some measure reversing roles. For they would then be making the greater effort, which generally falls to the subordinate; and they would speak French badly, whereas the subordinate generally speaks English pretty well." [14]

Language ignorance serves to set the dominant group apart from the subordinate and to minimize social contacts between the two groups. On the other hand — and this is vital — the earlier English families in this community knew a good deal of French.[15] In other words, before the new industrial order came to the community, bilingualism developed as a natural aspect of an equality of status and neighborly relations. Precisely this same observation can be made of Anglo-Hispano relations in the Southwest. "Before the railroads came," Anglo-Americans often spoke Spanish, frequently intermarried with Hispanos, and the two groups were quite intimate;

[14] *Ibid.*, p. 83.
[15] *Ibid.*, p. 34.

but the intimacy ceased the moment one group was able to acquire dominance over the other.[16]

Language, however, is but one of many techniques of dominance. A dominant group will always show extreme concern about relationships which are likely to lead to, or to create, *divided loyalties*, that is, divided group loyalties.[17] In Quebec the British seek to avoid all relationships with French-Canadians which might lead to courtship, marriage, and children of divided loyalties. Dr. Hughes points out that in certain social situations, French and British freely associate together; but the moment the relationship becomes of a character that might lead to marriage, the atmosphere undergoes a distinct change. With age, the ethnic hierarchy becomes more firmly entrenched and the social distance between the two groups even increases. "At present," he writes, "French and English mix little except at the golf-club affairs, held either at the club or in a large hotel." [18] In this divided world, if a Frenchwoman marries an upper-class Englishman, she becomes part of the English world; but if, as rarely happens, a lower-class Englishman marries a lower-class Frenchwoman, he joins the French-Canadian contingent.

To sum up: the English have maintained their dominant position in Quebec by a whole series of tactical measures and maneuvers which can only be understood as part of a strategy of dominance. The reality of this situation is not to be found in French or English cultural traits but in the relationship between French and English in the economy. In this context, it becomes absurd to say that the English do not intermarry more often with the French because they are "prejudiced." They are prejudiced because their policy is not to intermarry with the French. Throughout the entire range of French-Canadian society, an overwhelming numerical majority is

---

[16] *North from Mexico*, 1949, p. 291.
[17] *French Canada in Transition*, p. 160.
[18] *Ibid.*, p. 165.

dominated by a tiny minority. The tiny minority has the traits of a majority; the majority suffers from minority consciousness. The inferior position of the French-Canadians has little to do with culture and nothing to do with race; it is simply an aspect of a power relation between two groups, competing for place, power, and position.

In this instance, it is extremely important to note that French-Canadians have had full civil rights for many decades yet they remain in a subordinate position. For the inequality from which French-Canadians suffer has long since become part of the structure of the society in which they live; they would have to change or modify this structure before they could escape from British dominance. But should the French, a majority in Quebec, ever assert their political power in a manner that might endanger the economic dominance of the British, how long would the French continue to enjoy full civil rights? The answer is problematical but this much is clear: the present British indifference to local politics would cease overnight.

## 4. Intermediate Groups

In many industrial societies power is not completely parceled out between a "dominant" and a "subordinate" element; often an "intermediate" group may be found. The Irish in America are a classic example of an intermediate social group — that is, a group whose function it is to mediate. Mediation is of the essence of politics and the Irish skill and success in politics is proverbial. Dr. Milton L. Barron has come up with an intensely interesting explanation of the Irish as an "intermediate group." [19]

Historically the Irish occupied a "mean" position in the time sequence of American immigration. Although Irish immigration was both early and late, it was mostly concentrated in the last decades of the "old" European immigration from

[19] *Social Forces*, March 1949.

1850 to 1870. To a greater degree than those partaking in the older north European immigration, therefore, the Irish tended to concentrate in the northeast section of the country, which placed them directly in the path of the "new" immigration from southeastern Europe. But just as they occupied a "mean" position historically, so their cultural and demographic position was "intermediate." Culturally the Irish were in between the old European immigrants and the new; they really did not fit in either category. Unlike many north European immigrants, the Irish were Roman Catholics, largely illiterate, from a backward agricultural area, poor, and with the clannishness of a severely persecuted group. Some of these qualities or traits made them much closer to immigrants from southeastern Europe than to native Americans or north European immigrants. But, by a miracle, the Irish spoke English, which made them ideal interpreters or mediators between old and new among immigrants in America. Their Roman Catholicism identified them with the new immigrants; the fact that they spoke English gave them a foothold in the older groups. Occupying an in-between position, historically, culturally, and demographically, they became the natural go-betweens or politicians.

As the later or newer immigration arrived from southeastern Europe, the Irish were pushed up one or two rungs on the occupational hierarchy but not far enough to endanger those who occupied the upper-upper categories. The Irish thus became the natural foremen, straw bosses, and superintendents. And these, it will be noted, are jobs which confer political power over workers, that is, over the mass of voters. The Irish were "natural" foremen because they spoke English, but also because they had been here just enough longer than the new immigrants to know their way around. Capitalizing on their intermediate position, they became trade-union organizers, policemen, and firemen, all socially intermediate positions.

At the same time, the Irish were intermediate in their politics. The Federal-Whig-Republican elements were always mildly, and often actively, anti-Catholic; hence the Irish were driven into the Democratic Party. Many of the later Catholic immigrants naturally followed the Irish into this party, a fact which enhanced the power of the Irish. Nor was it long before the Irish came to occupy a highly strategic position as political brokers between old and new immigrants, and between the older native elements and the newer foreign elements. The Irish were not so much on the wrong side of the tracks; they were right on the tracks. That some Irish politicians have of late years begun to conduct brokerage operations in the ranks of the Republican Party only serves to indicate that the Irish have risen several degrees in status in the last few decades.

In the religious sphere, also, the Irish have occupied an intermediate position. They are Roman Catholics but they occupy a position between other Roman Catholics, those who came later and had to learn English, and the Protestants. It was only natural that the Church should turn to the Irish, as the first large Catholic contingent, for leaders as later and larger Catholic contingents arrived. Hence the American hierarchy became, and has remained, largely Irish-dominated — a fact which has, of course, greatly re-enforced the political power of the Irish. The older Americans have smiled at the Irish as Catholics who speak English, while the newer American Catholics have looked up to them as Catholics who have made good.

The intermediate position of the Irish is even reflected in the pattern of their spatial distribution. Various studies of eastern communities have shown that the Irish frequently occupy the intermediate zones between the old residents and the new. The characteristic Irish structure, in these cities, is the two-family residence. In the past the Irish have tended to live, quite literally, in between the two major white ethnic groups. Where two ethnic groups are to be found in a society, one dominant, one subordinate, the members of each group will tend to marry within the group to which they belong but with a strong secondary preference for some closely related intermediate cultural group. In a study of the Irish in Derby, it has been shown that the Irish were selected by the largest number of different groups in intermarriage. Intermarriage, in turn, has also re-enforced the political power of the Irish. In short the Irish have a large measure of political power because they happen to have more points of contact with all other groups than any one major group. To discuss an intermediate group of this kind solely in terms of its cultural traits, however, would be misleading. These traits are primarily significant in relation to the hierarchy of power in which the Irish function.

The spread of an industrial system of society has accentuated cultural and racial differences not only because these differences have become structured in the society and the plant but also because the stratification of industrial societies tends to make "strangers" of people who work in the same plant, get their pay checks at the same window, and see each other five days a week. In such a world, cultural and racial groups are separated and set apart by much the same process that individuals are "alienated" from the social order. To be sure, new forces are making for a new integration but the ethnic hierarchy cannot be rearranged overnight. The very nature of this hierarchy makes for a consciousness of cultural and racial differences and generates minority feeling. This feeling has nothing much to do with numbers; it stems from a relationship. "For minority feeling," writes Dr. Hughes, "is not so much a matter of number as of a felt disadvantage in some hierarchy, accompanied by the sense that strangers and strange institutions are wresting from one's people mastery over their own fate."

Studies have shown that the emergence of the highly prejudiced "authoritarian personality" is closely related to the emergence of a stratified, authoritarian social order. The authoritarian personality conceives of the world as a jungle, glorifies power, and identifies itself with privileged groups. The social order is thought of as a hierarchy of power in which one must avoid, at all costs, any identification with the underdogs. Society is seen as a chaos which can only be understood by falling back on stereotypy. For stereotypy "helps to organize what appears to the ignorant as chaotic . . . the opaqueness of the present political and economic situation for the average person provides an ideal opportunity for retrogression to the infantile level of stereotype and personalization." [20] Stereotypy is intimately related to personalization: stereotyped explanations lead naturally to the tendency to blame some group, to find a scapegoat. But, as these same studies also show, it is authority more than anything else that structures the world of the prejudiced individual. "The existence of power and privilege," writes Dr. T. W. Adorno, "demanding sacrifices of all those who do not share in the advantages, provokes resentment and hurts deeply the longing for equality and justice evolved throughout the history of our culture. In the depth of his heart, everyone regards any privilege as illegitimate."

## 5. Spotlight on Africa

At mid-point in the twentieth century, both America's race problem and its world-wide counterpart, the colonial problem, have passed into a new phase: permanent crisis. This is not to imply that two separate and unrelated problems have now merged or intersected; on the contrary, these have always been one problem. The racial problem is as old as the problem of colonialism. Both problems had their inception about four hundred years ago when European peoples dis-

[20] *The Authoritarian Personality*, p. 665.

covered the rest of the world and, because of the emphasis in their cultures on navigational skill, military organization, refinement of lethal weapons, and commercial efficiency, proceeded to enslave non-European peoples, most of whom were "colored." [21]

Today the identity of the weapons by which European peoples have, for four hundred years, maintained their dominance over colonial peoples is quite clear. The strategy of dominance used by colonial powers is the same as that used by the white majority in the United States in its relations with colored minorities. The main tactical weapons, defined by Raymond Kennedy, include the drawing of the color line or color bar; the denial of political democracy as long as possible; the continued economic subjugation of the native or colored people; the maintenance of a low level of development for the social services, with more emphasis on roads, public works, and sanitation than on education and welfare; and the development of a mutually exclusive social pattern as between the dominant and subordinate groups. In 1949 the United Nations issued a publication entitled *The Main Types and Causes of Discrimination* which documents, on a world-wide scale, the patterns or schemes which are everywhere used to maintain group dominance. It is through these methods that the world has been divided into colonial and noncolonial areas.

"Every institution of human society," as Kennedy pointed out in his analysis of the colonial problem, "is supported by a code of rationalization. Men must have reasons for the rules they follow and the institutions by which they live." [22] The "reason" may be irrational; it may be mythical; it may be false — but it becomes part of the system of belief on which the society is organized. Colonialism has its rationalization

[21] "The Colonial Crisis and the Future," by Raymond Kennedy, in *The Science of Man in the World Crisis*, 1945.
[22] *Ibid.*, p. 311.

in racism; in the notion of backward peoples; in manifest destiny based on the mission of the white, Christian Anglo-Saxon; in the theory that industrial nations have been given a mandate to rule nonindustrial nations. These are the same rationalizations — if not always stated in this precise form — which have always been used to support the pattern of racial discrimination in the United States. The American race problem is simply a special version of the world colonial problem, which, in the last analysis, is a problem involving the exploitation of labor.

It is unavoidable, therefore, that as a great crisis has developed in colonialism, so the racial problem should have reached a crisis in the United States. Both crises have a two-fold aspect: the traditional rationalizations or myths are being rapidly disintegrated through the emergence of the colonial peoples, thereby creating a division in white opinion; and at the same time continued exploitation and two World Wars have released a world-wide current of ferment and unrest in every colonial area. Lothrop Stoddard was right but for the wrong reason: a tide is rising in the world but it is a tide of social protest, not of color.

One might well use the Durban, South Africa, race riot, which occurred at almost the precise mid-point of the century, to mark the fusion of the racial and the colonial problems. In this "riot" 142 people were killed, 1087 were injured, and 650 stores and 1284 dwellings were destroyed. For the Durban race riot, indeed the whole pattern of discrimination in South Africa, represents a grotesque blend of the worst colonial abuses and pure Jim Crowism, southern style. South Africa's racism is the echo of American racism, in a crude, prehistoric, caricatured form. In other words, history seems to be winding up the colonial-racial issue where it began — in Africa.

In the wake of the Durban riot of January 1949, the South African government pushed through a policy of *apartheid* or legalized segregation which is clearly based on Dixie models.

*Apartheid* is to be carried into effect through the Group Areas Act which provides for restrictions on residential and land holdings on a racial basis; in fact it divides South Africa into racial zones or ghettos. The Group Areas Act is clearly American in origin; it is the quintessence of Jim Crowism distilled from hundreds of southern statutes and ordinances. In fact Dr. Daniel François Malan, the South African Prime Minister, is a kind of latter-day southern demagogue of the vintage of 1890; his prototypes were Vardaman, Tillman, and Tom Watson. The line of descent is so clear that South African racism might best be described as a nightmarish — a slightly more neurotic or distorted — version of the racism of Dixie.

The first thing the conquering whites did in South Africa was to seize the land from the natives, by force and without compensation. Land was seized not because it was valuable in itself but because the seizure could be used as a means by which the natives would be forced to work for the whites for a pittance, and thereby invest the land with value. In a three-year period after 1857 in Natal Province, 300 European immigrants appropriated 1,360,000 acres of land. Today natives have 26 acres per family; immigrants 3750 acres per family. Through land monopoly, and such techniques as penal sanctions, pass systems, segregation, and even direct subsidies to white labor, European industrialists acquired control of an inexhaustible supply of cheap native labor. To keep native labor unorganized and in the cheap unskilled categories, various systems of forced labor were used. The meanest white European in South Africa is paid a wage higher than the most skilled or efficient native; for example, in the mines the white workers start at a rate which is eleven times greater than the rate for native labor. The discrimination favoring the white worker is based not on racial loyalty or sentiment but on strategic considerations; in the absence of some such policy the continued gross exploitation of black labor would be impossible since the whites hold the blacks in line.

In South Africa there are today about 8,500,000 natives or blacks; around 2,500,000 whites or Europeans; a large mixed group known as colored, totaling around 844,440 (mostly Cape Colored or half-castes); and about 300,000 Asiatics, principally Indians. The Indians are mostly native-born, the descendants of indentured servants brought to South Africa in the latter part of the last century to work in the sugar plantations. Largely concentrated in Natal Province, the Indians — or a minority of them — perform many middle-class functions in relation to the natives; in fact they might be called the Jews of South Africa. Because of their exposed position, the Indians serve as a convenient stand-in target for the accumulated resentments of the natives; to many natives the Indians are "the cause of our misfortune." The Durban riot was between Indians and natives although it may well have been incited by Europeans.

The natives or blacks are employed in the diamond and gold mines; on the farms and railroads; and in all types of unskilled occupations. Except in Cape Province, the natives enjoy no political rights whatever; in Cape Province the natives have the privilege of voting for three *white* or European representatives in a parliament in which 2,500,000 Europeans have 150 representatives! Throughout South Africa, the natives are as thoroughly and as completely segregated as in the Deep South. Separate stands or docks are even provided for nonwhites in the law courts.

About South Africa's Jim Crow system there is no mystery whatever. G. H. Archambault, in a story in the *New York Times* of June 11, 1950, stated that, in the final analysis, "labor is the predominant factor"; the very essence of the problem relates to the eternal quest for cheap exploitable labor. Segregation is merely a means to this end. In fact the reason South Africa so closely resembles the Deep South is that the whites are not a tiny minority removed from direct competition with the natives but sufficiently numerous so that the pattern is more like a domestic racial minority situation than like a situation in which a mother-country elite exploit a colonial population.

But there is this difference between South Africa and the Deep South: the exploitation of cheap native labor in South Africa has been carried to the point where it has destroyed any hope of general prosperity. The general income level is so low that it has tended to hold all South Africans, white and black, to a much lower level than if the natives were paid, for example, even the substandard wages paid Negroes in the Deep South. Failing to see this, most observers have blamed "urbanization" and "industrialization" for the evils of South African society. Both processes, of course, have drawn thousands of black natives to the cities, where they have congregated in shack-town ghettos on the fringe of urban settlements. If paid a living wage, these natives would be a source of real prosperity to the towns and cities; but paid the pittances they receive, they are viewed as liabilities. Thus the Malan government has been trying to turn back the natives from the towns and cities and to force them back to their native reserves. A Southern Negro who receives $50 a month is well paid by comparison with these natives. The rationalization for this system, which compounds the evils of peonage and slavery, is that since the blacks outnumber the whites in the ratio of four to one, they must be kept in subjugation. Minister of Lands J. G. Strydom puts it this way: "Only segregation can prevent the bastardization of the white race." Unlike the situation in the Deep South, not the slightest pretense is made that this system will ever change. The Minister of Labor, Mr. Schoeman, has given this clear-cut statement about the meaning of *apartheid:*

Non-Europeans will never have the same political rights as Europeans; there will never be social equality; and the Europeans will always be *baas* (boss) in South Africa. At United

Nations meetings, General Smuts has explained the position of non-Europeans by saying that they had not yet reached the same level of civilization as Europeans. This was wrong, because logically it meant that when non-Europeans were on the same level as the Europeans, they would have equal rights. The Nationalist Party said they would never get these rights.[23]

When the mistreatment of Indians in South Africa was raised in the United Nations Assembly, that great "Christian" statesman, Jan Christian Smuts, returned to Pretoria full of angry words about what he called "all the rot about equality." "For the sake of peace and for the avoidance of pogroms in our country," he went on to say, "let us keep the races apart. . . . At the United Nations I heard nothing but the word 'equality.' Equality! I have been a student of history, politics, and philosophy but this is a new word to me. . . . If there were no discrimination in the world where would we be? There must be discrimination; you cannot run amok with a word like equality." [24] This, of course, is the attitude of the Dutch Reformed Church in South Africa.[25]

South Africa is important because there the battle for Africa is being fought out today. If Europeans in South Africa insist on *apartheid*, and enforce it, all Europeans may someday be driven from Africa. Today around 150,000,000 people live in Africa, speaking some 700 languages, divided into many societies and tribes; but the great bulk of them are colored and most of them live under colonial rule. If Europeans think they can *apartheid* these natives indefinitely, they are seriously mistaken. The strike of miners near Johannesburg in August 1946, the Durban riots in January 1949, the riots called in protest over the passage of the Group Areas Act, including the National Day of Mourning observed the day the act went into effect, all point to the conclusion that

[23] *The Crisis*, February 1950, p. 91.
[24] *New York Times*, December 21, 1946.
[25] *Ibid.*, May 30, 1950.

a new wind is blowing in African affairs. "In Africa today," writes Peter Abrahams, "there is the low rumble of voices raised for freedom. There is not a place on the African continent where the century-old values of empire, domination, segregation, and economic frustration are not being questioned, tested, challenged, resisted. Just as the First World War began the awakening of Asia, so the Second World War began the awakening of Africa. What was accepted without question is now being questioned. And when that kind of questioning starts, it is a matter of time only before the old is on the way out. That is where black Africa stands today." And just as the shameless labor exploitation of South Africa has become intolerable, indefensible, and ruinously wasteful (including a catastrophic waste of resources), so the model of this exploitation to be found south of the Mason-Dixon line has become intolerable in the United States. South Africa merely underscores the anachronism which is the Deep South. It may well be, however, that the descendants of African slaves in the United States may play a crucially important role in winning freedom for the peoples of Africa.

For as Africans struggle toward self-realization and political awareness, 13,000,000 American Negroes are emerging into full minority status, and at the same time the issue of discrimination has been raised from a local to a national, and now to an international, issue. But just as various nations have "freed" their colonies by granting them a hollow "political freedom," so we are now seeking to strike a bargain with racial minorities in the United States. The bargain is simply this: "civil rights" for "civil liberties." That is, legal discrimination will be abolished and full civil rights guaranteed, but on the implied condition that American Negroes, and other racial minorities, will not challenge the economic discrimination which is protected, not caused, by segregation. Segregation is simply a means by which the exploitation of Negro labor is facilitated; it is not synonymous with that exploitation. To grant racial minorities civil rights is, standing by itself, like granting the Philippines independence while retaining the economic controls over the islands' resources. The distinction between civil rights and civil liberties, which is stressed in the report of the President's Committee on Civil Rights, is an extremely handy ideological invention. On September 4, 1950, the United States was able to report to the United Nations that significant progress had been made in 1949 in combating discrimination and protecting basic freedoms for American citizens. In terms of civil rights for racial minorities, the statement was accurate; but the statement, and the report, completely ignored the devastating inroads which had been made in 1949 on the civil liberties of all American citizens, particularly of social, economic, and political dissenters.

Nevertheless the report of the President's Committee on Civil Rights, issued in November 1947, marks a turning point in the history of American racial minorities. Previously racial minorities in the United States had been struggling largely for recognition as minorities. Now that this recognition has been secured, the way has been cleared for more significant social gains. The granting of civil rights, in fact, might be said to be comparable to the granting of "dominion status" to a colony; it is not the end of exploitation but rather the beginning of the end. The Emancipation Proclamation did not "free" the Negro; it merely gave him a claim to freedom. Civil rights will not free Negroes; but the granting of civil rights will make it possible for Negroes to fight more vigorously than ever for freedom. The granting of civil rights — a concession which may be fully realized within the next decade — will be merely a way station, a mid-point, on the road to equality. The more civil rights racial minorities win, and the more thoroughly these rights are protected, the more rapidly will the old habits of exploitation cease to be rewarding to those who practice them. Profit or advantage is the motive force of group discrimination. The conflict between groups, as the conflict between individuals, is not rooted in nature; it is not due to a difference in race or culture. On the contrary, it is an aspect of the competitive social order in which we live. There is doubtless real social value in competition but to be valuable the competition must be real, not faked. Only hypocrites and crooks stack a deck of cards and then call upon their rivals to "compete." Competition can only have value where there is a real equality of opportunity, in a society in which co-operation is the norm and in which privileged hierarchies no longer have the power to create a sense of felt disadvantage in any group.

# Acknowledgments

I should like to acknowledge my great indebtedness to a number of individuals who have been of immeasurable assistance in the preparation of this manuscript. My thanks, then, to Mr. Hugh Calkins, Mr. Eshrev Shevky, Mr. Allen Harper, Dr. Joaquin Ortega, Dr. W. Lloyd Warner, Mr. William Hoy, Mr. Carlos Bulosan, Mr. Loren Miller, Mr. Edwin Bates, Miss Margaret Kalisch, Mr. Samuel Lee, Mr. Lim P. Lee, Mr. Albert J. Evers, Dr. Michael Pijoan, Mr. S. J. Oki, Dr. George Sanchez, and Mrs. Lorene Pearson. None of these individuals, needless to say, is in any manner responsible for any statements or opinions expressed in the text. In preparing this new edition, I am indebted to Dr. Leonard Broom, Dr. Arthur Katona, Helen Parker Mudgett, Dr. W. G. Steglich, and Dr. John C. Belcher, among others, for helpful comments and suggestions. I am particularly indebted to Dr. Alfred G. Fisk of San Francisco State College for helpful comments and also for having suggested the idea of this revision to me. Although my indebtedness to Dr. Everett C. Hughes, of the University of Chicago, should be apparent from the text of the last chapter, it is a pleasure to acknowledge it in a more explicit fashion. To my mind, his study, *French Canada in Transition*, is one of the most illuminating studies of majority-minority relationships in print. I should also like to point out that *The Puerto Rican Journey*, a study of New York's newest migrants, by C. Wright Mills, Clarence Senior, and Rose Kohn Goldsen, appeared too late to have served as a reference in the chapter on Puerto Rico but it should be consulted by those in quest of detailed information on the Puerto Rico–New York migration.

# *Index*

# Index

ABBOTT, DR. EDITH, 90
Abolitionists, 70, 197, 265
Abraham, Peter, 344
Acadians, 328
*Acheson v. Murakami*, 167
Actors' Equity Association, 52–53
Adams, Brooks, 303
Adams, Henry, 288, 301–305
Adams, John, 301
Adams, John Quincy, 196
Adirondacks, 289
Adorno, Dr. T. W., 304, 337
Africa, 62, 272, 344. *See also* South Africa
Aguinaldo, Emilio, 229, 230
Alabama, 46, 47, 56, 98
Alaska, 41, 85, 140, 214, 219, 227, 237, 300
Albizu Campos, 219
Albuquerque, 114
Alexander & Baldwin, 186
Alien Land Acts (1913, 1920), California, 147, 153, 155, 167, 248
Alien Registration Act (1940), 244
Allegheny Mountains, 67
Alpha Chi Sigma, MIT Chapter, 55
Alpha Phi Alpha, 54–55
Amarillo, Texas, 86
American Academy of Political and Social Sciences, 276
American Association of University Women, 53
American Council on Race Relations, 18, 20
American Factors, 186
American Legion, 162
American Party, 100
American Revolution, 171, 284, 328

*Americans Betrayed* (Grodzins), 159
Amherst College, 53
Anacostia Park, Washington, D. C., 57
Anderson, Albert, 34
Anderson, California, 95
Anglos, 114, 116, 118, 119, 120, 121, 122, 123, 126, 127, 131, 132, 135, 136, 137
Anglo-Saxons, 179, 181, 200, 230
Anti-Defamation League, 291
Archambault, G. H., 341
Arizona, 84, 114, 115, 118, 121, 123, 125, 133, 137–138, 147, 208, 216
Arizona State College, 86
Arizona Supreme Court, 84
Arkansas, 47
Arkies, 128
Armenian Gregorian Monophysites, 282
Armenians, 283
Armstrong, Reverend Richard, 172
Army, U. S., 9
Arnall, Ellis, 31
Arthur, Chester A., 92
Arts and Crafts Act (1935), 81
Ashkenazic Jews, 285–286
Asia, 89, 90, 92, 324, 344
Associated Farmers, 162
Associated Negro Press, 34
Atlanta, 30, 31, 32, 43, 51, 270, 272
Atlanta Christian College, 50
Atlanta University Studies of the Negro, 273
Atomic Energy Commission, 85, 138
Auburn, California, 95
Austin, Mary, 119

Austin, Texas, 133
Australia, 45, 89
Austria, 285
Azores, 184

BACON RESOLUTION, 231
Bahr, Herman, 306
Baker, Ray Stannard, 270
Balboa, C. Z., 220
Baltimore, 105
Bancroft, George, 100
Banks, Oregon, 242
Baptist World Alliance, 50–51
Barbados, 318
Barber, Joseph, 182, 183
Bargain of 1876, 265–267, 269
Barron, Dr. Milton L., 333
Beals, Carleton, 200
Beard, Charles, 257
Beaumont, Texas, 3
Beecher, Henry Ward, 289
Beeson, 67
Begay, Florence, 86
Bellingham, Washington, 248
Belloc, Hilaire, 288
Berea College, 55
Berger, Morroe, 15–16
Berry, Theodore, 18
Beta Sigma Tau, 54
Bethune, Mary McLeod, 18
Big Five, 182, 186–187, 191
Bilbo, Theodore G., 10, 11, 32, 33
Bill of Rights, 267
Binns, Dr. Walter Pope, 50
"Black Cabinet," 18
Black Codes, 92, 259
Blaine, James G., 178
Blanshard, Paul, 207, 214, 220, 222
Boer War, 304
Border Patrol, 128
Borneo, 90
Boston, 105, 165, 293
*Boston Post*, 42
Boudin, Louis, 296
Boxer Rebellion, 97
Brazil, 45, 61, 63, 252
Bremerton, Washington, 8
Brewer & Company, Ltd., C., 186
British, 196. *See also* England, Great
  Britain

British Columbia, 248
British West Indies, 201, 214
Brooklyn, 217
Broom, Dr. Leonard, 157, 158, 165–
  166
Brown, John, 41, 273
Brown, Dr. Warren, 218
Brownsville, Texas, 131
Bryan, William Jennings, 147
Buaken, Manuel, 248
Buchanan, James, 198
Buck, Dr. Paul, 270
Bulosan, Carlos, 233
Bureau of Colored Troops, 256
Bureau of Immigration of Hawaii,
  189
Burgess, John W., 177, 179
Burlingame Treaty (1868), 93
Buss, Dr. Claude A., 247

CALHOUN, JOHN C., 196
California, 69, 134, 138, 154, 180, 184,
  198, 274; American Indians in, 60,
  71; discovery of gold, 66, 141, 173;
  anti-Chinese agitation, 91–92, 93,
  94, 95, 109; influence of, in Chinese
  exclusion, 97–98, 99–104; concentration of Chinese in, 105, 106; contribution of Chinese to culture of,
  112; Spanish-speaking in, 114, 115,
  116, 117–118, 125; Anglo-Hispano
  relations, 121; Okies and Arkies,
  128; wetbacks, 129; Westminster
  School case, 132; racial tensions,
  140; Japanese immigration, 141–
  144; California-Japanese War, 144–
  150; Japanese adaptability and success, 150–154; Little Tokyo, 155–
  159; mass evacuation of Japanese,
  159–164; Filipinos in, 235–241; anti-
  Filipino agitation, 241–242, 244;
  Hindus in, 248–249
California Farm Bureau, 162
California Federation for Civic
  Unity, 18
California Supreme Court, 15, 52
Campbell, Albert A., 223, 225
Canada, 89, 141, 145
Canal Zone, 208, 219–222, 300
Cape Province, 341

Cariaga, Roman R., 188
Caribbean, 62, 180, 206, 214, 216, 220, 223
Caroline Islands, 228
Carpenter, Senator, 99
Carson, California, 95
Casserly, Senator, 69
Castle & Cook, Ltd., 186
Catholic Church, 51–52, 120–121, 180, 226, 334, 335
Catholic Committee of the South, 52
Catholic International Council, 52
Catskills, 289
Caucasians, 189, 191, 193, 194, 213, 219
Celebes, 90
Central Africa, 45
Central America, 61, 62, 104, 198
Central Asia, 283
Central Pacific Railroad, 93, 101–102, 106
Ceylon, 90
Chambers, R. L., 136
Chamorros, 226, 228
Chapman, John Jay, 304
Chattanooga, Tennessee, 56
Chavez, J. Francisco, 134
Cherokee Indians, 66, 69
Chester, Pennsylvania, 6
Chicago, 3, 6, 29, 34, 57, 105, 165, 285, 301
Chico, California, 95
China, 45, 76, 147
Chinatown, 107–112
Chinese, 120, 143, 144, 158, 167, 190, 282, 324; immigration barriers, 89–91; technique of exclusion, 91–97; politics of exclusion, 97–104; geographical and occupational distribution, 105–112; in Hawaii, 183–184
Chinese Exclusion Act (1882), 89, 92–94, 105, 183, 185
Ching Chao Wu, 94, 104, 107
Christian College, 50
Church, racial discrimination and, 49–52
"Church and Race, The," 49–50
Cincinnati, 50, 165, 285

Cincinnati Bible School, 50
Civic unity councils, 19
Civic unity movement, 17–22, 313–315
Civil Rights Act, 214, 259, 277
Civil Rights cases, 267
Civil Rights Message, Truman's, 41, 48
Civil Service Commission, 44
Civil War, 4, 15, 16, 30, 39, 51, 70, 92, 99, 146, 174, 198, 255, 259, 262, 266, 270
Clark, Tom C., 38
Cleveland, Grover, 177, 181
Cleveland, Ohio, 165
Cloverdale, California, 95
Coast Guard, 10
Cohen, Felix S., 97, 210, 279
College of the Bible, 50
Collier, John, 72, 74, 76, 80, 81, 82, 87, 210
Collier's, 148
Collins, Orvis, 321
Colombia, 89
Colón, 219
Colorado, 66, 68, 114, 115, 116, 137, 147, 275
Columbia, Georgia, 31
Columbia, Tennessee, 29–30
Columbians, Inc., 32
Columbus, Christopher, 62, 140, 201, 278
Columbus, Ohio, 49
Commission on Civil Rights, 41
Commission on Human Rights, United Nations, 37, 38
Commissioner of Indian Affairs, 63
Committee on Civil Rights. See President's Committee on Civil Rights
Committee on Equality of Treatment and Opportunity in the Armed Services, 44
Communism, 194, 291
Compromise of 1876, 199, 200
Congress of Industrial Organizations, 8
Congressional Medal of Honor, 138
Conkling, Roscoe, 232
Connally, Tom, 26

Constitution of the United States, 170–171, 175
Cook, Captain, 172
Coolidge, Mrs. Mary Roberts, 96, 97, 98
Copenhagen, 50–51
Cox, Oliver C., 107, 185, 254, 255, 308
Creek Nation, 80
Creoles, 196
Cristóbal, 220
Crosswaith, Frank, 23
Cruikshank case, 267
Cuba, Cubans, 99. 117, 195, 196–201, 229, 231
Culver-Stockton College, 50

DACHAU, 160
Danes, 223–224
Das, Taraknath, 249
Davie, Dr. Maurice R., 257
Davies & Co., Ltd., T. C., 186
Davis, Jefferson, 53
Dawes, Henry L., 73
Day Law, 55
Debo, Angie, 78
Debs, Eugene V., 303
Declaration of Human Rights, United Nations, 37
Declaration of Independence, 284
Deep South, 8, 11, 18, 48, 179, 206, 224, 341, 342, 344
Delaware, 47, 147, 275
Delgado case, 132
Delta Tau Delta, Amherst Chapter, 53
Democratic Party, 8, 27, 28, 36, 43, 101, 230, 263, 264, 335
Denman, Justice William, 160, 167
Denmark, 222
Denver, 116, 133, 165
Department of Interior, 222
Department of Labor, 275
Detroit, 3, 105, 301
Deveaux, Jean, 226
Dewey, Admiral George, 179, 229
DeWitt, General J. L., 159, 160
Dickerson, Earle, 37
Dillingham, Walter, 193
District of Columbia, 17, 41

Division of Negro Economics, Department of Labor, 275
Dixiecrat movement, 42
Dixon, California, 95
Dominican Republic, 210
Don system, 134
Douglas, Stephen A., 198, 199
Dred Scott case, 255
Dreyfus, Alfred, 304
Du Bois, Dr. W. E. B., 37, 38, 252, 260, 262, 265, 273
Durban, South Africa, 339, 341, 343
Durkheim, 252
Dutch Reformed Church, 343

EAST ST. LOUIS, ILLINOIS, 5–6
East Toledo Neighborhood House, 21
Eastern seaboard, 61, 64
Eastland, James O., 28
Eckenrode, H. J., 263, 265, 266
Ecuador, 89
Egypt, 45
Electoral College, 8, 42, 265
Elizabethtown, New York, 41
Ellender, Allen J., 33
Ellis Island, 90
El Paso, 116
El Salvador, 89
Emancipation Proclamation, 23, 24, 99, 199, 250, 256, 345
Emden, Paul H., 298
Emerson, Dr. Haven, 76
England, 296, 299, 300, 303. See also Great Britain
English-Canadians, 327, 329, 330
Epstein, Sam, 309–310
Eskimos, 219
Essex County Courthouse, New York, 41
Ethical Culture Society, 309
Europe, 62, 83, 254
Evansville, Indiana, 3
Executive Order No. 8802, 23, 24; No. 9066, 159; No. 9346, 24; No. 9808, 34

FAIR EDUCATIONAL PRACTICES ACT, 24
Fair Employment Practices Commission, 23–29, 36, 41, 43

Fairgrounds Park, St. Louis, 57
Far East, 104, 112
Faris, Dr. Ellsworth, 15
Federal Council of Churches, 49, 50
FEPC. *See* Fair Employment Practices Commission
Fergusson, Erna, 114
Fifteenth Amendment, 100, 174, 175
Fiji, 182
Filipino Laborers Association, 186
Filipinos, 104, 184; in Hawaii, 187–189; in Micronesia, 228. *See also* Philippine Islands
Fillmore, Millard, 141
First World War. *See* World War I
Fisk University, 257
Fiske, John, 179
Flagstaff, Arizona, 86
Fletcher, Elroy, 32–33
Florida, 46, 47, 117, 242, 263, 265, 266
Flowers, Montaville, 148
Ford, Henry, 291
Fort Cobb, Indian Territory, 68
*Fortune*, 292, 297
Fourteenth Amendment, 49, 56, 91, 92, 259, 267
Fowler, Ruth, 149
France, 24, 65, 300, 303
Frank case, 291
Frazier, Dr. E. Franklin, 252, 254, 269
Freedmen's Aid Societies, 256
Freedmen's Bureau, 256, 257–259
Freedom Train, 38
Freeland, Carolyn, 247
French-Indo China, 190
French West Indies, 201
French-Canadians, 120, 327–333
Freyre, Gilberto, 59, 62, 63, 64, 75, 253

*Gaines* v. *Canada*, 47, 48
Gary, Indiana, 29
Geary Act (1892), 95–96, 107
General Allotment Act (1887), 73
Geneva, Switzerland, 38
Gentlemen's Agreement (1907), 145, 146, 184, 234

Georgia, 30, 31–32, 47, 66, 160, 181, 291, 320
German-Jews, 285, 286, 287, 288, 289, 290
Germany, 300, 303, 306, 317
Glynn, Georgia, 35
Gold Run, California, 95
Gold Rush, 101, 103, 117, 125
Gompers, Samuel, 231
Gonzales, David, 138–139
Gooks, 168
Gordon, Maxine, 204–205, 206
Governors' Interstate Council on Indian Affairs, 85, 87
Graham, Frank P., 28–29
Grant, Madison, 276
Grant administration, 261, 264
Great Britain, 61, 65, 98–99, 178–179. *See also* England
Great Plains, 66
Great Wall of China, 89
Greek-Americans, 283
Greenville, South Carolina, 35, 39
Greenwood, Mississippi, 33
Gregg, David L., 174
Gregg, Josiah, 116
Grodzins, Morton, 159, 162, 163–164
Group Areas Act, 340, 343
Groveland, Florida, 57
Grower-Shipper Vegetable Association, 162
Guadalupe Hidalgo, Treaty of, 118, 122–123
Guam, 219, 226–227, 228
Guatemala, 89
Gupta, Kedar Nath Das, 249

HAAS, BISHOP FRANCIS J., 24
Hacker, Louis M., 262
Hamada, Hikozo, 143
Hampton Institute, 257
Harlan, Justice, 267
Harlem, 3, 219
Harper, Allen, 77, 138
Harpers Ferry, 41, 273
Harris case, 267
Harrison, Benjamin, 177
Hastie, William, 18, 225
"Hate strikes," 9, 29
*Hawaiian Gazette*, 177

Hawaiian Islands, 145, 201, 207, 208, 219, 227, 300; statehood for, 41; Chinese excluded from, 96; competition in, 140; Japanese in, 141, 160, 163, 164; annexation of, 170–176, 177–181; Republic established, 176–177; racial and cultural defeat of natives, 182–189; race relations, 189–194; contrasted with Puerto Rico, 212–214; immigration from, 216; Filipinos in, 234–235, 244
*Hawaiian Star*, 180
Hawaiian Sugar Planters Association, 141, 234
Hawaiian-Japanese Labor Convention (1886), 185
Hawley, Senator, 93
Hayes, Rutherford B., 92, 175, 265, 266
Healdsburg, California, 95
Heco, Joseph, 143
Heithaus, Reverend Claude Herman, S. J., 51
Henderson case, 49
Hendrickson, Robert C., 28
Hill, Lister, 28
Hill, T. Arnold, 18
Hindus, 37, 219, 248–249, 282, 341, 343
Hiroshima, 26
Hispanos, 114, 120, 121, 122, 123, 125, 126
Hoar, George F., 171
Hobart, Garrett A., 231
Holland, 284, 299
Hollister, California, 95
Honolulu, 173, 184
Hood River, Oregon, 242
Hooker, Georgia, 56
Hopi Indians, 82, 88
Horne, Frank, 18
House of Representatives, 25, 26, 43
Houston, Texas, 6, 10
Howard University, 257
Hughes, Dr. Everett C., 318–319, 324–327, 329, 330, 332, 336
Huguenots, 283

Ickes, Harold L., 226, 227
Idaho, 147, 260

Idaho Falls, Idaho, 165
Illinois, 274, 275
Illocanos, 188
Immigration Act (1924), 96, 129, 146, 147, 155, 184, 217, 275, 287
Immigration Service, 129
Imperial Valley, 153, 161, 242, 249
India, 45, 76, 90, 248
Indian Bureau, 74, 77, 84
Indian Personality and Administration, Final Report on, 87
Indian Reorganization Act (1934), 81
Indian Service, 81, 82, 86, 87
Indian Territory, 71
Indiana, 262, 275
Indians. *See* Hindus
Indians, American, 12, 114, 160; world's oldest colonial problem, 59–60; geographical distribution and race relations, 60–65; development of American Indian policy, 65–66, 67–71; Plains tribes, 66–67; cultural attack on, 71–79; New Deal for, 79–82, 86; since World War II, 82–88; relations of Spanish-speaking with, 118
Indo-China, 90
Industrial Revolution, 208, 254; present-day, in South, 45–47
Institute on Race Relations and Community Organization, 20
Intellectuals, 230
Intermountain West, 85
International Longshoremen's and Warehousemen's Union, 193
Irish, 286, 321, 333–336
Irwin, Wallace, 148
Irwinton, Georgia, 57
Issei, 159, 282
Italians, 296
Ives-Quinn antidiscrimination measure, 23

Jackson, Andrew, 66, 160
Jackson, Mississippi, 32, 42, 44
Jackson, North Carolina, 35
Jackson College, 32
Japan, 26, 90, 236

Japanese, 12, 90, 104, 120, 228; contact with Spaniards in New World, 140–141; immigration to California, 141–144; California-Japanese War, 144–150; capacity for assimilation, 151–154; contained status of, in California, 155, 159; mass evacuation of, 159–164; return to West Coast, 164–168; in Hawaii, 184–188

*Japanese Conquest of American Opinion, The* (Flowers), 148

Japanese-Americans, 7, 41, 283

Java, 90, 190, 236

Jefferson Military College, 53

Jews, 114, 149, 151, 152; as minority group, 280–283; America and, 283–292; position of, in American economy, 292–301; anti-Semitism as social growth, 301–311

Jim Crowism, 38; passing of, 46, 48–49; in California, 92, 98; in Canal Zone, 220–222; codification of, 271–272; in South Africa, 339–342

*Joan of Lorraine*, 52

Johannesburg, 343

Johnson, Dr. Charles S., 256, 268

Josey, Dr. C. C., 276

KAILUA, 172

Kansas, 197, 198, 274, 275

Kawakami, K. K., 92

Kennedy, Raymond, 338

Kentucky, 47, 55, 322

Kenya, 283

King, Primus E., 31

Kiwanis Club, Ahoskie, North Carolina, 52

Know-Nothing Party, 100

Korea, Koreans, 147, 168, 185, 189, 228

Ku Klux Klan, 6, 30, 31, 42, 56, 57, 146, 263, 275

Kyne, Peter B., 148

LA FARGE, OLIVER, 77, 83, 87

La Fayette College, 53

Laflore County, Mississippi, 33

Lahey, Edwin A., 44

Lake County, California, 242

Lake Geneva, Wisconsin, 54

Lake Success, 38

Lancaster, E. M., 18

Larrazolo, Octaviano, 135

Lasker, Dr. Bruno, 239, 246

Latin America. *See* Central America, South America, West Indies

LaViolette, Dr. Forrest E., 142

Lawrence, D. H., 68

League of Latin-American Citizens in Texas, 132

Lee, Rose Hum, 104, 106

Leong Gor Yum, 107

Lestchinsky, Jacob, 294

*Letters of a Japanese Schoolboy* (Irwin), 148

Leupp, Francis E., 73

Levin, Carl, 33

Lewisohn, Ludwig, 290

Lexington, Kentucky, 6

Leyburn, Dr. James G., 14, 278

Liholiho, Prince Alexander, 173–174

Lincoln, Abraham, 23, 24, 199, 237, 256

Lincoln, California, 95

Lincoln-Douglas debates, 199

Lind, Dr. Andrew W., 182, 184, 185, 189

"Little Marshall Plan," 83

Live Oak, California, 248

Lodge, Henry Cabot, 270

Logan, Camp, 6

London, 298

Longview, Texas, 6

Los Angeles, 84, 105, 131, 133, 138, 156, 157, 290, 301; "zoot-suit" race riots, 3; Negro community, 7; "hate strikes," 29; anti-Chinese agitation, 95; Spanish-speaking in, 116; Filipinos in, 237, 238, 239; German-Jews in, 285

Los Angeles Chamber of Commerce, 162, 238

Los Angeles County, 142

*Los Angeles Mirror*, 194

Louisiana, 7, 46, 263, 265, 266

Louisville, 285

Lowrie, Dr. Samuel Harman, 122

*Loyota v. United States*, 243

Luzon, 138

Lynch, Denis Tilden, 266
Lynchburg College, 50

MACARAIG, DR. SERAFIN E., 243
McCormick, Frederick, 140
McEnery resolution, 181
McKee, Ruth E., 143
McKinley, William, 229, 230, 303
McKinley Tariff (1890), 177
McLaurin, G. W., 48–49
Macleod, William Christie, 65, 67, 69, 75
McNickle, D'Arcy, 64, 65, 66, 67, 69, 77, 81, 82
McNutt, Paul, 246
Madeira, 184
Main Types and Causes of Discrimination, The, 338
Malan, Dr. Daniel François, 340, 342
Malaya, 183, 282
Mallery, 69
Manchuria, 189
Manifest destiny, 179, 180, 197, 270
Manila, 230, 234, 242
Manila Times, 243
Manila Bay, Battle of, 179
Mankin, Mrs. Helen Douglas, 31
Manlapit, Pablo, 186, 188
Marcantonio, Vito, 24, 219
March-on-Washington Movement, 23
Marianas, 228
Marine Corps, 9
Marr, Wilhelm, 307
Marshall Islands, 228
Marshall Plan, 83
Maryland, 47, 258
Mascerel, José, 133
Mask for Privilege, A (McWilliams), 304
Maslow, Will, 27
Massing, Dr. Paul W., 306
Massachusetts Institute of Technology, 55
Mayflower, 140
Mears, Helen, 151
Mecklin, John Moffatt, 269, 272
Me-Gook, 168
Melamed, S. M., 291
Melanesia, Melanesians, 75, 228

Melting Pot, 90
Memphis, 98
Menace of the Japanese, The (McCormick), 140
Mendel, Gregor, 148
Merced, California, 95
Meriam Report (1928), 79
Merriam, George S., 268, 271–272
Merton, Dr. Robert K., 326
Methodist Conference on Christian Education, 50
Mexican-American War, 122–123, 138
Mexicans, 12, 198, 322, 326; a forgotten people, 113–114; diversity of Spanish-speaking, 114–121; Anglo-Hispanic relationships, 121–130; changing status of, 131–139
Mexico, 45, 89, 119, 126, 145, 149, 198
Michigan, 218, 219, 228, 262, 274
Michigan Chronicle, 29
Michigan Council of Churches, 20
Miles, General Nelson A., 195
Millis, Walter, 200, 229
Ming, William, 37
Minorcans, 117
Mississippi, 32–33, 46, 47, 271
Missouri, 47, 274
MIT. See Massachusetts Institute of Technology
Mohammedans, 283
Monaco, 244
Monroe, Georgia, 31, 34
Monroe Doctrine, 178
Montana, 66, 260
Montreal, 329
Moon, Henry Lee, 18
Moore v. Dempsey, 275
Moors, 62
Morse, Wayne, 25
Morton, Senator, 102, 103
Mugwumps, 230
Mukden, 144
Mukerji, Dhan Gopal, 249
Muñoz Marín, Luis, 203, 204, 207, 214
Murray, Chief Justice Hugh C., 100

NAPA, CALIFORNIA, 95
Napoleonic Wars, 285

Natal Province, 340, 341
National Association for the Advancement of Colored People, 21, 22, 34, 37, 38, 40, 47, 86, 273, 276
National Association of Intergroup Relations Officials, 18
National Citizens Council on Civil Rights, 44
National Congress of American Indians, 86
National Humiliation Day, Manila, 242
National Interfraternity Conference, 54, 55
National Resources Planning Board, 115
National Student Association, 54
National Theater, Washington, 52
Native Sons of the Golden West, 162
Naturalization Act (1870), 99
Navajo Indians, 83–84, 86, 87, 88
Navy, U. S., 9, 222, 225, 226–227, 234
Nearing, Scott, 269
Nebraska, 147, 197, 198
Negroes, 61, 62, 101, 114, 138, 175, 219, 282, 318, 320, 322, 344; in race riots, 3, 6–7; migration of, in World War II, 7–8, 166; in World War I, 8, 9, 10; implications of interregional shifts, 8; economic and industrial gains, 8–11; changing attitude toward, 12–16; March-on-Washington Movement, 22–23; in crisis of 1946, 29–35; continuing injustice to, 35–41; in election of 1948, 42–45; influence of revolutionary change in South, 46–49; religious segregation of, 49–52; protests in favor of, 52–55; under reconstruction, 56–58, 259–267; as colonial problem, 59–60; Indians and, 68, 69–70, 79; Chinese issue and, 97–100; in Cuba, 196–197, 199; in Puerto Rico, 201–207; in Canal Zone, 220–222; in Virgin Islands, 222, 223; Emancipation Proclamation and, 250; discrimination against, as outgrowth of slavery, 250–256; as racial problem, 256–257; Freedmen's Bureau, 256, 257–259; segregation of, legalized, 267–273; struggle for minority status, 273–279

Nelson, Senator, 181
Netherlands West Indies, 201
Nevada, 260
Nevada City, California, 95
New Deal, 8, 18, 47
New England, 63, 172, 321
New Guinea, 90
New Jersey, 274
New Mexico, 79, 84, 114, 115, 116, 117, 118, 123, 138, 147, 198, 205, 208; Anglo-Hispano relations, 121; isolation of, 124, 125–126; population, 125; Mexican-Americans in politics, 133–137
New Orleans, 30, 52
New Spain, 61
New World, 81, 116, 140, 317
New York City, 29, 105, 110–111, 165, 216–219, 274, 300, 301
New York Herald-Tribune, 33
New York Post, 33–34
New York State, 23, 24
New York Times, 43, 44, 56, 168, 218, 226, 247, 341
New York World, 10
New Zealand, 89
Newmark, Harris, 290
Niagara Falls conference, 273
Nicaragua, 89
Nickerson, Hoffman, 288
Nigeria, 278
Nisei, 158, 159, 167, 168
North African campaign, 17
North America, 60
North American Review, 303
North Carolina, 28, 46, 47

Oahu, 186
Oakland, California, 95
Oceania, 190
Ohio, 262, 274, 275, 293
Okies, 128
Okinawans, 228
Oklahoma, 7, 47, 48
Olympia, Washington, 94
Omaha, 6

Open Door policy, 90
Oregon, 67, 68, 89, 90, 140, 142, 147, 180, 275
Ortiz, Fernando, 211
Ostend Manifesto, 197
O'Sullivan, John L., 197, 198
Oxnam, Bishop G. Bromley, 51
Oyama case, 167
*Ozawa* v. *United States*, 147, 243

PACIFIC COAST. *See* West Coast
Pacific Islands, 226–228
Pacific Mail Steamship Company, 93
Pacoima, California, 139
Palestine, 300
Panama, Republic of, 220
Panama City, 219
Panamanians, 221, 222
Papago Indians, 84, 88
Paris, Treaty of, 227
Park, Dr. Robert E., 89, 151
Park Manor, Chicago, 57
Parkes, James, 300
Parsees, 282
Pasadena, 95
Passaic, New Jersey, 293
Pattee, Richard, 208
Pearl Harbor, 148, 163, 187
Peirce, Dr. Paul Skeels, 256
Pell City, Alabama, 57
Penn, William, 80
Pennsylvania, 274, 275
Perez case, 52
Perlman, Philip B., 40
Perry, Commodore, 140, 141
Perry, Leslie S., 37, 268, 271
Persia, 45
Peru, 89, 140
Petaluma, California, 95
Petrullo, Vincenzo, 204, 212
Phi Kappa Psi, Amherst Chapter, 53–54
Phi Sigma Delta, 55
Philadelphia, 3, 34, 105, 165, 301
Philippine Independence Act (1934), 242, 243, 244
Philippine Islands, 171, 180, 181, 183, 184, 190, 207; immigration barriers, 90; Chinese excluded from, 96; im-
migration from, 216, 234–236; annexation of, 229–232, 245–248; Americanization of, 232–234; Filipinos in California, 236–241; anti-Filipino riots on West Coast, 241–242; agitation for exclusion and repatriation of immigrants from, 242–244; independence of, 242–244, 245, 246–248, 345; Filipinos in World War II, 244–245; treatment of Americans in, 245
Philippine Trade Act, 246–247
Phillips County, Arkansas, 6
Phillips University, 50
Phoenix, Arizona, 84, 86
Pi Beta Sigma, 54
Pickett, William P., 269
Pierce, Franklin, 143
Pittsburgh, 105, 293
Placerville, California, 95
Plains Indians, 66
Platt, Senator, 180
Platt amendment, 200
*Plessy* v. *Ferguson*, 15, 49, 267
Polish Jews, 287
Polynesia, Polynesians, 219, 228
Ponce, Puerto Rico, 217
Popham, John, 44
Populist Party, 269, 271, 303
Porter, Pleasant, 80
Portland, Oregon, 7, 94, 105
Portugal, Portuguese, 61–62, 184, 185, 299
Poston, Theodore, 18
Powell, A. Clayton, Jr., 23
Pratt, Dr. Julius W., 178, 181, 200
Presbyterian Church in the United States (Southern), 51
President's Commission on Higher Education, 38–39
President's Committee on Civil Rights, 31, 34, 35, 38–40, 53, 277, 312, 345–346
Price, Bem, 46
*Pride of Palomar, The* (Kyne), 148
Progressive Party, 44
Protestant Church, 49–51, 121, 180
Public Workers Union (CIO), 221
Pueblo Indians, 79

Puerto Rican Industrial Development Company, 218
Puerto Ricans, 185, 189
Puerto Rico, 171, 180, 184, 231, 300; acquisition of, 195, 229; racial issue in, 201–207; as American colony, 207–216; migration from, 216–219
"Pullman car" colonies, 7
Punjab, 248, 249

QUAKERS, 80, 180, 283, 298
Quebec, 120, 327–333
Queensberry, Marquis of, 27

"RACE PREJUDICE AT SUMMER RESORTS" (RHINE), 289
Randolph, A. Philip, 23
Rankin, John E., 10, 11
Reciprocity Treaty, Hawaiian, 175, 185, 262
Red Bluff, California, 95
Redding, California, 95
Redfield, Dr. Robert, 14–15
Redwood City, California, 34
Reed, Thomas B., 231
Reformers, 230
Rehabilitation Act, 246, 247
Repatriation Act (1935), 244
Republican Party, 26, 43, 44, 101, 230, 259–260, 261, 262, 264–265, 266, 335
Reuter, E. B., 207, 208, 209, 210, 211, 212, 214
Reynolds, Dr. Charles N., 149
Rhine, Alice Hyneman, 289
Rhodes, Charles J., 80
Rio Grande, 62, 116, 119
Rio Grande Valley, 60
Rippy, J. Fred, 212
Ritter, Archbishop Joseph E., 52
Rivers, W. H. R., 75
Roberts, Thomas, 18
Rock Springs, Wyoming, 94
Roosevelt, Franklin D., 23, 24, 25, 159, 244, 277
Roosevelt, Mrs. Franklin D., 23
Roosevelt, Theodore, 145, 146, 179
Rose, Arnold and Caroline, 284
Ross, Malcolm, 25, 26, 27
Rowell, Chester, 89

Royce, Josiah, 149
Rumania, 285
Rummel, Archbishop Joseph Francis, 52
Russell, Richard B., 25
Russia, Russians, 45, 76, 189, 285
Russian Jews, 286, 287
Russo-Japanese War, 144, 145

SACRAMENTO, CALIFORNIA, 95, 147
Sacramento Valley, 153
St. Augustine Normal School, 257
St. Barthelmy, 225
St. Croix, 222
St. John, 222
St. John's, Oregon, 248
St. Louis, 57, 105
St. Louis University, 51–52
St. Paul, 285
St. Thomas, 202, 222–226
Salinas Valley, 161
Salt Lake City, 84, 85, 165
Samoa, Samoans, 219, 227–228
San Antonio, 116, 133
San Buenaventura, California, 95
Sanchez, Dr. George, 83, 113, 117, 120, 128, 133, 135, 138
San Diego, California, 3
Sandmeyer, Dr. E. C., 94
San Fernando Valley, 139
San Francisco, 7, 26, 105, 108–110, 111, 143, 145, 146, 154, 166, 173, 184, 213, 236, 237, 266, 285, 293
San Francisco Board of Education, 145, 148
San Francisco Chronicle, 144, 153
San Francisco Housing Authority, 109–110
San José, California, 95
San Juan, Puerto Rico, 215, 217, 218
San Luis Valley, California, 116
Santa Barbara, 95
Santa Cruz, California, 95
Santa Fe ring, 135
Santa Rosa, California, 95
Sarah Lawrence College, 86
Saratoga Springs, 289
Saunders, Lyle, 123, 124, 131
Saveth, Dr. Edward N., 302, 303, 304
Scattergood, J. Henry, 80

Schmitz, Eugene E., 145
Schoeman, Mr., 342
Schreike, B., 99
Scott Act (1888), 95
Seattle, 8, 94, 105, 239
Second World War. *See* World War II
*Seed of the Sun* (Irwin), 148
Seligman, Jesse, 289
Seligman, Joseph, 289
Seligmann, Herbert J., 275
Senate, U. S., 25, 26, 33, 43
Senate Judiciary Committee, 28
Senate Rules Committee, 28
Sentaro, 141
Seoul, 168
Sephardic Jews, 284, 286, 287
Severson, Dr. A. L., 290
Shantung, 147
"Sharecroppers' riot," 6
*Shelley* v. *Kraemer*, 44
Shephard, Ward, 74
Sheridan, General Philip H., 68
Siam, 90
Siberia, 147
Siegfried, André, 269
Singapore, 183
Sino-Japanese War, 148
Sipuel, Ada Lois, 48
Smith, Alfred Edgar, 18
Smith, William C., 184, 191, 192, 194
*Smith* v. *Allwright*, 30, 31, 32, 36
Smuts, General Jan Christiaan, 343
Snipes, Macio, 31
Solid South, 30, 43, 45, 101
Sonoma, California, 95
Sonorans, 117
South Africa, 37, 267, 339–344
South America, 61–63, 104, 141, 206, 256, 284
South Carolina, 30, 35, 36–37, 46, 47, 175, 263, 265, 266
South Pacific, 140
South Sea Islanders, 184
Southern Regional Council, 18, 43, 157
Southwest, 45
Spain, Spaniards, 61, 62, 65, 66, 119, 140, 180, 184, 185, 199, 231

Spanish-American War, 229, 230
Spanish-Colonials, 117, 118–119
Statue of Liberty, 90
Stennis, John C., 28
Stephenson, Mrs. Gladys, 29
Stephenson, James, 29
Stevens, Sylvester K., 175, 176, 180
Stilwell, Hart, 130
Stockton, California, 237, 238, 239, 242
Stoddard, Lothrop, 276
Stone, Dr. A. H., 272
Stone Mountain, Georgia, 30
Stonequist, Dr. E. V., 68
Strong, Josiah, 179
Strydom, J. G., 342
Sumatra, 90
Sumner, William Graham, 12
Supreme Court, 16, 30, 40, 44, 47, 48, 49, 55, 56, 94, 146, 147, 167, 249, 267, 268, 275, 276
*Survey Graphic*, 234
Sutherland, Robert L., 276
Swainsboro, Georgia, 42
Sweatt, Herman Marion, 48
Syria, 45, 283

TACOMA, WASHINGTON, 94
Taft, William Howard, 237
Tagalogs, 188
Takahashi case, 167
Talmadge, Eugene, 31, 32
Taney, Chief Justice, 255
"Taxicab riot," 35
Taylor, Edmond, 59
Teller amendment, 229
Tennessee, 46, 322
Tennessee Valley, 46
Teutons, 179
Texas, 7, 43, 47, 48, 114, 115, 117, 118, 121–122, 125, 127, 129, 130, 132, 133, 134, 135, 137, 147, 180, 198, 208
Texas Christian University, 50
Texas Council of Church Women, 43
*Thaddeus*, ship, 172
Thomas, W. I., 15
Tilden, Samuel J., 175, 264, 265, 266
Tillman, B. R., 271, 340

Tobera, Fermin, 242
Tocqueville, Alexis de, 70
Tokyo, 147
Toledo Board of Community Relations, 20–21
Toledo Ohio Bell Telephone, Company, 21
Tongass Act (1947), 86
"To Secure These Rights," 38–39
To Secure These Rights in Your Community, 20
Towards Better Race Relations, 20
Toynbee, Arnold, 282, 296, 298
Trent, William, 18
Truckee, California, 95
Trujillo, Miguel H., 84
Truman, Harry S., 27, 28, 34, 35, 41, 42–43, 44, 83, 215, 277
Tulare, California, 242
Turner, Frederick Jackson, 67
Twain, Mark, 201, 229, 232
Tydings, Millard E., 246

UNCLE SAM'S SWEATSHOP, 210
Union Labor Party, 145
Union League Club, 289
Unitarians, 180
United Council of Church Women, 51
United Nations, 26, 37–38, 338, 342–343
United Nations Charter, 167
United States Employment Service, Oriental Division, 111
United States v. Wong Kim Ark, 92
Universal Jewish Encyclopedia, 300
University of Chicago, 20
University of Missouri, 47
University of Oklahoma Law School, 48, 49
University of Texas Law School, 49
University of Toledo, 21
University of Wisconsin, 54

VALENTIN, HUGO, 284
Vallejo, California, 95
Vancouver, Washington, 8
Vandenburg, Arthur H., 26
Vanderbilt, Cornelius, Jr., 148

Vardaman, James K., 10, 271, 272, 340
Veblen, Thorstein, 290, 298
V–E Day, 26
Verdict of Public Opinion on the Japanese-American Question, The, 148
Versailles, Treaty of, 147
Villard, Oswald Garrison, 40
Virgin Islands, 201, 208, 219, 222–226, 227
Virginia, 46, 251, 258
Viscayans, 188

WACO, TEXAS, 6
Walker, Francis, 63
Wallace, Henry A., 44
War Relocation Authority, 85
Waring, Judge J. Waties, 36–37
Warner, Dr. W. Lloyd, 295
Warren, Earl, 4
Washington, Booker T., 270, 272
Washington, D. C., 6, 10, 38, 57, 105, 165
Washington, State of, 140, 142, 147, 260
Watson, Tom, 271, 340
Watsonville, California, 242
Watterson, Henry, 200
Weaver, Dr. Robert C., 5, 9, 18
Webb, Dr. Walter Prescott, 261
Webster, Daniel, 232, 237
Welch, Richard, 242
West Coast, 7–8, 47, 60, 142, 154, 156, 236, 241, 248, 262
West Indies, 99, 202, 318, 325
West Point, 143
West Virginia, 47, 274, 322
Westerman, George W., 221
Western Growers Protective Association, 160, 162
Westminster School case, 132
Wetbacks, 129
Wheatland, California, 95
White, Nate R., 111
White, Walter, 23, 34
Whitefield, George, 320
Wickersham Report, 239
William Jewell College, 50
William Woods College, 50

**INDEX**

Williams, Eric, 197, 198, 201, 317
Williams, John, 187
Williams, Robert C., 33
Willkie, Wendell, 11
Wilmington, North Carolina, 269
Wilson, Captain H. A., 272
Wilson, Woodrow, 40
Wisconsin, 262
Wood, General Leonard, 200
Woodard, Isaac, Jr., 30
Woofter, T. J., Jr., 274
World War I, 5–6, 8, 9, 10, 147, 216, 275, 344

World War II, 3, 4, 5, 7–17, 22, 86, 128, 132, 193, 217, 219, 228, 245, 276, 278, 279, 300, 344
Wounded Knee, Battle of, 67, 195
Wright, Fielding L., 42

YAKIMA, WASHINGTON, 241
Yankees, 283, 321
Yellow Peril, 90
*Yick Wo* v. *Hopkins*, 92
Young, General S. B. M., 200
Young America Movement, 197
Yuba City, California, 95